MEASURING ENVIRONMENTAL QUALITY IN ASIA

PETER P. ROGERS

KAZI F. JALAL

BINDU N. LOHANI

GENE M. OWENS

CHANG-CHING YU

CHRISTIAN M. DUFOURNAUD

JUN BI

Published by

The Division of Engineering and Applied Sciences, Harvard University
and the
Asian Development Bank

Distributed by

Harvard University Press

363.7063
M484

ISBN Number 971-561-104-4
Library of Congress Cataloging-in-Publication (CIP) Data applied for.

alo

Sheet of Errata and Additional Notes

On Page 52

In Inequality (2.11) and Equation (2.12), S_m should be replaced with $\delta_m K_m$ and S_n should be replaced with $\delta_n K_n$.

In the first line of last paragraph, "Inequalities (2.11) and (2.12) ... " should read "Inequalities (2.10) and (2.11) ... ".

In the third line of last paragraph, ".. that rule (2.12) ... " should read " ... that rule (2.11) ... ".

On Page 77

In Equation (3.3), in the third component of the right-hand side, the operator in the numerator is a minus sign "-" rather than a multiplication sign "×".

On Pages 87 and 89

In Notes, Sector 1 should read "Water pollution control and supply, flood control", rather than "Water pollution control and supply, floor control".

On Page 110

In Figure 4.3, reverse the order of the legend, i.e. the darkest color represents 6-9% and the blank represents 1-3%.

On Page 121

In Table 5.5, under the column "Change of Coal Consumption," for the period between 1984 and 1985, the percentage "-1957.6%" indicates that Indonesia's coal consumption increased by 1957.6%. Since increased coal consumption has adverse impacts on the environment, it appears as a negative number in the table. There is NO calculation error with this result.

On Page 150

In the last line, "... (Table 6.3) that the annualized cost of ... " should read "... (Table 6.2) that the annualized cost of ...".

On Page 266

Equation (2.27) should be

$$C1 = 4.32Q^{0.7878}r^{1.234}$$

CONTENTS

Foreword vii
Preface ix
Acknowledgments xiv
Contributors xvii
Abbreviations and Acronyms xviii

CHAPTER I

Environmental Indicators: Issues and Problems 1
Definitions 2
Criteria for Developing Indices 4
Functions of an Indicator 6
Intended Indicator Users and Audiences 8
Framework for Indicator Creation 9
Computation of Indices 11
Weighting Factors in Indices 14

CHAPTER 2

urrent Status of Environmental Indicators 19
Environmental Components and Themes 19
Basic Environmental Indicators 20
Environmental Indices: A Review 23
Sustainable Development 43

CHAPTER 3

New Measures of Environmental Quality 57
New Environmental Quality Indicators 57
Principal Components to Find the Dimensionality of Indices 57
Cost of Remediation 60
Environmental Standards 64
Setting Environmental Standards 64
Development Diamonds—Environmental Diamonds 69
Environmental Elasticity 76
Computing Environmental Elasticity for OECD Countries 79

CHAPTER 4

Applications and Policy Implications of the Cost of Remediation Index 83
ADB's Environmental Expenditure Record 84
Estimation of Cost of Remediation 90
Applications of Cost-of-Remediation Indices 90
National Estimates of the Cost of Remediation 102

CHAPTER 5

Applications and Policy Implications of Environmental Elasticity and Developmental Diamonds 113
Characterizing Environmental Trends for Asian Countries 113
Assessing Environmental Trends in Asia 113
People's Republic of China 113
Philippines 116
Nepal 118
Pakistan 118
Indonesia 120
Cross-Country Comparison of Long-Term Environmental Trends 121
Computing EEs for Sixteen Asian Countries 127
Assessing the State of the Environment in Asia 132
Policy Implications of Environmental Elasticity and
Environmental Diamond 137

CHAPTER 6

Summary and Conclusions 139
Environmental Preferences 140
Proposed Indices: Their Advantages and Disadvantages 141
Application 1: Identifying Need of DMCs for Environmental
Investment and Internal-External Financing 143
Application 2: Investments in Environmental Remediation Across
Different Sectors—What Will $100 Million Buy? 149
Application 3: Financial Affordability of Environmental Standards—
Are They Feasible? 150
Environmental Elasticity 151
Identifying Priorities for Environmental Remediation 163

REFERENCES 165

APPENDIX 1

Compiling Emission Factors for DMCs: a Method for Rapid Assessment Using Secondary Data 173
1. Introduction 173
2. Some Conceptual Issues Related to Environmental Emissions 174

   3. Pollution Intensities (Emission Factors) 176
   4. Industrial Air and Water Emissions: A Comparison Between the
      US and PRC 182
   5. Vehicular Emissions: A Comparison between the US and the
      Philippines 193
   6. Emissions from Energy Consumption by Industries and Households . 197
   7. Emissions from Agricultural and Forestry Activities 202
   8. Solid Waste Generation by Industries and Households 203
   9. Summary 210

APPENDIX 2

Cost of Remediation 219
   1. Introduction 219
   2. Cost Functions 220
   3. Cost Functions—Air 222
   4. Cost Functions—Water 259
   5. Cost Functions—Land 278
   6. Cost Functions—Ecosystems 289
   7. Full-Cost Accounting 294
   8. Use of COR for Investment Decisions 294
   9. Commentary on the COR Index 298

APPENDIX 3

A Review of Environmental Indices 311
   1. Introduction 311
   2. Rationale for Environmental Indicator Development 312
   3. Early Development of Media-Specific Indicators 313
   4. A Modern Interpretation of Environmental Indicators 314
   5. Summary of Traditional Indices 319
   6. Institutions Engaged in Index Studies 352

APPENDIX 4

Some Theoretical and Technical Issues Regarding Environmental
Elasticity and Environmental Diamonds 369
   1. Issues Regarding Environmental Elasticity and an Alternative Index for
      Measuring Environmental Trend Relative to Economic Trend 369
   2. Issues Related to Alternative Ways of Sub-Index Aggregation 381
   3. Summary 384

This book is dedicated to the memory of

Myron Fiering

who worked so hard to get this research started,

but did not live to see it completed.

Foreword

Pressures of population growth, rapid urbanization, industrialization, and stress on natural resources provide new challenges to the Asian Development Bank (ADB) as it strives to incorporate the environment as a major element of sustainable economic development in the Asian and Pacific region. While ADB can provide policy guidance and technical assistance, the governments themselves must take the lead in providing the resources and policies needed to address effectively the rapidly changing environmental condition. How we measure the effectiveness of a country's performance in meeting the environmental challenge in Asia and the Pacific is the subject of this book.

By drawing on experiences in six Asian and Pacific countries, the authors have developed a series of methodological tools to assist others in assessing the state of environmental quality for air, water, soil, and biodiversity in developing countries. These tools can then be used to determine the financial resources needed to improve the quality of the environment. Comparisons using the environmental quality indices developed can be especially useful in guiding national action toward priority environmental issues as well as enabling governments to learn from the experiences of others.

This book is the product of a collaborative effort by the staff from Harvard University's Division of Engineering and Applied Sciences and the staff of the Asian Development Bank's Office of Environment and Social Development. It should be a useful guide for development practitioners, environmental scientists and governmental policy-makers in their efforts to shift development activities toward a more environmentally sound path.

Kazi F. Jalal
Chief, Office of Environment and
Social Development
Asian Development Bank

Preface

Asia is the home of more than 3 billion people, the majority of whom live in an impoverished economic and physical environment. Coupled with the explosive economic growth in recent years, the Asian and Pacific region is under tremendous environmental pressure. Two types of environmental degradation are widely prevalent in the region: poverty-induced and development-induced. The former includes lack of access to safe drinking water, to sanitary services, and related health impacts. The latter includes industrial air emissions, wastewater discharge, agriculture-induced soil erosion, deforestation for export of timber resources, and loss of habitat due to urbanization and agricultural activities. The dilemma facing many developing economies in the region is that lack of economic development causes poverty-related social and environmental degradation, while "unsustainable" economic development results in long-term environmental loss that could be irreversible and catastrophic.

The Asian Development Bank (ADB) is uniquely positioned to guide the region's economic development by bringing other multilateral financial institutions (MFIs) and its developing member countries together. ADB can directly influence the course of economic development through its lending and technical assistance activities. Until recently, environmental goals were not fully incorporated into ADB's formulation of lending strategies. Not unlike other MFIs, economic criteria often dominated policy decision-making. In the past several years, however, there have been dramatic changes in ADB's polices leading towards greater emphasis on environmental improvement. By 1995, the ADB adopted the goal that of total project lending 50 percent by number and 40 percent by volume must have an environmental objective. To achieve this goal, it became clear that ADB needed to monitor the state of the environment and assess the environmental impacts of economic development in its developing member countries on a regular basis. Such activities are not only essential for investing in remediation of the negative externalities of past economic development, but are also needed to ensure that future development projects have positive, or at least neutral, environmental impacts.

Beginning in 1994, the ADB and the Government of Norway co-financed a research project which was executed by Harvard University's Environmental Systems Program. The research team consisted of a group of researchers from Harvard University and senior staff members of the ADB; Dr. Kazi Jalal, Chief of OESD, Dr. Bindu Lohani, Manager of the Environment Division; and Dr. Gene Owens, project supervisor. The research team has developed a set of indices for monitoring environmental changes. Ideally, the indices developed should not only support the monitoring goals of the MFIs, UN-specialized agencies, and individual countries, as articulated in the 1992 Rio Conference goals outlined in Agenda 21, but should also help establish environmental investment budgets on a sectoral, spatial, and intertemporal basis. From the ADB's point of view, its country programs need standard tools for assessing the environmental quality of member nations, which are highly variable ecologically and geographically, ranging from the People's Republic of China to the Marshall Islands.

As a MFI, the question that faces ADB staff members on a regular basis, explicitly or implicitly, is where its next loan should be invested in order to achieve maximum developmental impact with minimum environmental damage, and preferably with environmental benefits. The question can also be rephrased as, how to compile an investment portfolio across different countries and sectors, to achieve the same effects. The economic efficiency criterion dictates that society should invest in environmental improvement to the point where the benefit brought out by the last dollar's investment is equal to the cost. While economists enthusiastically advocate this sound theoretical principle, they have so far failed to produce a satisfactory methodology for quantifying the benefits associated with environmental cleanup costs, largely due to uncertainties of the health impacts and other less quantifiable impacts of environmental pollution and degradation. In the meantime, relatively more is known about the costs of environmental remediation from an engineering point of view than the benefits from an economic point of view.

Instead of waiting for better methodology to come along, we believe that relatively rich, existing cost information may be utilized to assist policy-making at both national and international levels. It is in this spirit that this group of researchers developed an environmental index known as the cost of remediation (COR). This index reflects the cost of moving the environment from the present state to a more desirable level sometime in the future. As this volume will demonstrate, the COR index has strong policy implications for both national governments and MFIs because it reveals the amount of wealth that a society has to forgo to restore the environment to a more "livable" level. In particular, by expressing the total COR of a country in terms of a percentage of its total gross domestic product (GDP), one can obtain an indication of how much financial resource is needed from domestic, bilateral, multilateral, and private sources in order to improve its environment.

Although the COR index enjoys the advantage of being denominated in dollar values and, thus, can serve effectively as a counterweight to the traditional economic indicators such as GDP and national income, it is relatively data intensive and its estimation is complex. To meet the demand for simple but reliable indices for environmental monitoring purposes, we have also developed two supplementary indices, one for monitoring the environmental trend relative to the country's economic trend and the other for assessing the state of the environment by using four principal environmental components, air, water, land and ecosystem.

While the initiative for developing new environmental quality indices stems directly from ADB's need to monitor the environmental progress of the member countries, it is easy to lose sight of many previous attempts made by various national and international agencies in developing useful indices. Most notably, these efforts include the United Nations Development Programme's Human Development Index, the World Bank's Wealth of Nations Index and its use of development diamonds, the joint Organisation for Economic Cooperation and Development and Netherlands Government approaches, and the World Resources Institute's Environmental Quality Index. There are literally hundreds of existing environmental-economic indicators and indices. Unfortunately, many of them were developed in isolation and few attempts have been made to reveal the interrelation among them. Consequently, although there are many indicators, they provide little useful information—indicator-rich but information-poor. *The issue, therefore, is not that there are too few indicators, but rather that there are not enough simple, reliable, informative, and easy-to-appreciate indicators that serve as tools for communication and rational decision-making.* The synthesis of the literature provides the motivation for the development of the new indices presented and applied in the body of this volume.

The results presented in this volume represent a joint effort among staff of Harvard University, the ADB, and its collaborating agencies, comprising governmental and nongovernmental agencies in six Asian countries, namely the People's Republic of China, the Philippines, Pakistan, Nepal, Indonesia, and the Marshall Islands. Collaboration was essential not only because of the need to test the new indices among a range of countries with differing ecological/environmental patterns, but also to further the dissemination of the new methodologies and information among policy-makers within the developing countries of Asia and the Pacific.

Throughout this study, the authors have benefited from many useful exchanges with economists, engineers, various environmental groups, and policy-makers. Many constructive criticisms from these exchanges have been drawn, many of which have already been incorporated into the present volume. Nevertheless, many methodological uncertainties and data deficiencies undoubtedly remain. It is perhaps helpful to identify, in an unambiguous manner, what the new indices *are* and *are not* intended to achieve.

The new indices and methodologies developed in this study significantly expand the available environmental quality indicators and should help operationalize the fuzzy concept of sustainable development:

■ The indices will facilitate spatial and dynamic comparisons of environmental variables, across countries (regions), sectors, and over time.

■ The new indices can be used for decision-making, including issues covering environmental portfolio management and prioritization of types of environmental degradation and hazards within countries.

■ They facilitate comparisons among components of the environment, such as air, water, land, and ecosystems. We can determine how much money is theoretically needed to bring different components of environmental improvement or deterioration in line with a rational set of standards.

■ They enable comparison of environmental changes with economic changes using the same or similar terms.

■ Application of the COR index should encourage the setting of more realistic standards by countries. A current trend in many developing countries in the region is to simply adopt the United States' standards or some unrealistically high standards, just to be politically correct with no real intention of compliance.

The overriding function of the COR index is its usefulness in helping governmental regulatory agencies to set environmental standards that are both financially feasible and capable of lowering risks to human health, or as a minimum keeping such risks at fairly low levels. The willingness to accept environmental risks varies across different cultures and varies according to the economic wealth of countries. In many developing countries, poverty and hunger are the biggest risk of all and environmental hazards are considered secondary. For these countries, standards should be considerably more relaxed than for those countries that can afford to pay more to clean up the environment.

Due to constraints of time, resources, and data availability, this study is also subject to a number of limitations.

■ By focusing on only six Asian countries, this study should be viewed as a pilot effort in developing and testing the new methodologies for index development. Although extrapolations are made for other Asian countries based on the indicators used in these six countries, estimates are meant to provide an illustration of the potential usefulness of the new indices. More reliable estimates await in-depth studies for individual countries.

- Despite our special attention given to least-cost technologies in our COR estimation, the estimates contained in this study are not all necessarily least-cost estimates. The intent of least-cost estimation is further complicated by the fact that the least-cost technologies are changing rapidly over time as new technologies are developed.

- Much of this report is devoted to cost estimation. We argue in Chapter 3 that when environmental standards used in the COR estimation are considered optimal, the COR estimates represent the optimal benefits that society has to forgo to achieve those standards. Nonetheless, these cost estimates are not benefit estimates. In other words, the COR index is not based upon economic preference theory. Furthermore, the assumption of near-optimal environmental standards is rarely met, especially in developing countries which often adopt the standards of developed countries. While our cost estimates rely on "optimal" standards, to determine whether or not the standards are optimal requires both benefit and cost estimates. It is a classic dilemma.

- Because the indices are not based upon economic preference theory, the COR approach does not directly answer the question of where multilateral development banks should invest. To do so would require estimation of the benefits of the investment. Rather COR strives to determine how much finance is needed if a MFI, for instance, decides to invest in a particular country and a particular sector to achieve a specific environmental goal.

- This study focuses on index development primarily at regional and national levels, rather than at project level. However, in some cases, the cost functions collected and developed in this study (Appendix 2) may be used to derive the first approximation of the costs for specific projects such as a sulphur-removing facility or a waste management facility.

Finally, a detailed list of contributors, regional collaborators, and commentators is provided elsewhere in this volume; the authors would like to acknowledge their contribution here. Two persons, however, deserve special thanks. Dr. Gene M. Owens of the ADB and Dr. Chang-Ching Yu of Harvard are the ones who took the responsibility to develop the raw materials of the project report and convert them into this book. Without their prodigious efforts, carried out with great humor and intelligence over the past several months, and without the participation and collaboration of many people who contributed in the spirit of improving the welfare of the peoples of Asia, this volume would not have been possible.

Acknowledgments

Many people have made contributions at different stages of this study to whom we are deeply indebted. Our gratitude goes to the research team at Harvard University. Dr. Fiona Murray, who is currently teaching at Oxford University, United Kingdom, contributed greatly at all stages of the field research and at Harvard. She was the author or coauthor of several working papers and appendixes produced in the course of this project. Dr. Nagaraja Harshadeep, presently with the World Bank, was our main technical support and was responsible for pulling all the cost functions together in Appendix 2. Professor Joseph J. Harrington, at Harvard's Division of Engineering and Applied Sciences was, in part, responsible for identifying regional collaborators who were key to the success of this study; he also provided his expert opinions on cost functions particularly regarding wastewater treatment. Several Ph.D. candidates at Harvard University contributed to this volume. Xiang Yu was responsible for gathering and translating from Chinese literature, and processing much of the cost information that forms one of the main sources of such information in this volume. He was also the principal author of Appendix 4 which contains discussions on several theoretical and technical issues regarding environmental index development. Annette Huber was one of the main commentators on the early versions of the report. She was also responsible for editing the working papers which form the basis of this volume. Martha Crawford prepared the country report for the Marshall Islands and was actively involved in preparing the report of the study. Several undergraduate research assistants were also involved at different stages of the research, including Chris Legget, Trin Mitra, Angelina Zappia, and Alyssa Pei. Susan Morrison provided the administrative support for the project.

Several staff members in the Asian Development Bank have provided useful comments on the study. These include Mr. Peter N. King, Senior Project Specialist (Environment) and Dr. Piyasena Abeygunawardena, Environment Specialist. The interest and input provided by Mr. Bruce Murray, Programs Manager for the People's Republic of China, was very helpful. Staff comments and suggestions from the Bank's Economic Development Resource Center, and from Programs Departments in each of the countries represented in the study, were greatly appreciated. From the beginning of this study, we emphasized the engagement of potential users of the indices in the process of developing them. Our country collaborators in People's Republic of China, Philippines, Pakistan, Nepal, Indonesia, and the Marshall Islands, and our regional coordinator in Thailand, included the following individuals and their affiliated organizations.

PROFESSOR SHEN ZHANG
Chinese Academy of Sciences
Institute of Geography
Beijing, People's Republic of China

DR. MARIAN S. DE LOS ANGELES AND MS. LORETA RUFO
Resources, Environment and Economics Consultants, Inc.
Manila, Philippines

MR. ARUP RAJOURIA AND MR. VASKAR THAPA
King Mahendra Trust for Nature Conservation
Jawalakhel, Kathmandu, Nepal

MR. SYED AYUB QUTUB AND DR. SARFRAZ KHAN QURESHI
Pakistan Institute of Environment Development Action Research
Islamabad, Pakistan

DR. ROEHAJAT EMON SOERIAATMADJA
Bandung Institute of Technology
Bandung, Indonesia

MR. ABRAHAM HICKING AND MR. RIYAD MISTRY
RMI Environmental Protection Authority
Republic of the Marshall Islands

PROFESSOR CHONGRAK POLPRASERT
Asian Institute of Technology
Bangkok, Thailand

These individuals and institutions provided necessary technical and other support to our field studies and regional seminars, and prepared country reports for the study. Much of the material used in the formulation and testing of the environmental quality indices are drawn from the country reports.

The study also greatly benefited from other members of the Harvard community. Dr. Theodore Panayotou, of the Harvard Institute of International Development (HIID), participated in the commencement workshop and provided a written critique of the final report of the study. His persistence in developing indices from economic preference theories has led us to better assess the usefulness and weakness of dollar-denominated environmental indices and greatly sharpened our focus in pursuing such indices. Dr. Jack Spengler, of the Harvard School of Public Health, provided valuable comments in both the commencement and final workshops of the research project from the perspective of health impacts of pollution, and the importance of incorporating such impacts in index development.

We are very grateful to the following people with whom we had discussions on our research during the research period. This document, however, does not necessarily reflect their views. They are John Dixon, John O'Connor, Carter Brandon, and Richard Cambridge, of the World Bank; Joe Whitney, of the University of Toronto, Karen Polenske of MIT, Dun Tunstall of WRI, Anil Markandya of HIID, and Robert Dorfman of Harvard Universtiy.

Finally, our thanks go to Mr. Marc Kaufman and Mr. Bill Brinkly of Desktop Publishing & Design Co. in Boston, who have tirelessly worked with us on at least five different versions of this volume. Mr. Celso C. Amutan of Accents Graphic Arts in Manila did much of the typesetting work for the present volume. Mr. Jonathan Aspin, to whom we are most grateful, served as the technical editor for publication.

Contributors

DR. PETER P. ROGERS is Gordon McKay Professor of Environmental Engineering and Professor of City Planning, Harvard University, Division of Engineering and Applied Sciences. He is the principal investigator and project director of this research project.

DR. KAZI F. JALAL is the Chief of the Office of Environment and Social Development, Asian Development Bank.

DR. BINDU N. LOHANI is the Manager of the Environment Division, Office of Environment and Social Development, Asian Development Bank.

DR. GENE M. OWENS is a Senior Environment Specialist at the Office of Environment and Social Development of the Asian Development Bank, and the project supervisor and coordinating officer of this research project.

DR. CHANG-CHING YU is a post-doctoral fellow at Harvard University. He provided both field research services and served as the project administrator.

DR. CHRISTIAN M. DUFOURNAUD is a professor at the Faculty of Environmental Studies, University of Waterloo, Canada, and a senior member of the research team.

DR. JUN BI is a post-doctoral fellow at the Chinese Academy of Sciences and a member of the research team.

Abbreviations and Acronyms

AACR	average annual change rate
ADB	Asian Development Bank
Aeq	acidification equivalents
Air CHIEF	Air Clearinghouse for Inventories and Emission Factors
AIRS	aerometric information retrieval system
AIT	Asian Institute of Technology
AP	accelerated progress
API	Air Pollution Index
ASEAN	Association of Southeast Asian Nations
BAU	business as usual
BMPs	best management practices
BOD	biochemical oxygen demand
Ceq	Carbon Dioxide equivalents
CFCs	chlorofluorocarbons
COD	chemical oxygen demand
COR	cost of remediation
CRES	Conservation Reporting and Evaluation System
CRF	capital recovery factor
CSOs	combined sewer overflows
DD	development diamond
DENR	Department of Environment and Natural Resources (Philippines)
DMCs	developing member countries (of ADB)
DNC	depleted natural capital
DO	dissolved oxygen

DOE	Department of Energy (United States)
EAJ	Environmental Agency of Japan
ED	environmental diamond
EDI	Ecosystem Degradation Index
EE	environmental elasticity
EEC	Economic-Environmental Change
Eeq	Eutrophication equivalents
EGR	exhaust gas recirculation (system)
ENRAP	Environment and Natural Resources Accounting Project (Philippines)
EPDI	Environmental Pollution and Degradation Index
EPRI	Electric Power Research Institute (United States)
EQIs	Environmental Quality Indices
ESPs	electrostatic precipitators
FAO	Food and Agricultural Organization
FCR	forest coverage rate
FF	fabric filters
FGS	flue gas desulfurization
GDP	gross domestic product
GHDI	Green Human Development Index
GHG	greenhouse gas
GIS	geographic information systems
GNP	gross national product
GWP	greenhouse warming potential
HC	hydrocarbon
HDI	Human Development Index
HRI	Hierarchical Richness Index
IAPCS	Integrated Air Pollution Control System
ICDP	Integrated Conservation and Development Project
IDRC	International Development Research Center (Canada)
IET	Index of Environmental Trends
IMF	International Monetary Fund
IPCC	Intergovernmental Panel on Climate Change
IPPS	Industrial Pollution Projection System
ISIC	International Standard Industrial Classification

IUCN	International Union for the Conservation of Nature (World Conservation Union)
LPI	Land Pollution Index
MAQI	MITRE Air Quality Index
MFI	multilateral financial institution
MSW	municipal solid waste
MURC	Measure of Undesirable Respirable Contaminants (Index)
NAAQS	national ambient air quality standards (United States)
NAS	National Academy of Sciences (United States)
NCFEA	National Center for Economic Alternatives
NDP	net domestic product
Neq	number of people equivalents
NGOs	nongovernmental organizations
NIC	newly industrialized countries
NNP	net national product
NPAs	natural protection areas
NPDES	National Pollutant Discharge Elimination System (United States)
NSFWQI	National Science Foundation Water Quality Index (United States)
O&M	operation and maintenance
OECD	Organization for Economic Cooperation and Development
Oeq	ozone-depletion equivalents
OESD	Office of Environment and Social Development (of ADB)
PCA	principal component analysis
PIMs	perpetual inventory models
PM	particulate matter
POC	Particulate Organic Compound
PRC	The People's Republic of China
PSR	pressure-state-response
RCWP	Rural Clean Water Program
RMS	root-mean-square
SCOPE	Scientific Committee on Problems of the Environment
SCR	selective catalytic reduction

SCS	Soil Conservation Service (United States)
SNA	system of national accounts
SNCR	selective noncatalytic reduction
SPM	suspended particulate matter
SS	suspended solid
SSNNP	sustainable social net national product
TAC	Thermostatic Air Cleaner (system)
TOC	total organic compound
TRI	toxic release inventory
TSP	total suspended particulate
UNCED	United Nations Conference on Environment and Development
UNDP	United Nations Development Programme
UNEP	United Nations Environment Programme
UNESCAP	United Nations Economic and Social Commission for Asia and Pacific
UNSTAT	United Nations Statistical Agency
USEPA	United States Environmental Protection Agency
VOC	volatile organic compound
Weq	weight equivalents
WHO	World Health Organization
WPI	Water Pollution Index
WRI	World Resources Institute

1 ENVIRONMENTAL INDICATORS: ISSUES AND PROBLEMS

A concerted effort to enhance habitability of our planet is unlikely to succeed unless we know "where we are" and "where we want to go." To answer these questions, we must first consider exactly what we include in the term "environment." If we restrict our definition to overly simplified definitions, such as the amount of a specified pollutant in the air, we have very little difficulty in measuring the environment. However, as we broaden our definition to include all the physical components, or all the physical and biological, or all the physical, biological, and cultural ones, environment becomes exponentially more difficult to describe.

THOMAS, 1972, p.1.

The above quotation summarizes the real difficulties experienced by multilateral development agencies, whose mission requires characterization of environmental parameters of widely varying parts of the world. A consistent methodology for environmental characterization would assist overarching efforts to promote wise investment and management of resources in developing countries by providing valuable information relevant to economic growth, reduction of poverty, equity, health care, and environmental management. What is needed is an index for the environment that would offer the resonance that GDP has had for political and economic development.

Recent changes in the multilateral banks' strategies and policies and an added emphasis on environmental and social sectors have given rise to the need for new methodologies and procedures for assessing the status of sustainable development. With a greater emphasis on country programs and the consequent need for comparative assessment of country performances, the Asian Development Bank initiated a study[1] at Harvard University to develop tools for the monitoring of environmental change.

One reason that the developmental community needs environmental quality indices (EQIs) is to estimate how much environmental improvement can be drawn from investment in a particular sector in a given country. In particular, the development agencies need to know not only how good or bad the environment is in an absolute sense, but where on the environmental learning curve that particular country is located and how much environmental improvement is likely to occur for a given cost at the margin.

In addition to the timing issue of *when* to invest, there is the question of geographic heterogeneity and the consequent need to decide *where* to measure the environment and how to translate the measurements into an investment plan or set of policies. The environments of many Asian countries differ vastly between urban and rural areas. The elements of an EQI in Bangkok are likely to be different from those in a Thai coastal fishing village, and both sets are likely to be different from those in a highland village far from the sea. Integration of these components into a truly representative national scalar value is a daunting task, not easily managed merely by assigning weights based on population, land areas, or other metrics.

Any serious attempt to develop policy-relevant indices must be based on an expression of the objectives of the user. At a minimum, the following questions concerning the purpose of environmental indices must be addressed:

- Are they to be used to promote good environmental management by promoting development in those countries which have already invested heavily in the environment?

- Is the developmental agency primarily interested in the remediation of environmental degradation as an abstract entity benefiting future generations, or should environmental quality be weighted, perhaps by current populations?

- Is the developmental agency primarily interested in a longitudinal assessment with which to maintain the environmental performance of any given country over time? Or, will it be making a sequence of simultaneous cross-sectional assessments in which the countries are ranked against each other and from which the relative (not absolute) rank of any country can be tracked over time?

Definitions

Much of the original work on environmental indicators began in the early 1970s, as attention was being focused on the state of the environment in both the United States and Europe. With the creation of the President's Council on Environmental Quality in the United States, demand grew for systems of measuring progress toward environmental goals, and pollution control targets were in demand. Much of that work was compiled in 1978 by Wayne Ott in his comprehensive book *Environmental Indices*. Ott brought together indices on air and water pollution, and described several indexing approaches, including quality-of-life and environmental-damage functions. It is clear from Ott's work that environmental indicators, as conceived in the 1970s, were tools to describe the level of environmental quality in a particular medium for a particular region. Interregional comparisons were an important focus of this work.

After Ott's study, there was a surprising and significant lull in the literature regarding this subject matter. Only since the late 1980s and early 1990s, especially in the light of the UNCED meeting and Agenda 21, has interest once again focused on defining environmental indicators. Over the intervening period, however, the expectation placed upon indices has changed radically. Originally, environmental indicators were closely linked to environmental monitoring, with the intent being that they give insight into environmental conditions and provide a yardstick with which to judge the efficacy of environmental regulatory programs. By the 1990s the emphasis had changed to decision-making and to setting objectives.

Work in this area is currently led by international institutions such as the World Bank, the Organisation for Economic Cooperation and Development (OECD), the United Nations Development Programme (UNDP), the United Nations Statistical Agency (UNSTAT), and the Food and Agriculture Organization of the United Nations (FAO), in conjunction with active nongovernmental organizations including the World Resources Institute (WRI) and the National Center for Economic Alternatives (NCFEA). National environmental institutions have varied in their commitment to the formulation of environmental indicators, although the Netherlands and the Canadian environment ministries and the US Council on Environmental Quality, have been major forces in this work.

The World Bank describes an indicator as "a performance measure that aggregates information into a usable form" (O'Connor 1994). However, issues of valuation, intertemporal variations (discount rate), and uncertainty remain unresolved in terms of their definition and motivations of indicators. OECD describes indicators specifically in reference to some stated final objective(s); that is, indicators are envisaged as a set of information used to measure (environmental) performance with respect to a defined level of environmental

---

Indicators and Indices

Wayne Ott, in his 1978 book *Environmental Indices: Theory and Practice*, describes an environmental indicator as a single quantity derived from one pollutant variable, used to reflect an environmental attribute. According to Ott, these indicators can be aggregated in some way to form an environmental index. An index is therefore derived from information about more than one pollutant.

More recently, only the Japanese have explicitly tried to define the difference between an indicator and an index. A 1992 study for the Environment Agency of Japan notes that "most efforts [are]...aimed at the development of indices (or final single index) to quantify the quality of [the] local environment, rather than a set of indicators to characterize the state and the trends of the environmental quality." (WRI, 1992.) In current indicator/index work, these distinctions are somewhat arbitrary and not widely used.

quality. The WRI perceptively remarks that "indicators represent an empirical model of reality, not reality itself," (WRI, 1995, p. 1).

The Netherlands Environment Ministry defines both normative and descriptive indicators: Descriptive indicators present a certain state of the world, while normative indicators enable valuation by comparing a descriptive indicator with a standard acting as a norm, a so-called (environmental) performance standard. Accordingly, a normative indicator is not simply a measure of a state variable, but rather a measure of progress to show change.

In the literature, the term "indicators" and "indicies" are sometimes used interchangably, although some have tried to differentiate between the two (see the text box in this section).

Criteria for Developing Indices

The basic purpose of the indices formulated in past work was to facilitate the objective and precise determination of the state of the environment and humanity's impact upon that state. The application of indicators to policy debates and their use by decision-makers are not made explicit, in part, because the modeling and simulation techniques required to develop scenarios of future environmental quality under a set of possible policy choices have not been sufficiently developed.

Recently, confidence has risen in humanity's ability to predict the incremental effects of environmental policies and technologies. Furthermore, institutions are concerned with making rational choices between environmental policies and investments, given budget constraints and other limits to environmental management activities. Therefore, all agencies focus on the fact that indicators should be useful for making decisions and setting objectives. The Environment Agency of Japan (EAJ) suggests that indicators be "strategic, precautionary and systematic, multidimensional, and comprehensive," although their exact nature should depend upon their context. As the agency cautions, "we had better not seek almighty indicators" (EAJ 1992).

A paper that addresses the desirable qualities of an EQI (Tunstall et al. 1992) sets the following four criteria for an ideal indicator:

1. it is a reliable statistical measure;

2. it is measured in comparable fashion over time and space;

3. its changes can be assessed against a scientifically valid norm or standard; and

4. it bears upon a clearly identifiable social goal.

The first three criteria are vaguely stated. Presumably, what is meant by reliable is that the index should be statistically robust, and should characterize the relationship between environmental quality and resource depletion, which it is designed to monitor. The second criterion follows from the first and requires that an index be temporally and spatially replicable. The third criterion also follows from the first and defines the need for an environmental index to say something about how environmental quality compares to standards. A parameter that could be added to the list is that an index should allow for comparison of the environmental quality in geographically and ecologically dissimilar places. For example, the environmental quality of two countries may be deteriorating but one may be destroying the ambient air quality in its major cities while the other is depleting its resource base. Both countries are involved in a different process of environmental change but both are debasing the environment. An EQI should be able to capture both forms of deterioration.

OECD's stated criteria for the development of an index are that it must:

1. be relevant, i.e., serve a clearly defined purpose;

2. be reliable, i.e., have a sound scientific basis; and

3. be realizable, i.e., be measurable using available data.

The World Bank suggests that an indicator also be tolerant to inconsistencies that arise from aggregation and valuation and, more stringently, keep all the implications of the original information while decreasing the amount of information. The World Bank also suggests that indicators be empirically-based and driven by operational interests, but stresses that indicators be agreed upon so that their compilation and the necessary data-gathering is undertaken to the fullest extent possible by all agencies. The United Nations Environment Programme (UNEP) concurs that careful conception and general consensus on the indicators are important, but cautions that indicators should be free of value judgments and biases. The Earth Council echoes the search for general acceptance, calling for indicators that:

1. stand up to scientific scrutiny;

2. are amenable to aggregation and disaggregation at different levels; and

3. are clear and understandable.

The theme of comprehensibility is further developed by the US Environmental Protection Agency (USEPA), which suggests that indicators be simple enough to provide a vehicle for public debate in the setting and meeting of goals. On a more practical note, the International Development Research Center (IDRC) of Canada suggests that indicators should also:

1. be sensitive to interventions;

2. demonstrate change over time;

3. be reliably and reproducibly measured with limited resources; and

4. permit examination of ethical and equity considerations through disaggregation.

In general, the current debate suggests that indicators must have utility, efficiency, and effectiveness. It is also acknowledged that a solid database and information foundation is an important prerequisite for indicator development.

Reflecting current concern that development be sustainable, Dorfman (1977) calls for the development of indices that have social relevance. He claims that it makes no sense to present information on resource depletion or pollution emission away from the context in which the consequences of sustaining an improving level of human existence are seen. He suggests discussion on three aspects which EQIs should reflect: commercial and industrial productiveness, healthfulness, and amenities. The interest people have in the environment centers on their use of natural and environmental resources to advance one or more of these goals. It is considered axiomatic in this discussion that EQIs should reveal changes in the sustainability and further enhancement of human welfare. This anthropocentric perspective underpins our research and the presentation of alternative EQIs in the next chapter.

Functions of an Indicator

Traditionally, environmental indicators have been closely linked to environmental monitoring, so that they offer insight into environmental conditions and provide a yardstick with which to judge the effectiveness of environmental regulatory programs. The role of indicators as described by Train in 1973 is still appropriate today:

> For top management and public policy development, monitoring data must be shaped into easy-to-understand indices that aggregate data into understandable forms. Much more effort must be placed on the development of…indices than we have in the past. Failure to do so will result in suboptimum achievement of goals at much greater expense.

At the time Train was writing, the National Academy of Sciences (NAS) of the United States played a central role in promoting environmental indicators. A 1975 NAS report concluded that: "despite strong statements of need from all three branches of government, progress toward the development and use of methods for evaluating environmental quality has not been satisfactory." Recommendations for improving indicators focused on the role of indicators in six major areas:

1. financial resource allocation;

2. ranking of locations;

3. enforcement of standards;

4. trend analysis;

5. public information; and

6. scientific research.

Today, indicator functions are more closely focused on the interaction between the natural environment and socioeconomic decision-making. According to the World Bank, an environmental indicator is meant to be used in conjunction with socioeconomic indicators and oriented toward the specified aims of the decision-makers. The World Bank hopes to use indicators in a "bold effort to squeeze more policy relevance from the data that exist" (O'Connor 1994), with the objective of improving current practices in the analysis of traditional projects, public expenditures, and investment reviews. The indicators should also set the context for economic-sector work as well as for sectoral and structural adjustment operations. The indicators will then be used to identify the environmental impacts of national economic policies, to choose policy instruments for environmental protection, and to evaluate the environmental and economic impacts of projects.

In contrast, the functional value of indicators for OECD is more in line with older definitions and is intended to facilitate attempts to create environmental performance reviews for member countries and to help improvements in individual and collective environmental management. However, since the purpose of such OECD reviews is to integrate economic and environmental decision-making at a macro level, the final policy-related objectives of indicator use are similar, although on a different scale, to those that exist at the World Bank. In using and developing indicators, the Earth Council and other institutions are following the mandate of Agenda 21, set at UNCED in Rio de Janeiro in 1992:

> Commonly used indicators such as GNP and measures of individual resource and pollution flows do not provide adequate indications of sustainability. Methods for assessing interactions between different sectoral environmental, demographic, social, and developmental parameters are not sufficiently developed or applied. Indicators of sustainable development need to be developed to provide solid bases for decision-making at all levels and to contribute to a self-regulating sustainability of integrated environment and development systems (Chapter 40.4).
>
> Relevant organs and organizations of the UN system, in cooperation with other international governments should use a suitable set of sustainable development indicators and indicators related to areas outside of national jurisdiction, such as the high seas, the upper atmosphere and outer space. The organs and organizations of the UN system could provide recommendations

for harmonized development of indicators at the national, regional and global levels, and for incorporation of a suitable set of these indicators in common, regularly updated, and widely accessible reports and databases, for use at the international level (Chapter 40.7).

At the scale of national governments, the function of indicators seems to lie in the coordination of data collection and assessment of progress toward environmental goals (national and international). For example, USEPA considers indicators to be a means of characterizing the environment and environmental goals and a means to facilitate data-gathering. In Japan, local-level indicators have been extended to indicators at the sectoral and national levels. These are being incorporated into national accounts and used for international environmental assessments. The Netherlands Government has taken these ideas a step further with the intention of creating policy-oriented indicators that can be used to make decisions and to present yearly trends and progress. They have set goals based on policy relevance, analytical soundness, and measurability, and are using indicators to aid Parliament in assessing progress.

Intended Indicator Users and Audiences

Coate and Mason wrote in 1975 of the role of the user in formulating indicators:

> It is absolutely necessary that the user be identified. The scientist, administrator, elected official, and general public cannot usually be satisfied by the same environmental measure. The administrator needs to see the resource allocation implications and the scientist needs to see the cause-and-effect implications. Who the user is will also affect the geographic or political aggregation of data and the decision to highlight or obscure inter-jurisdictional comparisons.

Currently, the use of EQIs is generally confined to public information (for example, daily reports of air pollution in a local newspaper). Ott (1978) has suggested that very few of the indicators developed in the scientific literature had found their way into routine use by pollution control agencies.

During the present wave of activity in environmental indicators, all institutions in the process of developing or using environmental indicators seem to have the policy-maker or decision-maker in mind. It is clearly stated that the indicators should have policy relevance and should make the links between the environment and certain economic and policy actions more transparent and measurable.

In the World Bank, the staff are the decision-makers, but their decisions encompass project evaluation, sectoral and national policy structuring, advice to a member country's decision-makers, and institution building. As such, indicators must have "policy relevance" on a number of scales—at the scale of evaluating the environmental impacts of a range of options or formulations at the project level, sectoral investments and restructuring, and national macro-economic strategy.

At OECD, while similar considerations are echoed, the predominant focus is on policy-making at the national scale. Communicability is also an important consideration (probably through inclusion in state-of-the-environment reporting) and OECD acknowledges the importance of environmental policy objectives and sectoral environmental policies in implementing national-level environment improvements. FAO is trying to use indicators to put such policies into action, working with environmental decision-makers at all levels to improve efforts in the area of agricultural policy. It stresses that little of the work on indicators to date has been applicable to developing countries or useful for on-the-ground applications. FAO has utilized existing technology, augmented with environmental data through the integration of indicators into decision-support models (DSMs). This is an approach that the World Bank is also considering.

National environmental agencies have different concerns and different proposed users. For them the audience is particularly critical. Indicators provide a means of defining and communicating progress toward environmental goals and facilitating public participation in environmental management. The user is the decision-maker in the environmental agency on the one hand, and in the national government on the other. Therefore at a national level, project, sectoral, national, and international scale indicators are all necessary for making strategic choices about environmental management.

Framework for Indicator Creation

Ott identified two steps in developing indices: calculation of values for environmental quality indicators and subsequent aggregation of these subindices into an overall index. The formulation of different indices within this framework relies on the almost infinite capacity to generate different mathematical functions for both subindex and index formulation (Ott 1978). More recently developed frameworks are more elaborate and reflect the growing concern to integrate the environment with a range of socioeconomic issues. The most widely accepted today is the pressure-state-response (PSR) framework, originally developed by OECD. This framework has been adopted by, or is being considered by, a number of institutions, including the United Nations Commission on Sustainable Development.

The PSR model assumes that the state of the environment is linked to the state of the economy; that human activities impose pressures on the environment, but also depend upon it for natural resources; and that, as a result of feedback mechanisms, there is a human response to the state of the environment. Within this framework, OECD envisages the integration of sectoral-level data to link economics and the environment in key sectors.

FIGURE 1.1

Modified Pressure—State—Impact—Response Paradigm

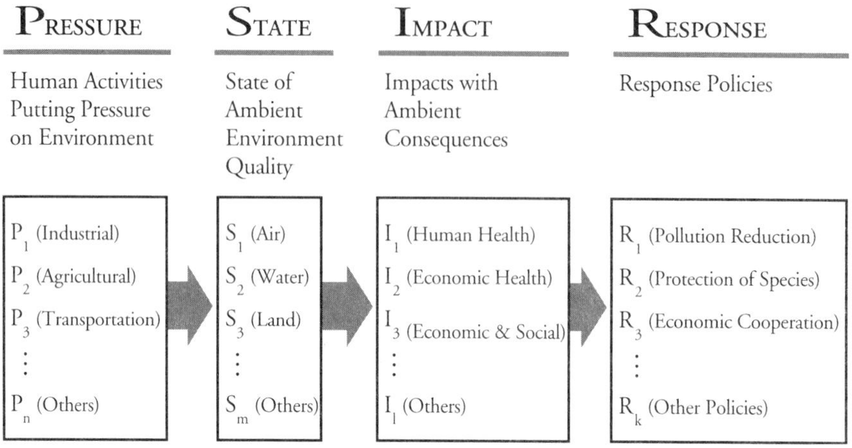

PRESSURE	STATE	IMPACT	RESPONSE
Human Activities Putting Pressure on Environment	State of Ambient Environment Quality	Impacts with Ambient Consequences	Response Policies
P_1 (Industrial)	S_1 (Air)	I_1 (Human Health)	R_1 (Pollution Reduction)
P_2 (Agricultural)	S_2 (Water)	I_2 (Economic Health)	R_2 (Protection of Species)
P_3 (Transportation)	S_3 (Land)	I_3 (Economic & Social)	R_3 (Economic Cooperation)
⋮	⋮	⋮	⋮
P_n (Others)	S_m (Others)	I_l (Others)	R_k (Other Policies)

The Netherlands Ministry of Housing, Physical Planning, and Environment has elaborated on the PSR model and conceived a framework based on an integrated approach to problem-solving—internally, within the environment, and externally, with other policy areas—to avoid isolated solutions that overlook interconnections. The Ministry states that clearly specified goals are required so that performance indicators as value judgments can be determined. The PSR framework is used as a means of identifying the range of possible indicators, with performance-based goals pertaining to resource use, pollution patterns, and the state of the environment. Environmental themes with specified goals provide the key environmental indicators, which are linked to performance indicators such as impact on the economic sector. Sectors can themselves be disaggregated to assess the pollution pattern caused by each and to find their contribution to the environmental theme indicators.

In contrast, the Japanese have adopted a bottom-up approach, developing indicators at a local level before moving to a larger scale. They have completed a series of case studies to determine physical measures of the environment and are trying to find a means of monetization. In the Japanese framework, indicators are built up sequentially. They focus first on the natural environment, then on intergenerational equity, poverty and quality of life, and finally on a level of (monetized) welfare.

FAO, focusing on agricultural indicators, highlights the importance of the linkages between the environment and other variables and suggests a framework in which macro- , middle- , and microeconomic levels of agriculture— and the feedback mechanisms between them—are encompassed. FAO suggests linking data and indicators so that they provide clear and valuable signals of changes.

We here adapt the PSR framework to include impacts as an intermediate stage between the State and Response functions, as depicted in Figure 1.1. Essentially, n human activities marked P_1 through P_n create pressures upon the ambient environment which is characterized by m ambient quality measures, S_1 through S_m. These ambient qualities lead to l impacts (I) upon human and ecosystem health, the economic and social system, and aesthetic enjoyment of the environment, and, finally, these impacts cause responses of individuals and communities to adjust and ameliorate the pressures on the environment, through k policies, R_1 through R_k. Table 1.1 lists possible metrics for the indicators of each type, P, S, I, and R. The pressures, P, can be conventional emissions such as tons of (BOD) into the aquatic system or tons of particulate matter into the air. They can also be items such as the number of livestock introduced onto grazing land or the area of wetlands drained. The states, S, can be the usual concentrations of pollutants in the air or water, but they can also be measures of the total remaining wetlands or the state of the pasture lands. The impacts of the ambient states are fairly self-evident and are typically restricted to the four impacted health systems shown in Figure 1.1; namely, human health, ecosystem health, economic and social health, and aesthetic health. The sequencing here is, however, not so obvious. For example, human health expresses many of its impacts through the economic system. Ecosystem health also has major economic ramifications, for example, when the impacts are felt in commercial forests. The human and social responses to the impacts are more varied and difficult to characterize simply. They could range from emission restriction policies to policies aimed at the structure of industrial production processes to reduce emissions, to emission trading arrangements, to policies that simply protect humans and the ecosystem from the ambient environmental states (for example, hats and sunglasses to protect against the result of ozone depletion).

Computation of Indices

Computation of indices can proceed using a range of different aggregation methods and mathematical functions. As originally described by Ott (1978), subindices require the generation of a mathematical function by which to move from a set of data points to a subindex. Aggregation could be accomplished through addition, multiplication, power series, or a range of other methods. There is, however, little or no literature that describes the application of indicators to real problem-solving, either in the United States or elsewhere. Most of the indices generated in the 1970s were based on US and Canadian environmental statistics. The US Council on Environmental Quality publishes a set of environmental indices each year and different groups, from state agencies to local newspapers, calculate their own environmental quality indices. In the context of the present study, it is the methodology used in the formulation of indices rather than the actual index numbers themselves that

TABLE 1.1
Anatomy of Environmental Themes

Issues	Pressure	State	Response
Climate Change	GHG emissions	Concentrations of GHGs	Energy intensity; environmental measures
Ozone Depletion	Halocarbon emissions and production	Chlorine concentrations; O_3 column	Protocols; CFC recovery; fund contribution
Eutrophication	N, P water, soil emissions	N, P, BOD concentrations	Treatment investments/costs
Acidification	SO_x, NO_x, NH_3 emissions	Deposition; concentrations	Investments; agreements
Toxic Contamination	POC, heavy metal emissions	POC, heavy metal, concentrations	Hazardous waste recovery investments/costs
Urban Env. Quality	VOC, NO_x, SO_x emissions	VOC, NO_x, SO_x and concentrations	Expenditures; transportation policy
Biodiversity	Land conversion; land fragmentation	Species abundance composition relative to virgin area	Protected areas
Waste	Waste generation—municipal, industrial, agricultural	Soil/ground water quality	Collection rate, recycling; investments/cost
Water Resources	Demand/use intensity—residential industrial/agricultural	Demand/supply ratio; quality	Expenditures; water pricing; savings policy
Forest Resources	Use intensity	Area of degraded forest; use/ sustainability; growth ratio	Protected forest area, sustainable logging
Fish Resources	Fish catches	Sustainable stocks	Quotas
Soil Degradation	Land use changes	Topsoil loss	Rehabilitation/protection
Oceans/Coastal Zones	Emissions; oil spills; depositions	Water quality	Coastal zone management; ocean protection
Environmental Index	Pressure index	State index	Response index

Source: Hammond et al. 1995.

provides the valuable insights into the work of a whole generation of environmental scientists and policy-makers.

The literature goes to great lengths to address the importance of the spatial resolution and data needed to develop indicators that yield information useful in policy formulation. A case in point is USEPA (1995, p. 3), which states that it has been criticized for being "data rich and information poor." The developing nations, on the other hand, can be said to be information rich and data poor. The background database to calculate indices is often lacking. Missing data must be complemented by a theoretical model of the more relevant indices to use in the quest to develop useful indicators.

The World Bank has initiated a large project (*Monitoring Environmental Progress*, 1995) to operationalize the use of environmental indicators. However, it has also focused attention on developing theoretical solutions to issues such as valuation, discount rate, and intergenerational equity. To develop indicators it is using an eclectic approach that includes models, national-level indicators, and sectoral- and project-level studies.

In order to integrate environmental costs and benefits into national accounts, the World Bank is working with UNSTAT to develop national indicators of the environment, or green GNPs. The World Bank is using case studies (Costa Rica, Indonesia, and Mexico), traditional system of national accounts shortcut methods, and potential cost-of-cleanup or defensive expenditures. This approach focuses largely on the cost side, and is linked to the smaller-scale issues of project environment-economic relationships by cost-benefit analysis as a means of better assessing environmental impacts. Models are being used to find creative solutions to valuation and aggregation at all scales. Valuation attempts are highlighting the cost side, using full-cost pricing.

Multi-objective decision-making has been suggested as a means of choosing optimal investment options or policies, i.e., using a modeling approach to interactively navigate the user through decision variables and complex interrelationships (see Murray and Harshadeep 1994). In fact, O'Connor describes modeling efforts as "prerequisites for devising interim solutions to valuation and aggregation problems, without which the ever-growing mound of environmental statistics and indicators will become the analyst's tower of Babel," (O'Connor 1994). In Japan, sector-based studies are being used to illustrate the principles of indicator calculation but broadened to a national scale to consider the possible incorporation of the environment into economic indicators through the cost of pollution. The Japanese have also generated some simple indicators of performance based on compliance rates, emissions, treatment capacity, and budgets. The notion of environmental satellite accounts is also being explored through calculation on a sectoral basis.

At a smaller scale and with a similar project- and sector-oriented concern that highlights some of the World Bank's work, FAO is searching for indicators that will be relevant for a range of policy and planning options and that illustrate the environmental impacts of different decisions. Computer models are being used—developed from an existing planning assistance and training model—to augment commodities, macroeconomics, land uses, and other components with environmental and natural resource modules. Other development activities focus on data-gathering and the collection of a wide range of natural resource indicators in order to search for those that can be used to describe the performance of agricultural policy.

Weighting Factors in Indices

One of the most difficult problems in the social sciences is how to make rational choices among many different goods or services, each having different attributes. If all of the attribute values of one good are preferable to those of the others, then the problem is easy. In real situations, however, this rarely occurs. Often the value of attribute i of good j is preferable to the value of attribute i of good k, but the value of attribute m of k is preferable to the value of attribute m of j, leading to no clear dominance[2] of one good over the other. In situations like this it is necessary to create a weighting system to express relative preferences for each of the attributes and to have some sort of calculus for adding the effects of the weights and the values of the attributes together. The economics profession was among the earliest to address this problem and to settle on prices as the way to assess relative preferences for goods and services. As a result, it is now commonplace to draw comparisons between and among countries based upon measures of GDP, which depend upon economic accounting models that suitably report all of the goods and services in value terms (price times quantity). Despite some drawbacks with the measures of national income (notably publicized by "green economics"), it is hard to avoid the almost universal use of these measures for international and regional comparisons.

Dorfman (1977) criticizes earlier attempts at index development, such as that of Inhaber (1976), by arguing that indices aggregated into a single number through a weighting system are useful only if all the measures aggregated are changing over time in the same direction. Dorfman concludes that an index is not needed to observe such change, and argues further that if, over time, all the measures do not tend in the same direction, the weights become the determining factor, rendering the index useless as a device to monitor environmental change and resource depletion. This is the weighting problem faced by all aggregations of indices and the fundamental, and perhaps intractable, problem in developing indices for any kind of social, political, and environmental assessment.

Although problematic, weighting approaches have been developed and are commonly used. Economists, for example, use indices with varying weights to represent aggregate utility. In a Cobb-Douglas utility function, the weights

FIGURE 1.2

Schematic Diagram of Canadian Indices

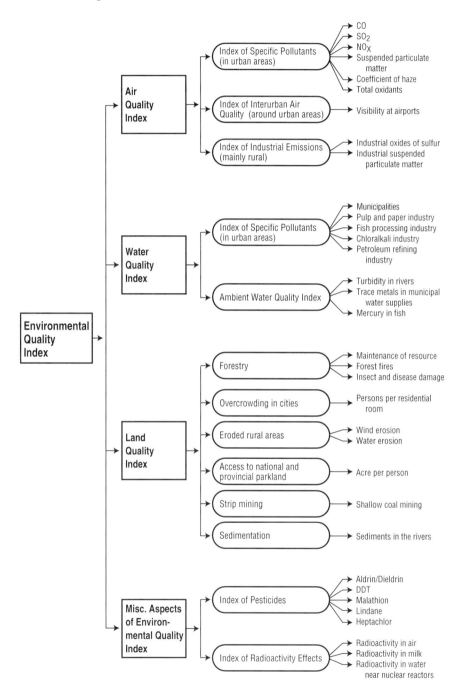

Source: Inhaber, 1976

represent the share of the individual budget allocated to the purchase of specific commodities. The utility function itself may represent the aggregation of many different products. Some weighting schemes can be justified on scientific grounds. Adriaanse (1993), for example, weights the contribution of global warming gases to a climate change index by the ability of various gases to inhibit the radiation of heat from the stratosphere. Dorfman's point remains instructive, however. We conclude that the use of a specific set of weights should be justified on scientific or socioeconomic grounds.

Such an approach has been taken by the Netherlands Ministry of Housing, Physical Planning, and Environment, which has developed a set of indicators for distinct environmental themes by gathering emission data and then weighting it according to scientific principles. Confining the data to specific themes limits the environmental issues. The target sectors are evaluated for their economic activity and environmental pollution pattern relative to each of the themes, as such determining an indicator for each sector with respect to

---

FIGURE   1.3
Canadian Indices

Air Quality Index

$$I_{air} = \sqrt{0.2\ I_{SO_2}^2 + 0.1\ I_{SPM}^2 + 0.1\ I_{COH}^2 + 0.2\ I_{CO}^2 + 0.2\ I_{O_x}^2 + 0.2\ I_{NO_x}^2}$$

where

I_{SO_2}	=	index for sulfur dioxide
I_{SPM}	=	index for suspended particulate matter
I_{COH}	=	index for coefficient of haze
I_{CO}	=	index for carbon monoxide
I_{O_x}	=	index for total oxidants
I_{NO_x}	=	index for oxides of nitrogen

Comprehensive Index of Environmental Quality

$$I_{EQI} = \sqrt{0.3\ I_{AIR}^2 + 0.3\ I_{WATER}^2 + 0.3\ I_{LAND}^2 + 0.1\ I_{MISCELLANEOUS}^2}$$

Note: All the above indices are based on the ratio of average annual concentrations in the atmosphere to a prescribed atmospheric standard.

Source: Inhaber 1974.

each theme. However, there is no unique weighting system with which to generate one indicator per sector.

A good example of the problems inherent in weighting the various aspects of the environment is based upon the first major attempt at creating an EQI. Inhaber and a team from Environment Canada began to develop an EQI for Canada in the early 1970s. Figure 1.2 schematically shows the four components that they thought appropriate for inclusion in the overall index: air, water, land, and a component called miscellaneous, which in effect represented pesticides and radioactive wastes. Each of these components, or subindices, was itself built up from a set of other subindices. Having derived the set of four subindices, one can see from Figure 1.3 how the subindices and the overall EQI are computed. The role that the weights play in arriving at the EQI and the subindices themselves is apparent from this figure.

Even if experts could agree on the monitoring and the return periods for measuring their own media-specific indices (in water and air, for example), it is unlikely that they would agree on the weights to be used to add them together. One can, therefore, imagine the difficulty in arriving at a sensible consensus on the weights to be used in each subindex in computing the overall EQI. Thus, the Achilles heel of index construction is laid out for all to see. How is it possible to ensure less arbitrary setting of weights at the subindex and EQI level? We believe that the major contribution of our research lies in how we have addressed this question, to which we will return later.

Notes

1 TA No. 5542-REG: *Regional Study of Environmental Indicators and Indices*, approved on August 16, 1993.

2 "Dominance" occurs when each of the attributes of i are preferred to each of the attributes of j.

2 CURRENT STATUS OF ENVIRONMENTAL INDICATORS

This chapter provides a critical review of the historical development and calculation of environmental indices, and describes current efforts in both the national and international community to use indicators. Activities undertaken by a number of international institutions are reviewed including those by the World Bank, OECD, and UNDP. We also report on the work of some of the more active national institutions—the Netherlands Ministry of Housing, Physical Planning, and Environment, USEPA, and the nongovernmental organization World Resources Institute (WRI) of Washington, DC which have contributed significantly to this burgeoning area of research.

Within the confines of this chapter it is not possible to do justice to the myriad environmental quality indices that have been created at the sectoral, national, or international scale. Hundreds of different indices have been suggested and more are under development by a growing number of institutions (see Tschirley 1992). In order to structure our discussion of progress in environmental index development, we start by reviewing the main environmental components and themes that define environmental quality. We examine the different methods used to aggregate and choose among different environmental indicators to develop indices. We review two broad approaches: methods that rely on the aggregation of theme-oriented subindices and those that try to supplement traditional economic approaches to the measurement of welfare with environmental considerations. Finally, we examine operational definitions of sustainability and how this concept impacts on index development.

Environmental Components and Themes

There is a broad consensus surrounding the different components of environmental quality across media. They include factors related to air quality or emissions, such as local air pollution, acid rain, global warming, and ozone depletion; water quality, including eutrophication, toxic contamination, wastewater etc.; land quality, including solid waste generation, soil degradation, and deforestation; and issues that include biodiversity, the quality of oceans, coastal zones, wilderness areas, and even the urban environment.

If we look again at Table 1.1 (in Chapter 1), we can see that these themes or issues are charted in the context of pressure-state-response. This list of environmental themes, perhaps more appropriately termed "black-list," provides a common basis for the discussion of environmental quality. However, it provides no direction as to how to measure each theme, compare the seriousness of the themes, prioritize the distribution of resources among them, or measure the progress of nations toward improving them. These tasks require environmental indicators and aggregated indices.

Basic Environmental Indicators

Ott (1978), Thomas (1972), and Inhaber (1976) are the best sources for detailed explanations of the basic approaches toward the development of simple environmental indicators. Examples of environmental indicators are numerous, especially in the area of air and water pollution, but we confine our discussion to a few illustrative examples.

One of the earliest air pollution indices was developed by Ridker (1967). His Air Pollution Cost Index attempts to describe economic damage as a function of air pollution intensity. The index divides damage into several categories, each corresponding to a different type of air pollution effect. The total costs of each type of damage are calculated by multiplying the damage per unit by the number of units affected, and by the monetary cost per damaged unit. Total air pollution costs are then obtained by summing over all damage types.

$$TC = \sum_{i=1}^{n} C_i Q_i F_i(S) \qquad (2.1)$$

where:

TC = total air pollution costs
C_i = cost per unit of damage type i
Q_i = number of units affected by damage type i
$F(S)$ = function describing how per unit damage of type varies with air pollution levels.

The Measure of Undesirable Respirable Contaminants Index (MURC) (Ott 1978) was used routinely in Detroit to report air quality data to the public in the 1970s. It uses only the coefficient of haze as an air pollution variable.

$$MURC = 70\, X^{0.7} \qquad (2.2)$$

where:

$MURC$ = measure of undesirable respirable contaminants
X = coefficient of haze

Five descriptors were assigned to various MURC ranges and were reported along with the numerical value of MURC:

MURC Range	Descriptor
0–30	extremely light contamination
31–60	light contamination
61–90	medium contamination
91–120	heavy contamination
>121	extremely heavy contamination

Similar index-policy approaches have been developed in other cities, including Taipei, although there has been limited use of this type of index in actual policy actions. More commonly, air quality indicators have been used to rank cities or other airsheds. For example, in a report of the MITRE Corporation (Ott 1978), the MITRE Air Quality Index (MAQI) makes use of national ambient air quality standards for five different pollutants to create an overall air quality index. A subindex is determined for each pollutant by using standards for several different averaging times. These subindices are then aggregated in the following manner:

$$MAQI = \sqrt{\sum_{i=1}^{5} I^2} \qquad (2.3)$$

where:

MAQI = MITRE air quality index
I_i = air quality subindex for pollutant i

The subindices for the MAQI are determined as follows, using, for example, sulfur dioxide:

$$I_5 = \sqrt{\left(\frac{X_a}{S_a}\right)^2 + \delta_1 \left(\frac{X_{24}}{S_{24}}\right)^2 + \delta_2 \left(\frac{X_3}{S_3}\right)^2} \qquad (2.4)$$

where:

X_a = sulfur dioxide concentration (annual arithmetic mean)
S_a = annual NAAQS for sulfur dioxide (S_a = 0.03ppm)
X_{24} = sulfur dioxide concentration (maximum 24-hr value)
S_{24} = 24-hr NAAQS (S_{24} = 0.14ppm)
X_3 = sulfur dioxide concentration (maximum 3-hr value)
S_3 = 3-hr NAAQS (S_3 = 0.5ppm)
δ_1 = 1 if $X_{24} \geq S_{24}$, 0 otherwise
δ_2 = 1 if $X_3 \geq S_3$, 0 otherwise

In the area of water quality, measures of pollutant stocks are used rather than the flows most commonly used to develop indicators in air pollution. For example, the National Science Foundation Water Quality Index (NSFWQI), developed in 1970 "as a means for communicating water quality information to the lay public and to legislative decision-makers," was among the most widely used of all water quality indices in the United States. In an attempt to avoid biases toward any single professional viewpoint or local situation throughout the country, the index was developed through the use of questionnaires, soliciting the opinions of a large number of water experts in a variety of geographic areas.

The panel of experts was first asked to choose variables that should be included in an index and the weight that each of them should be assigned. From the responses, eleven variables were selected: dissolved oxygen, fecal coliforms, pH, five-day biochemical oxygen demand (BOD_5), nitrates, phosphates, temperature, turbidity, total solids, toxic substances, and pesticides. Then, for the first nine variables, the panel members were asked to draw curves showing how they felt that subindices should vary with various levels of the pollutants. These curves were averaged to establish implicit nonlinear subindex functions. For toxic substances and pesticides, upper limits were established that could drive the NSFWQI to zero. The overall NSFWQI was then calculated by summing the products of subindices and their corresponding weights.

$$NSFWQI_a = \sum_{i=1}^{n} W_i I_i \qquad (2.5)$$

where:

$NSFWQI_a$ = additive National Science Foundation Water Quality Index
W_i = weight assigned to pollutant variable i
I_i = subindex for pollutant variable i

In other areas of environmental quality, there was less progress in indicator formulation. For land degradation, soil erosion has been addressed using comprehensive indicators, and these are all based on some version of Wischmeier's 1976 universal soil loss equation. This widely used empirical equation relates soil loss in a field (A) to rainfall (R), soil erodibility (K), length of slope (L), slope steepness (S), cropping system factor (C), and the support practice factor (P), that takes into account farming methods which reduce erosion:

$$A = R K L S C P \qquad (2.6)$$

In using the universal soil loss equation, it is important to keep in mind that it was developed *only* to measure soil loss on farms with slope S ranging from zero to seven degrees, and that it was to be applied only in the eastern and central United States. New applications require field calibration. Wischmeier cautions against the misguided application of his empirically derived equation to different circumstances.

Environmental Indices: A Review

As described in Chapter 1, even if basic environmental indicators can be developed, their aggregation into a single environmental index is difficult. The WRI Information Pyramid in Figure 2.1 shows the necessary relationship of indices to data and to the functional relationships between the various levels of indicators. It is with this empirical and theoretical model of environmental reality that many institutions are currently grappling. Many national and international institutions are setting up or have set up environmental monitoring programs whose information will contribute to the establishment of environmental indicators. As shown in Figure 2.2, international agencies such as the World Bank are moving toward indicators that have less of a basis in physical measures and place greater emphasis on socioeconomic implications. In OECD, for example, the focus has been on developing a series of natural resources accounts for member countries. Similarly, the World Bank has

FIGURE 2.1
Information and Indices Flows

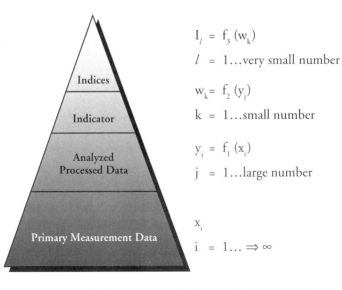

$$I_l = f_3 (w_k)$$
$l = 1...\text{very small number}$

$$w_k = f_2 (y_j)$$
$k = 1...\text{small number}$

$$y_j = f_1 (x_i)$$
$j = 1...\text{large number}$

x_i
$i = 1... \Rightarrow \infty$

Indices

Indicator

Analyzed Processed Data

Primary Measurement Data

$$I_l = f_3 (w_k) = f_3 (f_2(y_j)) = f_3 (f_2(f_1 x_i)) = f_3 (f_2(f_1(x_i)))$$

FIGURE 2.2
Schematic Representation of Activities in Indicator Development

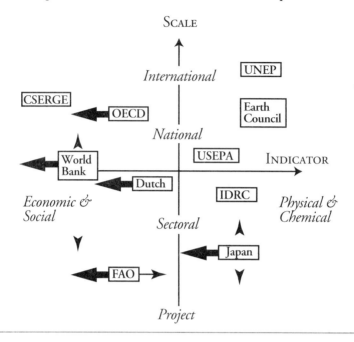

initiated data-gathering and environmental account development for Costa Rica, Indonesia, and Mexico (in collaboration with WRI). The World Bank also has indicator work under way at the project level: data assessment and indicator development are being incorporated into projects in agriculture, biodiversity (with WRI), coastal zone degradation, global climate change impacts (with WRI), and in forestry. On the industrial side, for which environmental pressures are better known and more effectively monitored, projects are underway to assess the risk intensity of manufacturing activities and to develop decision support systems for industrial pollution control. For example, the World Bank's prototype, Industrial Pollution Projection System (IPPS) calculates a multimedia pollution intensity index for each industrial sector of the economy.

In contrast, UNEP and, to some extent, USEPA remain in the physical chemical zone of indicator development in which much of the work involves the collection and limited analysis of environmental data in the absence of a policy-oriented framework. At a national level, both the Netherlands and Japanese Governments are developing indicators that are valuable in national environmental strategies. The Japanese Government places more emphasis on local and regional issues. Other national agencies have made less progress in indicator formulation, although they collect data, and the issue of concrete goals is raised more explicitly.

Some of these approaches are reviewed below. Some have obvious deficiencies, but are useful to highlight common problems faced in the generation of a useful, robust and representative index of the state of the environment and its improving condition.

The Netherlands Approach

The attempt by the Netherlands Ministry of Housing, Physical Planning, and Environment to develop indicators (see text box) is by far the most sophisticated study undertaken at the national level. The study by Adriaanse (1993), benefited from an existing set of national goals to reduce environmental emissions over the short to medium term. The study considered seven environmental themes: climate change, depletion of the ozone layer, acidification of the environment, eutrophication of the environment, dispersion of toxic substances, disposal of solid wastes, and disturbance of the local environment—each defined by several contributing factors. For example, in the case of climate change, a list of greenhouse gases included: CO_2, CH_4, N_2O, CFC-11, CFC-12, CFC-13, CFC-113, CFC-114, CFC-115, Halon-1211, and Halon-1301. These gases are weighted by the extent to which they inhibit the escape of long-wave radiation from the troposphere. All gases are brought to a common denominator by expressing them in terms of CO_2 equivalents. Some contribute to other themes: for example, CFCs also cause ozone depletion. Table 2.1 shows the components of the seven themes and how they are weighted to generate the individual pressure indices. Seven target groups that contribute to one or more of the themes are also identified: agriculture, traffic and transport, industry, energy, refining, building trade, and consumers and retailing. Agriculture, for example, contributes to acidification through emission of ammonia, to eutrophication through the use of phosphates, and to dispersion of toxic substances through use of pesticides.

T A B L E 2 . 1

Theme	Components	Weights	Basis
Climate Change (Ceq; Mtonnes)*	CO_2	1	Based on the greenhouse warming potential for all the GHG's, related to the GWP of CO_2, assuming a 100-year residency time.
	CH_4	12	
	N_2O	290	
	CFC's	5770 (average)	
Ozone Depletion (Oeq; tonnes)*	CFC-11, -12, -13	1	The weighting scheme depends upon the ozone depletion potential of the different compounds. This is measured relative to CFC-11.
	CFC-113	0.8	
	CFC-114	1	
	CFC-115	0.6	
	Halon-1211	3	
	Halon-1301	10	
Acidification (Aeq; ktonnes)*	SO_2	$10^9 * 1/64 * 2$	Weighting determined by the chemical composition of the acids formed by the cmpds —to give the moles of H+ produced, recalling that SO_2 produces 2H+ per unit of acid.
	NO_x	$10^9 * 1/46$	
	NH_3	$10^9 * 1/46$	
Eutrophication (Eeq; ktonne)*	P (phosphates)	1	Average ratio of P:N has been determined to be 1:10, from a range of natural ratios and is used as a weighting factor on the assumption that this is the "ideal" nutrient ratio.
	N (nitrates)	0.1	
Dispersion (Deq; Kg)*	pesticides	kg/MAC*t	The total mass of a chemical emitted is weighted by a Maximum Acceptable Concentration factor for air, water, and land, and also corrected for its half-life.
	priority compounds		
	radioactive	Bq/MAC*t	
Disposal (Weq; Mtonnes)*	solid waste	1	No weighting for different types of waste.
Disturbance (Neq; # people)*	noise	% population	The population % are combined to give a measure of the total number of people affected by disturbance.
	odor	% population	

*See Abbreviations and Acronyms at the beginning of this volume.

Source: Adriaanse, 1993

In order to aggregate the various contributing factors into a single number, each contribution is divided by a sustainable level of a particular substance expressed in the same units. Table 2.1 shows how this is implemented. The factors can be added to arrive at an impact measure (Ceq, Oeq, Aeq, Eeq, Deq, Weq, and Neq). The target is provided in the same units and the number is plotted over a period of time. This information is graphed along with targets and percentage change over time. In Adriaanse's words (1993), "An indicator consists of a single graph, one or more targets, and a single percentage." The graph is designed to show the trend over time. The targets show whether the trend is in the direction of the target and the percentage measures the extent to which the environmental pressure declined or increased over the time period considered.

The Adriaanse study (1993) is interesting in that it tells us the trend and the goal in a single graph. The user groups Adriaanse identifies are "decision-makers in the public and private sectors" (Adriaanse, 1993, p.1). He also states: "The essential points must be put forward in a clear and unambiguous fashion, divested of any minor details." Figure 2.3 shows such a graph for the climate change theme. It does not tell us the underlying consequences of directing the trend closer and closer to the target. For example, in the Netherlands, the government has set a target to stop using CFCs by the year 1995. The associated economic costs are not presented. Similarly, the 1995 goal for climate change, expressed in CO_2 equivalents, is 195. The sustainable level is 10 and, in 1991,

FIGURE 2.3

Change of Climate

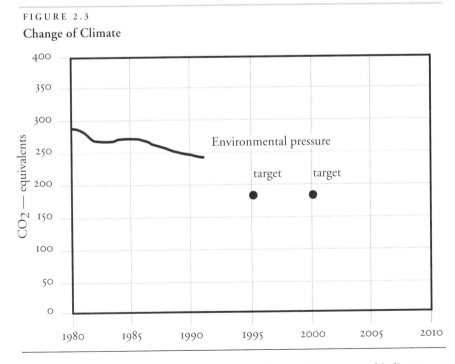

the level emitted was 231. The sustainable level for climate change emissions is probably too low to be achievable in the short-to-medium term. Also, 10 represents an arbitrary number since it is based on a *ceteris paribus* assumption. It may not be achievable under existing technology except at the cost of reducing industrial output. The sustainability level is so far removed from the 1995 target and current emission levels, that it can be used by groups on both sides of the debate on the merit—or lack thereof—of attaining it. Those who state that sustainability should be met will use this information to argue that it is time to implement stringent programs for emissions. They can argue that the 1995 target is a meaningless goal. Those who argue that the sustainability level cannot be met can use the present level of emissions to claim that it is an illusory goal and that the urgency to reach it has been overstated.

The progress that has been achieved in abatement, a 16 percent reduction over the period 1980 to 1991 (see Figure 2.3), is a number replete with problems. There is no indication that this level of reduction is possible in the next few years or that it is particularly wise to try to maintain that marginal rate of decline. In fact, strictly considering CO_2 emissions, a rise of 8 percent is reported. The index of climate change declines because other emissions are falling. Granted, Adriaanse makes the case that other gases, especially halons, are far more able to inhibit escaping heat, hence are attributed a higher weight in the climate change index. In the economy, the real problem is curtailing CO_2 emissions and we must conclude that the weighting scheme obscures this essential problem. It is more costly in terms of GDP lost to reduce CO_2 emission than it is to reduce the emission of halons. So what does the climate change index tell us? How do policy-makers use this information? Is the information presented correct, or are the results achieved through a contrived weighting scheme? Decision-makers want to know that they are gaining or losing ground on an index. If they suspect that the answer is determined by the choice of weights (Table 2.2), they will dismiss the indicator.

Turning to the disposal of solid wastes, the study develops a measure termed the waste equivalent (Weq) in order to quantify this aspect of emissions. An 8 percent drop in the Weq over the period 1980 to 1991 (see Figure 2.4) is shown. In the Netherlands, there is a year 2000 target of 5 Weq, while in 1991 the number hovered around 14.1 Weq. It is difficult to see how a 65 percent drop over the period 1991 to 2000 might occur if the Weq declined by only 8 percent over the period 1980 to 1991. We are assuming that the reductions become harder and harder. Furthermore, the waste products used to construct the Weq include domestic solid waste, household refuse, water treatment sludges, construction and demolition waste, and fly ash from coal-fired plants. Though the study recognizes that the toxicity levels of these wastes differs and that the products should be weighted accordingly, this is not done. Allowing for an equal weighting, it is a simple matter to arrive at the Weq by adding up the tonnage in millions of metric tons. While weight is a relevant feature of the

TABLE 2.2
The Netherlands' Model

Theme	⇒	Theme Indicators	⇒	Target Group Indicators	⇒	Indices
Change of climate		f (CO_2, CH_4, N_2O, CFC, etc.)		Agriculture		Weighted by targets
Acidification of environment		g (SO_2, NOA, NH_3)		Traffic and transport industry		Weighted by sustainability levels
Eutrophication of environment		f (P, nitrates as N)				
Dispersion of toxics		f (pesticides, priority subs, radioactivity)				
Disposal of solid wastes		f (emissions, solid wastes)		Energy sector		
Disturbance of local environments		f (noise, odor)		Refineries		
Dehydration of soils				Building trades		
Squandering of resources				Consumers and retail		
Depletion of ozone layer		f (CFC, halons)				

Year 2000 targets	(Ceq.	x	Mton)
1. Climate change	CO_2		173
	CH_4		10.1
	N_2O		11.6
	CFCs		0.0
	HCFCs		0.0
	SO_2		75 Kt
	NO_x		238 Kt
	NH_3		82 Kt
3. Eutrophication	P		47 Kt
	N		48 Kt

Source: Adriaanse, 1993

FIGURE 2.4
Disposal of Solid Waste

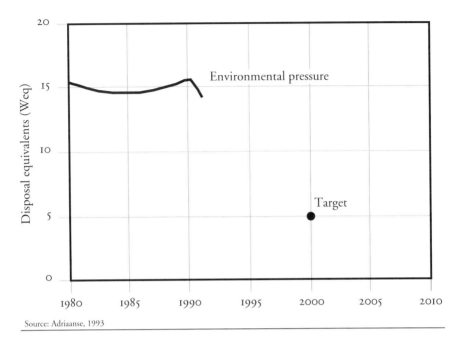

Source: Adriaanse, 1993

substances considered in the Weq, toxicity is much more important. Much of the waste identified recycles quite well, though the lack of success of recycling is borne out by the 8 percent decline figure, which is modest considering that much of the waste is simply paper.

Despite its limitations, the Netherlands approach is appealing in many ways. It recognizes the link between problem, stress created, environmental state, and policy options for environmental issues. This causal chain is relevant for all locations, though different countries will want to emphasize different problems. Climate change is an issue which the developing countries are unlikely to want to emphasize. Also, with solid waste disposal, recycling is practiced on a much larger scale in the Philippines, for example, than it is in the Netherlands. What passes for waste generation in the Netherlands may contribute to GDP in another country. Any useful index or set of indices for the developing world must be built around the notion of what is given up to meet environmental targets.

World Resources Study
Another significant attempt to construct an index of environmental quality was by the World Resources Institute under the principal authorship of Allen Hammond (1995). They define their "index of resource depletion" as:

...the value of the decline in the natural resource stocks in a country relative to the value of gross (or net) investment in man-made capital during the given year. Roughly speaking, the index indicates the degree of departure from sustainable resource use, assuming that the depletion of resource stock is sustainable if their use leads to the creation of other assets of equal value. The index is normalized so that an index of one indicates that the increase in man-made capital is offset exactly by the depreciation of the nation's national assets. And index much less than one indicates that resource depletion is small compared with the increase in man-made assets (a desireable circumstance).

This, they recognize, could also be described as a "weak sustainability" criterion (the concept of sustainability is examined later in this chapter). They argue that the index uses the concepts of "green accounting." Figure 2.5 provides indices calculated for Costa Rica and Indonesia over time for the whole economy. It shows that Costa Rica appeared to be more sustainable than Indonesia (much less than one), though Indonesia appeared to be improving over time. One problem, however, as shown in Figure 2.5, is that the graph for Indonesia exactly tracks the price of oil on the world market over the period 1970 to 1984. There is clearly a problem here, in that it is widely accepted that the price of oil over this period did not reflect the physical scarcity of the resource, though the index suggests exactly that. Furthermore, since the index attempts to relate resource depletion to gross fixed capital formation, and if it is assumed that capital formation is expensive, it must be true that the artificially high price of oil caused the index to portray an unsustainable situation. In fact, as is well known for Indonesia, capital formation was paid for by selling off oil reserves, but it was not until the price of oil rose significantly that Indonesia was able to finance such large capital expenditures. The more serious problem for Indonesia, which is not captured in the index, is the capacity to sustain the use of man-made capital acquired at the price of its oil resource. We are left with the obvious conclusion that "resources are not, they become," which is exactly what has happened in Indonesia. Leaving the oil reserves untouched would have made the development of man-made capital impossible. There is another concern here, namely that oil is depleted in one cycle, but capital is depreciated over several years. The index WRI presents does not reveal anything about the present value of the usefulness of the capital required and the role of the price of oil. Would such an adjustment make all trade-offs between resource depletion and the development of man-made capital appear beneficial?

There are other anomalous aspects of the index. Costa Rica, for example, is shown in the aggregate to use its resources in a sustainable pattern. When the same index is developed specifically for the agriculture, forestry, and fisheries sector (Figure 2.6), the country appears to be consuming resources in a much less sustainable pattern. The index for Costa Rica's whole economy in Figure

FIGURE 2.5
Resource Depletion Index: Depreciation/Gross Fixed Capital Formation

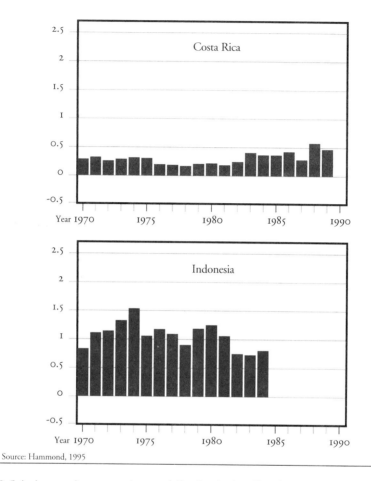

Source: Hammond, 1995

2.5 is improving over time; while the index for the sector in Figure 2.6 is deteriorating over time.

Organisation for Economic Co-operation and Development Indices

OECD has had an EQI program in place since about 1990. Its program evolved out of an OECD Council request to undertake a "next generation programme on environmental economics that would integrate environmental and economic decision-making more systematically and effectively as a means of contributing to sustainable development," and from an obligation to provide its members with "periodic reporting on the state of the environment." OECD defines indicators in reference to some stated final objective(s), that is, indicators are envisaged as a set of information used to measure (environmental) performance with respect to a defined level that would illustrate changes

FIGURE 2.6
Resource Depletion Index: Depreciation/Sector Domestic Product
(Agriculture, forestry, and fisheries sector)

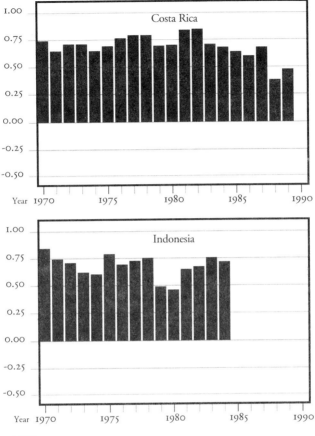

Source: Hammond, 1995

made in reaching that level. We have already mentioned OECD's PSR framework, which we have adopted to guide our own search for indicators.

OECD collects data on many different variables, and for the G7 members there exists a longtime series of data covering the period from 1970 to 1990. Nevertheless, even for the G7 member countries, certain data shortages over time are apparent. Data lacunae will turn out to be a very serious obstacle to EQI development.

National Center for Economic Alternatives Index
In an attempt to measure the effectiveness of the actions that the world's major economic powers have taken to protect the environment, the National Center for Economic Alternatives (NCFEA, 1995) has developed a composite,

aggregated index of environmental quality, known as the Index of Environmental Trends (IET). The index is an aggregate of 21 environmental change indicators for air, land, and water quality; chemical and waste generation; and energy use since the 1970s, as summarized in Table 2.3. The index was compiled for four periods: 1970–1975, 1970–1980, 1970–1985 and 1970–1990. For each period, the percentage change of each indicator was calculated. The sign of the percentage change is determined by the nature of the indicators. For example, if CO_2 emission increases by 20 percent during a given period, the value of the indicator takes a negative sign, i.e., –20 percent, since the increase of CO_2 causes adverse environmental impacts. Conversely, if the total forested area increases by 20 percent during a given period, the value takes a positive sign because the increase is considered an environmental plus. The aggregate index for each sector and for the overall environmental quality is a simple mean of all the indicators in each category, assuming an equal weight for all indicators. NCFEA computed the index for each of the six sectors separately and for all the sectors combined for four periods. This allows decision-makers and the general public to examine environmental progress in any given country, in air, water, land, and the overall environmental quality for different periods. Based on the aggregate index for all sectors combined for the period between 1970 and 1990, NCFEA ranked nine countries in terms of the least to the most environmental deterioration (see Table 3.3 in Chapter 3).

There are a number of points that are not adequately addressed in the NCFEA report (1995). First, as described in Chapter 1, the weighting of different indicators in the composite index is particularly critical because it can alter the results, including the country rankings. Second, some indicators are emission indicators (pressure indicators in OECD terminology), such as the air pollution indicators. Others are ambient concentration indicators (state indicators), such as water pollution indicators. The impacts of mixed types of indicators are not clear. Third, the progress, or lack thereof, in environmental quality measured in some indicators may be related to economic growth. For example, total CO_2 emission is related to energy consumption, which is related

TABLE 2.3

Indicators Used by NCFEA

Air	Water	Chemical	Waste	Land	Causal
CO_2	DO	Fertilizers	Municipal	Grasslands	Automobiles
NO_X	Nitrates	Pesticides	Nuclear	Woods	Energy
SO_X	Phosphorous	Ind. Chemical			
CO	Ammonium				
Particulate	Metals				
VOC or HC	Withdrawal				

Source: NCFEA, 1995

to economic growth. A country that achieves economic growth while decreasing or holding environmental emissions constant is obviously more successful than another country experiencing economic decline and environmental deterioration. The report attempts to tackle this issue by presenting two different scenarios: one with zero-economic growth and the other with a 4 percent economic growth rate across all countries. It computed the so-called "standardized pollution level" based on GDP; that is, the pollutant:GDP ratio, for those indicators believed to be related to GDP such as air emissions, fertilizer uses, and energy consumption. Total emissions were estimated by multiplying the pollutant:GDP ratios by the estimated total GDP under the two different economic scenarios. The estimated total emissions were then incorporated into the index and two sets of new indices were computed. The purpose of this exercise is to explore the environmental-economic linkages. In Chapter 3 of this report, we will explore these linkages using the same set of data but with a new concept known as environmental elasticity (EE).

Finally, the index is formed by freely comparing the values of stock and flow environmental indicators, (e.g., SO_2 emission and forest area) and may mean little.

The Green Index

The Green Index is the contribution of the Institute for Southern Studies (Hall and Kerr, 1991). It is an effort to assess environmental quality on a state-to-state basis in the United States. The Green Index collects 256 indicators in 8 environmental sectors. Table 2.4 summarizes its contents.

To minimize the difference in the sizes or population of the states, the indicators are given in the form of per capita or per acre or a similar ratio. Based on each of the 256 indicators and the proponents' value judgments on "good" and "bad," the Green Index ranks all 50 states. In addition, the index features several composite rankings, derived by adding together the ranks a state receives for each indicator in a subset, such as air pollution or water pollution, to produce a composite score. The composite scores are then ranked with the lowest total receiving the best "composite rank." Using a similar method, the final Green Index score is the sum of any state's ranks for all 256 indicators, with each indicator carrying equal weight.

The main purpose of the Green Index is to draw public attention to the overall environmental performance of each state. By heavily emphasizing state rankings, the Green Index largely achieves its purpose. A few points should be made regarding the index methodology. First, it is based upon a very large and comprehensive data set from detailed governmental records and other sources. Such a comprehensive database is unlikely to exist in developing countries. Furthermore, the index developers seem to be more concerned with the total number of indicators included than with the covariance structure of the indicators. Many air emissions and energy consumption indices, used here, are

TABLE 2.4
Indicators in the Green Index

Sector	# of Indicators	Examples
Air Sickness	18	Total toxic chemicals released to air per capita, ozone-depleting emissions per capita
Water Pollution	24	Pesticide-contaminated groundwater; % investment for sewer needs to year 2008
Energy Use and Abuse Vehicle	38	Oil production; persons per automobile
Toxic, Hazardous, and Solid Waste	30	Total toxic chemicals released to environment; hazardous waste generated per capita
Community and Workplace Health	23	Cancer cases per 100,000 pop.; workers in high-injury industries
Farms, Forests, Fish, and Fun	46	Cropland erosion (tons/acre) wetlands lost since 1780s
Congressional Leadership	4	Score for voting record on nuclear issues; contributions received from energy-related Potential Action Committees
State Policy Initiatives	73	"Renew America" score on 17 policies including forest management, waste recycling
Composite Green Index	256	

Source: Hall and Kerr, 1991

highly correlated. By including such variables, the overall amount of the information carried by the Green Index is not as comprehensive as sheer numbers suggest. Second, the Green Index adopts a method of adding ranks to derive the composite index. Not only is the equal weighting implied by the method questionable, but the meaning of the composite index, or sum of the ranks, is as well. For example, California is ranked fourth among all 50 states by the final Green Index score. If air pollution indicators were given more weight than "score for voting record on nuclear issues," the results may be different. Finally, in the PSR framework, the Green Index includes all three types of indicators in one index.

UNDP's Human Development Index

The success of macro-level indices (such as GNP) in economics has led the development community to seek similar macro-level indices. One index that has recently attracted much attention is the Human Development Index (HDI) first formulated by UNDP in its 1992 *Human Development Report.* This index, based on three indicators of human well-being—life expectancy, educational level attained, and income—appears to many potential users to be a good way to characterize the status of human development in different countries. More than anything else it appears to ameliorate the emphasis on GNP found in most intercountry and interregional comparisons. For example, using HDI instead of GNP per capita as an index for ranking the member countries of the United Nations moves Saudi Arabia from 31st to 84th place, and Cuba from 101st to 75th place. The same index, when applied to regions within countries, also shows wide variability; for example, in India the scale for the wealthy but socially backward state of Uttar Pradesh is one third lower than the national average of HDI for the whole country.

HDI combines the three attributes of longevity, knowledge, and income. It measures longevity by life expectancy at birth. It measures knowledge by a linear combination of adult literacy and mean years of schooling, weighing the former variable by two-thirds and the latter by one-third. To measure income, HDI uses the well-known Atkinson formulation reflecting the diminishing value of additional income. This is given as:

$$W(y) = \frac{1}{1-\varepsilon} y^{1-\varepsilon} \qquad (2.7)$$

where ε is the elasticity of the utility of income with respect to income. The HDI applies equation (2.7) by defining the poverty level of per capita income as y, and dividing the range of national incomes into multiples of the poverty level of income. Table 2.5 shows how HDI is calculated.

One surprising feature of the determination of the utility of income is that it does not alter the ranking of a country from what it would be if the unadjusted income per capita figure is used. By itself, this transformation is meaningless as it preserves the ranking and maintains the "more income is better" axiom. Combined with other measures, the specific marginal transformation becomes more important.

Unfortunately, three of the four variables retained in HDI are invariant over a typical environmental policy planning period of about four to five years. These are life expectancy at birth, adult literacy, and mean years of schooling. The consequence is that to change the ranking of nations according to HDI, other variables must be included. The fourth variable, GDP per capita expressed in purchasing power parity, is more likely to change over time. It seems then that to discrediting GDP as a single revealing measure of human welfare, UNDP has produced an index where GDP is the only variable capable of changing the ranking of different countries. The developers of HDI recognize that it is impossible to naively compare HDIs over time. They give an example of a country which improves its HDI relative to a previous period, but since the best and worst countries have also improved, the country's absolute improvement registers as a relative decline. UNDP avoids this problem by defining minima and maxima for a period of time. One must question the necessity of this attempt at intertemporal comparison given that HDI is unlikely to vary over time.

TABLE 2.5
Human Development Index

HDI	=	f {Longevity, Knowledge, Income}		
Longevity	∫	Life Expectancy at Birth (LE)		
Knowledge	∫	O (% Adult Literacy) + N (Mean Years of Schooling)		
Income	∫	Utility of Income W(y)		
	=	$\dfrac{1}{1-\varepsilon}\, y^{1-\varepsilon}$		
$1-\varepsilon$	=	Marginal Utility of Income		
$1-\varepsilon$	=	1 for poor countries		
$1-\varepsilon$	=	½ for countries 1 to 2 times poverty level		
$1-\varepsilon$	=	⅓ for countries 2 to 3 times poverty level		

Each factor is scaled by max and min; e.g., for longevity:

$$\frac{\max LE - LE}{\max LE - \min LE} = \frac{78.6 - LE}{78.6 - 42.0}$$

Source: UNDP, 1992

Several follow-up studies have been done to modify HDI to make it more gender sensitive, for example, and more "green" (Desai, 1994; Pfliegner, 1995). The Green Human Development Index (GHDI) eliminates from consideration the question of human welfare as measured by life expectancy at birth. The three variables retained for the computation of GHDI are greenhouse gas emissions per capita [G], water withdrawal as a percentage of annual internal renewable water resources [W], and energy consumption per constant US$ of GNP 1979–1989 [E]. The developers of GHDI argue that:

> It is tempting at this stage to add up these indicators [the three environmental variables] as was done in the case of the HDI. It is prudent, however, to be cautious. With respect to each variable, it is possible to say that a low value of the index is better than a high value...The optimal level of index for any country depends on many variables and, relative to income, population, structure of output, complexity of production processes, etc. ...an appropriate level could perhaps be defined. However, until the environmental literature is clearer on many of these aspects, it is best to proceed with caution. (GHDI, p. 10)

The World Bank's Wealth of Nations Index

Since its introduction in the Brundtland report (Brundtland Commission, 1987), the concept of sustainable development has been widely referred to in choosing the course of economic development. It describes a scenario for improving the well-being of the current generation without compromising the welfare of future generations. The inadequacy of the traditional economic indicators such as GNP in terms of measuring sustainable development has long been recognized; that is, its inability to account for human and environmental values. There have been a number of efforts to modify the situation. Most recently, the World Bank (1995) has developed a new measure of a country's wealth.

According to the proponents of the new measure at the World Bank, a nation's wealth contains four ingredients: natural capital (such as soil, atmosphere, forests, water, wetland, minerals); man-made capital (houses, roads, factories, ships); human capital (people, their education, their health and capacity); and social capital (institutions, cultural cohesion, collective information, knowledge). The total wealth of a nation at any given time is thus the sum of all kinds of capital measured in a unified unit, i.e., dollars. To attach monetary values to each kind of capital, the authors adopted the following strategies:

- Tradable natural capital including forest, oil, minerals, and coal was estimated by multiplying the total known reserves by 50 percent of the prevailing international prices. Water was valued at 1 US cent per gallon of fresh water available for human use.

- The value of nontradable (immobile) natural capital—i.e., land of different uses—was assumed to be proportional to per capita income of a country; e.g., the weightings given to one hectare of cropland, forest, pasture, and other land are 2, 1.75, 0.75, and 0.25 times per capita income, respectively.

- Man-made capital was estimated using perpetual inventory models (PIMs), which accumulate annual estimates of fixed capital formation while retiring some fraction of the produced assets.

- The weighting of human capital was assumed to be the expected lifetime earnings of today's population computed as the residual of per capita gross national income after deducting earnings accounted for by natural and man-made capital multiplied by the average years of life remaining to the current population. When the residual is negative, the case for 19 of 192 nations, a minimum value is assigned to human resources, i.e., one third of the value of produced assets and land.

- Social capital was "excluded" from this accounting process, due to difficulties of quantification.

Examining these methods in detail, the assumption of fixed prices for all the tradable natural capital is reasonable in the sense that one barrel of crude oil is assumed to have the same value in all countries. The study did not provide justifications for why 50 percent of the prevailing international prices was assumed. Such prices should ideally be determined by the quality of the resource, such as grades of ore, thickness of trees, and composition of soils. An important factor that is excluded is that resource prices are strongly affected by the current production scale in the sense that a mass increase or decrease in supply will decrease or increase the price substantially. In addition to uncertainties related to prices, total known reserves are also likely to change over time as technologies advance.

Looking at the assigned water prices, 1 US cent per gallon appears to be too high. The typical US rates for irrigation and municipal drinking water supply are 0.01 and 0.15 cent per gallon, respectively. The cost of desalinizing seawater is only about 0.75 cent per gallon. The assigned price of water will inflate the value of water by at least a factor of 6 in favor of those nations with rich water resources, e.g., Canada.

The assumption used for estimating land value is perhaps most problematic. The total land assets (excluding forest stocks) of Japan and Sweden were valued at $1,240 billion and $1,109 billion respectively, compared to only $215 billion for the People's Republic of China. Despite the legitimate argument that the return from land uses per hectare is generally higher in developed countries than in developing countries, such a dramatic result is difficult to comprehend for anybody with a notion of the size differences of these three countries. The assumption that land values are proportional to a nation's per capita income is based on the belief that land is immobile and cannot be traded on an international market. Although true, it is also true that other capital can move to where land exists.

Another methodological flaw is the method of computing the value of human resources. Human capital is valued as the expected lifetime earnings of the current population in the home countries computed as the residual of per capita GNP, after deducting earnings accounted for by natural capital, multiplied by the average number of years left to the current population. Such an approach raises a long-debated question: Does a person living in Switzerland have the same value as a person in Nepal with exactly the same qualifications? The answer, according to this new index, is no. The solution to this dilemma lies in the conceptual framework proposed for the index. Since total wealth consists of four components—natural, man-made, human, and social capital—the residual, i.e., per capita GNP after deducting the part accounted for by natural and man-made capital, is human capital plus social capital for one year. In the desire to "exclude" social capital from the current accounting process, the authors view the residual as human capital only. However, if one allows social capital to be negative—interpreted as social and economic institutions that prevent people from realizing their economic potential, as in centrally planned economies—we can conceptually define human capital solely based on qualifications, not nationalities. This method lets "social capital," not "human capital," account for the cross-country variations of the residuals.

To recapitulate, most of the methodological and conceptual problems just discussed discriminate against developing countries by underestimating their capital. Therefore, although the new index corrects GNP by adding environmental and human dimensions to the measure, it also magnifies the inherent problems of GNP by relating human and environmental variables to it.

Despite the clear need to develop a more appropriate ranking system for nations, it is important to ask how much new information a new index carries. One of the illustrations of this index was to rank the 192 nations. A simple statistical correlation analysis shows that the Spearman rank correlation between the ranks of the nations using per capita GNP (which we have known for years) and those based on the estimated per capita wealth is 0.96. (This correlation is 1.00 if the two rankings match exactly.) In other words, the new order of 192 countries produced by this new method is not statistically different from that based on per capita GNP. The values of the estimated wealth per capita are much larger than per capita income because the new measure also includes human and natural capital. It appears that the estimated wealth of rich countries generally increases much more than that of poor countries. For example, using per capita GNP, the top ten richest countries in the world have an average per capita GNP roughly 200 times that of the ten poorest nations. By comparison, using the newly estimated per capita wealth, the top ten richest countries have an average per capita wealth roughly 250 times that of the ten poorest nations.

It should be mentioned that steps have been taken to correct some of these problems and a new set of the estimates has been recently released (World Bank 1997).

The World Bank's Development Diamonds
In another attempt to characterize much of the economic, social, and environmental information gathered by the World Bank, its publication on social indicators of development (World Bank, 1994) defined a "development diamond" for a given country constructed from four indicators: per capita GNP, life expectancy, gross primary enrollment, and access to safe water. By plotting these values on four separate axes, the resulting shape can be compared to the best or the average of that country grouping (although the use of diamonds to represent such indicators is topologically problematic, as addressed by Yu and Rogers 1995). This concept is illustrated in Figure 2.7, which highlights the development diamonds for four of the six developing member countries (DMCs) considered in our study. (The data for the Marshall Islands and the Philippines are currently missing.) The position of each nation is shown relative to the average for low-income nations. PRC can be seen to fall very close to the average, although this is hardly surprising, since it is the largest member of the

FIGURE 2.7
Developmental Diamonds

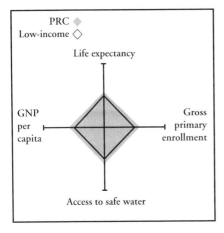

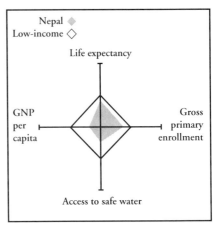

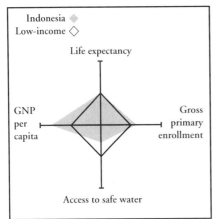

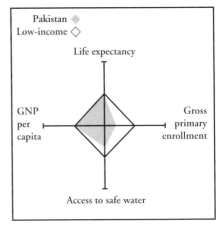

Source: World Bank, 1990

low income group. Nepal is below average on all four measures, while Indonesia is above average in terms of GNP per capita but below for access to safe water.

Development diamonds are a simple, but powerful concept for highlighting the interrelationships between four variables. It requires only a small stretch of the imagination to see that this could be a very useful graphic technique for analyzing environmental issues. A preliminary application of this concept (Rogers and Jalal 1994) to the environment used the four variables of the ecosystem identified by the Principal Components Index (discussed further in Chapter 3) namely, air, water, land, and ecosystem.

Sustainable Development

Sustainable development is a vague concept. Its many definitions usually defy attempts to explain what it actually implies in concrete terms. However, it is a powerful concept in that it addresses the issues of our responsibility to future generations and the trade-off between economic development and environmental quality. If sustainability is to become more than a mere buzzword and be operationalized in the development choices we make in this generation, we need to understand the concept in more concrete terms.

Pezzey (1992) has cited over 50 definitions of sustainability. These definitions range from vague notions to concrete steps. Even if we use the traditional "assuming" powers of economics to say (for illustrative purposes) that we can define, measure, and operationalize the concept of sustainability, the most important question to address before attempting to operationalize sustainability is the problem of spatial and temporal aggregation. For example, sustainable development for a country may imply that some of its regions are sustainable and others unsustainable. If one desires sustainable development on a global scale only, can some nations be sustainable and others not? Similarly, can spatial entities be sustainable some of the time and not all of the time?

"We do not inherit the earth from our forefathers, we borrow it from future generations" goes an ancient saying sometimes attributed to Native Americans. Sustainable development is primarily about our responsibilities to future generations and taking into account how our actions today would affect their situation in the future. *The Limits to Growth* (Meadows et al. 1972) made dire predictions about the economy and survivability of mankind due to the exhaustion of nonrenewable resources and "overshoot and collapse" by employing simplistic models of systems dynamics without taking into account technological development, changing needs, and the availability of substitutes. Also, exhaustible resources do not simply become depleted, rather, more effort has to be expended to extract them or find substitutes. A follow-up publication, *Beyond the Limits* (Meadows, Meadows, and Randers 1992) essentially reiterated the findings of its predecessor two decades earlier.

At the time of the publication of *The Limits to Growth* and the Stockholm Conference on Environment and Development in 1972, the view was still primarily that of a choice between environmental protection and economic growth. In the 1980s, the focus shifted to stressing the complementarity between environmental improvement and economic growth (Markandya and Richardson 1993). The Brundtland Commission produced a highly influential report in 1987 entitled *Our Common Future* that highlighted the intertwining of the environment and the economy, especially in developing countries, and stressed the need to find alternative development paths that reflected this interdependence and the inter- and intragenerational equity issues. It produced perhaps the most-quoted definition of sustainable development as a process which "meets the needs of the present without compromising the ability of future generations to meet their own needs." The landmark UN Conference on Environment and Development in Rio de Janeiro in 1992 reinforced this view and managed to attract world attention back to the concept of sustainable development.

Robert Repetto (1986) defines sustainable development as:

> ...a development strategy that manages all assets, natural resources, and human resources, as well as financial and physical assets, for increasing long-term wealth and well-being. Sustainable development as a goal rejects policies and practices that support current living standards by depleting the resource base, including natural resources, and that leaves future generations with poorer prospects and greater risks than our own.

Daly (1987) distinguishes between the concepts of economic *growth* and *development* by defining the former as a quantitative increase in the scale of the physical dimensions of the economy and the latter as the qualitative improvement in the nonphysical characteristics of the economy. He suggests that traditional neoclassical economic concepts would not be valid if we are near the biophysical or socioeconomic limits to growth. He suggests that sustainability requires increasing the moral knowledge or ethical capital of mankind.

Pezzey (1992) draws the distinction between survivability (that requires welfare to be above a threshold in all time periods) and sustainability (that requires welfare to be nondecreasing in all time periods). Munasinghe (1993) highlights three approaches to sustainability: the *economic* approach that maximizes the flow of income that could be generated while maintaining a constant or increasing stock of capital (natural and manmade); the *ecological* approach that attempts to maintain the resilience and robustness of the biological and physical systems; and the *sociocultural* approach that seeks similarly to maintain the stability of social and cultural systems (including concepts of inter- and intragenerational equity).

The application of the concept of sustainability to project selection is also discussed in detail in Pearce, Barbier, and Markandya (1990) and Murray and Harshadeep (1994).

We can consider sustainable development to be an optimization problem, where we are collectively trying to maximize our overall welfare subject to a set of constraints. Our objective function, our overall welfare, would reflect our relative preferences for the consumption of various goods (including the environment) discounted over the generations as necessary. Pearce, Barbier, and Markandya (1990) suggest that development is a vector of desirable social objectives, and that sustainable development implies that the development so defined is nondecreasing over time. The constraints would reflect the availability of resources, the rate of change of demands for resources and their supply, etc. In addition, it has been suggested that sustainability constraints could be added on to control the rate of change in consumption and welfare. We have to keep in mind that sustainability needs to be feasible before it can be implementable. The sustainable development intertemporal framework maximizes the current value of welfare by choosing the optimal values of current controls (such as consumption and portfolio of investments).

Many researchers (such as Solow 1974; Krutilla and Fisher 1975; Dasgupta and Maler, 1990; Nordhaus 1992; and Dorfman et al, 1996) have employed analytical models of optimal economic development with environmental considerations. The prominent empirical parameters in these models are usually the elasticities of substitutions, rate of technological change, population growth, stocks of natural resources, income elasticity, rate of stock depletion per unit of output, costs of goods, rate of GDP growth desired, pollutant emission factors, etc. Sometimes, some of these are endogenous variables, but often critical assumptions have to be made in the estimation of these parameters. Uncertainty of their values precludes the development and use of very complicated models, and their utility is primarily in demonstration and investigation of system links.

How *does* one make development sustainable? The suggestions have been many:

■ Let future generations have as much access to our resources as we do.

■ Do not discount for future welfare.

■ Minimize consumption of exhaustible resources.

■ Maintain current stocks of renewable resources.

If these were to be truly operationalized, we would consume no non-renewable resources today as we spread these scarce resources out over an essentially infinite horizon. And, as the welfare of our future generations is as dear to us as our own welfare (with a zero intertemporal discount rate), we would save for the future by dropping our own consumption of exhaustible resources to essentially zero. The *Limits to Growth* authors (Meadows et al. 1972) recommend that we minimize the use of nonrenewable resources and maintain renewable resources at current levels (although they assert that these "piecemeal" approaches are no substitute for a cessation of economic growth!). Boulding (1966) reminds us that it is a well-known phenomenon that we discount the future, even in our own lives. If we discount our future, it is not unreasonable to discount posterity's future, especially given that it is always a little hard to find a convincing answer to the person who says, "What has posterity ever done for me?" In addition, we have little idea about the preferences, needs, and availability of substitutes and technologies in future generations. This can be visualized by the analogy of a person in the last century deciding upon what the needs of the current generation would be.

Stavins (1992) remarks that the *Limits to Growth* concept of "overshoot and collapse" can make sense in the case of a subset of renewable resources— biological ones, such as species, because of a threshold population or critical dispensation of some species that are required to ensure the survivability of the species. He also makes an interesting observation—that the "exhaustible" resources (such as minerals and fossil fuels which are really quite inexhaustible in economic terms and better named nonrenewable resources) are actually not threatened because their price reflects their scarcity; on the other hand, the "renewable" resources (such as clean water, forests and some biota) are most threatened due to mismanagement of these usually common property resources.

■ *Leave everything in its pristine state or return it to its pristine state.*
This strong suggestion would essentially stop all developmental activity, including all construction, mining, etc. This would certainly stop pollution; however, our aim is finally to increase the present value of our welfare, which would be severely negatively impacted by such a step.

■ *Develop so as not to overwhelm the carrying capacity of the system.*
The concept of carrying capacity has been proposed by many as an upper limit on the development, for example, by estimating the amount of waste that the earth can absorb. Foy and Daly (1989) cite misallocation of resources, inequitable distribution of resources, and an excessive scale of resource use that overwhelms the carrying capacity as the primary factors contributing to environmental problems and unsustainability. However, the concept of *carrying capacity* is extremely fuzzy and does not lend itself to any practical interpretation for implementation. For example, the carrying capacity in terms of the number of people a particular region will support can only be determined by making the same kinds of Mathusian assumptions as made by Meadows et al. (1992) about scarcity of resources.

■ *Sustainability will take care of itself as economic growth proceeds.*
The controversial concept of *Kuznet's Curve* implies that if cross-sectional data from different countries were plotted with an indicator of environmental quality (such as SO_2 emission per capita) on the ordinate and a measure of economic activity (such as per capita GDP), the curve would look like an inverted "U." This implies that countries with very low economic development cannot afford to pollute (i.e., their economic activity is not high enough to generate pollution); however, as their development proceeds, their pollution increases. In addition, there is another effect that tends to reduce pollution— both due to the inevitable increase in efficiency of newer plants that pollute less per unit of output and to the increased demand for environmental resources (if the environment is considered a sort of a luxury good). This leads to a threshold per capita GDP corresponding to the maximum level of pollution beyond

which the environment starts improving. The problems with the Kuznet's Curve concept are that: not all pollutants behave in this manner; the environment is assumed to be a luxury good; a correlation is extrapolated into a cause-and-effect relationship; and empirical data to validate these curves are hard to come by. Most important, it may not be necessary for a country to follow this inverted "U" path in its development and technological advances; diffusion of technology and better policies could help a country bypass its "destiny" as suggested by the curves.

■ *The polluter and victim can arrive at an efficient solution by themselves.*

This view was proposed by Coase (1960), who, in his classic paper, argues that initial allocation of property rights does not affect the achievement of an efficient outcome achieved by bargaining. It has since been realized that this is only under stringent assumptions including the availability of perfect information on emissions, transport, damages, and costs of control, the negligibility of transaction costs, and the possibility of the nonexistence of a core allocation in the case of more than two parties.

■ *Let the markets take care of it.*

■ *Internalize the externalities.*

These classic anthems of economists are simple to understand but difficult to operationalize. If the economic impacts of all the pollution and other unaccounted-for externalities to the system defined were reflected in prices, this would lead to a full-cost pricing system. In the case of pollution, this is restated as the "polluters pay" principle and can be achieved by environmental regulations and economic incentives for pollution prevention. It is true that market mechanisms may be more efficient than traditional command and control regulations; however, it is not reasonable to expect private profit maximizers working with high discount rates to be entrusted with the responsibility of keeping the welfare of future generations in mind. In addition, it is difficult to identify, cost, and assign environmental assaults to particular sources. But most important, many environmental goods do not have a robust market (Baumol and Oates 1975). It is possible, however, to let market mechanisms work to implement innovative approaches to environmental management, such as tradable permits. The problem is that these approaches have limited applications; in addition, the cost of tradable permits is not easily predetermined. Effluent charges and taxes would also encourage innovation and efficiency as compared to more traditional regulations, but there would be uncertainty in the amount of environmental improvement achieved. Market mechanisms are extremely difficult to implement in the face of the large uncertainty in the emissions, the standards and the costs, efficiencies, and reliability of control technologies. The following two quotations illustrate the failure of markets and the need for government intervention in environmental problems:

> ...the disassociation between scarcity and price, benefits and costs, rights and responsibilities, actions and consequences. This disassociation exists because of a combination of market and policy failures. The prevailing configuration of markets and policies leaves many resources outside the domain of markets, unowned, unpriced and unaccounted for and more often than not, it subsidizes their excessive use and destruction despite their growing scarcity and rising social cost. This results in an incentive structure that induces people to maximize their profits not by being efficient and innovative but by appropriating other people's resources and shifting their own costs onto others.... Preventing prices from rising in line with growing scarcities and rising social costs distorts the signals that in a well-functioning market would have brought about increased efficiency, substitution, conservation and innovation to restore the balance between supply and demand.
>
> Panayotou (1992)

> Efficiently managing environmental resources...requires replacing the invisible hand of markets with the visible hand of government. There are no simple approaches to setting environmental policies wisely. Governments face thorny choices in four distinct areas: selecting the appropriate areas for intervention, finding the right level of intervention, choosing the most efficient tools for minimizing the net economic harm from externalities, and coordinating policies where international spillovers occur.
>
> Nordhaus (1992)

An extension to this section is the fact that environmental goods must be imputed prices that reflect not only the cost of extraction but also the shadow prices or opportunity costs of the environmental good in situ (Dasgupta and Maler 1990). These shadow prices are thus the sum of their use value and their option value (Arrow and Fisher 1974).

■ *Let the national economic accounting system reflect environmental defensive expenditures.*
Traditional economic indicators such as GDP and GNP have been criticized for their lack of representation of the depletion of natural resources and environmental pollution. It has been suggested that a good accounting system that includes opportunity costs reflecting scarcity would internalize the depletion of natural resources in the form of increased prices. However, it is necessary to compute the defensive expenditures for preventing environmental pollution and include them into the national accounting system to compute an updated net national product (NNP) (Ahmad, El Serafy, and Lutz 1989; Lutz 1993; Repetto et al. 1989; Mäler 1991). Such a system would involve the computation of the currently implemented portion of the cost of remediation.

■ *Reinvest the rents from non-renewable resources.*

John Hartwick of the Queen's University of Canada outlined this policy (also called Hartwick's Rule) to help guarantee a simple economy the ability to have a constant or increasing capacity to consume in perpetuity. Simply stated, it requires a society to reinvest the rents it collects from natural resources into physical capital. This simple concept has been generalized, adopted, modified, and applied by a number of researchers since it was first published. One attempt by Pezzey (1992) extends Hartwick's Rule as maximizing a suitably aggregated index of world consumption and spending only current income on consumption, while keeping an aggregated index (of natural and manmade capital) constant over time.

Dasgupta and Heal (1974) determined that an economy could fully deplete a resource if there were a renewable or manufacturable resource whose elasticity of substitution for the exhaustible resource was greater than unity. It is under these conditions that Hartwick's Rule is applicable.

Dorfman (1996) shows with the help of simplified control models that simply accumulate large amounts of manmade resources need not compensate for environmental deterioration, and specific attention to repairing or protecting the environment would generally be needed to sustain a desirable level of social welfare indefinitely.

Foy and Daly (1989) comment further on the substitutability of natural and manmade capital. They state that *weak sustainability* requires that we maintain the sum of these two forms of capital constant over time; *strong sustainability* requires that we maintain each constant separately. Pearce, Barbier, and Markandya, (1990) have alternative definitions of these terms: they define strong sustainability as a situation when the development vector must monotonically increase in every time period, and weak sustainability as a situation when this is not necessarily true in every time period (either as a constraint on only the trend of the development vector or the present value of development benefits being positive).

Hartwick's Rule has been tested regionally for Malaysia and for Indonesia as a whole (Vincent 1990) by comparing consumption with (environmentally) adjusted net domestic product or the investment with capital consumption allowances. This method suffers from the assumption of substitutability between manmade capital and environmental resources, and, like the "green GNP" approaches, relies on market prices to determine the value of environmental resources.

■ *Leave future generations the option or the capacity to be as well off as we are.*

This is a suggestion by the Nobel Laureate Robert M. Solow in a landmark speech (Solow 1991). Although this sounds like a laudable goal, he reflects upon the problems with operationalizing such a desire. Problems include the fact that in our haste to sacrifice, we have no idea of the tastes, preferences, needs, and capabilities of future generations. Solow contrasts this vagueness with the more concrete issues of our present resource use and what we leave behind in terms of resources and built environment (including productive capacity and technical knowledge). This highlights the important concept of the substitutability among and between manmade and natural capital. This fungibility of such resources implies that sustainability does not require the preservation of any *particular* species of trees or minerals in our consideration of future generations. And, as we have no idea of future needs and capabilities, we need to make robust decisions to ensure reasonable intergenerational equity. Thus, sustainabilty is reduced to a choice between current consumption and providing for the future. However, to avoid free-riding at the expense of future generations, Solow comments that governmental environmental regulations are necessary in addition to market forces. He suggests that current environmental protection contributes to sustainability if it is at the expense of current consumption and not at the expense of investment in future capacity. He further expands on Hartwick's Rule to suggest that environmental protection can be regarded as an act of investment; hence, we could ensure some kind of sustainability if at least the rents gathered from nonrenewable resources were reinvested into human and manmade capital. However, he suggests a paradox here between intergenerational and intragenerational concerns: that the concern for the disadvantaged denizens of the future should reflect itself in a concern for the disadvantaged denizens of today, which would then suggest an increase in consumption and go against the notion of sustainability.

Sustainability and National Accounts
It appears generally accepted (ignoring intragenerational equity issues temporarily) that any economic development path that is sustainable is by definition "good." The vagueness of this concept becomes obvious when we consider that there may be good reasons for a society to deplete a resource as part of an intertemporal trade-off which sets it on a more sustainable path later. In short, sustainability makes little sense when it is applied at the level of a single resource or even a single nation over a short time span.

The search for an index equivalent to GDP, that has an environmental focus, has led economists to look at some of the shortcomings of GDP as a measure of development. The search led back to Hicks and his 1946 definition of income, which is "the maximum value that a person can consume during a time period and still expect to be as well off at the end of the period as he was at the beginning." Note that this definition involves both stocks and flows (Daly 1987). Stocks are involved in that capital is invested and depreciation takes place during the given period. Flows are involved as the income generated from the existing capital stock is modified by investments and/or depreciation. Daly (1987) refers to this as "sustainable" income, and he suggests two ways of adjusting net national product[1] (NNP) to make it more nearly reflect Hicks's concept of income. The first is to extend the concept of depreciation to cover natural capital stocks depleted through productive activities (DNC) and the other is to subtract "defensive" expenditures necessary to defend against unwanted side-effects of production and consumption (DE). Hence, "sustainable social net national product" (SSNNP) is the net national product (NNP) minus the environmental defensive expenditures and the depreciation of natural capital, or

$$SSNNP = NNP - DE - DNC \qquad (2.8)$$

This approach is called environmental or green accounting and is based upon the sustainable development principle that along a sustainable path, "the income-generating capacity of the stock of capital assets in the future is no less than it is today." This approach looks like an attractive way to use conventional national accounts as an indicator of environmental quality for a nation or region. Unfortunately, there are few examples of attempts to measure such indices. The World Resources Institute (1992) mentions attempts to measure these indices in Costa Rica, Indonesia, and Mexico. Repetto et al. (1989) give the details of one such attempt based in Indonesia, where they tried to assess the depreciation in the three major natural resource sectors: petroleum, forestry, and agriculture. They used the GDP, instead of NNP as the base upon which to compute their own definition of net domestic product (NDP), which only considered the depreciation in each of the natural resource sectors. They demonstrated how to estimate the depreciation due to loss of soil, loss of timber resources, and loss of petroleum reserves. They showed that over the period 1971 to 1984, Indonesian GDP, which was claimed to be growing at 7.1 percent per annum, really reflected only a 4.0 percent rate of growth when natural resource depletion was taken into account.

Savings and Depreciation

Given the key role of savings in this discussion, a more detailed examination of the concept is warranted. Economic development is a process whereby a society dedicates a portion of its national product to the goal of sustaining consumption into the future. The quantity and the quality of savings is what determines the sustainability of a level of consumption. Notice that savings do not only take expression in quantitative terms. For example, a society which saves its coal reserves is saving a resource which may never be used in the future. A society which saves its oil equally may be saving a resource which is at the end of its product lifecycle.

One way of conceptualizing savings is given in Pearce and Atkinson (1993). They disaggregate savings (S) into three components: human knowledge (H), and man-made (M) and natural (N) capital. Let us suppose that all three forms of capital are expressed in the same unit, for example, dollars. A simple rule, suitably modified to define sustainability, is given by them as:

$$\frac{S}{Y} - \frac{\delta_H K_H}{Y} - \frac{\delta_M M_M}{Y} - \frac{\delta_N K_N}{Y} \geq 0 \qquad (2.9)$$

Y is defined as total national income and the expression states that the proportion of savings out of national income minus the proportion of depreciation of H, M, and N must be greater than or equal to zero to ensure sustainability. At any point in time, a society must have a net capital gain greater than or equal to zero. There is some debate about whether H can be depreciated. The critical variable is S. It must be sufficiently high so that the ratio remains positive. In economic terms, it is an endogenous variable which can be modified by human action.

There are many problems with this rule, but the most damaging is that it is far too restrictive. There may be good reasons not to save for a period of time. A very poor society may be much more concerned with consumption in the present than with consumption in the future. The rule overemphasizes intergenerational equity at the cost of ignoring intragenerational equity. If one accepts the premise that there is a declining utility of additional income as is used in the HDI, it can be argued that a greater social optimum derives from richer societies saving a greater proportion of their income than poorer ones, including, and perhaps essentially, their natural capital.

Another problem is the requirement that all forms of capital be translated into equivalent units. This problem also places in the foreground the difficulty of ascribing value to N. If N is very expensive it will be conserved more but does its price reflect its physical scarcity?

The degree of substitution among H, M, and N is an equally important issue and one that Pearce and Atkinson address. If one does not accept that H and M are even imperfect substitutes for N, they reduce the rule to:

$$\frac{\delta_N K_N}{Y} \leq 0 \qquad (2.10)$$

$$\frac{S}{Y} > \left[\left(\frac{S_m}{Y} \right) + \left(\frac{S_n}{Y} \right) \right] \qquad (2.11)$$

$$Z = \frac{S}{Y} - \left(\frac{S_m}{Y} + \frac{S_n}{Y} \right) \qquad (2.12)$$

Inequalities (2.11) and (2.12) are presented in Pearce and Atkinson (1993) as discriminating between weak and strong sustainability. We do not believe that rule (2.12) represents an operational criterion of strong sustainability. Depreciating resources up to some point does not necessarily lower the sustainability of an alternate pattern of consumption into the future. The level of human knowledge is a critical factor in the strong sustainability criterion. One would have preferred the following expression:

$$\frac{\iota_H K_H}{Y} - \frac{\delta_N K_N}{Y} \geq 0 \qquad (2.13)$$

where l_H represents increments to human knowledge. We add the caveat that we do not accept that H is a perfect substitute for N.

Inequality (2.13) states that the rate of capital accumulation resulting from increases to human knowledge minus the rate of depreciating natural capital must be greater than or equal to zero. The time frame to justify this rule is critical. Within some extended time period, N may be depreciated and there may be increments to H. We argue that rule (2.13) should hold over some extended period of time. That time period is itself determined endogenously by the urgent needs of the current generation. A society may be more able to reduce the depreciation of N once it has raised its per capita consumption.

Inequality (2.13) says little about the cost to society of economic development. There is a cost associated with a chosen course of development by the current generation. Broadly, this cost can be defined as the cost of remediation, or the cost of restoring the environment to its initial state, or some other desirable state. The magnitude of these costs is an indication of the importance of the environmental damage caused by economic development. The cost of repair provides a measure of the extent to which natural capital is depreciated given a fixed level of man-made capital. A sharply rising cost of remediation is a serious indication of an unsustainable development path.

We conclude that it is important to observe the extent to which a development plan leads a society away from sustainability. It is equally important to understand the cost of rehabilitating the environment. The cost of remediation is an alternative indicator of the sustainability of an economic development path with an advantage over criterion (2.13), in that it determines how much consumption must be given up by society to achieve economic development. It allows us to determine something even more important, the rate of change in the costs of rehabilitating the environment. The level of H determines whether these costs will continue to rise or fall in the future. An example of this is the banning of CFCs in the world. The inconvenience caused by having CFCs was later softened by the introduction of new transport catalysts far less damaging to the ozone layer.

In Table 2.6, Pearce and Atkinson (1993) compare and contrast several countries using the concept of weak sustainability. The surprise in this table is the conjunction of Brazil and the United States with Costa Rica, the Netherlands, and Japan in the list of sustainable economies, and the inclusion of the Philippines with the United Kingdom in the marginally sustainable countries.

Sustainability and This Study

The multitude of definitions and approaches that we have outlined above demonstrate that no one approach is completely satisfactory in making the concept of sustainable development operational. Some approaches are either too vague for definition, and others are so narrow that they blindly grasp only a portion of the environment. Most require the collection of large quantities

TABLE 2.6

Weak Sustainability

Country	S/Y	δ_m/Y	δ_n/Y	Z
Sustainable Economies				
Brazil	20	7	10	+3
Costa Rica	26	3	8	+15
Czechoslovakia	30	10	7	+13
Finland	28	15	2	+11
Germany (West, pre-unif.)	26	12	4	+10
Hungary	26	10	5	+11
Japan	33	14	2	+17
Netherlands	25	10	1	+14
Poland	30	11	3	+16
USA	18	12	3	+3
Zimbabwe	24	10	5	+9
Marginally Sustainable				
Mexico	24	10	12	0
Philippines	15	11	4	0
United Kingdom	18	12	6	0
Unsustainable				
Burkina Faso	2	1	10	-9
Ethiopia	3	1	9	-7
Indonesia	20	5	17	-2
Madagascar	8	1	16	-9
Malawi	8	7	4	-3
Mali	-4	4	6	-14
Nigeria	15	3	17	-5
Papua New Guinea	15	9	7	-1

Source: Pearce and Atkinson, 1993.

of data on environmental costs (of control and cleanup) and damages. Such data are prone to uncertainty and the results so obtained may be suspect. We propose avoiding the whole valuation issue until the science is more developed, and focusing our efforts on getting better estimates of the costs of remediation to a certain standard, as proxy for environmental response to investments.

Weitzman (1992), in reviewing a paper by Nordhaus (1992) that reviews the *Limits to Growth* concept (Meadows et. al 1972, and Meadows, Meadows, and Randers 1992), identifies a gap in the current literature on sustainability. He says that we need to estimate how much it is really costing us to prevent local environmental deterioration. He states that when the elasticity of environmental improvement with respect to environmental spending is high (i.e., the environment responds positively and readily with an increase in spending), then greater environmental spending is sufficient to counter the adverse environmental consequences of economic activity. In this case, he asserts that the income spent on environmental improvement (or the cost of remediation) is a relatively good proxy for the appropriate social cost of preventing environmental deterioration. If the elasticity of environmental response is not that high, the environmental spending underestimates the degree of the "environmental drag." This effect, combined with the fact that some environmental goods may be omitted from a practical cost of remediation computation, may lead to an undervaluing of the environmental drag.

As Hammond (1993) sums up, the concept of sustainability is probably less important than the keeping of proper accounts. The cost of remediation is one such account that is perhaps the least controversial and most useful. We shall examine this in more detail in Chapter 3.

Note

1   Net national product is gross national product minus depreciation. Gross domestic product is the gross product of resources located inside the nation's boundaries.

3 NEW MEASURES OF ENVIRONMENTAL QUALITY

New Environmental Quality Indicators

In Chapter 1 we developed a framework for the development of new EQIs and introduced the fundamental problems raised by weighting systems. We have suggested the so-called cost-of-remediation (COR) approach to obviate the worst of the weighting problems. In this chapter, we describe three measures of environmental quality we have developed: cost of remediation, the environmental diamond (ED), and environmental elasticity (EE). We pay particular attention to the theoretical rationale behind each index and the technical aspects of index development. In Chapters 4 and 5 we will shift our focus to the applications and policy implications of the three measures in the context of Asian countries.

Principal Components to Find the Dimensionality of Indices

The intellectual foundation for each of our indices is the exploitation of the correlation structure among the different variables used in describing different aspects of the environment, and, ultimately, in index construction. This approach is based upon the statistical method of principal components analysis (PCA) using existing environmental indicators. The main purpose of PCA is to summarize information and to derive statistical dimensions of environmental problems to serve as a theoretical basis for index development. Although some suggest that PCA scores can also be viewed as an "index," in this study we employ PCA as a statistical tool, not as an index, to summarize the main environmental issues our three new indices need to address. It is beyond the scope of this volume to provide a detailed description of the PCA techniques. Interested readers are referred to various statistical textbooks for the technique in general and to one of the working papers produced in this study (Yu et al. 1995) for the details of this analysis. The following discussion will briefly introduce the methodology but will mainly focus on the conclusions and implications of the analysis.

The past two or three decades have witnessed a tremendous boom in the number of environmental indicators and indices developed and published annually by various international institutions such as the World Bank, World Resources Institute (WRI), United Nations Environment Programme (UNEP), and United Nations Development Programme (UNDP). One cannot evaluate the usefulness of EQIs based merely on the sheer number generated since many of these indicators are mutually correlated. On the contrary, too many indicators may be counterproductive by overwhelming and even confusing decision-makers and the general public.

The environment is a multidimensional concept consisting of air, water, solid wastes, forests, soils, wildlife, and other biota. One of the first questions we encountered in developing environmental indices is how many indices we need in order to characterize environmental quality. The objective is to construct the least number of indices possible which yet give adequate account of this object which we refer to as the "environment." The development of EQIs is a process involving data simplification and reduction of effective dimensionality (Ott, 1978, p. 2). Dimensionality reduction not only helps cut down the high costs of gathering additional information, but also avoids the problem of overwhelming decision-makers with hundreds of indicators.

PCA is a dimensionality reduction technique that transforms correlated original variables into a new set of uncorrelated variables. The new variables are linear combinations of the original variables and are sorted in descending order according to the amount of variance that they account for in the original set. Each new variable accounts for as much remaining total variance in the original data as possible and cumulatively all the new variables account for 100 percent of the variation.

PCA is used to achieve parsimony by removing noise in the data to highlight the simplest covariance structure. As an example, deforestation may increase both soil erosion and CO_2 emissions. It follows that the cost of controlling erosion through afforestation may also bring benefits of reduced CO_2 emissions. A new index that employs all three variables, i.e., deforestation, soil erosion, and CO_2 emissions, carries less information content than what the proponents of the index might expect. Another well-known example is the Human Development Index (HDI) developed by UNDP (1992). As discussed in Chapter 2, HDI uses four variables: life expectancy at birth, adjusted gross domestic product (GDP) per capita, adult literacy rate, and school enrollment. It is easy to see that these four variables are correlated in that richer countries generally have higher life expectancy and educational attainment. Aggregating correlated variables in the same manner as aggregating independent variables not only reveals little new information, but can also be misleading. One needs to take a critical view of data before employing them to develop aggregate indices. The PCA helps find the interrelationships and the effective dimensionality of data, and determines their suitability for use in developing environmental indices.

Earlier works using this approach for index development include those by Lohani (1980), Lohani and Todino (1984), Lohani and Mustapha (1982), and Fiering (1992). They used PCA to develop indices of environmental quality with an emphasis on air and water quality. Compared with previous efforts, our analysis focuses on the macro scale (national level) and is more inclusive in terms of the types of environmental indicators chosen for analysis. A total of 79 indicators for 146 countries were selected from documents published by UNEP (1989/1990), UNDP (1992), World Bank (1991a,b) and WRI (1992/1993). The range of indicators selected encompassed air pollution (emissions and ambient concentrations), water pollution (concentrations), changes in land uses, energy consumption, biodiversity, social and economic welfare, and health statistics. The types of indicators selected include "pressure indicators," i.e., environmental emissions, and "state indicators," i.e., ambient concentrations, species endangered, and human health statistics (see Chapter 1).

Using the above database, we conducted a number of PCAs using different combinations of variables (indicators) to investigate the interrelationship among these variables. One such analysis employs 32 environmental variables covering air emissions, water quality, deforestation and erosion, and endangered species. The analysis indicates that the first four principal components account for 64 percent of the total variation, suggesting that there is a large "redundancy" in the 32 environmental indicators.

Furthermore, the first principal component has large coefficients with such indicators as per capita industrial emissions of CO_2, CFC, Particulate Matter, CO, NO_2, etc., leading one to believe that the first principal component primarily represents the *air dimension* of environmental stress or quality.

The second principal component is relatively difficult to interpret because a large number of variables are correlated with it. However, it appears to have large coefficients mainly with those indicators related to deforestation, e.g., per capita roundwood cut for industrial uses, forest cover, change of forest cover and pasture land, and deforestation-related soil erosion, e.g., sediments in rivers, and emissions of CO_2 due to loss of forest as a carbon sink. In general, the second principal component primarily represents the *land dimension* of the environment.

The third principal component is closely related to the number of different species threatened per thousand sq. km., including mammal, bird, higher plant, and reptile. It unambiguously represents *biodiversity* or *endangered species*.

Lastly, the fourth principal component has large coefficients with, among other indicators, change of forest cover, average values of BOD, electric conductivity, dissolved chlorides, suspended solids, and sediment for selected rivers. Thus, the fourth principal component appears to represent *water quality*.

To recapitulate, the first four principal components account for 64 percent of the total variation exhibited in the 32 original environmental indicators, and represent air, land, biodiversity, and water, respectively. It should be stressed, however, that the principal components often contain mixed indicators of related environmental issues. For example, although the second principal component primarily represents deforestation and erosion, it also has water quality indicators such as river sediment as its significant component because rivers are the main recipients of the eroded soil. The indicators on number of species threatened appear in all four components because different species are affected by different environmental factors.

It should also be clearly understood that there are major data lacunae in these sources and major definition problems surrounding the variables used that are typical of these kinds of databases. To test the robustness of the conclusions drawn from such analyses, Yu et al. (1997) conducted a statistical procedure called "bootstrapping" to test how the PCA results vary by using different sub-sample sets which are generated randomly from the original data set. The results indicate that the above conclusions are statistically robust.

Based upon these findings and the literature, we believe that four components or factors, namely, air, water, land, and ecosystem (biodiversity), can adequately describe environmental quality. In our research work we have decided to limit ourselves to indices describing these four components.

Cost of Remediation
Development of the Cost-of-Remediation Methodology
Inhaber (1976) commented upon the ease of acceptance of complicated economic indices such as the GNP by the general public and political decision-makers, even though most of them would find it hard to explain just what the GNP measures; they have the perception that it provides an unambiguous measure of what the economy is doing. The success of such measures may be due to the fact that economists have been working on them for more than two hundred years, but a much more likely explanation is that they are denominated in currency terms. They have a common numéraire: the dollar, the yen, the pound, the mark, or other currency. It is plausible to add up the activities of different sectors of an economy when expressed in dollar terms instead of the physical units of production; shoes and ships and sealing wax, etc.

A scheme that generates considerable interest is the use of environmental cleanup costs as an index of environmental degradation. This approach was first suggested in the late 1960s by Ridker and in the early 1970s by Inhaber (1976), Herfindahl and Kneese (1974), and Fiering and Holling (1974), and it is a major part of the new "environmental economics" that emphasizes the inclusion of depreciation of environmental capital in estimates of national income (see Leontief 1970; Repetto et al 1989).

In describing this approach, we follow Inhaber (1976) and report the costs in terms of aquatic systems, air resources, and ecosystems, amended by our own work of principal component analysis of existing environmental variables discussed above, which added another component: land.

In using the cost-of-remediation approach it is important to carefully structure the algorithms for calculating costs. The costs are based on the idea that there are three major ways to meet standards: *process change, prevention,* and *cleanup after the fact,* as documented in the Fiering-Holling study cited above. In reality, however, estimation of the costs for process change and prevention suffers from a number of difficulties. One is lack of such data. The other is the issue of "joint costs." It refers to the phenomenon that the costs associated with process changes bring about multiple benefits simultaneously, i.e., improvement of production efficiency and reduction of emissions. Depending on different proportions allocated to the economic and environmental benefits, the costs for environmental remediation could vary dramatically. This study focuses primarily on the cleanup costs after the fact, or more customarily referred to as "end-of-pipe" treatment costs. They are admittedly crude, but can serve as a lower bound of the true costs. Wherever possible we have also utilized least-cost alternatives to cleanup such as fuel switching for domestic heating.

Another important point on the cost estimation is that the total cost varies across countries, but basically, the cost of capital equipment is about the same everywhere and the major differences arise in labor costs and in operation-and-maintenance costs. The relatively stable capital costs across different countries may allow the use of cost information from one country to make some "educated guess" for other countries with similar economic development level, with or without some adjustments. This is crucial because the cost information simply does not exist in many developing countries in Asia and must be "borrowed" from alternative sources. In Chapters 4 and 6 we will discuss this issue in greater detail.

Cost functions are a key to construction of the cost-of-remediation index. The engineering-economics literature is replete with generalized cost functions for most, if not all, human activities. Appendix 2 provides the generic cost functions obtained from different sources. We consider the cost of remediation under four separate "accounts:" air, water, land, and ecosystem. A total of six types of cost functions are included: (1) air pollution (stationary sources), (2) air pollution (mobile sources), (3) water pollution (industrial and households), (4) solid waste management, (5) soil erosion control, and (6) ecosystem protection.

In order to compute the costs, it is necessary to estimate in some detail the potential and actual losses due to various activities in a country. In a generic sense, these can be estimated by first deciding upon the environmental assault per unit of activity (typically called emission factors) and then estimating the unit cost to deal with the assault so as to meet a prespecified standard of environmental quality. Appendix 1 provides details on compiling emission factors for developing countries. In particular, a rapid assessment method is developed for those countries without adequate data using secondary data sources such as the US emission data.

The significant contribution that COR can make for various sectors is that it can determine the amount of current well-being that must be given up to restore the environment to its pristine state, or to some other acceptable state. COR is a measure of the increase in defensive expenditures that a society must undertake in order to leave to future generations environmental assets equivalent in quality to the ones the current generation received. These expenditures are indicative and we are not arguing that they all need to be made now. Whether they are made or not, however, they are an indicator of the magnitude of resources that would have to be committed once a political decision has been made to restore or improve the environment.

Advantages and Disadvantages of the Cost-of-Remediation Approach

We argue that the cost-of-remediation approach incorporates the best features of both the economic and the environmental approaches discussed above. Some advantages are that:

1. It is a cardinal measure. This means that all of the aggregation problems of the other types of indicators that are sensitive to scaling parameters and ambiguous weighting parameters are avoided. It can be added, subtracted, and multiplied at will.

2. It uses the same units as the conventional economic evaluation calculus; therefore, it can be used directly in project and program evaluation. Moreover, it allows for comparison of sectoral or project investments in dollars with the state of the environment.

3. It uses data and studies usually required by national and international agencies in carrying out their normal business. In order to plan for the future these types of data are absolutely required.

4. It makes use of traditional environmental indicators to signal the levels of the required cost of remediation. It also uses traditional methods and data from industrial and agricultural engineering.

5. It uses highly disaggregated data by region (rural/urban) and type of industry (manufacturing, agriculture, forestry, mining, and energy exploitation). Even when these data are aggregated, if the need arose the cost associated with the smallest jurisdiction could be generated by disaggregation back to the smallest units.

6. It can be incorporated in the cost of repairing damage, or potential damage, to human health and ecosystem health.

7. It can be used to evaluate the financial feasibility of various existing environmental standards. Many developing countries have adopted their environmental standards directly from developed countries, particularly the US. Although these standards conform to "political correctness" and look good on paper, the enforcement of such standards is lacking. In addition to low institutional capacities, another reason for lack of enforcement is that they are too expensive to implement. The cost of remediation can be used to provide an indication of the costs of implementing a set of proposed environmental standards. This will help governments to establish environmental standards that will not only achieve significant improvement in environmental quality, but are also financially affordable for the countries.

Unfortunately, there are also some of disadvantages to using this approach, namely that:

1. Although the cost-of-remediation approach can be used to evaluate the financial feasibility of a set of proposed environmental standards, the use of cost of remediation as an index for cross-country comparison requires the acceptance of a standard or baseline. Should this be a uniform standard over the entire Asian and Pacific region? Should there be one standard for the richer countries and one for the poorer? There are ecological differences between countries that make it unfair to apply the same quantitative standards for components such as suspended particulate in the air; some arid regions have much higher background levels than more humid regions.

2. There are problems assigning repair costs to habitat loss and intrinsic values if the goal is complete remediation, because under this situation there are, by definition, no habitat and intrinsic losses under the ex ante situation. It is generally not possible to conceive of a return to a true ex ante situation; therefore, only the habitat and intrinsic value losses incremental over what would be remedied by meeting the standards need to be estimated.

3. The costs are not independent of the actual technologies assumed for the cost functions. So a technology choice is also implicit in the cost function choice.

4. It may not capture joint products or externalities in the repair approach chosen. For example, many water treatment technologies use some form of incineration that will impact air quality and many air pollution

technologies use scrubbers that add heavy particulate loads to the aquatic ecosystem.

5. It is difficult to incorporate important social impacts such as equity and the role of women into this framework.

6. The approach requires large amounts of data.

Environmental Standards

In order to use the COR index we need to explain the types of standards typically used, to comment upon how they may be set, and finally to discuss the intellectual foundations of COR. The text box on the next page describes different types of environmental standards.

In dealing with the quality of the environment, including the conventional (brown) and non-conventional (green) aspects, it is important to define standards in as broad a sense as possible. Although there are many commonly accepted standards for air and water quality, for land and ecosystems the standards are much less clearly articulated. In these latter areas, various governmental and nongovernmental agencies articulate norms, or desiderata; an example is the forestry goal of the People's Republic of China of reaching a 20 percent forest cover for the nation as a whole. In ecosystem protection these norms often take the form of minimum size limits on habitat set aside for endangered species, or limits on the size of fish catches. In order to calculate precisely a COR index, the norms and standards must be clearly articulated.

Setting Environmental Standards

Standards are the critical link which determine how much remediation is to be attempted (and therefore determine the cost of remediation) and the economic and social benefits associated with environmental improvement. However, setting standards has always been more an art than a science. The standards in existence today sometimes have scientific roots, but often tend either to be chosen under the influence of political or narrow cost concerns, or to be set through the adoption of standards existing elsewhere or even for some other pollutant. Sometimes, standards are too lax, allowing pollution to go unchecked; more often, however, especially in some developing countries, they are so unrealistically high that there is no hope of proper enforcement. What, then, should the optimal standard be?

Lack of data is most often a reason for setting arbitrary standards. Let us assume we had all the data we needed at hand, which admittedly in the real world is rarely the case. How would we sensibly set standards? Let us consider the case where we knew what the pollution control costs were at all desired levels of ambient concentrations (this implies that we also know perfectly the relationships between ambient concentrations and emission levels). Let us further assume in this information-rich world that we knew the cost of

Types of Environmental Standards

Environmental standards can be of many kinds, but as the following demonstrates they have been almost exclusively used for control of conventional ("brown") pollutants, rather than for "green" issues, such as preserving biodiversity:

1. Risk Standards

Using estimates of the risk associated with various systems, it is possible to construct a standard for risk that we wish to achieve; this is similar in concept to the one-in-a-million-risk yardstick that is often quoted for cancer. Such a risk standard can be too anthropocentric and ignore risks to other parts of the ecosystem.

2. Personal Exposure Standards

These are relatively new concepts, and have been used primarily for radiation exposure standards in nuclear plants, and for indoor and outdoor air pollution. They have the advantage of being closest to human health through respiratory and dermal exposure. Widespread use of personal exposure monitoring badges could result in new standards for personal exposure by various socioeconomic groups.

3. Ambient Standards

These are standards that are set for the concentration of a pollutant in an environmental medium, for example, a standard on the concentration of SO_2 in the atmosphere. Air pollution control programs in the United States are based on uniform National Ambient Air Quality Standards (NAAQS), unlike water pollution control programs, which have ambient standards that vary from state to state (Ott 1978).

4. Emission Standards

Ambient and personal exposure standards may be set, but for actual implementation, we need to set standards directly on what we can control. This leads us to a common form of command and control regulation: standards based on emissions. In order to set emission standards, it is desirable to know how much effect a change in emissions from a source has on the ambient concentration of a pollutant, and conversely, how a desired change in ambient concentrations can be achieved by means of change in emissions. This can be done by using *rollback models* that define the relationship between emissions and ambient concentrations. Emission standards can be set in terms of the total amount, or the concentration, of a pollutant discharged. These standards may vary spatially, temporally, and by the kind of emitting industry, but due to the many uncertainties involved and the fallibility of rollback models, the emission standards set may not always translate to a cleaner environment. In addition, emission rules may have to be revised when new pollutants are introduced. There have been various innovative economic instruments proposed for administering emission ceilings efficiently, including the concepts of bubbles, offsets, banking, tradable permits and emission (effluent) charges. Many of these innovations are more suitable for well-mixed air pollutants than for water pollutants, where location of the source in relation to the water body is a critical factor.

5. Technology Standards

It is common to mandate the use of certain kinds of pollutant control technology. Examples of this are the stipulation of secondary treatment of effluent, or a requirement that automobiles use a catalytic exhaust converter. Such rules are applied for nonpoint source control of water wastes and for forest management. This kind of requirement has the advantage of being predictable to the polluter, but by fixing on an existing technology it has the major disadvantage of not encouraging technological exploration for new and potentially more efficient methods of dealing with a pollutant.

6. Performance Standards

A performance standard regulates the amount of pollutant discharged per unit of output in say, a factory. It provides a strong incentive for pollution prevention, leaving the method to be chosen up to the polluter. There can be difficulty in specifying the meaning of "output" in particular situations, such as forestry, erosion control, and endangered species preservation.

7. Probabilistic vs. Deterministic Standards

Most standards are deterministic, but the trend in developed countries is toward probabilistic standards. Practically, it is impossible to design a regulatory program that can guarantee that any reasonable standard will *never* be violated, and there is a growing awareness that probabilistic concepts should be an integral part of the standard-setting process. From a scientific point of view, standards should be set taking into account the stochastic nature of the quantities being regulated.

pollution damages, meaning that the pollutant's effects on all health and ecosystem risks are known exactly and can be monetized. How, then would one set the standards?

Figure 3.1 depicts the known information in this hypothetical data-rich case. We want to minimize the total costs, both damage costs and control expenditures. This suggests that the value C* be the ambient standard for the pollutant in question. Setting a less demanding standard than C* means that we are neglecting an additional degree of control that would cost less than the damages it would avert. If the standard is set more stringently than C*, the cost of the extra control required would be greater than the decrease in damages achieved.

The focus of COR is the cost-of-control curve; this does not mean that the equally important (and usually much more difficult to compute) damage cost curve has been neglected. Setting an appropriate standard (at the point where total costs are minimized) takes into account not only the control costs, but also the damages, and results in the right amount of remediation. This is then reflected in the cost of remediation.

However, given the very different actuality of current data availability, in real life the smooth curves of Figure 3.1 usually become a few points scattered

---

FIGURE 3.1

Determination of Optimal Standard

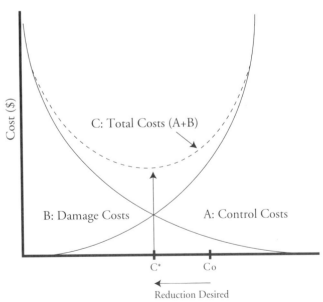

Ambient Pollutant Concentrations (μg per cubic meter)

Equivalence Between Benefits and Cost of Remediation

Consider two different approaches to the same problem, one based upon maximizing net benefits and one based upon maximizing benefits subject to constraint on environment. In each case there is a benefit function, B(E), which is a function of the environmental quality, E. In the first case, the problem is to maximize the benefits due to quality level E subject to the constraint that the environmental quality exceed some level, E^M. In the second case, the goal is to maximize B(E) minus the damages, D(E), caused by the environmental quality being at level E.

Model 1

Max B(E)

subject to $E > E^M$

In the solution let the shortfall be S.

Then $E - S = E^M$

and the Lagrangian becomes

$L = B(E) - \lambda(E - S - E^M)$,

and the first order conditions for a maximum are

$\partial L/\partial E = \partial B/\partial E - \lambda = 0$

$\partial L/\partial S = \partial B/\partial S + \lambda = 0$. Hence,

$\partial B/\partial S = \partial B/\partial E = \lambda$.

Model 2

Max U = B(E) - D(E)

where D(E) is a function representing economic damages associated with environmental quality level F.

The first order conditions for a maximum now become;

$\partial U/\partial E = \partial B/\partial E - \partial D/\partial E = 0$,

$\partial B/\partial E = \partial D/\partial E$.

These two different approaches to the same problem demonstrate the equivalence between the marginal cost of remediation, $\partial B/\partial S$, and the marginal damages, $\partial D/\partial E$, as

$$\partial D/\partial E = - \partial B/\partial S.$$

In other words, if the environmental standards, E^M, are optimal then estimating the cost of remediation is equivalent to estimating the economic damages. A priori we do not know if or when the standards are optimal; one would have to know the economic damages in order to establish them. However, given the difficulties associated with estimating the damages, the approach taken here is to assume that society has some notion of what the optimal standards ought to be and the cost of remediation is then an estimate, albeit imperfect, of the economic damages. In many cases, we would argue that it will be a lower bound on the estimates of economic benefits.

across an undefined and poorly understood data and process landscape. Even if remediation costs are known, the extent and value of environmental damage are not, so that standards of repair must be set in a pragmatic way suitable to each situation, rather than on total cost minimization which would be ideal in a situation of full data availability. In setting standards in the real world, perhaps the hardest issues are:

■ Even if we know exactly the costs of controlling emissions in the most efficient manner, matching the control effort to different levels of ambient concentration requires the use of poorly understood rollback models. A given discharge of automotive carbon monoxide will create a different ambient level in the closed valley where Kathmandu is located than in Manila, located on a bay swept by ocean winds.

■ It is very difficult to assign damages to specific levels of a particular pollutant. For example, health impacts can often be attributed to any one of several different pollutants (complicated by synergistic effects); it is difficult to separate out which pollutant is responsible for what effect. The entire analysis is complicated when additional pollutants, sources, media, and receptors are considered.

■ Although damages may be identified and their extent known, damage costs are extremely difficult to estimate as they involve valuation of non-monetary goods (such as deterioration of wetlands, species extinction, illness, and death). Surrogate measures (such as lost wages during illness) have been suggested for some of these effects, and often there is no alternative to their use, but they do not fully capture the true damage cost.

We can now appreciate why standard-setting is sometimes more of an art than a science. Where it is possible to learn from one's mistakes without irreversible damage, standards should be set in an iterative manner, starting off with a reasonable value and changing as the results are observed.

It is evident that in the implementation of control measures to achieve these standards, the least-cost technology or set of options should be used to minimize the cost of remediation. Indeed, there should be a steady search to minimize the costs of avoiding or remediating pollution, and in principle, as such remediation costs go down, the standard of environmental quality to be sought can rise.

The box above provides a simple mathematical formulation which shows the equivalence between measuring benefits and measuring costs.

Some Examples from PRC

The most difficult, and arguably the most useful, indices are to be found in the cost-of-repair and cost-of-remediation concepts. One of the major thrusts of this research on environmental quality indices is the development of these indices in the Asian context. The cost functions are hard to compute without extensive data sets; however, we have obtained a set of studies on the cost of remediation in cities in PRC and use these to compute the component and total costs of environmental remediation (Bao and Chen 1993).

For example, for the city of Shenyang the environmental planners looked for the "best" ways to meet the proposed year 2000 quality standards. They did not rely solely upon "end-of-pipe" methods to repair the effects; when considering the air environment, they chose cost-effective combinations of district heating to reduce reliance on small coal furnaces, the production of town gas from coal, and the provision of methane and LPG from new industrial projects, in addition to source reductions and emission controls. Conceptualizing and computing air, water, and land components is relatively straightforward; the ecosystem component is the most difficult. They have used a compromise approach based upon building parks, planting trees, and increasing vegetative cover in the city environs.

In Table 3.1a we show the total cost of remediation for each city by component of the environment. Shenyang has the largest cost of $407,661,000,

TABLE 3.1a
Cost of Remediation in Six Cities in PRC ($000)

City	Air	Water	Land	Ecosystem	Total
Shenyang	220,198	113,513	31,333	42,617	407,661
Taiyuan	167,362	66,690	9,361	46,905	290,318
Changsha	103,697	50,660	16,807	6,002	177,166
Lanzhou	110,444	7,779	8,067	35,151	161,441
Shaoxing	18,544	21,409	7,803	3,001	50,757
Dandong	3,902	31,212	5,882	624	41,620

TABLE 3.1b
Cost of Remediation in Six Cities in PRC (per capita $)

City	Air	Water	Land	Ecosystem	Total
Shaoxing	77.3	89.2	32.5	12.5	211.5
Taiyuan	112.3	44.8	6.3	5.5	168.9
Changsha	98.8	48.2	16.0	5.7	168.7
Shenyang	71.1	36.7	10.1	13.8	131.8
Lanzhou	79.5	5.6	5.8	5.5	96.4
Dandong	6.0	48.2	9.1	0.9	64.3
Average	74.2	45.5	13.3	7.3	140.2

followed by Taiyuan with $290,318,000. Dandong has the smallest total cost of $41,620,000. These figures are misleading because Shenyang is the biggest city and has the largest population, Taiyuan the next largest, and Shaoxing has the smallest population. A much more meaningful number is the cost per capita (Table 3.1b). Now Shaoxing has the highest figure with $212 per capita and Shenyang drops to 4th place with $132 per capita. On the per capita basis, Dandong ($64) has the highest environmental quality in terms of cost of remediation. In other terms, for an expenditure of capital resources of $64 per capita the city of Dandong can be made to meet its year 2000 environmental quality goals.[1]

The discussions and example on COR in this chapter have focused on methodological development and illustration. In Chapters 4 and 6, we will apply this methodology for estimating the cost of remediating the environment including air, water, land, and ecosystem at both city and national level for Asian countries.

Development Diamonds—Environmental Diamonds

A simple graphical approach for comparative assessment of environmental performance of countries may be adapted from the World Bank's report on the Social Indicators of Development, which defines a "development diamond"

TABLE 3.2

Indicators Used for Constructing the Environmental Diamonds (Around 1990)

Country	Air Indicators		Water Indicators				Land Indicators			Ecosystem Indicators		
	Ind.CO₂ Emi. kg/capita	Com. Energy Cons. Gigajoules/capita	%Urb Access to Safe Drinking Water	DO mg/l	BOD mg/l	E. Coli MPN/l	Forest Area as % of Total Area	% Land Area Degraded	Annual Fertilizer Use (kg/ha, 1990)	Prot. Area as % of Total Area	Threat. Sp. Per 1000 ha.	% Wetlands Threatened
Bangladesh	133.22	2.30	39	6.80	2.7	188	15	7.4	101	0.7	0.00691	82
PRC	2,204.98	23.71	87	7.60	1.5	1,153	14	30	284	3.3	0.00048	39
India	831.43	9.47	86	8.50	2.0	11,000	23	49	73	4.4	0.00492	45
Indonesia	925.05	10.39	35	3.20	2.5	175,000	61	24	109	10.7	0.00281	37
Pakistan	579.81	8.74	82	6.20	2.0	230	4	17	89	4.7	0.00080	50
Philippines	714.08	12.12	90	6.70	3.3	1,400	35	16.8	65	1.9	0.00926	69
Thailand	1,845.21	23.43	67	6.10	1.0	1,400	28	38.7	39	12.7	0.00161	47
Average	1,033.40	12.88	70	6.44	2.1	27,196	25	26.1	109	5.5	0.00383	56
Maximum	2,204.98	23.71	93	8.50	3.3	175,000	61	49	284	12.7	0.00926	82
Minimum	133.22	2.30	35	3.20	1.0	188	4	7.4	39	0.7	0.00048	39

Note: The four environmental components: air, water, land, and ecosystem, are derived statistically using the principal component analysis technique.

Source: Data for this table are mostly derived from WRI report *World Resources 1992–1993*, except DO, BOD, E. Coli which were taken from a working paper by K.F. Jalal (1996).

(DD) for a given country constructed from four variables: GNP per capita, life expectancy, gross primary school enrollment, and access to safe water (see Chapter 2). This approach is not without shortcomings.[2] Similarly, once we give the operational definitions of the four environmental dimensions: air, water, land, and terrestial ecosystem (including biodiversity), it is also possible to obtain a view of the environmental stress currently faced by a country (or region or metropolitan area), and the relative sources of the stress by employing such a diamond. A preliminary application of this concept to the environment (Rogers and Jalal 1994) used the four environmental dimensions derived from the PCA: air, water, soil, and ecosystem as the four variables.

The major contribution of the environmental diamond is that it is integrative in nature. It reveals a general picture without concealing the multiple dimensionalities of environmental quality by presenting the picture relative to norms or average values of the four environmental components. It partially eliminates the need to aggregate different subindices to form a single index since it allows an observer to look simultaneously at the four components, although, as will be demonstrated below, aggregation of the four subindices is also possible through mathematical manipulations.

To construct environmental diamonds, the first step is to select appropriate variables or indicators that best characterize the environment for each of the four components. In reality, though, the choice of indicators is often dictated by data availability. Table 3.2 has a total of 12 indicators to characterize the environmental stress/quality for seven Asian countries. A number of other indicators were also considered but ultimately dropped due to lack of data. In addition to the environmental diamond, another index correlating changes in the environment with changes in the economy—termed environmental elasticity—has been formulated (see following section).

To characterize environmental stress for air quality, for example, we selected two indicators: annual industrial CO_2 emissions per capita and annual commercial energy consumption per capita. The energy consumption indicator was chosen based upon our statistical analysis which indicates that it is highly correlated with the emissions of several other major air pollutants such as suspended particulate matter (SPM), SO_2, and NO_x. Therefore, by including this indicator, we effectively account for most air emissions in these countries. An important point regarding the indicator selection is that, due to data constraints, we have included both "pressure" and "state" variables in the OECD pressure-state-response (PSR) indicator classification scheme. For example, the two air indicators chosen are emission-related and, thus, are considered pressure indicators. Most of the water quality indicators chosen i.e., dissolved oxygen (DO) concentration, biological oxygen demand (BOD) and E. Coli., are state indicators. For some indicators, large values are "bad" and vice versa for others. For example, in terms of water quality, large DO values are desirable while small BOD is desirable. Similarly, for land quality, a high percentage of forest coverage improves land quality while a high figure for annual fertilizer use is undesirable since the fertilizer has some adverse effect on soil quality and its use is also indicative of poor soil fertility. Finally, for the ecosystem component, a large percentage of protected land is obviously a plus for protecting the species while a large number of threatened species per 1000 hectares of land and a large percentage of wetlands threatened are direct indicators of biodiversity threat or loss.

Once the individual indicators are chosen, the next step is to "standardize" the values to derive some kind of scores that are indicative of environmental pressure or quality. To be consistent with the World Bank's development diamond, we adopted its approach of standardization. In particular, the score of each country with each indicator is expressed in terms of percentage of the group averages i.e., seven countries in this case. We follow the principle, "Small is Good" and "Large is Bad." Consequently, for those indicators for which the reverse is true, we adopted its opposite indicator. For example, for the indicator: "percentage of urban population with access to safe drinking water," we adopted its opposite indicator, "percentage of urban population without access to safe drinking water." The same method was also applied to "forest area as a percentage of total area" and "protected area as a percentage of total area."

The third step is to aggregate the individual scores to derive an average index for each of the four principal environmental components based on a weighting scheme. Ideally, the weighting scheme should reflect policy priority and health effects. For simplicity and demonstration, we adopt equal weighting for all the indicators. The results are displayed in Table 3.3.

The last step is to draw the diamonds on a Cartesian system of axes using the indices in Table 3.3. In Figure 3.2, the square "diamonds" indicate the 7-country average i.e., 100 percent and the overlay shaded diamonds reflect the environmental situation in individual countries. As indicated earlier, along each dimension, larger values indicate either worse environmental quality or added environmental stress.

TABLE 3.3
Aggregated Indices for Constructing Environmental Diamonds

	Air (%)	Water (%)	Land (%)	Ecosystem (%)	RMS (%)	RMS Ranking
7-Country Average	100	100	100	100	100	
Pakistan	62	64	92	71	73	1
India	77	64	120	104	94	2
Bangladesh	15	106	79	144	98	3
Philippines	82	70	71	157	101	4
Thailand	180	67	94	73	113	5
PRC	199	51	164	62	135	6
Indonesia	85	294	82	90	165	7

FIGURE 3.2

Environmental Diamonds

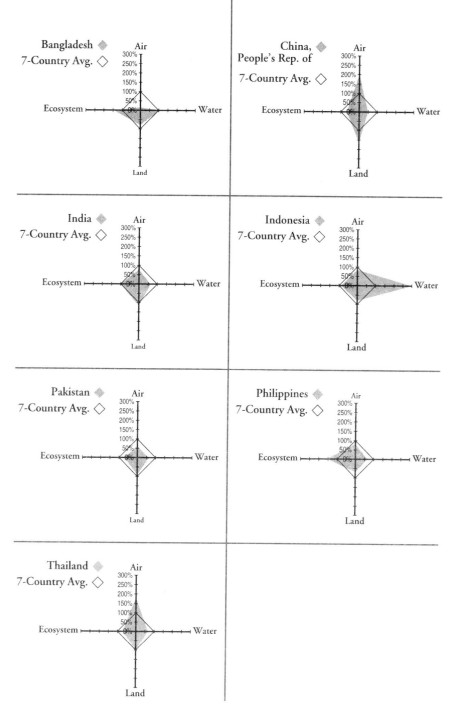

Why Diamond?

The decision to adopt the four principal dimensions of environmental quality to construct the environmental diamond was based on the following considerations. First, as shown by the PCA discussed earlier in this chapter, the first four principal components account for 64 percent of the total variations of the 32 environmental indicators used for the PCA. Second, the first four principal components represent air, land, biodiversity, and water quality, respectively. These four dimensions reflect the most urgent environmental issues across all countries. Third, the interpretation of the subsequent principal components is considerably more difficult than the first four since the subsequent principal components tend to be correlated, much more randomly, with different types of environmental indicators, with no particular group of indicators dominating their loadings. Fourth, compared to other types of polygons such as a triangle or a pentagon, a diamond is perhaps the most effective tool to present the orthogonality of the axes on a two-dimensional space. The principal components, by definition, are perpendicular to each other.

Environmental diamonds are appealing as they are easy to construct, keep individual components separate, and graphically are a good way of presenting the result especially for cross-country or cross-region comparisons. For example, from Figure 3.2, one quickly obtains an impression that Bangladesh is near or within the average in all environmental components except ecosystem. By comparison, PRC does very poorly with respect to air quality (mostly from coal combustion) and land degradation (due to severe soil erosion and desertification). Indonesia is at the average in terms of air, land, and ecosystem, but does extremely poorly in terms of water quality.

As mentioned earlier, the principal advantage of the environmental diamond is that it partially eliminates the need for aggregation by presenting the four "corners" or subindices in a single picture (see the text box). However, if one is still not satisfied with this integrative approach, it is also possible to aggregate the four subindices through mathematical manipulation of the data. An obvious option is to calculate the area within a diamond and use the diamond area as an indication of the environmental stress or quality. However, we do not recommend this method due to the fact that the environmental diamond is "topologically" incorrect in that when the four axes are switched, the diamond area will change (see Appendix 4). Another alternative, advocated by Ott (1978), which has the virtue of indifference of axis orders, is the root-mean-square (RMS) method, which takes the following form:

$$RMS = \sqrt{W_1 \, (airindex)^2 + W_2 \, (waterindex)^2 + W_3 \, (landindex)^2 + W_4 \, (ecoindex)^2}$$

The RMS values, based on equal weighting for the four environmental components, and the ranks of the countries based on the RMS values are shown in Table 3.3. The ranking results seem to indicate that the South Asian countries, with relatively slower economic growth rates, receive better environmental ranking. Pakistan, with the lowest RMS value, ranks the best, followed by India and Bangladesh. The Southeast and East Asian countries, Philippines,

FIGURE 3.3
COR/Capita for Six Cities in PRC as a Percentage of the Average

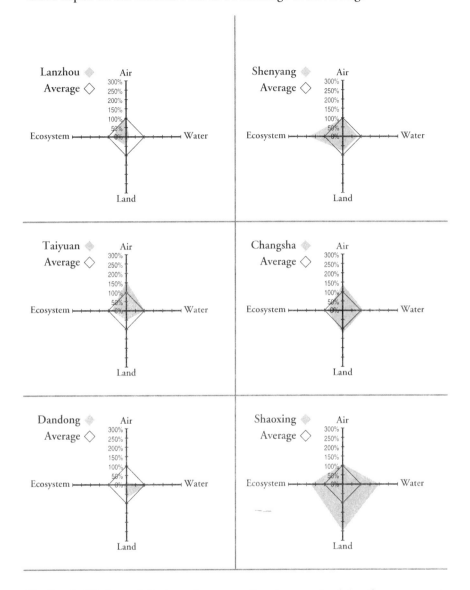

Thailand, PRC, and Indonesia, generally characterized by fast economic expansion, receive relatively poor environmental ranking.

As a graphic tool, the environmental diamond is flexible in terms of the types of subindices adopted to form the four corners. Figure 3.3 provides another type of environmental diamonds drawn using the COR estimates for the six cities in PRC derived in the previous section. In these diamonds each of the cities is compared with the difference from the average cost on each dimension, hence, the larger the diamond the lower the environmental quality index. The diamonds show the clear lead of the city of Dandong in this comparison, but they also show that Lanzhou does extremely well on two dimensions, water and land, but fares very poorly on the air and ecosystem dimensions. The environmental diamonds using COR estimates present the type and magnitude of environmental problems facing a city or a country in monetary terms. This sort of information should help inform decisions concerning sectoral allocation of remediation funds.

Environmental Elasticity
The Concept of Environmental Elasticity
The environmental diamond introduced in the previous section is designed to capture the state of the environment of a city or a country. Asia is facing rapid economic environmental changes and an index depicting its environmental trends with respect to economic trends is also highly in demand. In an attempt to monitor environmental trends and correlate changes in the environment with changes in the economy, we have utilized the economic concept of elasticity to develop another index known as environmental elasticity (EE). It is defined as the percentage change in an environmental aggregate as a function of a 1 percent change in an economic aggregate, or:

$$E_t = \frac{N_t}{D_t} \qquad (3.1)$$

where:
N_t = aggregate environmental change (percent),
E_t = aggregate economic change (percent)

The numerator, aggregate environmental change, is given as:

$$N_t = \sum W_k \cdot \frac{X_{t,k} - X_{t-1,k}}{X_{t-1,k}} \qquad (3.2)$$

The weights, W_k, in equation (3.2) must sum to one. The variables we would like to use, X_t, are listed in the column entitled State in Table 1.1 of Chapter 1. The numerator of EE can be used to describe the state or the pressure of the environmental system. In many cases, the state of the system is identical to the pressure of the system, but there are exceptions. For example, on the issue of biodiversity ecosystem, the pressure is land conversion, but the environmental state is species abundance. The amount of land converted from forest land to agricultural land is not necessarily a negative environmental indicator, while the reduction in species number is more clearly a negative environmental indicator. For this study, the variables we retain are dictated by availability. Note that the problem of selecting appropriate weights in EE still remains.

The economic variables in the denominator can be aggregated in several ways. The basic scheme is as follows:

$$D_1 = W_{GDP} \left(\frac{GDP_t - GDP_{t-1}}{GDP_{t-1}} \right) + W_{POP} \left(\frac{POP_t - POP_{t-1}}{POP_{t-1}} \right)$$

$$+ W_{\frac{GDP}{POP}} \left(\frac{\dfrac{GDP}{POP_t} \times \dfrac{GDP}{POP_{t-1}}}{\dfrac{GDP}{POP_{t-1}}} \right)$$

(3.3)

The weights, W, in equation (3.3) can take any value between zero and one and must sum to one. The central issue in economic development is how much of GDP goes toward raising per capita incomes and how much goes to sustaining a rapidly growing population at a constant level of consumption. The environmental impact of population growth is primarily mediated through increases in the GDP and the end use of GDP, although there are exceptions to this argument. Human waste generation, land conversion, and erosion are environmental pressures that do not register as changes in GDP per capita.

What constitutes an "appropriate" set of weights has been the subject of a great deal of debate. Should the weights reflect a country's priorities in the environment and the economy, the presumption being that these reflect urgent environmental problems and economic goals? Or, should the weights reflect a more universal set of priorities? An example of divergence between the two might be that the Philippines identifies urban air pollution as an urgent environmental problem requiring attention while outside observers view deforestation as a problem of paramount importance because of its global repercussions. The problem of determining a universal set of weights is not solved in EE. There is preliminary evidence of the importance Asian nations place on environmental problems in the ADB's 1994 report entitled "The Environment Program of the Asian Development Bank" (see Table 6.1 in Chapter 6).

Environmental elasticity can also be used to rank the countries. Since environmental elasticity deals with environmental changes relative to economic changes, Figure 3.4 graphically illustrates the four possibilities (quadrants) in which a country can be located in the economic-environmental space.

Quadrant I (both economic and environmental changes are positive) is clearly the most preferred situation and Quadrant III (both the economic and environmental changes are negative) is clearly the least preferred situation. However, the choice between Quadrants II (positive environmental change but negative economic change) and IV (positive economic change but negative environmental change) is less than clear-cut. As will be seen below and also in

FIGURE 3.4

Map of Environmental Elasticity

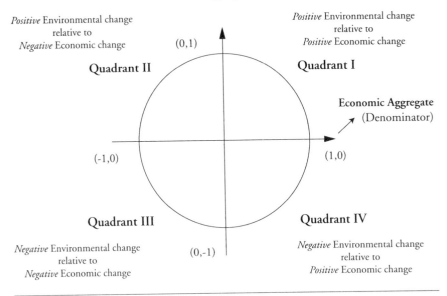

Environmental Aggregate (Numerator)

Positive Environmental change
relative to
Negative Economic change (0,1)

Quadrant II

Positive Environmental change
relative to
Positive Economic change

Quadrant I

Economic Aggregate
(Denominator)

(-1,0) (1,0)

Quadrant III Quadrant IV

Negative Environmental change
relative to
Negative Economic change (0,-1)

Negative Environmental change
relative to
Positive Economic change

Chapter 5, most of the countries included in our analysis seem to prefer IV to II: assigning more weight to economic development than environmental improvement. However, we also know that many former Soviet republics are currently located in Quadrant II, experiencing drastic economic, particularly industrial, decline which is accompanied by a substantial decrease of industrial emissions, and by air, water, and land quality improvement. We argue that environmental improvement can only be achieved and sustained with a certain level of economic development as a foundation. We also believe that most countries currently located in IV (positive economic change but negative environmental change) are more likely to move into I (positive economic and environmental changes) after a prolonged period of economic development, rather than into II (positive environmental change but negative economic change).

The principal merit of environmental elasticity is its dynamic nature. It uses data for two points in time to compute the change over that period of both the environmental aggregate in the numerator and the economic aggregate in the denominator. The weights used in the numerator to generate the aggregated indices could reflect the urgency with which a region or nation faces specific environmental stresses. Like the environmental diamond, the environmental elasticity can also be used for cross-country or cross-region comparisons. However, there is a profound difference between environmental elasticity and the environmental diamond. The latter is static in that it focuses on the state of the environment, rather than the change of the environment.

Below we provide an example illustrating how to compute and interpret EE and how to use EE to rank the countries. Since the focus of this chapter is to highlight the methodology, we use OECD countries as examples because the data required for these countries, especially time-series data, are much more complete than those for developing countries. In Chapter 5, however, we will focus our attention to applying EE to Asian countries.

Computing Environmental Elasticity for OECD Countries

This section discusses EEs computed for nine major industrialized OECD countries. These countries were chosen to demonstrate that EE can be readily calculated for countries that have the typical databases available to modern developed societies. It also allows us to make comparisons with other types of indicators that have already been calculated for these same countries. The data for the analysis are taken from a study made by the National Center for Economic Alternatives (NCFEA, 1995). As discussed in Chapter 2, the Index of Environmental Trends (IET) by the NCFEA failed to uncover the environmental-economic linkages. The EEs to be presented below using the same data attempt to examine a country's environmental deterioration in relation to its economic progress.

Nineteen of the 21 indicators used by the NCFEA were also used for computing the environmental elasticities (see Table 3.4). Two indicators in the "Causal" sector, i.e., automobiles and energy, were excluded because they tend to be strongly correlated with indicators for air emissions. For simplicity, the changes of total GDP were used as the denominator of the EEs. The EEs are computed for the four 5-year intervals and for the period 1970–1990. The results for the 1970–1990 period are summarized in Table 3.5.

Let us assume equal weighting for the 19 indicators. In other words, the total environmental changes are the simple average of the percentage changes of individual indicators falling into each category. For example, for the air sector, if CO_2 increases by 15 percent, i.e., -15 percent, and NO_x decreases by 20 percent, i.e., +20 percent, the net result is (-15 percent+20 percent) / 2 = 2.5 percent. The same rule also applies across different sectors, which effectively assumes that 10 percent of improvement in air quality will be offset by 10 percent deterioration in water quality or another sector. This approach assumes that the same percentage increase of environmental stress in all sectors causes about the same amount of damage. This is most definitely not true because the marginal impacts of additional environmental stress have to do with its existing level. To modify this situation, unequal weightings are used for different indicators. For example, global pollutants such as CO_2 could be given less weight (Table 3.4).

Weighting Scheme for EEs

Sector	Indicator (unit)	Weight
Air	CO_2 (tonnes)	0.1
	NO_X (tonnes)	0.2
	SO_X (tonnes)	0.2
	CO (tonnes)	0.2
	Particulate (tonnes)	0.2
	VOC or HC (tonnes)	0.1
	Sectoral weight in the total	0.25
Water	DO (mg/l)	0.3
	Nitrates (mg/l)	0.1
	Phosphorous (mg/l)	0.2
	Ammonium (mg/l)	0.1
	Metals (micrograms/l)	0.2
	Withdrawal (mil. cu. m.)	0.1
	Sectoral weight in the total	0.25
Chemical	Fertilizers (tonnes)	0.2
	Pesticides (tonnes active ingredients)	0.4
	Ind. Chemical (trend data)	0.4
	Sectoral weight in the total	0.20
Waste	Municipal (tonnes)	0.4
	Nuclear (tonnes heavy metal)	0.6
	Sectoral weight in the total	0.15
Land	Wetlands (sq. km)	0.4
	Woods (sq. km)	0.6
	Sectoral weight in the total	0.15

T A B L E   3 . 5
Country Rankings Based on IET and EE (1970–1990)

Country	IET (Rank)	EE Equal Weighting (Rank)	EE Unequal Weighting (Rank)
Canada	-38.1% (8)	-0.30 (8)	-0.22 (8)
Denmark	-10.6% (1)	-0.15 (4)	-0.15 (6)
France	-41.2% (9)	-0.55 (9)	-0.47 (9)
W. Germany	-16.5% (5)	-0.17 (5)	-0.08 (4)
Japan	-19.4% (6)	-0.00 (1)	-0.01 (2)
Netherlands	-11.4% (2)	-0.00 (1)	0.04 (1)
Sweden	-15.5% (4)	-0.21 (6)	-0.17 (7)
U.K.	-14.3% (3)	-0.07 (3)	-0.03 (3)
U.S.A.	-22.1% (7)	-0.21 (6)	-0.13 (5)

The EEs have altered some of the country rankings based on IETs. The rankings based on IETs and EEs (total) for 1970–1990 are shown in Table 3.5. The most notable changes are found in Japan, which jumps from sixth place in the IET ranking to first place in the EE equal weighting ranking and second place in the EE unequal weighting ranking, and in Denmark, which slides from the first place to the fourth and sixth places, respectively. Other changes are relatively minor. In general, countries with greater GDP growth rates over the 20 years tend to improve their positions and vice versa. Japan, for example, had a very high economic growth rate, 126 percent, between 1970 and 1990. The main difference between EEs and IETs is that EEs demonstrate the trade-off between natural capital and produced capital. Based on equal weighting, the EEs show that all nine countries fall into the range of $-1 < EE < 0$. This resembles the "weak sustainability" scenario described in Chapter 2. In our study, weak sustainability refers to a scenario in which environment experiences negative changes but these changes are not enough to offset positive economic growth. With unequal weighting, the Netherlands scores a positive value, 0.04. This is classified as "strong sustainability," which refers to the scenario in which the economy and environment improve simultaneously. The validity of this result is debatable due to several reasons. First, weighting is obviously an important factor, particularly when slightly different weighting schemes result in the sign changes of the values from negative to positive or vice versa, since the conclusions to be drawn from the results are fundamentally different. Another reason lies in the inherent assumption of the perfect substitutability of environmental quality in different environmental sectors. More specifically, improvement in land quality is assumed to provide justifications for degradation of water quality. To obtain a better sense in this regard, one needs to examine the EEs in each of the five different sectors. Furthermore, a country may be sustainable in one period and not sustainable in another.

It should be pointed out that missing values are prevalent, especially for the earlier years. If the data for a particular indicator are missing for a country and a period, the indicator is excluded from the index. The average indices for different countries, thus, may be the aggregates of different indicators for the same sectors. In addition, when time intervals are shorter, e.g., five years rather than 20 years, random "noise" in the data such as changes caused by temporary setbacks (strikes, price fluctuations), may be a major influential factor. All these require a certain caution in interpreting the results.

Across different sectors, most OECD countries have achieved remarkable improvements in air and water quality since the 1980s. The Chemicals and Wastes sectors are where most countries consistently experienced deterioration. This means that the economic growth of the countries is largely accompanied by an increase in the use of fertilizers, pesticides, and industrial chemicals, and in the amount of municipal and nuclear wastes generated. In terms of land uses, it appears that the number of countries that experienced loss of wetlands and forest exhibited a mild increasing trend since 1970.

Across different countries, France and Canada consistently score low points in almost all accounts during the 1970s. Certain progress has been made during the 1980s in air and water quality, but not enough to offset the deteriorating trends. For France, waste generation, particularly nuclear wastes, is a main concern. At the other end of the spectrum, no country receives consistently high scores for all accounts in all periods. The Netherlands appears to be a winner in part because of its great improvements in air and water quality. Japan and the UK receive a boost from improvement in air and land quality and are the only two countries that experience a net gain of wetlands and/or forests over the 1970–1990 period. The differences among the remaining countries are relatively minor. All countries, with an exception of the Netherlands, appeared to be located in Quadrant IV (see Figure 3.4) for the 20-year period, experiencing economic growth but environmental deterioration.

It appears that in the period 1970–1990 most of the countries greatly reduced their air emissions and improved their water quality, but were not very effective in the other sectors of Chemicals, Wastes, and Land. This reflects the tremendous expenditure devoted to improving air and water quality by both public and private sectors in the period. The general public considers air and water essential to quality of life once economic needs have been met. The pressure on governments and industry has translated into policies and regulations and, in turn, net improvements. In contrast, the attention paid to the sectors of Chemicals, Wastes, and Land, though increasing, has not yet seen as many results, in part because these sectors were or are considered less crucial for people's well-being.

Notes

1   This is restricted to the capital costs and does not reflect the operating and maintenance costs necessary to sustain these capital investments.

2   For example, per capita energy (safe, conventional and nonconventional) availability may have been a more appropriate indicator of sustainable development than accessibility to water.

4 Applications and Policy Implications of the Cost-of-Remediation Index

Until recently, the criterion of economic efficiency and economic development has been a top priority in the identification of opportunities for investment by multilateral financial institutions (MFIs) such as the World Bank, International Monetary Fund, and Asian Development Bank. However, there is a new emphasis on projects related to the environment. For example, although insignificant in the past, the proportion of environmentally-related loans at ADB is steadily rising and is expected to reach 50 percent of the annual $5 billion total in the near future. In addition, there is increasing awareness of the environmental impacts of projects traditionally supported by MFIs. In order to operationalize the concept of sustainable development, there is a need to develop a set of indicators that can represent various components of the environment. The Environmental Quality Indices (EQIs) developed in this study are intended to help devise investment or lending policies to achieve environmental goals without compromising economic efficiency, or at least to highlight the trade-offs involved. We have developed the environmental diamond (ED), environmental elasticity (EE), and cost-of-remediation (COR) indices to address major environmental themes: air pollution, water pollution, land degradation, and ecosystem protection. The question that faces MFIs on a daily basis is in which sector and country should their next loan be invested in order to best realize their economic, social, and environmental goals? The ED index was shown in Chapter 3 to support the national and international comparison of environmental performance between components. The EE and COR indices address this question from two different perspectives. The EE indicates whether or not a country is on a sustainable path for different time periods. If, for example, the EE index indicates that a country is unsustainable in the use of its land resources, the COR index will provide some estimates of the relative source of these unsustainable activities and the methodology for estimating the costs associated with achieving a more sustainable land-use pattern. The two types of EQIs are, thus, complementary tools for devising MFIs' lending strategies. In this chapter we will illustrate the use of COR indices in assessing environmental loans with specific examples for different Asian countries.

ADB's Environmental Expenditure Record

In order to assess ADB's lending practices with respect to the environment, it is useful to review its past environmental expenditure. To a certain extent, past investment in environmental areas reflects ADB's perceptions of the benefits that accrue from such investment, in that it represents the amount that ADB was willing to loan to prevent or remediate the environmental damage in Asian countries. The damage is caused by negligence of environmental consequences in the drive for development or, more precisely, economic growth.

Table 4.1 breaks down ADB's investment in environment-related projects for different periods. It shows that the investment has exhibited an increasing trend since 1970.

Tables 4.2a and 4.2b summarize ADB's environmental-oriented loans for two different periods in a cross-tabular form. The tables break down the total loans by 21 countries and 11 sectors. Table 4.2a covers the period from 1968 to 1989, and Table 4.2b the period from 1990 to 1993. It should be noted that Tables 4.1 and 4.2 could be misleading, because the amounts represented in both tables are not discounted to a base-year level. However, our main concern is the relative proportion of the investment in each category, rather than the absolute values.

Table 4.2a shows that from 1968 to 1989, roughly 35 percent of the ADB's total environmental loans went into water-related projects, followed by urban development and environmental improvement (20 percent); fishery, aquaculture and marine resources protection (17 percent); forestry and afforestation (13 percent); and land- and agriculture-related projects (8.3 percent). These

TABLE 4.1

ADB Environment-Oriented Loans in Different Periods

Period	Investment ($ m)	% Increase over Previous Period
1970–1974	142	na
1975–1979	597	320
1980–1984	841	41
1985–1989	1,740	107
1990–1993	3,678	111

na = not available

1994 data are not yet available.

Source: ADB, 1994.

five sectors together account for over 93 percent of all the environmental loans. It is rather surprising that, during this period, ADB did not spend any money explicitly on energy conservation and air pollution control (Sector 4), or biodiversity and ecosystem protection (Sector 7). Comparing countries, Table 4.2a indicates that before 1990, the top three borrowers of ADB's environmental loans were Indonesia (26.99 percent), the Philippines (24.80 percent), and Pakistan (16.07 percent). Other countries accounted for relatively small proportions. Notably, India and the PRC (which became a member country in 1986) did not receive any such loans.

For the period from 1990 to 1993, Table 4.2b indicates a dramatic reversal of ADB's lending practices in terms of both sectors and countries. Energy conservation and air pollution control (Sector 4) replaced water pollution control and supply (Sector 1) as the most heavily invested environmental sector of ADB, accounting for 28.82 percent of the total investment. The water sector investment went from 34.84 percent for the pre-1990 period to 25.78 percent for the post-1990 period. Other notable changes of the sectoral weight of investment are found in forestry and afforestation (Sector 2), which saw a decline from 13.05 percent to 4.82 percent, and fishery, aquaculture, and marine resources protection (Sector 5), which also experienced a marked decrease from the previous 16.90 percent to 2.98 percent. Since 1990, the ADB has initiated investments in biodiversity and ecosystem protection (Sector 7). Although the total amount is insignificant (0.66 percent), it represents an important milestone in ADB's lending practices. After 1990, PRC overtook Indonesia as ADB's largest borrower of environmental loans (18.01 percent), followed by Indonesia (16.46 percent) and India (14.81 percent).

It appears that before 1990, most of ADB's environmental investment went into water pollution control and supply, fishery, and afforestation plus urban development. These investments are mostly resources-related and often bring about immediate social and economic benefits. Only since 1990 has ADB invested in large projects, each costing roughly $100 million, in energy conservation and air pollution control. Only two countries received such loans—PRC and India. Other areas for which benefits are less tangible and more long-term-oriented, i.e., biodiversity and ecosystem protection, have not yet received the same amount of assistance as water and air pollution control. ADB funded only one such project in Indonesia.

The uneven sectoral distribution of environmental investment in favor of water management has also been recognized in *Financing Environmentally Sound Development*, a book published by ADB (Owens 1994). In it, Weatherly quoted the World Bank estimates that "the levels of public investment in water and sanitation have, on a worldwide basis, remained at a level equivalent to approximately one half of one percent of GDP." National governments and MFIs have long histories of giving strong support to water and sanitation, long before these sectors began to be seen as key elements of the sustainable use of

TABLE 4.2a

ADB Environment-Oriented Loans by Country and by Sector (1968–1989) ($ million)

	Sector 1	Sector 2	Sector 3	Sector 4	Sector 5	Sector 6	Sector 7	Sector 8	Sector 9	Sector 10	Sector 11	TOTAL
Bangladesh	14.40	54.50			55.46			6.20				130.56
%	0.43	1.64			1.67			0.19				3.93
Bhutan	3.30											3.30
%	0.10											0.10
PRC												0.00
%												0.00
Fiji										4.40		4.40
%										0.13		0.13
India												0.00
%												0.00
Indonesia	121.64	61.30	62.40		113.70	536.85						895.89
%	3.67	1.85	1.88		3.43	16.18						26.99
Lao PDR	6.00	16.00										22.00
%	0.18	0.48										0.66
Malaysia	114.11	54.00	25.40			16.00			48.20			257.71
%	3.44	1.63	0.77			0.48			1.45			7.77
Marshall Islands												0.00
Micronesia, Fed. States of %												0.00
												0.00
Myanmar	28.00	50.00			55.80							133.80
%	0.84	1.51			1.68							4.03

TABLE 4.2a continued

	Sector 1	Sector 2	Sector 3	Sector 4	Sector 5	Sector 6	Sector 7	Sector 8	Sector 9	Sector 10	Sector 11	TOTAL
Nepal	24.00				22.80					34.00		112.40
%	0.72				0.69					1.02		3.39
Pakistan	146.50		171.00		94.50	121.20						533.20
%	4.41		5.15		2.85	3.65						16.07
Papua New Guinea	18.90											18.90
%	0.57											0.57
Philippines	425.60	154.00			156.34					79.00		822.94
%	12.82	4.64			4.71					2.38		24.80
Solomon Islands	1.65				8.90							10.55
%	0.05				0.27							0.32
Sri Lanka	30.00	10.00	16.70		33.87							90.57
%	0.90	0.30	0.50		1.02							2.73
Thailand	217.60				11.11			39.00				267.71
%	6.56				0.33			1.18				8.07
Vanuatu												0.00
%												0.00
Vietnam	4.60				8.50							13.10
%	0.14				0.26							0.39
Western Samoa		1.74										1.74
%		0.05										0.05
TOTAL	1,156.30	433.14	275.50	0.00	560.98	674.05	0.00	45.20	48.20	117.40	8.00	3,318.77
%	34.84	13.05	8.30	0.00	16.90	20.31	0.00	1.36	1.45	3.54	0.24	100.00

Source: ADB, 1994.

Notes:
a. The sum amount contained in this table is a gross amount in current year dollars without being discounted to a base-year value.
b. Sector:
   1. Water pollution control and supply, floor control.
   2. Forestry, afforestation.
   3. Land, agriculture (erosion control, salinization prevention and restoration, irrigation, etc.).
   4. Energy conservation and air pollution control.
   5. Fishery, aquaculture, marine resources protection.
   6. Urban development and environmental improvement.
   7. Biodiversity and ecosystem protection.
   8. Mineral resources exploration.
   9. Regional development.
   10. Rural development.
   11. Others (NGO credits, tourism, etc.).

TABLE 4.2b
ADB Environment-Oriented Loans by Country and by Sector (1990–1993) ($ million)

	Sector 1	Sector 2	Sector 3	Sector 4	Sector 5	Sector 6	Sector 7	Sector 8	Sector 9	Sector 10	Sector 11	TOTAL
Bangladesh	179.50			95.00								274.50
%	4.86			2.57								7.43
Bhutan												0.00
%												0.00
PRC			305.00	107.00			253.00					665.00
%			8.26	2.90			6.85					18.01
Fiji												0.00
%												0.00
India				547.00								547.00
%				14.81								14.81
Indonesia	47.40		125.10		33.00	263.00	24.50		85.00	30.00		608.00
%	32.10		3.39		0.89	7.12	0.66		2.30	0.81		16.46
Lao PDR	32.10	11.00										43.10
%	0.87	0.30										1.17
Malaysia	105.00		43.00									148.00
%	2.84		1.16									4.01
Marshall Islands	0.70				6.95							7.65
%	0.02				0.19							0.21
Micronesia, Fed. States of					70.00							70.00
%					1.90							1.90
Myanmar												0.00
%												0.00

TABLE 4.2b *continued*

	Sector 1	Sector 2	Sector 3	Sector 4	Sector 5	Sector 6	Sector 7	Sector 8	Sector 9	Sector 10	Sector 11	TOTAL
Nepal		40.00	20.00			12.00					10.40	82.40
%		1.08	0.54			0.32					0.28	2.23
Pakistan	299.60	41.60										341.20
%	8.11	1.13										9.24
Papua New Guinea	11.30											11.30
%	0.31											0.31
Philippines	97.60	75.00	48.00						58.00			278.60
%	2.64	2.03	1.30						1.57			7.54
Solomon Islands												0.00
%												0.00
Sri Lanka	70.00	10.50				27.00						107.5
%	1.90	0.28				0.73						2.91
Thailand	45.00			315.60					70.00			430.60
%	1.22			8.55					1.90			11.66
Vanuatu						14.00						14.00
%						0.38						0.38
Vietnam	64.00											64.00
%	1.73											1.73
Western Samoa												0.00
%												0.00
TOTAL	952.20	178.10	541.10	1,064.60	109.95	569.00	24.50	0.00	213.00	30.00	10.40	3,692.85
%	25.78	4.82	14.65	28.83	2.98	15.41	0.66	0.00	5.77	0.81	0.28	100.00

Notes:
a. The sum amount contained in this table is a gross amount in the current-year dollars without being discounted to a base-year value.
b. Sector:
1. Water pollution control and supply; floor control.
2. Forestry, afforestation.
3. Land, agriculture (erosion control, salinization prevention and restoration, irrigation, etc.).
4. Energy conservation and air pollution control.
5. Fishery, aquaculture, marine resources protection.
6. Urban development and environmental improvement.
7. Biodiversity and ecosystem protection.
8. Mineral resources exploration.
9. Regional development.
10. Rural development.
11. Others (NGO credits, tourism, etc.).

Source: ADB, 1994.

environmental resources, or before they were classified as "environmentally-oriented" projects. In contrast, air quality affected by electric power generation, transportation activities, and industrial emissions has received much less attention, reflected by the much smaller investment worldwide. Even less attention has been paid to the ecological side of environmental protection, i.e., biodiversity.

Estimation of Cost of Remediation
Past Efforts
If remediation is defined broadly, it would imply not only repairing the damages of past environmental injury, but also making sure that future growth is sustainable and that society reaches some level of general environmental welfare. This definition has expanded the mandate of COR from that of hindsight to also foreseeing the environmental investments needed to achieve some general standard of the environment. This implies that, for example, we consider new investments in expanding water supply and sanitation to meet unmet demand or expanding capacity for a burgeoning population as part of the COR. Estimates of the total environmental investments required by all the Asian countries by the year 2000 were made by Weatherly (in Owens, ed. 1994) for 12 different types of environmental problems (sectors) based on two scenarios: "business as usual" (BAU) and "accelerated progress" (AP). The details of the estimation are subject to many questions; however, it is useful to explicitly examine the assumptions underlying these estimates, summarized in Table 4.3.

Weatherly's estimates represent a milestone in estimating the costs of remediating past environmental damages in Asia. For example, he arrived at an estimate of $85 billion for the BAU scenario and $417 billion for the AP scenario for the ten-year estimated period (1991–2000). Interestingly, he arrives at an estimate of $80–90 billion each for air pollution and water and sanitation in the AP scenario. As will be demonstrated, we improve on these estimates through the following measures. First, we focus our attention mainly on four sectors—air, water, land, and biodiversity, rather than Weatherly's 12 sectors. Second, we use localized data wherever possible rather than international averages. Third, we use generally nonlinear cost functions rather than average cost ratios.

Applications of Cost-of-Remediation Indices
This section addresses the application of the COR approach related to MFIs' lending policies and strategies. The discussion focuses on the four accounts mentioned above via four examples: one each on air and water pollution, one on land degradation and pollution, and one on biodiversity and ecosystem conservation. Our main objective is to illustrate how to use the COR approach through specific examples, which may involve a city, a sector, or a nation as a

Estimation of Cost of Abatement and Key Assumptions

Sectors	Key Assumptions	Estimated Total Cost ($ million) by the Year 2000 Net Present Value (5%)
Water Supply	BAU: $2.60 and $8.00 per m3 required to provide safe drinking water for rural and urban areas, respectively	41,208
	AP: the same cost ratios but assuming increased number of persons served with safe water	54,578
Sanitation	BAU: $17 and $128 per capita required to provide sanitation for rural and urban areas, respectively	7,223
	AP: the same cost ratios but assuming higher percentage of population with sanitation	26,337
Electric Power	BAU: no pollution controls	0
	AP: 1. assuming no retrofitting of existing capacities, pollution reduction achieved all through adopting new low-polluting technology—50% adoption rate by 2000	62,499
	2. he cost differential for an 80–95% reduction of NOx, SO^2 and PM is between 10–12% over the cost of current technology ($2500 per kilowatt)	
Transportation	BAU: no pollution control	0
	AP: the capacity to produce low-polluting vehicles and to introduce clean fuels grows at 7% per year, thereby reducing emission by 10%	22,528
Industrial Wastes	BAU: no pollution control	0
	AP: 5% extra for low pollution control technology and 50% of industries will adopt such technologies by 2000	21,292

TABLE 4.3 continued

Sectors	Key Assumptions	Estimated Total Cost ($ million) by the Year 2000 Net Present Value (5%)
Agriculture	BAU: no erosion control	0
	AP: 1% of agricultural output used for erosion control at $400 per ha	12,116
Forestry	BAU: the 1980s rates of plantation will continue at a cost of $800 per ha	15,455
	AP: in addition to BAU, $50 per ha required for upgrading management of closed, natural forest	28,577
Population Programs	BAU: $0.89 per capita	20,795
	AP: $1.51 per capita for enhanced population programs	35,396
Education	BAU: n/a	0
	AP: cost of educating women to the same level as men at $38 per capita for primary education and $67 for secondary education	128,685
Acid Rain	BAU: n/a	0
	AP: 20% reduction of SO^2 at $50 per tonne	4,033
Global Climate	BAU: n/a	0
	AP: 20% reduction of carbon emissions at $30 per tonne	21,125
Biodiversity	BAU: maintaining existing national parks at $2 per ha (assuming a 4% annual increase of per ha cost)	510
	AP: maintaining existing parks at $2 per ha and building all proposed national parks by 2000 at $4 per ha	614
Total	BAU	85,000
	AP	417,000

Source: Weatherly, in Owens 1994.

whole. The examples used are intentionally simplistic; in reality, more complex analysis is needed, especially when aggregating for large regions or countries.

The structure of the examples is generally first to describe an environmental problem and estimate its magnitude; next, to specify a standard; and finally, to show simple computations that help us arrive at an order-of-magnitude estimate of the cost of improving the environment to that standard.

The environmental problems addressed could vary from air, water, and land pollution to deforestation to biodiversity loss and ecosystem protection, but are all addressed in this consistent manner. The key is the setting of the standard. It is not enough to use international or national standards; one should set realistic standards based on rational approaches, accounting for human and ecosystem health concerns and economics. This is especially true because we are comparing different components of the environment. Note that standards cannot be conceived of independently of the temporal scale. At times, we may have to achieve standards to reach a particular level of stock or flow of an environmental good by a particular year or annually. We could derive more statistically-based measures such as how many times and by what magnitude we can allow violations of some (say, ambient air pollution) standards. In addition to the temporal disaggregation, the spatial lumping of the standards is also a very important issue; the heterogeneity in the regions within a province or country is sufficient to justify the imposition of different standards. This will avoid spatial "hot spots" caused by the problem of spatial lumping.

The remediation cost can be computed in a number of ways depending on the solution proposed. We assume here that we are always interested in the least-cost alternative or most cost-effective manner to achieve the standard specified. We can use other utility measures such as maximizing the net economic surplus, but this would involve the thornier, tricky questions of valuing the environmental benefits for each case. This can be done at a later stage if the data and resources are available and projects are being more thoroughly appraised.

For example, in the case of a region whose industries are emitting a certain kind of pollutant, say SO_2, we desire to find the cost of remediation up to a particular standard. We can achieve this in a variety of ways depending on the policy options considered. If we desire to mandate the same percentage of control for all sources, we can proceed as follows. The amount of SO_2 reduction can be estimated for the region to achieve the standard set (using a rollback model if the standard is on ambient concentration). This reduction can be apportioned to all the sources to achieve the same level of reduction in all these sources and the cost of doing this can be computed. Note that this is not the least-cost way to achieve the standard, but it might be so if other policy alternatives were not considered. Another method is to consider the use of some economic instruments or modified command-and-control measures that would achieve a more efficient solution. This may involve determining the marginal costs of control for each of the sources, and then solving an optimization problem that minimizes the overall cost while determining to what level each source reduces its emissions, so that they meet the standard overall.

Listed below are a few simple examples of the COR approach. More details can be found in Appendix 2.

Example 1: Costs of Reducing Air Pollution from Household Energy Use in Beijing, PRC

Problem

Emissions from energy-consumption activities by industries and households (stationary sources) are a major source of air emissions. A good example is the city of Beijing where coal forms the main energy source for both industries and households, i.e., heating and cooking. The situation gets worse during the winter season when many residential heating stoves are in use. Coupled with air inversions that occur frequently during the winter, the ambient air pollutant concentrations can reach dangerously high levels.

Appendix 1 (Appendix Tables 1.10 through 1.13) contains emission factors for different types of fuels. With these tables, one can calculate total emissions for a given fuel using a particular device. For example, assume Beijing residents currently consume 1 million tonnes per year of coal using coal stoves. Using Appendix Tables 1.12 and 1.13 in Appendix 1, the annual carbon monoxide (CO) emission from residential coal burning is calculated as:

1,000,000 tonnes/year × 22 GJ/tonne × 3,580 grams/GJ = 78,760 tonnes/year.

This level of pollution is deemed unacceptable for humans and there is a need to reduce this level to a more sustainable one.

Standards

Before we estimate the remediation costs, we need to specify a standard for CO emissions. Note that standards are usually set for ambient concentrations of gaseous pollutants, but using a rollback model, we can compute the corresponding emission standards. Let us say that in this case, we need to bring the level of CO emission to about 250 tonnes per year. Of course, in a real case, this standard would need to be set for the emissions in each household to counteract the indoor air pollution threat; however, for simplicity of demonstration, let us assume that we can fully account for the environmental damages by means of an overall constraint.

Estimation of the Cost of Remediation

Let us propose that one of the least-cost solutions to the severe air pollution problem in Beijing is to switch fuel from coal to natural gas. Natural gas is produced in Shaanxi province approximately 900 km away. Suppose that the Government of PRC is proposing a project to switch to centralized residential heating using natural gas boilers. To obtain the equivalent amount of heat, the total annual natural gas requirement would be (from Appendix Table 1.13 in Appendix 1):

(1,000,000 tonnes/year × 22 GJ/tonne)/(46 GJ/tonne) = 478,261 tonnes/year

However, since we can assume that natural gas can be used more efficiently in gas burning units than coal, and we can estimate that the efficiency is perhaps 2 times greater for natural gas than for coal combustion, the amount of natural gas actually required is only:

(478,261/2) tonnes/year = 239,131 tonnes/year.

which corresponds to a volume of:

(239,131 tonnes)/(850 tonnes/million m³) = 281 million m³ (annual volume of natural gas).

The annual CO emission would be (using Appendix Table 1.10 in Appendix 1):

239,131 tonnes/year × 46 Gj/tonne × 19 grams/Gj = 209 tonnes/year.

One can see that switching from coal stoves to natural gas boilers for households will cut Beijing's annual residential CO emission from 78,760 tonnes to 209 tonnes, which is below the assumed standard and which will certainly achieve a dramatic improvement of the city's air quality. The key to the feasibility of such a project is an estimation of the cost, including the cost of producing and transporting (over 900 km) the 239,131 tonnes of natural gas per year required, and the costs of the municipal gas distribution system, including installing the boilers.

To determine the costs of switching from coal to natural gas, a number of different costs must be calculated, including costs of producing natural gas required, construction of the gas pipeline, and development of the gas distribution system within the city. The three basic costs provided in Appendix 2 are for gas production, the pipeline, and the distribution system. These can be scaled up to provide the total costs as follows:

Production: 1400 yuan/million m³ x 281 million m³
  = 0.393 million yuan
Pipeline: 1100 yuan/km-million m³ x 900 km x 281 million m³
  = 278 million Yuan
Distribution: 4.25 million yuan/million m³ x 281million m³
  = 1,194 million yuan
Total Costs: 0.393 + 278 + 1194 = 1,473 million yuan
  = $177 million ($1= 8.3 yuan).

Additional costs would include annual costs of gas production and annual operation and maintenance costs for pipeline and distribution system maintenance. However, with gas systems, the largest cost incurred is the up-front cost of system development. In addition, for a true cost-benefit analysis with and without the project, we have to consider the cost savings of not using coal. Another important factor is the cross-pollutant control effects. For example, such a switch would result in not only emission reductions for CO but also for sulfur dioxide and particulate (in the range of 11,000 tonnes/year for SO_2 and 8,500 tonnes/year for TSP). Hence, the calculation of a yuan/tonne of pollution abated cost for CO removal is misleading and cost apportionment by unit of different pollutants controlled needs to be determined. The emission reductions from fuel switching are significant and could be compared to the cost of retrofitting existing coal boilers with pollution control and efficiency improvements, which in total would give similar emission reductions (although in fact the overall reductions would be difficult to achieve with these techniques).

Example 2: Costs of Industrial Wastewater Treatment in the Philippines

Problem

The water quality in the Philippines, especially in urban centers such as Metro Manila, has become a concern for the Government and MFIs. The most frequently cited example is the Pasig River, which is classified by some as "biologically dead." The existing concentration data depend heavily on where and when the samples are taken. During the dry season, the Pasig River water quality is just slightly better than that of lightly diluted raw sewage. The highest biochemical oxygen demand (BOD) levels and the lowest dissolved oxygen (DO) levels, which occur in the upper stream reach, are 40–120 mg/l and 0.0 mg/l, respectively, while the DO saturation level for this stream is 7.5 mg/l and the maximum allowable BOD level is 20–30 mg/l (JMM, Inc. 1992). The magnitude of the problem is instantly obvious to a casual visitor to the Pasig River in the form of noxious odors of sewage. The severe water pollution is by no means unique to the Pasig in the Philippines. Rivers in many other cities in

TABLE 4.4
BOD Loads by Source for the Philippines (1992)

	BOD load (tonne/year)	Percentage of the Total
Primary Industry	738,118	11.77%
Manufacturing	174,981	2.79%
Services	1,551,083	24.72%
Domestic	3,809,520	60.72%
Total	6,273,702	100.00%

Source: Orbeta and Indab, 1994

Asia such as the Suzhou Creek in Shanghai, PRC, also exhibit similar water quality.

Industrial and household wastewater are the largest sources of BOD discharges in the Philippines. JMM, Inc. (1992) estimated BOD loadings for several catchment basins. Industrial wastewater and domestic sewage contribute 38 percent and 40 percent of the total BOD loads, respectively, with the rest attributable to solid waste disposal in the rivers. Table 4.4 shows the estimates made by Orbeta and Indab (1994) for the country as a whole. The industrial activities, including primary, manufacturing, and services, contribute to roughly 40 percent of total BOD discharge.

As detailed in Appendix 2, the cost functions developed in this study for BOD treatment fall into two categories: industrial and municipal. For the Philippines, only data on the costs of industrial wastewater are available. Appendix 2 contains cost functions of treating industrial BOD based on such data from the Philippines. Two types of cost functions are given: (1) cost as a function of flowrate, removal rate, and BOD concentrations; and (2) cost as a function of daily BOD removal, with both types of cost functions derived for individual sectors and for the economy as a whole. For the purpose of illustration, we take the simplest cost function, cost as a function of daily BOD removal for the economy as a whole:

$$C = 59.80 \ M^{0.76} \qquad (4.1)$$

where:

C = the total cost of BOD removal for an average industrial facility in the Philippines, including the capital and O&M costs (pesos)

M = the BOD removed daily (kg/day).

Standards

Let us assume that to achieve a sustainable environmental water quality, we need to reduce the BOD loading by 50 percent. Note that this is a traditional command-and-control approach; other solutions with performance-based standards with or without using economic incentives could be considered to achieve the same result at a lower cost.

Estimation of the Cost of Remediation
With equation (4.1), it is possible to make some quick estimates of the total cost of BOD treatment in the Philippines, given a desired treatment level. First, from Table 4.4 we know that industrial activities (primary, manufacturing, and services) discharged 2,464,182 tonnes BOD in 1992, or 9,856 tonnes daily (assuming 250 working days a year). Assume that we wish to reduce the discharge by 50 percent, that is, 4,928 additional tonnes of BOD need to be removed per day. Assume that there are a total of 10,000 industrial establishments in the Philippines in 1992. The average additional daily BOD removal required is thus 492.8 kg per day per plant. Assume also that in 1992 on average 20 percent of BOD was already removed. The new daily removal rate required (M) is thus:

492.8 kg/day/plant (1%–20%) = 394.2 kg/day/plant.

To enter these values in equation (4.1), we obtain the cost of achieving 50 percent BOD reduction for an "average" plant as follows (in 1992 pesos):

$$C = 59.80 \times (394.2)^{0.76} = 5{,}616.2 \text{ pesos/day/plant.}$$

The total annualized costs of 10,000 plants is ($1 = 25 pesos):

250 days/year × 10,000 plants × 5,616.2 pesos/day/plant = 14,040,000,000 peso/year = $561,600,000/year.

In other words, the annual cost of 50 percent industrial BOD reduction in the Philippines is approximately $561 million. Since industrial BOD accounts for roughly 40 percent of total BOD loads, 50 percent reduction of industrial BOD represents 20 percent of total BOD reduction.

The above example is crude by its nature. Several measures may improve the accuracy as suggested in Appendix 2. First, we need to obtain more accurate information on the current BOD removal rates and current BOD discharge, ideally, by different economic sectors. Second, given the information, we should use cost functions for different economic sectors and then aggregate the cost estimates to derive the total cost. Despite its approximate nature, the example not only provides a rough estimate of the cost of industrial BOD abatement, but also illustrates how decision-makers at all levels might use the COR approach to determine the appropriate amount of investments needed once they have decided to invest in a country's wastewater treatment.

Example 3: Costs of Solid Waste Management in Kathmandu, Nepal

Problem

Compared to air and water emissions, solid waste generation and management have generally received less attention in Asian countries. However, the solid waste situation is no less of a problem. The famous "smoky mountain" in Manila, and garbage dumped along major streets in Kathmandu, Nepal, and along the Yangtze River banks in Chongqing, PRC, are the results of poor solid waste management. The health effects of poor management—methane emission, disease vectors, underground water pollution—are equally acute as those of other forms of pollution.

Standards

Let us assume that we need to collect and dispose all of the wastes generated in Kathmandu, i.e. 100% collection and disposal.

Estimation of the Cost of Remediation

The costs of solid waste management are incurred mainly in two categories of activities: waste collection and public cleansing (street cleaning), and waste management facilities (disposal). In most developing countries, about 95 percent of the solid waste management costs are attributable to collection and public cleansing. In comparison, in industrialized countries, about 60 percent of the solid waste management costs are attributable to collection and public cleansing (street cleaning) and 40 percent to managing the facilities and for disposal. The cost functions for solid waste management are given below.

The values of $COST_{col}$ and $COST_{disp}$ are determined as follows:

$$COST_{wm} = COST_{col} + COST_{disp} \qquad (4.2)$$
$$COST_{col} = MSW(0.90p_h + 0.10p_l + t\,p_t) \qquad (4.3)$$
$$COST_{disp} = c_i MSW \qquad (4.4)$$

where:

$COST_{wm}$ = the total waste management cost per year
$COST_{col}$ = waste collection cost per year
$COST_{disp}$ = waste disposal cost (facility cost) per year
MSW = the quantity of municipal solid waste (not including industrial wastes)
p_h = the cost of collecting one tonne of household waste
p_l = the cost of public cleansing per tonne
p_t = the cost of transferring one tonne of wastes at transfer stations = the percentage of total MSW sent for disposal via transfer stations
c_i = the cost of waste disposal per tonne, where i = sanitary landfilling, incineration, composting, etc.

The two parameters in equation 4.3, 0.9 and 0.1, are the proportions of total MSW collected through curbside collecting and public cleansing, respectively, estimated by the World Bank for developing countries.

We now provide an example of how to use equations 4.2 through 4.4 to estimate the costs of solid waste management. In 1991, the city of Kathmandu had a population of 675,341. At a garbage generation rate of 0.2t/c/a or 0.54 kg/c/day (see Appendix 1: Emission Factors), it generated 135,068 tonnes of MSW annually. In Appendix 2, we estimated that, for Nepal, the cost of collecting and transporting one tonne MSW from curbside (p_h) = $20, the cost of collecting one tonne of wastes from public cleansing (p_l) = $40, and the cost of disposing of one tonne of MSW through sanitary landfill (c_i) = $2. We assume no transfer station is needed in Kathmandu or t = 0. The total annualized solid waste management cost through sanitary landfill for Kathmandu is:

$$COST_{wm} = 135,068 \text{ tonnes/year} (0.9 \times \$20/\text{tonne} + 0.1 \times \$40/\text{tonne} + \$2/\text{tonne}) = \$3,241,637/\text{year}.$$

The above estimate includes the annualized capital and O&M costs.

Example 4: Costs of Ecosystem and Biodiversity Protection in Indonesia

Problem

Compared to the "brown" types of environmental problems discussed earlier, the costs of the "green" issues such as ecosystem and biodiversity protection are more uncertain and subject to more controversy. This is largely because of the complexity of the ecosystem itself. For example, no one can say with confidence which species should be protected and which should not be based on the "values" (to humans) of the species and the economic conditions of a particular country. There are also many uncertainties regarding protection of species. Different approaches imply different degrees of protection and, thus, costs. In this study, we adopted an approach of using the costs of building and managing national parks as a proxy for the costs of ecosystem and biodiversity protection. The advantage of this approach lies in its simplicity and practicality in the sense that the cost information is relatively easy to obtain and the total estimated costs are directly relevant to lending practices in this area by MFIs. In Appendix 2, we adopted this approach to estimate the costs of ecosystem protection. Below, we will briefly illustrate this methodology with an example from Indonesia.

As of 1993, the total protected area (IUCN categories I–V) in Indonesia was 19.3 million hectares, accounting for 10.2 percent of its total land area. The current expenditure on protected area is averaged at $0.75/ha/yr, which is regarded as inadequate.

Standards
The Indonesian official goal is to increase the total protected area by 68.7 million hectares by the year 2000. This has been deemed necessary from a sustainability viewpoint.

Estimation of the Cost of Remediation
The costs of biodiversity and ecosystem protection consist mainly of two parts: in situ conservation, and ex situ conservation. In situ costs can be further divided into two categories: (1) costs of protected area management, including the costs associated with managing the land area, e.g., land acquisition, zone development, and management facilities; and (2) costs of integrated conservation and development projects (ICDP), including the costs of managing the people being affected, including relocation, training, and education. Ex situ costs include such items as inventory of plants, inventory of animals, gene banks, and research and training. Consequently, a linear generic cost function for building and running national parks can be constructed as follows:

$$COST_{bio} = COST_{InSitu} + COST_{ExSitu} \qquad (4.5)$$

$$COST_{InSitu} = a\ AREA + b\ PEOPLE \qquad (4.6)$$

$$COST_{ExSitu} = COST_{InvPla} + COST_{InvAni} + COST_{Res} + COST_{Other} \qquad (4.7)$$

The subscripts of the symbols used in equations (4.5) through (4.7) are self-explanatory. In particular, AREA refers to the total protected area and PEOPLE refers to the number of people being affected. The main parameters that need to be estimated empirically are "a," area management costs per hectare of land protected; and "b," ICDP costs per capita.

Tables 4.5a, b and c provide the detailed cost estimates for the next ten-year period for Indonesia.

Table 4.5a shows that the value of a protected area falls in a range between $0.50 and $5 per hectare per year, depending on the type of reserves with higher degree of protection generally incurring higher costs. Table 4.5b indicates that b has a value range between $7.50 and $30 per capita per year. Table 4.5c gives the values for terms in equation (4.7). The values are not proportional to either AREA or PEOPLE and, thus, no ratio cost figures are given. Note that the total costs are all calculated as the net cost for ten years, rather than the annualized costs as expressed by equations (4.5) through (4.7). The total ten-year net cost for realizing the Government's goal by the year 2000 is 1030 + 900 + 1033 = $2,963 million.

TABLE 4.5a

In Situ Measures: Protected Area Management

Type of Protected Area	AREA (m ha)	a ($/ha/yr)	Duration (yrs)	Net Cost ($ mil)
Key top priority reserves	12.5	5	10	625
Other top priority reserves	6.2	2.5	10	155
Proposed marine reserves	17.4	0.5	10	87
Hydrological protection forests	30.3	0.5	10	151.5
Other reserves	2.3	0.5	10	11.5
Total	68.7	—	—	1030

TABLE 4.5b

In Situ Measures: ICDP

Intensity of Input	PEOPLE (mil)	b ($/c/yr)	Duration (yrs)	Net Cost ($ mil)
Most	1	30	10	300
Medium	2	15	10	300
Least	4	7.5	10	300
Total	7	—	—	900

TABLE 4.5c

Ex Situ Measures

Measures	Year "1" Cost ($ mil/yr)	Year 2–10 Cost ($ mil/yr)	Net Cost 1 ($ mil)
Inventory of plants	75	50	525
Inventory of animals	154	26	388
Gene banks, research, & training	12	12	120
Total	241	88	1033

National Estimates of the Cost of Remediation

The previous section dealt with computation of CORs on a sector or project basis; three of the four examples involved estimating CORs at the city level. However, there is also a need to arrive at aggregated estimates of the CORs at the regional (provincial) and even national levels. In the remaining section of this chapter, we will illustrate the estimation of National CORs via case studies for the Philippines and PRC. Compared to other Asian countries, these two countries have relatively complete cost data. Wherever data permit, we will attempt to estimate the CORs for air, water, land and ecosystem, the four principal environmental components. Furthermore, in Chapter 6, we will extrapolate these results to other Asian countries through a set of assumptions.

TABLE 4.6
Current Annual COR for the Philippines

Category	COR ($ billion)
Air	0.67
Water*	1.36

*including cost of soil erosion control

Philippines

The estimation of the CORs for the Philippines was made by Resource, Environment and Economics Consultants Inc. who served as our regional collaborator of the Philippines. It included only the air and water dimensions due to data constraints.

Table 4.6 provides the estimate of annual COR by two categories: air and water. The total annual COR amounts to roughly $2 billion. For air, the costs of emission reduction were estimated for both stationary (particulate matter, PM) and mobile sources (PM, SO_x, NO_x, VOC, and CO). The standards were set at 90 percent reduction of the current emissions. The control options for stationary sources included the control of PM by electrostatic precipitators (low and high efficiencies), baghouses, and mechanical collectors. The options for mobile sources included fuel reformulation, inspection and maintenance, engine modification and catalytic converters for gasoline-fueled vehicles. The control costs were based primarily on estimates from the Environment and Natural Resources Accounting Project (ENRAP) and assumed to be 90 percent capital costs and 10 percent O&M costs at a 15 percent discount rate.

For water, estimates of the cost of pollution reduction for BOD_5 and Suspended Solids were also made assuming 90 percent capital and 10 percent O&M at a 15 percent discount rate. As in the case of air pollution, the standard was set at 90 percent removal. Options for household wastewater treatment included primary treatment methods (septic tanks). The industrial cost of remediation was estimated by using Philippine data but adopting PRC wastewater treatment cost functions. The Philippine water COR also included the cost of erosion control, which might be better placed in estimating the land COR. The emissions were estimated for BOD_5, SS, TDS, N, P, and oil and grease for a variety of sectors including households, sanitary and similar services, gold and copper ore mining, livestock production, food, beverage and tobacco manufacturing, public administration and defense, food manufacturing, forestry, urban runoff, and community, social, and personal services.

People's Republic of China

Compared to other developing Asian countries, PRC possesses relatively rich cost data. PRC is also among the earliest in implementing the concept of cost

TABLE 4.7
Decade COR for PRC

Category	Decade COR ($ billion)		
	1991–2000	2001–2010	2011–2020
Air	16.5	22.7	31.3
Water	9.5	30.2	59.8
Land	10.7	12.9	14.2
Ecosystem	5.8	5.8	8.1
Total	42.5	71.6	113.4

Source: Han, et al, 1993

of remediation. A report published in 1993 (Han et al.) contained estimates of the costs of achieving a set of predetermined environmental objectives at decade intervals starting in 1990. The study determined costs according to nine categories (sectors) which were aggregated into our four categories (Table 4.7). Table 4.7 indicates an increasing trend of the cost of remediation over the 1990–2020 period as the economy grows, with $43 billion, $72 billion and $113.4 billion required for the first, second, and third decades, respectively. Below, we provide an alternative set of estimates made by the Chinese Academy of Sciences as a part of this research project.

The estimation was made for the four principal environmental components, namely, air, water, land, and ecosystem. The cost data are not only available at the national level, but also at the provincial level. This allowed the estimation of the CORs to be made for all of the provinces which is crucial in view of the diversity of PRC in terms of both socioeconomic and physical environment.

For the first two sectors, i.e. air and water, we estimated COR based on environmental emission levels and currently available pollution control technologies. For land, we estimated the total cost of soil erosion control in PRC. For ecosystems and biodiversity protection, we employed the percentage of forest coverage as a proxy for the ecological quality of a country and estimate the total costs of increasing the percentage to a specified level. In order to derive the COR estimates, we need data on current emission levels, environmental standards, costs of treatment, and other socioeconomic data related to emissions control.

Because of the significant diversities of the physical environment in different regions of PRC, it is difficult to link the environmental quality standards with the permitted environmental emissions. To simplify the problem for the first application of the methodology, we have adopted a 90 percent reduction across the board for air and water pollution abatement. In other words, the COR is the cost of removing 90 percent of the current emissions for all the air and water pollutants included. Furthermore, many air and water pollution control technologies are available including different pollution prevention measures, the so-called clean production technologies, and end-of-pipe pollution abatement. Presently, little data are available for the clean production type of technologies. Hence, the estimation reported here is for end-of-pipe pollution control only.

For air quality, suspended particulate matter (called dust in the PRC literature) and sulfur dioxide are two pollutants that contribute most to the deterioration of air quality in PRC. For dust control, cost functions have been developed for boilers of different capacities. The data were derived from a nationwide survey. The capital costs include direct cost (equipment, transportation, and installation of distribution systems) and indirect costs (design and other administrative charges). The O&M costs include electricity, purchase or production of compressed air, water use, and maintenance costs. Using the national survey data, we have developed cost functions for industrial boilers, domestic boilers, and industrial furnaces separately. The total cost was estimated using the weighted average of the costs for different boilers based on the percentage of each type of boiler.

The cost functions for sulfur dioxide removal systems were adopted from Han et al. (1993). The unit capital and O&M costs were calculated to be 1000 and 150 yuan[1] per tonne of sulfur dioxide removed, respectively.

The current estimation of air pollution control costs does not include cost of mobile source emission control due to insufficient data, although mobile sources are increasingly important for contributing to urban air pollution in Chinese cities.

For water pollution, data from 30 provinces were used to calibrate a regression model. The dependent variables are O&M cost and capital cost for treating all the pollutants. The independent variables are the amounts of different pollutants removed. Eleven pollutants are included:—COD, SS, S^{2-} (sulfide), Oil, ROH (phenols), CN–, Hg, Cd, $Cr^{6}+$, Pb, and As. Since data on water pollution control costs in PRC are available at the facility level and municipal level (for wastewater treatment plants), cost functions at these two levels were developed using this method. The base year is 1993.

The regression results indicate that chemical oxygen demand (COD) removal is the most significant factor for determining both O&M and capital costs. Other factors have varying statistical significance for the costs. For simplicity, we have adopted the most parsimonious model which has COD removal as the only independent variable. Data on COD emission are widely available for most provinces in PRC. It is the main water pollutant and also the most important indicator of pollution control by the enterprises and municipal wastewater treatment plants. It should be stressed that although COD removal was employed as the only variable for estimating the costs, due to the high correlation between COD and other pollutants, the costs estimated this way also represent the costs for treating these other pollutants. Capital cost was

TABLE 4.8
Unit Costs of Different Erosion Control Measures (yuan per hectare)

Control Measures	North	South
Earth Dam Terrace	6,750–9,000	9,000–12,000
Stone Dam Terrace	—	15,000–22,500
Water Protection Shelter	3,750–4,500	6,000–9,000
Grass Planting	1,200–1,800	—
Check Dam	10–15% of whole cost	—

added to the present value of O&M costs. The total annual COR for a province was estimated assuming 50 percent of total wastewater is treated by industry and the other 50 percent is treated by municipal wastewater treatment plants.

Due to data constraints, we estimated the COR for land quality based upon soil erosion control only. The country was divided into two broad regions: North and South. Huanghe (Yellow River) watershed in the North and Changjiang (Yangtze River) watershed in the South are the two areas subject to the most serious soil erosion in PRC. Within these two watersheds, we took the Loess Plateau to represent the North and the Three Gorges to represent the South. Each region has 15 provinces. The data for soil erosion come from a national remote sensing survey conducted in the early 1990s. Since the total area of soil erosion reported in this survey is larger than the data reported in the National Statistical Yearbook, an adjustment factor has been adopted to maintain consistency. Only the cost of controlling water soil erosion was estimated for two reasons: it is the dominant type of erosion in PRC and few data on the costs of controlling wind erosion are available.

According to the survey, water erosion in PRC is divided into six types. For each type, some of the following erosion control measures may be feasible. These measures include earth dam terraces, stone dam terraces, check dams, grass planting and water protection shelters. According to an in situ survey and feasibility study carried out in the Loess Plateau and the Three Gorges area, the unit erosion control costs vary dramatically across different regions and measures. For estimation purposes, we assume that 70% eroded area should be controlled within ten years to achieve 70–90% erosion reduction. Costs of remediation for erosion control for different provinces are calculated separately. As an example, Table 4.8 provides the unit costs of different control measures used in the estimation.

Data on costs of ecosystem and biodiversity protection are extremely scarce for developing countries and PRC is no exception. We adopt a very simple approach—to use forest coverage rate (FCR) as a proxy to represent the ecological quality of a province. The rationale behind this assumption is that forest habitats for many species are the most important ecosystem. For

TABLE 4.9
Current Annual COR for PRC

Category	Annual COR ($ billion)
Air	3.17
Water	1.43
Land	9.94
Ecosystem	1.06
Total	15.60

simplicity, we assume that 20 percent of FCR is a threshold for all provinces, above which most of the species will be protected and no further COR is needed. The afforestation cost per hectare, i.e., $179/ha is derived from a study conducted by Han et al. (1993)

Using the cost data outlined above, the COR for air, water, land, ecosystem and a total are estimated for all the provinces and autonomous regions of PRC. The aggregated national total is given in Table 4.9. Compared to Han's estimates (Table 4.7), there are significant differences due to different estimation techniques used and different components included. The average annualized COR for 30 years estimated by Han et al is approximately $8 billion while our estimate is about $16 billion.

To obtain an overview, Figure 4.1 provides a chart of the total regional COR by type and by province. It indicates that for most provinces, soil erosion control and ecosystem protection account for most of the total COR. The proportion for these two types exhibits an increasing trend as one moves from the more economically developed eastern provinces, e.g., Guangdong, Jiangsu, to the west less economically developed provinces, Ningxia, Xinjiang. By comparison, the COR for air and water presents an opposite trend—larger for eastern developed provinces and less for western underdeveloped provinces. Figure 4.2 collapses the provinces into six major regions and shows these trends—increase of COR for erosion control and ecosystem protection and decrease of COR for air and water as one moves from east to west. To obtain a better sense of these spatial variations, Figure 4.3 provides a thematic map. The same regional data are shown as environmental diamonds in Figure 4.4 which clearly show the advantages of the diamond as a tool for visual presentation of the multidimensionality of environmental quality. In these diamonds, each of the regions is compared with the difference from the average cost on each dimension; hence, the larger the diamond the lower the environmental quality index. For example, it is clear from these diamonds that Northwest is beset with ecosystem and land degradation, characterized by large per capita COR for these two dimensions; while South Central seems to be performing very well all around with the exception of its water quality.

FIGURE 4.1

Total COR for Different Provinces of People's Republic of China ($ Million)

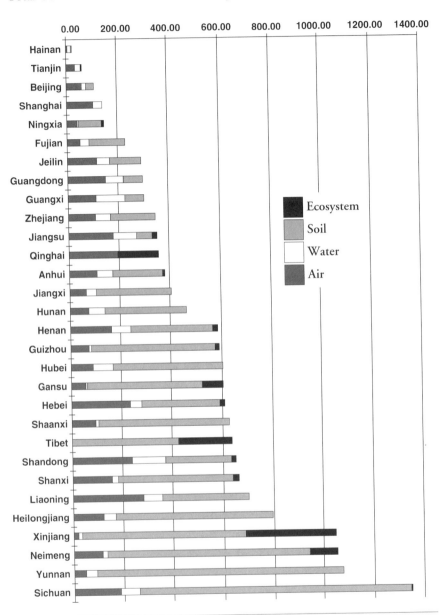

To summarize, although air and water pollution have been very serious in PRC, especially in the eastern provinces, the ecosystem degradation seems to be more pressing overall, particularly in the west. This point may be of particular interest to the government and the MFIs when planning investment in different provinces and environmental sectors in PRC.

We also calculated the COR per unit area, COR per capita, and COR per dollar GDP Shanghai, Tianjin, and Beijing have the highest COR values per hectare, although their total CORs are relatively low. In terms of COR per capita, Tibet ranks the highest, indicating that the autonomous region has low population density and severe environmental problems. The annualized COR amounts to roughly 4 percent of GDP for the whole country. Compared to the present economic growth rate, roughly 9 percent, this value is very significant. Had the environmental damage measured by COR been taken into account, the real wealth growth rate (net of economic growth and COR/GDP ratio) would have been only 5 percent. This conclusion highlights the inadequacy of the economic indicators such as GDP and the usefulness of money-denominated environmental indicators such as COR. In terms of spatial variations of

FIGURE 4.2

COR of Four Sectors for Different Regions of People's Republic of China

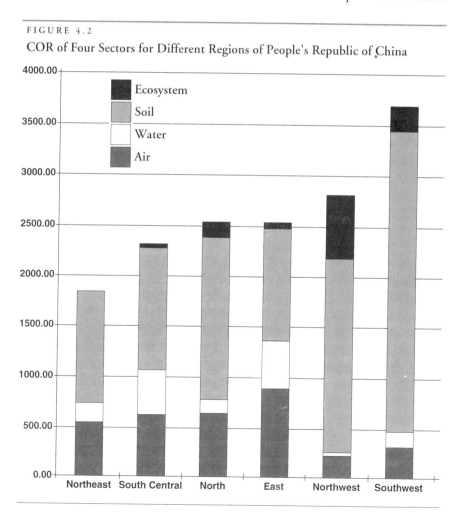

FIGURE 4.3

Total COR as % of GDP for Different Provinces of People's Republic of China

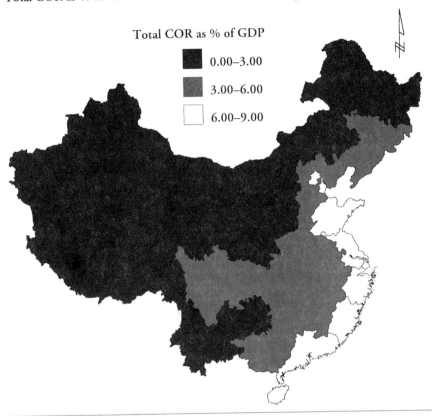

the COR/GDP ratio, as expected, the eastern provinces generally have low ratios because of their relatively high GDP, not necessarily because they have less environmental damage. The highest COR as a percentage of GDP is 142.56 percent for Tibet, representing an annual environmental "deficit"; the annual cost of remediation is greater than the GDP! In contrast, richer Guangdong and Shanghai have very low COR/GDP ratios, 0.77 percent and 0.80 percent, respectively. Clearly, the western provinces with high COR/GDP ratios need much more financial assistance than the eastern provinces in reversing their negative environmental trends.

This section has highlighted the strength of COR as an environmental index. For a large country like PRC, both economy and environment exhibit strong regional disparities. Different provinces also have different types of environmental problems. Due to the relatively complete databases available in PRC, we are able to compute CORs for 30 provinces and four environmental sectors. In Chapter 6, we will further illustrate that COR can be a very powerful tool for both environmental planners in developing countries and MFIs in

FIGURE 4.4

Diamonds Based on COR per Capita for Different Regions of People's Republic of China

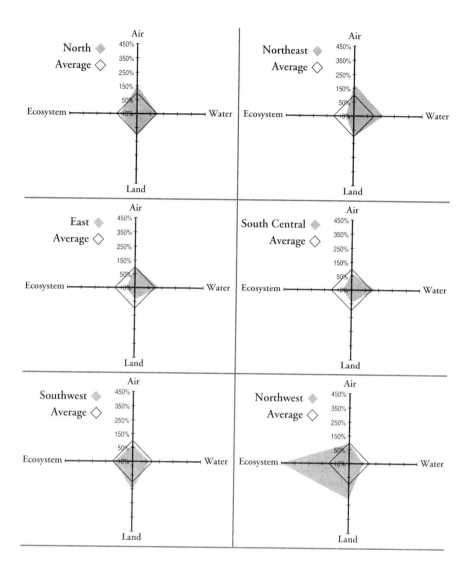

cross-country comparisons, identifying investment opportunities, and assessing the need for environmental loans.

Note

Exchange rate: 8.30 yuan = $1.

5 Applications and Policy Implications of Environmantal Elasticity and Environmental Diamonds

Characterizing Environmental Trends for Asian Countries

In Chapter 3, in addition to our principal index—cost-of-remediation—we also introduced two supplementary measures of environmental performance, namely, the concepts of environmental elasticity and environmental diamond. Examples were given to illustrate the methodological aspects of the two supplementary measures. In this chapter, we further expand the discussions of Chapter 3 to focus on the applications of environmental elasticity and environmental diamond in a policy context particularly for Asian countries. As noted in Chapter 3, the environmental elasticity is principally designed to assess the environmental trend relative to economic development and the environmental diamond is created to graphically describe the state of the environment.

Assessing Environmental Trends in Asia

Computing EE for Five Participating Countries

This section draws data from our country reports. As mentioned in Chapter 1, a sample of six Asian countries were chosen for index development and testing in this study, including the PRC, Indonesia, the Marshall Islands, Pakistan, the Philippines, and Nepal. However, insufficient time-series data are available for the Marshall Islands which is, therefore, excluded from the following time-series discussion.

People's Republic of China

A 13-year time series of environmental and economic data was obtained and used in computing EE to reflect the environmental trends for the period between 1981 and 1993.

Annual growth rate of GDP per capita was used as the denominator. For the numerator, four categories of environmental indicators are used in the analysis—air, water, land, and ecosystem quality. The specific indicators are air pollution index (API), water pollution index (WPI), ecosystem degradation index (EDI), and land pollution index (LPI) (equations 5.1 through 5.4). Each subindex consists of several variables considered important in PRC. API is indicated by four variables: sulfur dioxide (SO_2), nitrogen oxide (NO_x), total suspended particulate (TSP), and dust. For the water pollution index (WPI) chemical oxygen demand (COD), biochemical oxygen demand (BOD), ammonia nitrogen (NH_4-N), volatile phenol (ROH), and cyanide (CN-) are selected. Forest coverage rate is used as a proxy for ecosystem quality. Meanwhile, industrial solid wastes, urban domestic solid wastes, fertilizer used, and the area of the soil erosion are adopted as the indicator of land pollution and degradation. While calculating the subindices, we adopt the option of equal weighting for all environmental variables, though unequal weighting may be preferable. The four subcategory indices are then used to calculate the overall environmental pollution and degradation index (EPDI) (equation 5.5). The calculation process is outlined below.

$$API = \sum_{i=1}^{4} w_i \frac{C_i}{C_{i0}} \qquad (5.1)$$

Where:

C_1, C_2, C_3, and C_4 represent sulfur dioxide, nitrogen oxide, TSP, and dustfall (the concentrations averaged from 130 cities) respectively;

C_{i0} is the Class III Quality Standard for Air Pollutants i.

$$WPI = \sum_{i=1}^{5} w_i \frac{C_i}{C_{i0}} \qquad (5.2)$$

Where:

C_1, C_2, C_3, $C_{4,}$ and C_5 represent COD, BOD, NH_4-N, R-OH and CN– respectively;

C_{i0} is the Class III Quality Standard for Water Pollutants i.

$$LPI = \sum_{i=1}^{4} w_i \frac{C_i}{C_{i0}} \qquad (5.3)$$

Where:

C_1, C_2, C_3, and C_4 represent the area of industrial solid wastes storage, urban domestic solid wastes produced, fertilizer used, and area affected by soil erosion respectively;

C_{i0} is the value of variable i in 1981.

$$EDI = \frac{C_0}{C_i} \qquad (5.4)$$

Where:

C_1 represents forest coverage (as a percentage of total land area); C_0 is the objective of the government in the year 2000.

Note that all the environmental indicators above are defined in such a way that larger values indicate worse environmental quality because they are an indication of more environmental stress. For the ecosystem component, a very simple proxy approach is taken—using forest coverage percentage as the only indicator for ecosystem quality. The overall EPDI, in equation 5.5, is the simple mean of the change rates of all four indicators (equal weighting or $w_i = 0.25$ (i=1, 2, 3, 4)).

$$EPDI = w_1 \, API + w_2 \, WPI + w_3 \, LPI + w_4 \, EDI \qquad (5.5)$$

Table 5.1 provides the results including the change rates of per capita GDP, the change rates of the four environmental quality indicators and the overall EQI and EE. Note that the change rates of environmental quality indicators in Table 5.1 are obtained by multiplying the change rates of environmental

TABLE 5.1

Environmental Elasticity for People's Republic of China

Year	Change of GDP/c	Change of Air Quality Index	Change of Wat.Quality Index	Change of Land Quality Index	Change of Ecol. Index	Change of Overall EQI	EE
1980–81							
1981–82	6.00%	4.68%	0.00%	-15.63%	1.15%	-2.45%	-0.41
1982–83	6.19%	7.86%	60.68%	-3.77%	1.06%	16.46%	2.66
1983–84	13.08%	6.99%	-273.89%	-8.45%	1.13%	-68.56%	-5.24
1984–85	11.25%	-1.69%	22.99%	-8.88%	1.12%	3.39%	0.30
1985–86	6.84%	5.65%	-7.18%	-0.24%	1.10%	-0.17%	-0.02
1986–87	9.31%	-2.96%	-20.93%	-8.72%	1.17%	-7.86%	-0.84
1987–88	9.48%	5.29%	29.60%	-3.53%	1.08%	8.11%	0.86
1988–89	2.78%	8.85%	10.62%	-5.44%	1.07%	3.78%	1.36
1989–90	2.45%	11.69%	30.45%	-6.05%	1.06%	9.29%	3.79
1990–91	6.59%	7.01%	-64.33%	-7.61%	1.05%	-15.97%	-2.42
1991–92	12.28%	-4.04%	-2.14%	-6.14%	1.69%	-2.66%	-0.22
1992–93	12.13%	-0.85%	-14.47%	-4.73%	2.08%	-4.49%	-0.37

pollution and degradation indices, defined in equations (5.1) through (5.5), with "-1."

For the periods 1982–83, 1984–85, and 1987–90, the EE indicates that PRC may have followed a sustainable course with positive values for both economic and environmental aggregates. However, for most of the period, the EE has negative values with a negative numerator or EQI, indicating that the environment was declining but the economy was improving. More specifically, for the period 1981–82, the EE value is -0.41, indicating that every 1 percent GDP growth was achieved at the expense of 0.41 percent decline of environmental aggregate or EQI. As discussed in Chapter 3, we describe this situation as "weakly sustainable," a scenario in which the economy is improving and the environment is declining, but the environment is declining at a rate slower than economic growth.

One can gain much insight by analyzing the underlying political (policy) and economic factors that contribute to the temporal changes of "sustainabilty." For example, Table 5.1 indicates that PRC was experiencing positive changes for both the economy and environment from 1987 to 1989. This corresponds to a period of economic "slowdown" marked by slower GDP growth rates. It is conceivable that slower economic growth may have slowed the rate of environmental degradation, although other factors such as more aggressive environmental policy implementation could also have played an important role.

Philippines

In deriving environmental elasticity, the economic indicator used was real GDP per capita. The environmental variables used to compute EE include ambient levels of particulate matter (PM), sulfur dioxide (SO_2), and carbon monoxide (CO) in Metro Manila, forest cover of the country, and the levels of suspended solids (SS) and dissolved oxygen (DO) in Laguna Lake. Not all of these variables have a long time-series data available for the period 1970–1993. Moreover, some of the variables were measured differently over time. For example, PM was measured by both light-scattering and gravimetric methods at different times and may account for some of the change in PM levels. Forest cover estimates depended on the type of method used (aerial photographs, satellite imagery, interpolation, and inventory systems).

Table 5.2 shows the computation of EE using real GDP per capita in dollars in the denominator. For the period 1970–1993, the dominant quadrant was Quadrant III (see Figure 3.4 in Chapter 3), showing that over the time period the Philippines has shown very unfavorable economic and environmental performance for most of the years i.e., negative changes for both economic and environmental changes. This happened during the early 70s, the early and mid-80s, and the early 90s. The next dominant quadrant was Quadrant IV which shows that the Philippines was able to post economic growth at the expense of

TABLE 5.2
Environmental Elasticity for the Philippines

Year	% Change in Per Capita GDP	%Change in Environ. Aggregate	EE	Ecological Variables Used*
1970–71	4.00%	-0.15%	-0.04	1
1971–72	-1.10%	-1.28%	1.17	1
1972–73	4.70%	-11.34%	-2.41	1
1973–74	0.30%	-1.47%	-4.89	1
1974–75	-3.40%	-1.56%	0.46	1
1975–76	2.70%	7.85%	2.91	1,2,3,4
1976–77	3.30%	1.92%	0.58	1,2,3,4
1977–78	2.90%	-2.49%	-0.86	1,2,3,4
1978–79	2.70%	3.71%	1.37	1,2,3,4
1979–80	0.50%	0.49%	0.98	1,2,3,4
1980–81	-4.10%	-5.22%	1.27	1,2,3,4,5,6
1981–82	-6.50%	6.23%	-0.96	1,2,3,4,5,6
1982–83	-23.60%	-11.42%	0.48	1,2,3,4,5,6
1983–84	-39.80%	-4.74%	0.12	1,2,3,4,5,6
1984–85	-18.80%	-34.12%[#]	1.82	1,5,6
1985–86	-7.90%	-3.02%	0.38	1,5,6
1986–87	1.00%	-2.57%	-2.57	1,5,6
1987–88	1.70%	-24.38%[#]	-14.34	1,2,3,5,6
1988–89	0.70%	-10.45%	-14.92	1,2,3,5,6
1989–90	-10.80%	7.34%	-0.68	1,2,3,5,6
1990–91	-14.00%	-0.14%	0.01	1,2,3,5,6
1991–92	5.70%	-3.03%	-0.53	1,2,3,5,6
1992–93	-6.20%	-7.49%	1.21	1,2,3,5

*Ecological Variables
  1. Forest Cover
  2. Particulate Matter (Metro Manila)
  3. Sulfur Dioxide (Metro Manila)
  4. Carbon Monoxide (Metro Manila)
  5. Dissolved Oxygen (Laguna Lake)
  6. Suspended Solids (Laguna Lake)
Numbers are correct.

the environment. However, there are periods which show that the country was performing very well (Quadrant I) in both economy and environment and performing well only in the environment but not in economy. Therefore, there is really no trend in the values of the EE, i.e., the country swings among different quadrants without any direction. This lack of trend may be brought about by inconsistencies in the measurement of environmental variables and fluctuations in the exchange rate. Also, it should be noted that not all environmental data are available for every period to compute the EE.

TABLE 5.3
Environmental Elasticity for Nepal

Year	Change of Real GDP/Capita	Change of Fuelwood Consumption	Change of Agri- Residue	Change of Animal Waste	Change of Coal Consumption	Change of Petro-Prod. Consumption	Change of Overall EQI	EE
1985–86	-2.20%	-1.63%	-2.73%	-2.40%	-63.30%	-12.10%	-16.43%	7.47
1986–87	4.35%	-2.36%	-1.88%	-2.10%	-2.74%	-16.14%	-5.04%	-1.16
1987–88	1.57%	9.43%	-41.15%	-45.40%	17.52%	12.90%	-9.34%	-5.95
1988–89	1.83%	-9.78%	27.90%	-26.60%	83.14%	5.64%	16.06%	8.78
1989–90	2.20%	-2.65%	-1.06%	-2.70%	-434.25%	-36.96%	-95.52%	-43.42
1990–91	17.49%	-0.87%	-3.00%	-1.50%	-23.00%	-22.62%	-10.20%	-0.58
1992–92	-7.57%	-0.93%	-1.00%	-1.50%	2.10%	-41.74%	-8.61%	1.14

It is important that the environmental consequences of the investments be interpreted in economic terms. The EE reveals that a trade-off between the two forms of capital (natural capital represented by the numerator or environmental aggregate, and man-made capital represented by the denominator or per capita GDP change) has characterized the period 1971–1990 in the Philippines and that trade-off is dependent on the temporal scale used.

Nepal

Since time series data on various pollutants are lacking in Nepal, calculation of EE based on emission intensity of various pollutants is not possible. Hence a proxy method is adopted to address environmental change by using energy consumption data over the years. The rationale behind using these energy data for the environmental change is that they serve as a rough approximation of the emissions of the various air pollutants like CO_2 and NO_x (Yu et al. 1995). An obvious drawback of the environmental aggregate so defined is that it will only account for changes in air quality and ignores other notable environmental degradation such as soil erosion in hilly arable land, water pollution, and loss of biodiversity. For assessing the change in the economy, we adopt the growth rate of real GDP per capita as the economic indicator.

The results are given in Table 5.3. The EE indicates that Nepal experienced some dramatic fluctuation in its environmental changes relative to economic changes and it in general performed poorly during the periods marked by some very "large" negative EE values.

Pakistan

Per capita GDP was used as the economic indicator in the case of Pakistan. Three categories of environmental quality indicators—air, water, and ecosystem—were used to calibrate the environmental aggregate.

Air quality indicators include vehicular emissions and industrial emissions. Four pollutants, i.e., SO_2, CO, HC, and NOx) were included and each was given an equal weight (1/4). Note that no weight has been given to CO_2 which is primarily considered a global pollutant rather than a local pollutant. Water quality is affected by a number of factors, including industrial and municipal effluent. Other important sources of water pollution include agrochemical residues and sedimentation from upland erosion. A time-series of industrial effluent generation was developed using production values and industrial water use and wastewater coefficients. Municipal effluent has currently not been included in the water category. Forests are the richest and most diverse of terrestrial ecosystems. As such, the loss of forest cover can be broadly equated with loss of biodiversity. While threats to species may be generally related to forest habitat loss, two caveats may be noted:

■ Secondary forests in general, and monocultural plantations in particular, are not areas rich in the variety of life. In fact, they may be quite sterile.

■ The posited relationship may not hold for the thinning of gene pools for domesticated plants and animals. Agricultural practices are more responsible for the thinning of the gene pool of plants and animals. Pakistan is not a world center or a threatened hot spot for biodiversity in general, except for cereal cultivars, and perhaps soil organisms.

A methodological problem is that the area surveyed in Pakistan has expanded over time to encompass the forest-rich northern mountains that included formerly quasi-independent princely states. Thus, the territorial extent of forests seems to increase particularly around 1969–1970, when many of the states were amalgamated with routinely administered districts, leading to erroneous interpretations of the ecosystem index. However, no other simple measure was available. Forest habitat loss was used as a surrogate for biodiversity loss and the ecosystem indicator.

Finally, arable land expansion, increase in area and volume of irrigation supplies, excessive logging and fuelwood collection, overgrazing, and land pollution from industry and municipal activities are among the major causes of land degradation in Pakistan. However, due to lack of data, land quality indicators are excluded from the current EE computation.

Table 5.4 gives the EEs for Pakistan from 1982–1983 to 1992–1993. In all years, there has been growth in the economy, except 1991–1992, a year of heavy floods. There has also been a deterioration in the environment in all years except 1985. Under EE the results for all years except 1985 are in Quadrant IV. Only in 1985 did Pakistan appear to be on the path of sustainable development. EE provides a powerful tool to inform policy-makers about the shape of development in the country. On the one hand, it relates closely to the traditional perception of policy-makers that the mid-1980s was a period of

TABLE 5.4

Environmental Elasticity for Pakistan

Year	Change in Air Quality	Change in Forest Quality	Change in Water Quality	Change in Environment	Change in Economy Per Capita	EE
1982–83	-15.18%	-1.22%	0.30%	-5.36%	0.85%	-6.31
1983–84	-14.52%	-1.49%	-9.52%	-8.51%	5.44%	-1.56
1984–85	-6.78%	-1.78%	10.28%	0.57%	3.16%	0.18
1985–86	-17.22%	-2.11%	2.22%	-5.71%	2.64%	-2.16
1986–87	-9.03%	-2.48%	-13.62%	-8.38%	3.23%	-2.60
1987–88	-14.25%	-2.89%	0.00%	-5.72%	1.66%	-3.45
1988–89	-8.23%	-3.36%	2.16%	-3.14%	1.44%	-2.18
1989–90	-18.00%	-3.90%	-0.18%	-7.36%	2.39%	-3.07
1990–91	-9.81%	-4.52%	-2.49%	-5.61%	4.47%	-1.25
1991–92	-10.12%	-4.74%	-4.26%	-6.37%	-0.70%	9.05
1992–93	-12.16%	-5.48%	1.00%	-5.55%	0.94%	-5.92

relative prosperity for Pakistan. On the other hand, it sharpens the perception that the subsequent slowdown in the economy has also been accompanied by a continuing environmental deterioration.

Indonesia

Time-series data for characterizing the environmental trends are particularly lacking for Indonesia. Although we have obtained some data on total solid waste and liquid waste generation, these data are only available for two years, (1991 and 1993) and only for West Java. Again, we adopt a proxy approach which uses only total crude oil and total coal consumption as environmental indicators. As in Nepal's case, the rationale for this choice is that energy consumption is highly correlated with air emissions, particularly GHG such as CO_2. However, other prevalent environmental problems in Indonesia such as loss of biodiversity, soil erosion, and water pollution are not addressed by the current EEs. We use per capita GDP as the economic indicator in the indices.

Table 5.5 provides the results of the EE computation for Indonesia. As shown by the changing rates of per capita GDP between 1980 and 1989, Indonesia experienced a strong economic boom during the period. Along with the economic development, energy consumption also surged. As a result, EEs exhibit negative values for many of the years.

Environmental Elasticity for Indonesia

Year	Change of GDP/c	Change of Crude Oil Consumption	Change of Coal Consumption	Change of EQI	EE
1980–81	17.30%	-0.50%	-15.20%	-7.85%	-0.45
1981–82	3.50%	6.40%	-14.70%	-4.15%	-1.19
1982–83	22.30%	-1.70%	14.40%	6.35%	0.28
1983–84	13.20%	-11.10%	75.40%	32.15%	2.44
1984–85	5.90%	-6.50%	-1957.60%*	-982.05%*	-166.45*
1985–86	4.00%	-8.40%	-121.70%	-65.05%	-16.26
1986–87	18.40%	1.30%	-2.00%	-0.35%	-0.02
1987–88	11.10%	-8.20%	23.80%	7.80%	0.70
1988–89	15.10%	29.70%	-47.60%	-8.95%	-0.59

* Numbers are correct.

Cross-Country Comparison of Long-Term Environmental Trends

The above EE computation was conducted for individual countries and for multiple one-year intervals. This approach has a number of drawbacks. First, because the time span is set at one year, the shortest time interval possible, the data on economic and environmental changes may be more susceptible to "noise" in data collection and compiling rather than as a reflection of policy and economic changes. As a result, for most countries, no identifiable temporal pattern of environmental-economic changes exists and the EE seems to fluctuate dramatically from one year to another. The second drawback of setting the time interval at one year is that it prevents comparison of different countries in terms of their longer-term environmental trends.

To overcome these shortcomings and to obtain a better perspective on relative performance of the five countries, we also conducted the following two types of exercises: (1) computing EEs for the entire time spans for which the data are available, and (2) graphically plotting the environmental trends. It should be noted that the time spans for which the EEs are computed are slightly different for different countries, as indicated by Tables 5.1 through 5.5, but cover most of the 1980s for all countries.

In Table 5.6, the right column, i.e., EE maps, shows the location of a country in the economic-environmental space (the shaded area) (see Figure 3.4). For example, the first four countries: PRC, Pakistan, Indonesia, and Nepal, all have a negative environmental elasticity. The EE maps show that they are all located in Quadrant IV: positive economic growth but negative environmental change. They are ranked according to their values of environ-

TABLE 5.6
Environmental Elasticity

Ranking	Country	Value	EE Map
1	People's Republic of China	-0.43	
2	Pakistan	-1.68	
3	Indonesia	-2.63	
4	Nepal	-5.70	
5	Philippines	0.94	

mental elasticity. The Philippines is a special case as the only country in the group that is located in Quadrant III; experiencing both negative economic change and negative environmental change for the time period, a clearly unsustainable scenario. It is ranked last even though it has a positive value. No country in the group is found in Quadrant II, an indication that most countries choose to develop the economy first before improving the environment. PRC receives the highest ranking in the group with a value of –0.43, indicating that for every 1 percent economic growth, the environmental aggregate deteriorates by 0.43 percent. With an EE smaller than one in absolute value, PRC is the only country in the group for which the rate of environmental deterioration is slower than the rate of economic growth, a situation some may characterize as "weakly sustainable." By contrast, for Nepal, 1 percent of per capita GDP growth has been achieved at the expense of 5.7 percent decrease of the environmental aggregate. The environmental elasticity quantitatively demonstrates the trade-offs that the countries are making in their efforts to develop their economies.

Apart from computing EEs, another way to observe the environmental trends for the countries is simply to plot the EQIs and economic indicators on a two dimensional space. We illustrate this by using the same data used for computing the EEs for the five countries (Figures 5.1 through 5.5). Overall EQI, which is the equally-weighted average of all the environmental variables used for EE is normalized to unity for the starting year, is used as the y-axis. Per-capita GDP, which is also normalized to unity for the starting year, is used as the x-axis.

FIGURE 5.1
Environment vs Economy—People's Republic of China
(EQI & GDP normalized to one for 1980)

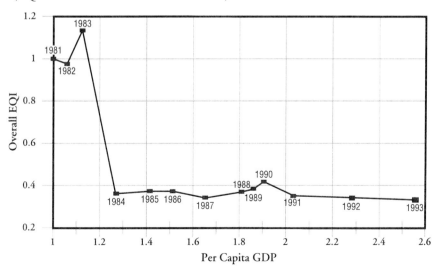

FIGURE 5.2

Environment vs Economy—Indonesia (EQI & GDP normalized to one for 1980)

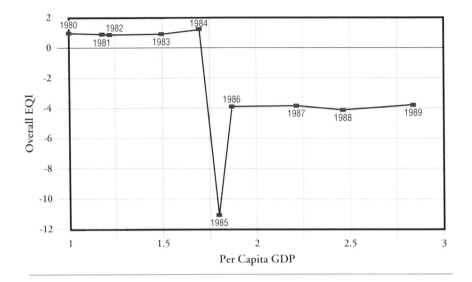

FIGURE 5.3

Environment vs Economy—Philippines (EQI & GDP normalized to one for 1980)

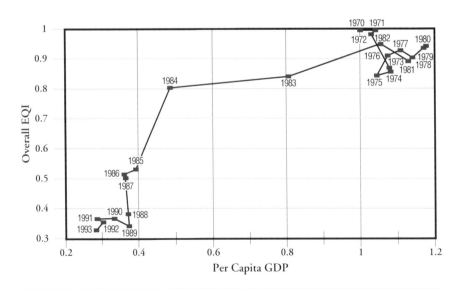

FIGURE 5.4

Environment vs Economy—Pakistan (EQI & GDP normalized to one for 1980)

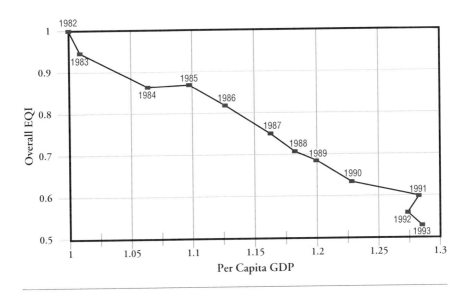

FIGURE 5.5

Environment vs Economy—Nepal (EQI & GDP normalized to one for 1980)

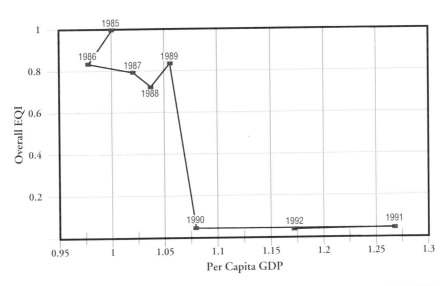

FIGURE 5.6

Environment vs Economy—1970–1993 (EQI & GDP normalized to
one for Year One)

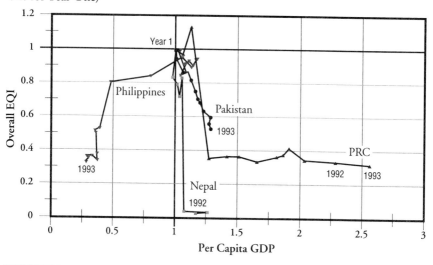

Compared to the year-to-year EEs discussed earlier, the graphs better
illustrate both yearly changes and long-term trends for the environment and
the economy. In contrast, the year-to-year EEs tend to better reveal short-term
changes only. Take PRC (Figure 5.1) and Pakistan (Figure 5.4) as an example.
Figure 5.1 shows that during the period between 1981 and 1984, PRC's
environment took a plunge, from 1 to approximately 0.35, and then stabilized
between 1984 and 1993, despite the rapid economic growth for the period. By
comparison, Figure 5.4 shows that Pakistan's environment has continuously
deteriorated between 1982 and 1993, at a much more moderate pace, while the
economy also grew at a moderate pace during the same period. The Philippines
is another interesting case. Figure 5.3 indicates that during the 1970s, the
country was essentially stagnant environmentally and economically. It then
swirled backward during much of the 1980s and has been stagnant again
entering the 1990s. For Nepal, Figure 5.5 reveals that the economy has
experienced considerable amount of "up-and-down" while the environment is
also declining.

To get an intercountry perspective, we have plotted all of the participating
countries but Indonesia in one single graph (Figure 5.6). Indonesia is excluded
because its dramatic decline of environment tends to skew the whole picture.
Figure 5.6 presents an interesting comparison of the different economic-
environmental "paths" the countries took during the periods. All the countries
start from Year One (in the center of the chart; note that the base year is different
for different countries due to data constraints) for which both EQIs and per

capita GDP are normalized to one. PRC moved upwards first and then took a plunge towards the lower-right direction. Pakistan and Nepal also moved toward a similar direction, although at a much more moderate pace. These three cases symbolize economic growth but environmental deterioration. However, PRC's economy grew much faster than Pakistan and Nepal which move almost straight down except for the last three years, which means environmental decline and economic stagnancy. By contrast, the Philippines moved towards the lower-left direction (deterioration in both environment and economy), which is the least-preferred scenario.

Due to the fact that the environmental variables used in constructing the EQIs are different for different countries due to data limitations, we are obliged to standardize the EQIs with Year One as unity. This prevents us from obtaining a sense of the relative locations of the state of the environment and the economy of different countries in the economic-environmental space in the same years. However, Figure 5.6 does show the relative directions that the countries took in their economic and environmental development. Together with the EEs, these diagrams provide a good overall assessment of the environmental-economic trends in these countries.

Computing EEs for Sixteen Asian Countries

The data used for computing the EEs for the five countries participating in this study were generated as part of this study. The same data are not available for other Asian countries for which there is also a need to assess their environmental trends. To meet such a need, we employ some more commonly used environmental indicators to compute a new set of environmental elasticity for 16 Asian countries.

Table 5.7 presents variables used to compute the environmental elasticity over the period between 1980 and early 1990 for the 16 Asian countries. The economic indicator or the denominator employed is the average annual change rate (AACR) of total GDP (based on exchange rate) for the period between 1980–1993. Change of total GDP was chosen as the denominator because economic activities such as energy consumption and manufacturing, represented by the GDP, normally cause the most environmental damage by either overutilizing resources or polluting the environment.

The numerator or change of environmental aggregate is an average annual change rate of four environmental indicators, each representing the four principal environmental components: air, water, land, and ecosystem. For air, we use commercial energy consumption because, as mentioned in Chapter 3, our statistical analysis indicates that total air emissions of a country including SO_2, NO_x are closely related to its total commercial energy consumption. For water, we use percentage of population with safe drinking water. For land and ecosystem quality, we use fertilizer use per hectare of arable land and forest cover, respectively. Fertilizer use is indicative of a country's soil quality. A

TABLE 5.7

Average Annual Change Rates (AACR) of Selected Environmental-Economic Indicators

Country	Tot. Com. Eng. Use AACR (1980–93)	% Pop w S.D.W. AACR (1980–91)	Fertilizer Use/ha AACR (1980–93)	Forest Cover AACR (1980–90)	Env. Aggregate AACR (1980–early 90)	Total GDP AACR (1980–93)
Vietnam	2.6%	2.91%	36.21%	-1.44%	-9.34%	7.10%
Nepal	8.1%	15.90%	23.31%	-1.07%	-4.15%	5.00%
Bangladesh	7.9%	9.45%	9.75%	-2.73%	-2.73%	4.20%
Lao PDR	2.6%	2.92%	-2.12%	-0.90%	0.39%	4.80%
India	6.7%	7.31%	2.13%	-0.62%	-0.53%	5.20%
Mongolia	2.2%	-3.09%	4.35%	-0.86%	-2.62%	3.80%
Pakistan	6.8%	3.77%	6.98%	-2.69%	-3.18%	6.00%
P.R. China	5.1%	5.45%	7.75%	-0.65%	-2.01%	9.60%
Sri Lanka	1.9%	10.16%	0.72%	-1.50%	1.51%	4.00%
Myanmar	-0.8%	5.45%	-2.38%	-1.22%	1.85%	0.80%
Indonesia	7.5%	7.51%	7.01%	-1.00%	-2.00%	5.80%
Philippines	3.5%	7.08%	3.15%	-2.91%	-0.62%	1.40%
Papua New Guinea	2.4%	9.84%	8.32%	-0.30%	-0.29%	3.10%
Thailand	10.5%	1.25%	20.21%	-2.91%	-8.09%	8.20%
Korea, Rep.	9.5%	0.25%	2.10%	-0.15%	-2.87%	9.10%
Singapore	7.7%	0.00%	0.14%	0.00%	-1.96%	6.90%
Average	5.3%	5.38%	7.98%	-1.40%	-2.31%	5.17%

Source: World Bank, 1995

country with severe soil erosion and population pressure is inclined to use more fertilizer. Further, the excess use of fertilizer itself also has some adverse effects on soil quality. Forest cover is considered important for ecosystem quality because forest, particularly natural forest, is perhaps the most important ecosystem and serves as habitats for many species.

The aggregation of the four variables was conducted through equal weighting for simplicity, though unequal weighting may better reflect reality in terms of policy priorities. Furthermore, for some variables, i.e., commercial energy consumption and fertilizer use, increase of their values are undesirable and, thus, a negative sign is assigned to them in calculating the environmental aggregate. In contrast, for percentage of population with safe drinking water and forest cover, the increase of their values are desirable and no sign adjustment is needed in the aggregation.

Table 5.8 shows the ranking of the countries based on environmental elasticity computation. Again, the fourth column, i.e., EE maps, indicates the location (quadrant) of a country in the economic-environmental space (also see Figure 3.4 in Chapter 3). The three top ranked countries, Myanmar, Sri Lanka, and Lao PDR, all have positive environmental elasticity and they are all located in Quadrant I: positive economic growth and positive environmental changes. This is clearly the most preferred scenario because it indicates that their economic growth has been accompanied by positive change of environment aggregate. In Table 4 (last column), we characterize this group as "Group A: Sustainable." All the other countries have negative elasticity values and are located in Quadrant IV: positive economic growth and negative environmental change, suggesting that the economic growth in these countries have been accompanied by negative changes in environmental quality. However, with the exception of Vietnam, all the other countries have negative elasticity values with absolute values less than one, indicating that although their environment deteriorates as their economies grow, the deterioration rates appear to be slower than the growth rates of their economies. We characterize this group as "Group B: Weakly Sustainable." Vietnam has a value of -1.32, larger than one in absolute value, indicating that its 1 percent GDP growth may be achieved at the expense of more than 1 percent decrease of environment aggregate. We classify it as "Group C: Unsustainable."

Interestingly, in the earlier computation of EE for five countries (Table 5.6), the Philippines experienced both negative changes of per capita GDP and negative environmental changes during the period between 1970 and 1993. In the present computation, we have adopted total GDP, rather than per capita GDP, and we have changed the time frame to 1980–1993. The average percentage change of total GDP for the 1980–1993 is positive for the Philippines in contrast to the negative per capita GDP growth rate for the period between 1970 to 1993. This could be due to the fact that the Philippines has a very high population growth rate, higher than total GDP growth rate, resulting a net decrease of per capita GDP over the period.

Some countries may jump from one quadrant to another over different time periods and policy can affect the courses of the development. Although the top three countries, Myanmar, Sri Lanka, and Lao PDR, were shown to be on a sustainable course for the time period, they may be on a different course in the future when their economic growth accelerates without benefit of sound environmental policies. In contrast, many former Soviet republics in central Asia can be currently found in Quadrant II, experiencing drastic economic, particularly industrial decline which is also accompanied by massive decrease of industrial emissions and noticeable improvement in air and water quality. However, this is clearly not a sustainable scenario, either, because the environmental improvement has been achieved at the expense of people's economic welfare, which was at its bare minimum to start with.

Environmental Elasticity (1980–early 1990)

Rank	Country	Value	EE Map	Group Characteristics
1	Myanmar	2.32	+ Env. / + Eco	A
2	Sri Lanka	0.38	+ Env. / + Eco	A
3	Lao PDR	0.08	+ Env. / + Eco	A
4	Papua New Guinea	-0.09	+ Env. / + Eco	B
5	India	-0.10	+ Env. / + Eco	B
6	People's Republic of China	-0.21	+ Env. / + Eco	B
7	Singapore	-0.28	+ Env. / + Eco	B
8	Korea, Rep.	-0.32	+ Env. / + Eco	B

TABLE 5.8 *(continued)*

Rank	Country	Value	EE Map	Group Characteristics
9	Indonesia	-0.35	+ Env. / + Eco	B
10	Philippines	-0.44	+ Env. / + Eco	B
11	Pakistan	-0,53	+ Env. / + Eco	B
12	Bangladesh	-0.65	+ Env. / + Eco	B
13	Mongolia	-0.69	+ Env. / + Eco	B
14	Nepal	-0.83	+ Env. / + Eco	B
15	Thailand	-0.99	+ Env. / + Eco	B
16	Vietnam	-1.32	+ Env. / + Eco	C

Assessing the State of the Environment in Asia

While the EE is created to assess environmental trends that may affect future environmental quality, the third type of measuring tool developed in this study is the environmental diamond, which is designed to evaluate the state of the environment. In Chapter 3, we introduced the theoretical foundations and the methodology for constructing the environmental diamonds via an example for seven Asian countries (see Tables 3.2 and 3.3, and Figure 3.2). Below we construct environmental diamonds for 16 countries using the same four variables used to compute the EEs as shown in Tables 5.7 and 5.8. Employing the same variables for environmental elasticity and environmental diamond allows one to examine the environmental trends and state of the environment on the basis of same indicators for the 16 countries.

Table 5.9 presents the data on the four variables. Specifically, for air, we use commercial energy consumption per capita. For water, we use percentage of population with access to safe drinking water. For land and ecosystem, we use fertilizer use per hectare of arable land and forest cover, respectively. Note that the difference between the data presented in Table 5.9 and those used for

TABLE 5.9

Selected Environmental Indicators for Environmental Diamonds

Country	Energy Consumption kg/c (oil eq), 1993	% Pop w Safe Drinking water, 1991	Fertilizer Use 100g/ha 1993	Forest Cover (%) 1990
Vietnam	77	50%	1347	25.0%
Nepal	22	37%	391	35.5%
Bangladesh	59	78%	1032	5.6%
Lao PDR	39	28%	42	55.7%
India	242	75%	420	15.7%
Mongolia	1089	66%	108	8.9%
Pakistan	209	50%	1015	2.4%
P.R. China	623	71%	3005	13.0%
Sri Lanka	110	60%	964	25.8%
Myanmar	39	33%	69	42.7%
Indonesia	321	42%	1147	57.5%
Philippines	328	81%	540	26.0%
Papua New Guinea	238	33%	308	77.8%
Thailand	678	72%	544	24.8%
Korea, Rep.	2863	78%	4656	65.7%
Singapore	5563	100%	5600	0.0%
Average	444	69%	1217	21%

Source: World Bank, 1995

computing environmental elasticity (Table 5.7) is that the data for elasticity (Table 5.7) are expressed in the forms of change rates over time because of the dynamic nature of environmental elasticity. In contrast, the data in Table 5.9 are "static" since environmental diamonds are created to indicate the state of the environment.

To standardize the values of the indicators, the score of each country per each indicator is expressed in terms of percentage of the group averages, i.e., 16 countries in this case. Due to the vast size difference of the countries being compared, we use weighted average using total population (for per capita energy consumption and percentage of population with access to safe drinking water), total land area (for forest cover) and total arable land (for fertilizer per hectare of arable land). In addition, the principle "small is good and large is bad" was followed. Consequently, for those indicators for which the reverse is true, its "opposite" indicator was utilized. To illustrate, for the indicator "percentage of urban population with access to safe drinking water," its opposite indicator, "percentage of urban population without access to safe drinking water" was used. The same method was also applied to the indicator "percentage of land with forest (forest cover)" for which "percentage of land without forest" was used. Table 5.10 provides the "standardized" values.

TABLE 5.10
Scores for Constructing Environmental Diamonds

Country	Air (Energy Use/c)	Water (% Pop w/n S.D.W)	Land (Fertilizer Use/ha)	Ecosystem (% Land w/n Forest)
Vietnam	17%	159%	111%	95%
Nepal	5%	200%	32%	82%
Bangladesh	13%	70%	85%	120%
Lao PDR	9%	229%	3%	56%
India	54%	79%	35%	107%
Mongolia	245%	108%	9%	115%
Pakistan	47%	159%	83%	124%
P.R. China	140%	92%	247%	110%
Sri Lanka	25%	127%	79%	94%
Myanmar	9%	213%	6%	73%
Indonesia	72%	184%	94%	54%
Philippines	74%	60%	44%	94%
Papua New Guinea	54%	213%	25%	28%
Thailand	153%	89%	45%	95%
Korea, Rep.	645%	70%	383%	43%
Singapore	1253%	0%	460%	127%
Average	100%	100%	100%	100%

The last step is to draw the diamonds on a Cartesian system of axes using the indices in Table 5.10. In Figure 5.7, the square diamonds indicate the 16-country average, i.e., 100 percent and the overlay diamonds reflect the environmental situation in individual countries. As indicated earlier, along each dimension, larger values indicate either worse environmental quality or added environmental stress. We exclude the Republic of Korea and Singapore in Figure 5.7 because these two countries seem to be in different development and technological levels from the rest of the group. For example, we use energy consumption as a proxy for air emissions, assuming the countries have more or less similar pollution abatement levels. However, although Singapore has the largest per capita energy consumption level, its air quality is among the best of the Asian cities.

Environmental diamonds are as appealing as they are easy to construct. They keep individual components separate, and are graphically a good way of presenting the result, especially for cross-country or cross-region comparisons. By examining Figure 5.7, one quickly obtains an impression that Bangladesh is near or within the average in all environmental components except ecosystem. In comparison, PRC does very poorly with respect to land quality (heavy fertilizer use) due to severe soil erosion, and air quality due to its heavy coal burning. Indonesia is at the average in terms of air, land, and ecosystem, but scores worse than average in terms of providing its citizens with safe drinking water.

In Chapter 3, we suggested a method of aggregating the four sub-indices forming the environmental diamond to derive an overall index: the root-mean-square (RMS) method, which takes the following form:

$$RMS = \sqrt{w_1 \text{ (air index)}^2 + w_2 \text{ (water index)}^2 + w_3 \text{ (land index)}^2 + w_4 \text{ (eco. index)}^2}$$

Table 5.11 ranks the countries according to their RMS values based on equal weighting of the four subcomponents. The countries are divided into two groups: lower-than-average and higher-than-average (the average is 100 percent). The Philippines receives the best rank with an RMS value of 70 percent, closely followed by India (74 percent), Bangladesh (81 percent), and Sri Lanka (89 percent). At the other end of the spectrum, Mongolia scores 146 percent and PRC scores 159 percent. Finally, as mentioned earlier, the two newly industrialized countries (NICs), i.e., the Republic of Korea and Singapore, receive unfavorable rankings using this set of indicators. However, they appear to be in a different level of economic development and technology from the rest of the group which calls for cautions when interpreting the above results.

It is interesting to compare the cases of the Philippines and Myanmar. Figure 5.7 shows that the Philippines scores lower-than-average on three dimensions and about average on one dimension while Myanmar receives low or very low scores on three dimensions but a very high score on the fourth

FIGURE 5.7
Environmental Diamonds

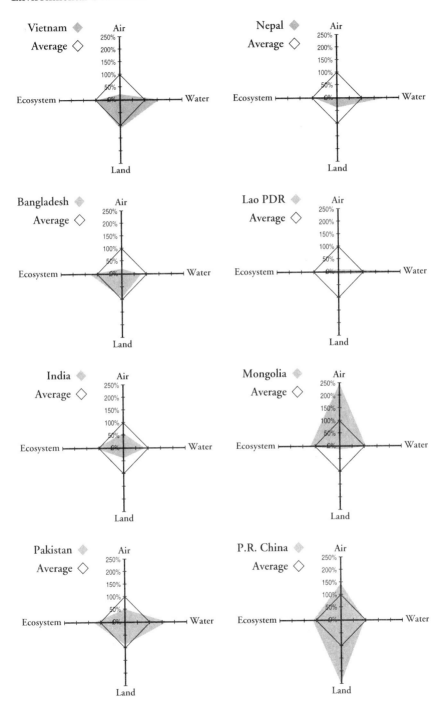

FIGURE 5.7 *(continued)*

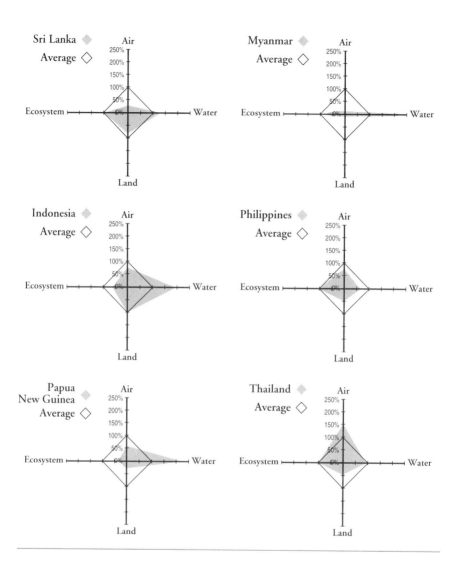

dimension (water). However, Table 5.11 ranks the Philippines as the best and Myanmar the distant 10th in the 16-country group. Such a dramatic difference of the ranks is largely due to the fact that RMS is extremely sensitive to large values (outliners) and favors those countries which score moderately on every dimension. In other words, if a country scores particularly badly on any one dimension, it is likely to receive a very low overall ranking even if it may score favorably on the other three dimensions. One of the arguments in favor of adopting this method in environmental index development is that environmental quality is often determined by extreme values, such as severe air and

TABLE 5.11
Country Rankings Based on Root-Mean-Square Values

Rank*	Country	Root-Mean-Square Total (eq. wt)	Group Characteristics**
1	Philippines	70%	A
2	India	74%	A
3	Bangladesh	81%	A
4	Sri Lanka	89%	A
5	Thailand	103%	B
6	Vietnam	108%	B
7	Nepal	109%	B
8	Papua New Guinea	111%	B
9	Pakistan	111%	B
10	Myanmar	113%	B
11	Indonesia	113%	B
12	Laos PDR	118%	B
13	Mongolia	146%	B
14	P.R. China	159%	B
15	Korea, Rep.	377%	B
16	Singapore	670%	B

  * First is the best.
 **A: Less than average.
   B: More than average.

water pollution, which may cause the most damage. The index, therefore, should reflect this fact by being sensitive to the extreme values.

Policy Implications of Environmental Elasticity and Environmental Diamond

By assessing both environmental trend relative to economic trend and the current state of the environment of a country, the environmental elasticity and environmental diamond provide simple but useful tools for policy-makers in achieving a balance between economic development and environmental improvement.

Compared to the cost-of-remediation approach discussed in Chapters 3 and 4, the EE and ED enjoy the advantage of being simple and less data intensive. They can be constructed and computed on a regular basis to provide policy-makers and the general public with an assessment of the state and the trend of the environment. For example, in this chapter, we have observed through the environmental diamond that the PRC's state of the environment is poor. However, the environmental elasticity computation shows that its environmental degradation seems to have slowed, compared to other countries in Asia. This in part reflects the moderate success of the PRC Government's policies and efforts towards balanced economic development and environmental improvement. The improvement of air quality in some northern Chinese cities during the winter season is quite obvious for local residents and visitors who have the opportunity to compare the present air quality with that of ten years ago. The improvement is largely due to the increase of district heating and wider use of natural gas for cooking. In contrast, the environmental diamond indicates that although the state of the environment in the Philippines and Vietnam is better than or at the average, environmental deterioration may occur at an alarming rate, which calls for greater attention from the governments and MFIs.

Finally, the environmental elasticity shows that the Lao PDR, Myanmar, and Sri Lanka seem to have been on a relatively sustainable course in the 1980s. However, a cautionary message is in order: the trend may change for the worse when their economic growth accelerates since higher economic growth tends to cause more environmental damage.

6 Summary and Conclusions

The former Indonesian Minister for Population and Environment, Emil Salim, is reported to have made the following remarks in 1986:

> "In my policy-making I need an indicator in money terms for losses in environment and resources, as a counterweight to the indicator for production, namely national income. If a theoretically sound indicator is not possible, then think up one that is rather less theoretically sound."[1]

Those of us concerned with index construction hope that it is possible to create effective indicators of environmental quality that are also theoretically sound. However, it must be stressed that the end purpose of developing environmental indicators is improved decision-making. The above remark suggests two important points. First, there is an urgent demand for useful environmental quality indicators in day-to-day environmental and resource management. Partially due to the lack of such indicators, environmental benefits and costs that tend to be less tangible and more long-term-oriented are often inadequately accounted for. Economic criteria often dominate the decision-making processes, in part because the tools used, including traditional economic indicators such as GDP, have been developed exclusively for making economically wise decisions. The second point is that any environmental indicators that have a chance to "counterweight" economic indicators such as GDP must be expressed in the same currency, for example dollars, or relate to monetary terms in some direct way.

To measure environmental costs and benefits in monetary terms is not to fully endorse the existing economic indicators such as GDP whose many deficiencies are increasingly obvious. Rather, it is dictated by the reality that most of the actual identification and evaluation of investment opportunities are carried out, by governments and multilateral financial institutions or MFIs, e.g., the World Bank, International Monetary Fund (IMF), and ADB, in terms of monetary values. For example, one of the methodologies for evaluating the policies on production and export of timber is to assess their impact on increasing a country's domestic income or job creation. In order for a minister of environment to object to such a policy, he or she needs to prove that the costs of exporting trees, including the costs of replanting trees, restoring habitats, and controlling deforestation-induced erosion, are substantial, or at least not as small as typical production economics studies alone might suggest.

It is this policy orientation that leads the research team to search for sound and useful environmental quality indices (EQIs). Such EQIs ought to be capable not only of describing environmental pressure, the state of the environment, and possible responses, which, as discussed in Chapter 2, many existing indicators strive to do, but also be able to provide an indication of the costs of adopting a particular response.

There are two fundamental problems that the proposed EQIs overcome and that distinguish them from others in the literature. First, using cost of remediation (COR) the weighting problem is partially solved; the need to aggregate indicators measured in different units is one of the major obstacles to using EQIs. In addition, the environmental diamond (ED) also tackles the weighting issue by keeping the four subindices separate and, thus, avoids the need to aggregate them. Second, past attempts at EQIs do not present information on environmental change relative to economic gains, which is what environmental elasticity (EE) does. COR is at the heart of the new developments in our project. It defines the amount of consumption a society must give up in the present to restore the environment to a previous state or to a future desirable state. EE is essential to track environmental developments over time in an economic framework and ED is effective for presenting the state of the environment.

Environmental Preferences

The question addressed throughout this volume is how MFIs and governments could use EQIs to make decisions in the economic and political environment outlined above. In more concrete terms, this translates into how policy-makers choose investment projects. Given the new stronger emphasis on development projects related to environment and social issues, three uses for the indices are isolated:

1. to identify the need of developing countries for environmental investments and financing from both internal and external sources;

2. to identify worsening or improving environmental situations; and

3. to assess the present environmental state.

These three uses of environmental indicators can be addressed in the context of the overlapping interests of three stakeholders: developing countries, MFIs, and the global environmental community.

The interests of decision-makers in developing countries and the goals of the MFIs overlap significantly. The information in Table 6.1 comes from a report entitled, *The Environment Program of the Asian Development Bank* (1994) and shows which environmental issues have been identified by selected Asian countries and with what degree of urgency ("3" denotes the highest urgency). Among the ten issues highlighted there is conspicuously no mention of greenhouse gas emissions.

Nepal places urban congestion and pollution at a low level of priority when our fieldwork shows this to be a high priority for national decision-makers in Kathmandu. The Philippines is shown to attach a high priority to land and soil resource problems but a low priority to waste disposal. Land degradation is a huge problem in the Philippines, but waste disposal is a worsening problem. Nevertheless, Table 6.1 represents a useful insight into the priority of environmental issues as identified by selected Asian governments.

Developing countries are actively interested in curtailing environmental impacts that can affect their ability to create wealth in the present. They recognize that economic development contributes to other environmental issues and that they are affected by global environmental issues. For ADB, the historical pattern of environment-centered activities suggests that it has filled a niche that complements and overlaps the activities of developing countries. Its investments reinforce the national goals of developing countries and furthers the interests of the countries in environmental issues for which they do not have resources to address concurrently. It could be said that ADB represents two sets of interests, those of the developing countries and those of the global community, including these developing countries. The three uses of our EQIs underpin these two roles for ADB by revealing: (1) distance from acceptable norms as reflected in the averages in the ED; (2) change from an existing state as indicated by the EE; and (3) the cost of moving backward or forward from an existing state as expressed in the COR.

Proposed Indices: Their Advantages and Disadvantages

We have made a thorough review of significant earlier attempts to develop indices in general, and environmental indices in particular, including UNDP's Human Development Index, the World Bank's Wealth of Nations Index, the Netherlands Government's approach, the World Resources Institute's Environmental Quality Index, and the literature on environmental sustainability. As mentioned earlier, with special attention paid to the strengths and weaknesses of existing indices, we have developed and tested three sets of EQIs:

- cost of remediation,

- environmental elasticity, and

- environmental diamond.

TABLE 6.1

Perceived Priorities of Environmental Problems

	Rising Sea Level	Acid Rain	Waste Disposal	Marine & Coastal Resource Degradation	Industrial Pollution	Urban Congestion and Pollution	Pesticides and Fertilizers	Land Soil Resource Problems	Water Resource Problems	Deforestation
PRC	2	3	1	1	3	3	2	1	1	3
Indonesia	2		1	2	2	3	2	2	3	3
Nepal	n.a.			n.a.		1	1	3	1	3
Pakistan	1		1	1	1	3	2	3	2	2
Philippines	3		1	2	2	3	2	3	2	3

Note: 1 = low priority; 2 = medium priority; 3 = high priority
Source: ADB (1994)

All three indices have been developed on the basis of four principal environmental components: air, water, land, and ecosystem. The justification for choosing only four components is derived statistically from an examination of existing environmental indicators using principal component analysis techniques; they account for the bulk of the variability in the data set.

Each of the three new indices is designed to characterize different aspects of environmental quality. Each has different implications for data requirements. The technical complexities and methods for constructing each set of indices vary. The order in which they are listed above reflects a decreasing level of technical complexity in terms of methodological rigor and data requirements. The environmental diamond and environmental elasticity enjoy the advantage of, respectively, being expressive in characterizing the state of the environment and trends. They are easy to construct, especially if compared to the cost-of-remediation index. The latter provides additional information on the cost of moving the environment from a current state to a more desirable level but requires far more data and is more difficult to calculate. Together, these indices can support the goals of the MFIs and of individual countries to limit and redress environmental damage.

Cost of Remediation

The COR index provides a measure of the cost of moving from the present state of the environment to a more desirable level sometime in the future. The evaluation of the cost to remediate adverse environmental impacts forms the basis for this index. To operationalize the concept of cost of remediation, three steps were followed: (1) existing levels of environmental emissions and degradation were assessed; (2) a set of targets or standards for improvement were established; and (3) the costs of achieving these targets or standards using engineering cost functions were estimated. A strength of the COR index is that it puts environmental and economic outcomes on the single footing of a common metric—monetary values. It indicates the amount of wealth that a society as a whole has to forgo in order to realize its environmental goals. It is an indication of the magnitude of the environmental problems a country faces in monetary terms. The costs of remediation were estimated for each of the four major environmental components: air, water, land, and ecosystem.

Below we suggest three different ways of applying the COR approach to guide MFIs and governments in their efforts to invest in environmental improvement.

Application 1: Identifying Need of DMCs for Environmental Investment and Internal-External Financing

Table 6.2 contains the estimated cost of remediation for selected Asian countries broken down by the four principal environmental sectors. Due to data constraints, the COR of the countries outside our sample were derived

TABLE 6.2

Annualized Cost of Remediation for DMCs ($million in 1990 US Dollars)

Country[1]	Water[2]	Air[3]	Land (erosion)[4]	Land (MSW)[5]	Land (forest)[6]	Land (Total)	Ecosystem[7]	COR(total)	COR/Capita	Rank based on COR/cap	COR/GDP(%)	Rank based on COR/GDP
Bangladesh	13.70	30.34	199.21	99.87	22.38	321.46	52.39	417.89	3.92	1	1.95%	8
Bhutan	0.16	0.35	8.07	0.43	0.00	8.50	24.45	33.45	23.89	16	14.93%	19
Cambodia	0.31	0.69	72.84	5.26	0.00	78.11	30.85	109.97	12.94	9	5.62%	16
Lao PDR	0.26	0.58	34.19	4.27	0.00	38.46	33.18	72.48	17.68	13	7.43%	18
Mongolia	5.91	13.08	2517.62	6.14	249.50	2773.26	13.39	2805.64	1336.02	20	397.63%	20
Myanmar	3.56	7.87	208.42	52.32	0.00	260.74	65.20	337.36	8.11	3	1.23%	4
Nepal	0.78	1.74	93.10	12.43	10.07	115.60	48.90	167.02	8.84	6	5.32%	15
Pakistan	53.97	119.49	522.59	187.21	157.40	867.20	36.09	1076.76	9.58	7	2.57%	12
Sri Lanka	3.50	7.76	46.84	18.28	0.00	65.12	147.86	224.24	13.19	10	2.54%	11
Vietnam	12.97	28.71	134.56	66.19	0.00	200.75	251.48	493.91	7.45	2	7.30%	17
PRC	1430.13	3166.07	9939.10	1648.85	1070.02	12657.97	299.79	17553.96	15.48	12	4.88%	14
India	418.97	927.53	3630.67	1092.80	159.51	4882.97	852.23	7081.70	8.34	4	2.89%	13
Indonesia	100.10	221.61	675.93	277.99	0.00	953.92	296.30	1571.93	8.82	5	1.43%	7
P. New Guinea	1.73	3.82	9.61	3.33	0.00	12.94	70.44	88.92	22.80	15	2.39%	10
Philippines	39.59	87.65	184.76	134.91	0.00	319.67	160.67	607.57	9.88	8	1.40%	6
Thailand	67.00	148.32	477.85	68.03	11.75	557.63	47.73	820.68	14.71	11	0.83%	3
Fiji	0.52	1.16	6.03	1.45	0.00	7.48	20.37	29.53	39.69	19	1.97%	9
Korea, Rep. of	199.84	442.40	43.82	159.42	0.00	203.24	61.70	907.18	21.20	14	0.33%	2
Malaysia	43.15	95.52	98.22	40.55	0.00	138.78	329.48	606.93	33.91	17	1.32%	5
Singapore	24.42	54.07	0.02	14.40	0.23	14.65	14.55	107.70	35.90	18	0.24%	1
Total	2420.58	5358.76	18903.45	3894.143	1680.85	24478.44	2857.05	35114.83				

TABLE 6.2 (notes)

1. Data for Afghanistan, Maldives, South Pacific (including Marshall Islands), Hong Kong, and Taipei, China are incomplete or unavailable.

2. Cost data based on 90% water pollution reduction (COD and some heavy metals) for PRC are used and the total CORs of all the DMCs are assumed proportional to their total commercial energy consumption.

3. Cost data based on 90% air pollution reduction (TSP and sulphur) for PRC are used and the CORs for all the DMCs are assumed proportional to their total commercial energy consumption.

4. Unit cost data per ha. are derived from China and total area subject to erosion for all the DMCs is estimated assuming it is proportional to their total cropped and pasture areas. We assume that 70% eroded area will be controlled to conform to the PRC standard, i.e., 70–95% erosion reduction, in 10 years.

5. A fixed waste generation rate, 0.2 t per capita per year, and fixed costs for waste collection and waste management, $20/t for collection, and $2/t for sanitary landfill, are assumed for all DMCs. Only urban municipal solid wastes (MSW) are considered which do not include rural and industrial wastes.

6. PRC data on unit cost for tree plantation per ha., i.e., $179 per ha., is adopted and an universal target of 20% forest coverage rate is assumed for all DMCs. If a country's forest coverage exceeds 20%, no further cost is incurred.

7. Indonesia unit costs on building and running national parks and targets for the period 1991–2000 are used for all DMCs assuming the cost is proportional to the total number of species considered threatened, including mammals, birds, reptiles, amphibians, higher plants, and fish.

using the cost data for PRC and Indonesia based on a series of assumptions, given in the footnotes of Table 6.2. These estimates were based upon a specific set of environmental targets and for a specific time frame. For example, for air and water, we assumed that 90 percent reduction of the early-1990s total emission levels of the countries will be achieved within a ten-year period. For land, three components were included: erosion control, afforestation and solid waste management. For erosion control, the PRC unit cost was adopted and extrapolated to other countries assuming that 70 percent eroded area will be controlled to achieve 70–95 percent erosion reduction within a ten-year period. For afforestation, the objective was set to achieve 20 percent forest coverage rate within ten years for all countries. For solid waste management, we adopted the World Bank estimates of solid waste generation rate for developing countries, 0.2t/capita/year, and unit costs for waste collection and sanitary landfill, $20/t for waste collection and $2/t for sanitary landfill. The target for solid waste management was set so that all urban municipal solid waste (not including industrial and agricultural wastes) would be collected and landfilled. For the ecosystem component, we employed the Indonesian cost data and its ten-year target for building and operating national parks. The Indonesian estimates were then extrapolated to other countries proportional to the total number of species considered threatened in those countries. Due to lack of indigenous data, especially cost data, for most of the countries and the hypothetical nature of the assumptions used in the estimation, it is believed that these cost estimates are no more than a first approximation. More accurate estimates require in-depth country studies.

In Table 6.2, the term "annualized cost" is used because some of the costs are incurred unevenly during the ten-year period. For example, capital costs are typically up-front costs, and operation-and-maintenance (O&M) costs are incurred throughout the period. The annualized costs are the annual averages of the two types of costs for the entire period.

Table 6.2 indicates the COR breakdown across different environmental sectors and across different countries. Across the sectors, an alarming phenomenon is that, based on the assumption used, the "green" side of environmental degradation i.e., land and ecosystem, accounts for a much larger percentage of the total CORs required for virtually all countries. This forms a drastic contrast to the conventional thinking and investment pattern that have been primarily brown side-oriented i.e., water and air pollution control. The sectoral breakdown of the cost of remediation is helpful in allocating funds in different environmental sectors to achieve maximum returns. Across different countries, among those that participated in this study, PRC has the highest annualized COR of roughly $17.6 billion, followed by Indonesia with a total of approximately $1.6 billion. Nepal has the lowest COR of $0.17 billion. This order is to be expected due to the size difference of the countries. Table 6.2 also includes annualized COR per capita, annualized COR as a percentage of total GDP, and the country rankings based on these two measures.

Figure 6.1 provides a bar chart showing the distribution of annualized COR as a percentage in the total GDP across different countries. It appears that the COR/GDP ratio of a country can serve as an effective indicator for its priority need for external financial assistance. It also bears major implications for resource allocations within a country. For example, PRC currently spends approximately 0.7 percent of its total GDP on "environmental expenditure." This study indicates that this ratio for PRC should be raised to 4.8 percent. The Philippines currently spends up to 0.2 percent of total GDP on the environment while this study shows that the ratio required is 1.4 percent. It should be stressed that figures for actual environmental spending are highly variable depending on which expenditures are classified as "environmental." However, it is quite clear that both Philippines and PRC need a significant boost of their ratios of environmental expenditure in their total GDP. In addition, both countries, probably also need some financial assistance from MFIs in order to meet the environmental targets, particularly the PRC for which raising the COR/GDP ratio to 4.88 percent is quite unlikely in the short term.

The total economic wealth of a country inevitably affects how much the country can afford to spend on the environment without seriously compromising its economic welfare. Figure 6.2 shows the percentage of environmental expenditure as percentage of total GDP for several OECD countries for the period between 1990 and 1992. Note that these estimates include only the costs for air, water, and solid wastes and do not include costs for ecosystem protection. For the countries in Figure 6.2, the total environmental expenditure exceeds 1.2 percent, with Netherlands, Switzerland, and US spending approximately 1.9 percent of total GDP on environmental maintenance. We can probably assume that most of the countries in Asia can afford to allocate

FIGURE 6.1

Annualized COR as a Percentage of GDP

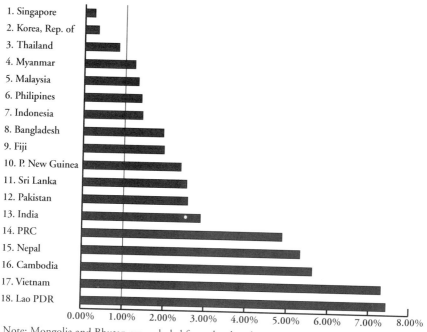

Note: Mongolia and Bhutan are excluded from the chart because their large CORs would skew the picture.

1 percent of total GDP on such an expenditure. We indicate this 1 percent cutoff value with a vertical line in Figure 6.1. The difference between this and the estimated required percentage represents the deficit/surplus of the environmental expenditure for a country.

In general, richer countries such as Republic of Korea, Singapore and, to a lesser extent, Thailand are characterized by very low COR/GDP ratios, indicating that these countries can essentially "buy" their own environmental cleanup if they choose to do so. In contrast, in order to maintain an acceptable environment, all other countries require certain amounts of external financial assistance to combat their environmental problems, with those countries higher in the chart probably requiring more assistance. Two countries, Mongolia and Bhutan, have been excluded from Figure 6.1 because their large COR values would skew the analysis. According to Table 6.2, Bhutan would have to allocate approximately 15 percent of its total GDP for environmental improvements—a scenario clearly impossible to realize. In the most extreme situation, Mongolia, with a very small population but vast territory, would require about 400 percent of its annual GDP to combat its environmental problems, mainly land degradation and low forest cover. However, these two countries are

FIGURE 6.2
Environmental Expenditure of Selected OECD Countries

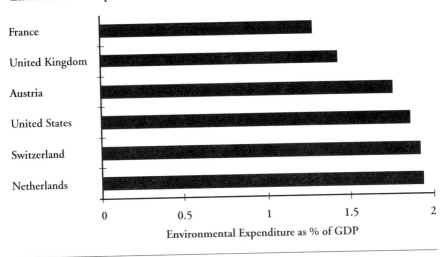

demographically and ecologically "unique" in the sense that Bhutan is a mountainous country and Mongolia is characterized by dry and cold weather, and both are characterized by extremely small populations relative to size of the ecosystem. Some of the environmental targets e.g., 20 percent forest coverage rate for all countries, assumed for calculating the COR may have been too unrealistic. This could explain the unusual large COR/GDP ratios for these two countries.

Below we use the COR/GDP ratio to suggest means of prioritizing investments based on the relationship between the overall COR required and the "maximum affordable" level of COR, i.e., 1 percent is assumed for all the countries in the region. It must be stressed that the discussion below is not meant to tell Asian countries what they need, but rather the order of magnitude of resources needed if they decide to clean up their environment to achieve the common standard assumed in this study over a ten-year period.

Countries with High Demand for Financial Assistance (COR/GDP: > 4.5 percent)

This group comprises Cambodia, PRC, Lao PDR, Mongolia, Nepal, and Vietnam. With the exception of Nepal, these countries are in a transition period from centrally-planned economies to market economies. They are experiencing rapid economic expansion which is generally associated with severe environmental degradation. In terms of environmental expenditure as a percentage of GDP, these countries have the greatest need for environmental investment. Roughly 5 percent or more of the GDP is required for environmental cleanup for these countries to achieve a balance between economic growth and environmental assimilation.

Countries with Medium Demand for Financial Assistance
(COR/GDP: 2–4.5 percent)

This group consists of India, Pakistan, Papua New Guinea, and Sri Lanka. The economic growth rates of this group are somewhat lower than those countries in the above category. This group has the highest poverty incidence in Asia. Both industrial pollution and the pollution associated with abject poverty or lack of development—such as polluted drinking water, indoor air pollution, and land degradation—are severe. These countries need to develop their economies in order to remediate or to resolve poverty-related environmental degradation, for which they require heavy investment. They also require a significant amount of external financing for environmental and economic improvement.

Countries with Low Demand for Financial Assistance
(COR/GDP: 1–2 percent)

This group consists of Bangladesh, Fiji, Indonesia, Malaysia, Myanmar, and Philippines. With a few exceptions, these countries have traditionally received much financial assistance from MFIs. Some, such as Malaysia, are increasingly capable of paying for their own environmental cleanup.

Countries with Diminishing Demand for Financial Assistance
(COR/GDP: < 1 percent)

Republic of Korea, Singapore, and Thailand have the lowest COR as a percentage of GDP (0.33 percent, 0.26 percent, and 0.83 percent, respectively) and therefore seem to be in a situation where they are capable of meeting their own costs of environmental remediation.

Grouping countries based on their needs for financial assistance clearly has strong policy implications for MFIs in compiling their environmental investment portfolios across different countries. Although better estimates can only be available through individual country studies, the current rough estimates indicate a pattern which suggests that MFIs should gradually shift resource flows from the more economically maturing economies to those newly emerging economies where environmental problems are increasing faster than resources allocated to environmental remediation.

Application 2: Investments in Environmental Remediation Across Different Sectors—What Will $100 Million Buy?

Another innovative way of applying COR index is to compare what can be bought with a fixed amount of investment, say $100 million, in different environmental and infrastructure sectors. For instance, in government decision-making about infrastructure investments there is often little to guide the policy-makers in making intersectoral allocations. Most decisions are made and analyzed sector by sector and most sector planners have a good sense of the relative worth of investments in their sectors. One good way of exposing the decision-making process to the ambiguities of infrastructure investments in various sectors is to tabulate how much "infrastructure" can be bought for a given amount of money. In Table 6.3 we compare what $100 million can buy in terms of various infrastructure investments and environmental improvements. One can now ask questions at the margin, "Would you rather have 80 rural hospitals or reduce SO_2 emissions by 2.7 million tons?" "Are 5 million home electrical connections preferable to 800,000 hectares of reforested land?"

Application 3: Financial Affordability of Environmental Standards—Are They Feasible?

Many developing countries have adapted their environmental standards from developed countries such as the US with little understanding of the capacity needed to implement them. Overly hefty standards incapable of being enforced tend to generate widespread disregard of the laws and result in added pollution. The COR approach can be used to estimate the costs of complying with a set of newly proposed standards or some existing standard. We refer to this type of cost as the "cost of compliance." For example, we have estimated earlier (Table 6.3) that the annualized cost of controlling erosion in PRC to achieve

T A B L E   6 . 3

What Can Be Bought for $100 Million?

Items	Contents
Environmental Goods	
SO₂ Reduction	2,796,800 tons
Particulate Reduction (Industrial Boilers)	7,087,400 tons
COD Reduction	601,000 tons
Afforestation	872,600 hectares
Soil Erosion Control	1,796,200 hectares
Infrastructure Investments	
Roads	
National Highways	170 kilometers
Rural Roads	5,600 kilometers
Irrigation	
Shallow Tubewells	688,500 hectares
Surface Irrigation	9,300 hectares
Electrification (Rural Connection)	5,000,000 houses
Schools (Four-Room Tin Shed)	9,700 schools
Rural Health Complex	80 hospitals

Source: Estimation of environmental goods is based on PRC's data, others from Government of Bangladesh, *Crop Agriculture Development: Trends, Issues, and Opportunities*, Dhaka: Ministry of Agriculture, Sector Monitoring Unit and Policy Planning Branch, January, 1994.

70–95 percent reduction is roughly $9.9 billion, accounting for 2.76 percent of China's total annual GDP in 1990. This is likely to be considered unfeasible by central planners who may opt for a more relaxed target which still results in significant improvement in soil quality. In contrast, Table 6.2 indicates that the annualized cost of reducing China's air emissions of TSP and sulfur is $3.17 billion, amounting to a moderate 0.88 percent of total GDP. This seems to be a much more realistic goal. The cost of compliance can be used to assess many other situations such as estimating the cost of installing catalytic converters if such a requirement is put into place, or the cost of mandatory solid waste collection and disposal by municipalities.

Table 6.4 is the major planned environmental targets for the ninth five-year plan period (1995–2000) for PRC (NEPA 1996). Bear in mind that these targets are based on the assumption that the economy is going to grow at roughly 8–10% annually for the period. The table shows that despite lack of benefit estimates, governments do need to set up environmental targets and try to implement them. The cost of remediation can be a very useful tool to assess the feasibility and implementability of these targets.

Environmental Elasticity

The second of the three EQIs is environmental elasticity (EE). It is used to monitor environmental trends and correlate changes in the environment with changes in the economy. EE is defined as the following ratio:

aggregate environmental *change* / aggregate economic *change*.

The numerator is defined as aggregate percent change of several selected environmental indicators over a particular time period. The denominator is defined as the percentage change of one or several selected economic indicators, e.g., per capita GDP, over the same time period. When multiple indicators are employed for numerator or denominator, the aggregation is normally done through a weighting scheme—equal or unequal weighting.

As demonstrated in Chapters 3 and 5, EE can be used to rank Asian countries. Based on the data presented in Chapter 5, three countries: Lao PDR, Myanmar, and Sri Lanka, appear to be in an ideal situation, all having positive EE. Analysis shows they are all characterized by positive economic growth and positive environmental change. We characterize this group as "Group A: Sustainable." All the other countries have negative elasticity values and are characterized as having positive economic growth and negative environmental change, suggesting that economic growth in these countries has been accompanied by negative changes in environmental quality. However, with the exception of Vietnam, all other countries have negative elasticity values with absolute values of less than one, indicating that although their environment deteriorates as their economy grows, the deterioration rates appear to be slower

TABLE 6.4

Major Environmental Targets for the Ninth Five-Year Plan Period for PRC

	1995	2000
Soot Emission ('000 tonnes)	7,440	17,500
Industrial Dust Discharge ('000 tonnes)	17,310	17,000
Sulphur Dioxide Emission ('000 tonnes)	23,700	24,600
Chemical Oxygen Demand (COD) ('000 tonnes)	22,330	22,000
Oil Pollutants Discharge (tonne)	84,370	83,100
Cyanide Discharge (tonne)	3,495	3,270
Arsenic Discharge (tonne)	1,446	1,376
Mercury Discharge (tonne)	27	26
Lead Discharge (tonne)	1700	1670
Cadmium Discharge (tonne)	285	270
Hexivalent Chromium Discharge	670	618
Industrial Solid Waste Generation ('000 tonnes)	61,700	59,950
Wastewater Discharge (billion tonnes)	35.6*	48
Industrial Wastewater Discharge (billion tonnes)	22.25*	30
Treatment Rate for Industrial Wastewater (%)	76.8*	74
Treatment Rate for Urban Sewage (%)	19	25
Treatment Rate for Industrial Air Emissions (%)	74	80
Rate of Recycling, Reuse and Recovery of Industrial Solid Waste (%)	40	45
Decontamination Rate of Urban Refuse (%)	43	50
Forest Cover (%)	13.92	15.5
Total National Conservation Area ('000 ha.)	71,850	100,000

* These do not cover town and township industries.

Source: NEPA, 1996

than the growth rates of their economies. We characterize this group as "Group B: Weakly Sustainable." Vietnam has a value of -1.32, larger than one in absolute value, indicating that its 1 percent GDP growth may be achieved at the expense of a more than 1 percent decrease of environment aggregate. We classify it as "Group C: Unsustainable."

Some countries may jump from one quadrant to another over different time periods and economic policy changes can affect the courses of the development. Although the top three countries, Lao PDR, Myanmar, and Sri Lanka, are shown to be on a sustainable course for the time period, this pattern may change in the future when their economic growth accelerates, if such growth is without the benefit of sound environmental policies. As a most unusual case, many former Soviet republics in central Asia may be characterized as experiencing economic decline concurrent with environmental improvement. This is due in part to drastic economic dislocation, particularly industrial decline, which is also accompanied by a massive decrease of industrial emissions and noticeable improvement in air and water quality. Inasmuch as environmental improvement has been achieved at the expense of an already low economic status, this, clearly, is not a sustainable scenario.

The principal merit of environmental elasticity is its dynamic nature. It uses data for two points in time to compute the change over corresponding periods for the environmental aggregate in the numerator and the economic aggregate in the denominator. The weights used in the numerator to generate the aggregated indices could reflect the urgency with which a region or nation needs to confront specific environmental stresses.

Environmental Diamond

The last measure formulated by the study, the Environmental Diamond (ED), shows graphically the state of the environment of a country or a city along each of the four statistically-derived principal components, namely, air, water, land, and ecosystem. The major contribution of the ED is that it is integrative in nature. It reveals a general picture without concealing the multiple dimensions of environmental quality by presenting the picture relative to norms or average values of the four environmental components. It partially eliminates the need to aggregate different subindices to form a single index since it allows an observer to look simultaneously at the four components.

EDs are easy to construct, keep individual components separate, and graphically present the results of single country or regional analysis in a simple format for cross-country or cross-region comparison. EDs are flexible in terms of the types of subindices used to construct the four corners of the diamond. In Chapters 3 and 5, we created three sets of EDs using different variables: two using conventional environmental indicators such as air emissions and water pollutant concentrations, and one using the cost of remediation index.

The four subindices that constitute the four corners of an environmental diamond can also be aggregated to derive an overall index indicating the state of the environment of a country. Chapter 5 ranked the countries using the "root-mean-square" aggregation method which will be discussed again in the section below on cross-country comparison of environment-economic performance.

Cross-Country Comparison of Overall Economic-Environmental Performance

Although each of the three indices can be used separately, as demonstrated in previous chapters, they may be best used in concert. In the following discussion all three indices are applied in conjunction with other existing social, economic and environmental indicators to conduct a preliminary comparison of overall environmental-economic performance for selected Asian countries (Table 6.5). It must be cautioned that this type of assessment is broad in nature and sometimes "subjective." It is not the intention of this group of authors to be controversial, but rather to illustrate.

The two existing indices employed here are GDP growth rate and UNDP's Human Development Index (HDI). HDI takes into account four socioeconomic indicators including per capita GDP, literacy rate, school enrollment, and life expectancy at birth. We also considered using the World Bank's Wealth of Nations Index in our cross-country comparisons, but opted against it. The Wealth of Nations Index is an effort to measure the total stock of a country including environmental and human resources, all in terms of monetary values. However, our statistical analysis for 20 Asian developing countries shows that the rank correlation between per capita GDP—a long-existing economic indicator which has been widely used to characterize a country's economic development—and the Wealth of Nations Index is 0.92, (the rank correlation would be one if the rankings of the countries based on two indices match completely). This suggests that Wealth of Nations Index does not provide much more new information than per capita GDP. As a comparison, the rank correlation between per capita GDP and per capita COR estimates for the same Asian countries is -0.49, much less significant. This indicates that COR as an environmental quality index provides a different perspective from that offered by per capita GDP.

The following patterns may be identified from Table 6.5. First, South Asian countries including Bangladesh, India, Nepal, Pakistan, and Sri Lanka in general score favorably based on the ED, indicating that the state of the environment does not deviate significantly from the norm for all countries in the region. Their COR/GDP ratios are also not very high, ranging from 2-3 percent with the exception of Nepal. The environmental trend with respect to economic growth varies dramatically among the group. India and Sri Lanka seem to indicate a favorable trend in which the environment either improves or deteriorates slightly as the economy grows. The main problem facing the region is lack of development characterized by relatively low HDI and GDP growth rates, much lower than those in Southeast and East Asian countries. Environmental problems associated with underdevelopment, such as lack of access to safe drinking water, may be more severe than environmental problems associated with industrialization and agricultural activities such as energy consumption/air emissions and toxicity from extremes in fertilizer and pesticide use.

Among the ASEAN countries, the Philippines has the best state of the environment based on comparative norms. Indonesia and Thailand, although ranking lower in terms of a regional environmental standard, show relatively low COR/GDP ratios due to their relatively high GDP. Compared to South Asian countries, with the exception of the Philippines, the economic growth rates are relatively high. All three countries score high points on HDI. For this group, the EE values show that environment deteriorated as their economies

Overall Comparison of Environmental-Economic Performance

DMC	COR/GDP	EE (%)	ED (%)	GDP Growth Rate (%)	HDI	Qualitative Assessment
Bangladesh	1.90	-0.65	81	4.2	0.365	Bangladesh has a better-than-average state of the environment, and fairly low COR as a percentage of GDP. Its environment deteriorates quickly relative to its slow economic growth. Its HDI is very low. The country, therefore, may need moderate investment in environmental improvement but significant investment in socioeconomic development.
India	2.89	-0.10	74	5.2	0.436	India has a better-than-average state of the environment, and moderate COR as a percentage of GDP. Although its environment appears to deteriorate, the deterioration rate is very slow compared to its economic growth rate. Its HDI is relatively low. The country should pursue a well-balanced policy that improves both the economy and environment. India requires massive amounts of external financing in environmental improvement due to its sheer size and medium COR/GDP ratio.
Indonesia	1.40	-0.35	113	5.8	0.64	Indonesia has a slightly worse-than-average state of the environment, and low COR as a percentage of GDP. Its environmental deterioration rate is moderate compared to its economic growth rate. Its HDI is relatively high. The country should pursue a well-balanced policy that improves both the economy and environment. Most of the financing for improving the environment should be self-generated due to its relatively low COR/GDP ratio.
Lao PDR	7.43	0.08	115	4.8	0.340	Lao PDR has a worse-than-average state of the environment, but a very high COR as a percentage of GDP due to its relatively low GDP. However, an encouraging observation is that its environment appears to be improving as its economy grows, though the economic growth rate is relatively low. Its HDI is also very low. All these suggest that the country should make socioeconomic development a priority, while maintaining its positive environmental trend. It will require significant amounts of external financial assistance for environmental improvement due to its high COR/GDP ratio.
Mongolia	397.63	-0.69	146	3.8	0.578	Mongolia has a much worse-than-average state of the environment, and very high COR as a percentage of GDP largely due to its poor land quality. Its environmental deterioration rate is high compared to its economic growth rate, which is among the lowest in the group. Its HDI is reasonably high. The country should focus on economic development. It requires a large amount of external finance for environmental improvement due to its very large COR/GDP ratio.
Myanmar	1.2	2.32	114	0.8	0.450	Myanmar has a worse-than-average state of the environment, and very low COR as a percentage of GDP. In addition, its environment seems to improve as the economy grows. However, its economic growth rate is the lowest among the 16 countries. Its HDI is about the average. The country should focus on economic and social development.

TABLE 6.5 (continued)

DMC	COR/GDP	EE (%)	ED (%)	GDP Growth Rate (%)	HDI	Qualitative Assessment
Nepal	5.32	-0.83	109%	5.0	0.332	Nepal has a slightly worse-than-average state of the environment. However, its COR as a percentage of GDP is high due to its low GDP. Its environmental deterioration rate is high compared to its economic growth rate, which is slightly lower than the group average. Its HDI is low. The country faces the challenge of both economic development and reversing the negative environmental trend; a substantial amount of external financial assistance is required due to its high COR/GDP ratio.
Pakistan	2.57	-0.53	111	6.0	0.442	Pakistan seems to be at the average in almost every measure. It has a slightly worse-than-average state of the environment, with about average COR as a percentage of GDP. Its environmental deterioration rate is relatively high compared to its economic growth rate, which is about the group average. Its HDI is also at the average. The country should pursue a balanced development policy which improves both economy and environment. It requires a significant amount of external financial assistance due to its medium COR/GDP ratio and its relatively large population size.
Philippines	1.40	-0.44	70	1.4	0.666	Philippines has the best state of the environment with a reasonably low COR as a percentage of GDP. Its environmental deterioration rate is high compared to its economic growth rate, which is the second lowest in the group. Its HDI is relatively high. The country is currently recovering from a period of slow economic growth. However, such economic recovery must be accompanied by sound environmental policies to reverse the current negative environmental trend. The financing of the environmental clean-up should be largely self-generated due to its relatively low COR/GDP ratio.
PNG	2.39	-0.09	111	3.1	0.504	Papua New Guinea has a worse-than-average state of the environment and about average COR as a percentage of GDP. Its environment is more or less stabilized, though its economic growth is relatively low. Its HDI is about average. The country faces the challenge of both economic development and environmental conservation, and it requires some external financial assistance for environmental improvement due to its medium COR/GDP ratio.
PRC	4.88	-0.21	159	9.6	0.609	PRC has a much worse-than-average state of the environment and a very high COR as a percentage of GDP. However, an encouraging observation is that the economy is growing at the highest speed among the 16 countries and its environmental deterioration seems to have slowed down. Its HDI is relatively high. The country faces tremendous environmental challenges in the face of fast economic expansion and it requires massive external financial assistance for environmental cleanup due to its sheer size and large COR/GDP ratio.

DMC	COR/GDP	EE (%)	ED (%)	GDP Growth Rate (%)	HDI	Qualitative Assessment
Korea, Rep. of	0.33	-0.32	377	9.1	0.886	The Republic of Korea scores very low points in terms of the state of the environment due to its high per capita energy consumption and fertilizer use. However, its COR as a percentage of GDP is very low due to its high GDP. Its environmental deterioration rate is moderate compared to its very high economic growth rate. Its HDI is very high. Although it faces tremendous environmental challenges, the country requires little external financial assistance for environmental improvement due to its low COR/GDP ratio.
Singapore	0.24	-0.28	670	6.9	0.881	Singapore also scores very low points in terms of the state of the environment due to its high per capita energy consumption and fertilizer use. However, its COR as a percentage of GDP is very low due to its high GDP. Its environmental deterioration rate is moderate compared to its economic growth rate. The country requires little external financial assistance for environmental improvement due to its low COR/GDP ratio.
Sri Lanka	2.54	0.38	89	4.0	0.698	Sri Lanka has a better than average state of the environment with an average COR as a percentage of GDP. The most encouraging observation is that its environment appears to improve as its economy grows. Its HDI is quite high. The main challenge that the country faces is to accelerates economic growth while maintaining the positive environmental trend through sound development policies. Some external financial assistance is required due to its medium COR/GDP ratio.
Thailand	0.83	-0.99	103	8.2	0.832	Thailand has an about average state of the environment and relatively low COR as a percentage of GDP. The country enjoys a very high economic growth rate. However, an alarming observation is that its rate of environmental deterioration is almost as high as its rate of economic growth. Its HDI is very high. The country must address its environmental problems in its economic development and it can achieve that with little external financial assistance due to its low COR/GDP ratio.
Vietnam	7.30	-1.32	108	7.1	—	Vietnam has a slightly worse-than-average state of the environment. However, its COR as a percentage of GDP is high due to its low GDP. Its environmental deterioration rate compared to its economic growth rate is the highest and is the only country in the group with an environmental deterioration rate higher than its economic growth rate. The country faces tremendous environmental challenges as its economy enters a high-growth era. It requires a significant amount of external financial assistance for environmental improvement due to its large COR/GDP ratio.

grew and the rate for Thailand was particularly fast. In their long-term development strategies, these countries must pay special attention to the deteriorating environmental trend as economies continue to grow rapidly. A major environmental issue is increased energy consumption and associated urban air pollution.

The former centrally planned economies including PRC, Lao PDR, Mongolia, and Vietnam, form the third group. All are experiencing a transition from planned economies to market economies. This group is characterized by high or very high COR/GDP ratios and relatively poor state of the environment. PRC, for example, shows particularly bad air and land quality. The environment in these countries generally deteriorated as their economies grew. Vietnam appears to suffer most in this regard—the environmental deterioration rate is higher than the economic growth rate, a seemingly unsustainable situation. As the economic growth rates within the group accelerate, special attention in terms of resource allocation for environmental remediation will be required by governments and MFIs. Both sound environmental policies and investments are needed to avoid environmental catastrophe and to maintain minimum environmental quality standards.

The two newly industrialized countries, a group comprising the Republic of Korea and Singapore, appear to be in a different economic development and technological level from others analyzed by the study. Although they receive unfavorable scores based on regional norms set by the environmental diamonds, this is largely due to their high per capita energy consumption. Their level of technology and economic wealth allow them to control emissions and other adverse environmental impacts of economic activities more effectively. Therefore, a cautionary note should be introduced regarding the strict interpretation of the environmental diamonds. In addition, as expected, both countries have very low COR/GDP ratio due to their large GDP values, and relatively high GDP growth rates and HDI values.

What Have We Learned and Where Do We Go From Here?

Asia is currently the fastest expanding region economically in the world and economists have predicted that it is likely to remain so in the foreseeable future. However, few can predict with confidence the magnitude of the environmental changes associated with such enormous economic expansion during the next 20 to 50 years. The pace of economic growth demands unyielding efforts by governments and multilateral financial institutions to monitor environmental change relative to economic growth. Failure to do this will result in a loss in real economic terms, as has been demonstrated in this study through COR estimates of the environmental damages caused by past environmental negligence and poor planning, or even irrecoverable environmental catastrophe. In Table 6.2, we estimated that at least $35 billion is needed every year for Asian countries to bring their environmental quality up to a more acceptable level and to maintain the environment at that level. With proper environmental planning and management, this money could have been conserved wholly or in part, and better spent elsewhere. The only way to ensure that the cost figures are within reach or to avoid potential catastrophe is to start to commit more resources for environmental remediation, backed by a consistent and comprehensive monitoring program. The three sets of environmental quality indices developed in this study, cost of remediation, environmental elasticity, and environmental diamond, provide useful tools to support the environmental monitoring goals of multilateral financial institutions and individual governments.

What distinguishes the EQIs developed in this study from others is that the new indices overcome several fundamental problems of index construction. First, with the ED and COR, we partially eliminate the need to aggregate individual indicators and, when we do have to aggregate using the COR method, we solve the weighting problem because the COR is a cardinal measure. The COR also links the magnitude of the environmental problems facing a country directly to investment decision-making by expressing it in monetary values. Second, past attempts at developing EQIs do not present information on environmental change relative to economic gains, an aspect accommodated within the concept of environmental elasticity. The environmental elasticity underscores the importance of gathering time-series data about environmental changes, which are currently lacking or inadequate. The complementary nature of the three indices dictates that they may be most effective when used together.

The principal merit of EE is its dynamic nature. It uses data for two points in time to compute the change over that period of both the environmental aggregate in the numerator and the economic aggregate in the denominator. The major contribution of ED is that it is integrative in nature. ED reveals a general picture without concealing the multiple dimension of environmental quality by presenting the picture relative to norms or average values on the four environmental factors of air quality, water quality, land resources, and ecosystem. ED is also visually appealing and easy to construct.

The concept of COR is not only theoretically sound but also bears very important policy implications. It should be stressed, however, that heterogeneity in information availability across different countries and sectors will always exist. There are sectors like wastewater treatment, for which much information on COR exists and other sectors, such as preserving ecosystem biodiversity, for which very little COR information exists. In addition, COR is typically an emission-based approach in the cases of air and water pollution abatement. That this can be misleading is given by the example of the ambient air pollution problem in Manila and Kathmandu. Though Kathmandu is a much smaller city than Manila and there are fewer vehicles, the air pollution problem is far more serious. Both cities must address the problem of the ambient quality of the air, but the policy-makers in Kathmandu face a more urgent crisis, or higher COR, because their city is in a valley that traps pollution. Situated on Manila Bay, Manila benefits from wind patterns that carry the pollutants further. This requires decision-makers to incorporate other factors such as wind patterns exogenously, when determining a desirable emission control level. This is due to the fact that many air quality standards should be set based upon the exposure or ambient air quality and then "rolled-back" to set emission standards. In the case of Kathmandu, they may need to increase the emission control level in order to achieve the same ambient air quality as in Manila.

Another limitation of COR lies in the fact that it does not directly address the benefits of environmental remediation. The estimation of benefits is compounded by many factors. There is a great deal of disagreement about the magnitude of the environmental damages that are incurred by a single new project or an ongoing program of raising living standards in a given country. For this reason, we have chosen in our work to use standards as proxies for benefits (or damage avoided).

In summary, we believe that the approaches used in this study would significantly expand EQIs and help the development community pursue its goal of environmentally sustainable development. The salient features of the three indices are:

- COR, EE, and ED enable comparison of environmental changes with economic changes on the same or similar terms.

- They enable comparison among various media (e.g., air, water, land, and ecosystem). We can determine how much money is theoretically needed to bring each of the different components of environmental deterioration to a certain set of standards.

- They estimate an upper bound of the cost of remediating for comparison with more innovative approaches. (The COR approach requires the use of the cheapest alternative to meet standards—source changes, process redesign, end-of-pipe treatment or remediation to estimate the COR; however, if better ways to achieve compliance to well-set standards are considered, for example, tradeable permits, this could be reflected in subsequent estimations of COR.)

- COR avoids the weighting problem that plagues most EQIs.

- The COR subcomponents would help determine environmental investment strategies by helping to maximize the environmental improvement (determined by COR subcomponent costs) that could be achieved for a given amount of investment.

- An interesting spin-off effect would be the setting of more realistic standards by countries. These standards could vary spatially, temporally and set by pollutant, sector or source and be based on emission, ambient, or performance criteria to reflect the inherent triage in environmental control in various media and with economic development and to reflect the impact of the different kinds of pollution. The standards would be set primarily to incorporate health risks or the risks to ecosystems. Note that these standards could be set at different levels of conceptual aggregation (e.g., project level, sectoral level, national level).

- They would enable spatial and dynamic comparisons—across countries or among various spatial regions (or sectors) within a country (or economy), and also over time—this would reflect any change in the environment, standards, economy or technological or policy innovations that affects the ease of compliance. This would enable these indicators to be used for ranking or prioritization purposes.

- These new indices could be used for decision-making purposes—such as environmental portfolio management, prioritization of pollution types, identifying target sectors, identifying "win-win" or other costless or low-cost solutions, assessing the utility of existing technological and policy options and identifying the need for future developments in these areas.

- By focusing on the costs of control, the computation of COR has been made much easier than for other EQIs that usually require much more extensive monitoring, modeling, weighting or controversial damage/benefit valuation. Well-set standards would reflect the environmental benefits or losses by dictating the degree of cleanup required.

- The new indicators attempt to capture the environmental pressures, states and responses in a unitary measure.

- Depending on the use, these indices could be developed at different levels of accuracy—from back-of-the-envelope computations for getting rough estimates for prioritization, to more detailed analyses for project appraisal.

- Their use would be enhanced with any rational set of traditional EQIs.

- The integrating nature of these indices is ideally suited to operationalize the fuzzy concept of sustainable development.

This study is also subject to a number of limitations:

- By focusing on only six Asian countries, this study should be viewed as a pilot effort in developing and testing the new methodologies for index development, rather than as all-inclusive index computation for all the Asian countries. Although extrapolations are made for other Asian countries using the data collected in these six countries, these estimates are meant to provide an illustration of the potential usefulness of the new indices. We caution overstatement of the significance of the specific values of these indices. More accurate estimates for each country call for individual country studies.

- Despite our special attention paid to least-cost technologies in our COR estimation, the estimates contained in this study are not necessarily least-cost estimates. The intent of least-cost estimation is further complicated by the fact that the least-cost technologies are changing rapidly over time as new technologies are being developed.

- Much of this book is devoted to cost estimation. We argue in Chapter 3 that when environmental standards used in the COR estimation are considered optimal, the COR estimates represent the optimal benefits that society has to forgo in order to achieve the standards. Nonetheless, these cost estimates are not benefit estimates. In other words, the COR index is not based upon economic preference theory. Furthermore, the assumption of near-optimal environmental standards is rarely met, particularly in developing countries that often adopt the standards of developed countries such as the US. While our cost estimates rely on "optimal" standards, to determine whether or not the standards are optimal require both benefit and cost estimates.

- Because of the fact that it is not based upon economic preference theory, the COR approach does not answer the question of where MFIs should invest; to do so would require an estimation of the benefits of the investment. Rather, COR strives to determine how much assistance is needed if MFIs decide to invest in a particular country and a particular sector.

- This study focuses on index development primarily at regional and national levels, rather than at the project level. However, in some cases, the cost functions collected and developed in this study (Appendix 2) may be used to derive the first approximation of the costs for specific projects such as a sulfur-removing facility or a waste management facility.

The methodological development and testing, as one of the objectives of this study, may be viewed as a milestone and the first step of what should be a continuous effort, by MFIs, governments, and academic communities, to monitor the environment, to assess progress or lack thereof, and the costs required to make progress. The effort should also be integrated into the wider context of formulating and financing Agenda 21. Among the three indices, the COR can play a particularly valuable role in devising financially and technologically feasible "priority" programs, across different countries and environmental sectors. The estimation of costs is also an important first step to determine how much finance is required domestically and internationally. Those countries with high demand for external financial assistance should also be identified and monitored on a periodical basis using the COR approach, as demonstrated in this study.

Both ED and EE are relatively easy to construct and less data-demanding than COR. They should be adopted by governments and international financial agencies, and published on an annual basis. The COR, though more data intensive and more technically complex to estimate, links the present state of the environment to a more desirable state of the environment by estimating the costs of moving between them. The cost figures may change more slowly and, therefore, may be estimated on a much longer time interval, perhaps every 10 years. Nonetheless, the COR has strong policy implications particularly for

MFIs such as the World Bank and ADB in compiling their investment portfolios, both across different countries and across different environmental sectors, to enable them to achieve maximum economic and environmental returns.

Identifying Priorities for Environmental Remediation

Aside from methodological development and testing, we have also identified several environmental "hot spots" in Asia which call for special attention by the international community. The countries facing particular environmental stress include PRC, in addition to Vietnam, Lao PDR and Cambodia. Their economies are developing at an unprecedented rate and the environment is often a part of the costs of economic growth. These countries should be closely monitored and given priority by international financial and technological donors to avert an environmental downward trend. The other area of environmental distress is found in South Asia including India, Pakistan, Bangladesh, and Nepal. The environmental problems associated with poverty and lack of development, such as polluted drinking water and uncollected solid wastes are particularly severe while environmental degradation accompanied by economic expansion is also on the rise. Although not reflected in the COR/GDP ratios, these countries may require more financial assistance than other countries to combat both poverty and environmental degradation. Lastly, this study indicates that the ASEAN countries, best exemplified by Thailand, are increasingly capable of paying their own bills for environmental cleanup. MFIs should gradually shift their focus of assistance away from these countries in order to more effectively target those newly emerged environmental hot spots.

There is also a wide range of opinions about the urgency of addressing different forms of environmental deterioration. We raised this point earlier in this chapter when we argued that developing countries may not be as interested in curtailing global warming gases as they are in addressing local pollution problems. The MFIs have distanced themselves from such a view. While they share with the developing country's desire to raise living standards, they cannot take a strictly national view of the problem of environmental change. This study has pointed out that a common problem facing most of the Asian developing countries is land degradation, which accounts for the largest proportion of total COR required by most countries. This implies that governments and MFIs may need to reprioritize their environmental investment from the more traditional projects such as water pollution control to projects that address land degradation problems including deforestation, soil erosion, and solid waste management.

Note

1 R. Hueting, p. 204, in Costanza (1991).

REFERENCES

Adriaanse, A. 1993. Environmental Policy Performance Indicators, A Study on the Development of Indicators for Environmental Policy in the Netherlands.

Ahmad, Y. J., S. El Serafy and E. Lutz, eds. 1989. Environmental Accounting for Sustainable Development. A UNEP-World Bank Symposium. Washington DC. World Bank, June 1989.

Arrow, K. J. and A. Fisher. 1974 "Preservation, Uncertainty and Irreversibility," in *Quarterly Journal of Economics*, vol. 88, no. 2, pp. 312–319.

Asian Development Bank, 1994. The Environment Program of the Asian Development Bank, Past, Present and Future, Manila, Philippines.

Bao Qiang and Chen Jian Zhi, eds., 1993. *The Quantification of Environmental Protection Strategy Objectives for the Year of 2000.* China Environmental Sciences Press, Beijing.

Baumol W. and W. Oates. 1975. *The Theory of Environmental Policy.* Englewood Cliffs, NJ:Prentice Hall.

Bi, J., S. Zhang, Q. G. Cai and Y. J. Tang. 1994. "Assessing the Feasibility of Developing New Environmental Indices in the PRC." Working paper no.11. Harvard University, Division of Applied Sciences.

Bi, J. 1995. "Temporal Variations of Pollution Intensities of Chinese Industries." Paper presented at the Interim Workshop, Asian Development Bank–Harvard Study of Environmental Indicators and Indices, Asian Institute of Technology, Bangkok.

Boulding, K. 1966. "The Economics of the Coming Spaceship Earth," in *Environmental Quality in a Growing Economy*, H. Jarrett eds. The Johns Hopkins Press for Resources For the Future, Inc.

Brundtland Commission (The World Commission on Environment and Development) 1987. *Our Common Future.* Oxford University Press, New York.

Coase R. 1960. "The Problem of Social Cost," in *Journal of Law and Economics*, 3, 1–44

Coate, E. L. and A. K. Mason. 1975. "Some Practical Problems in Developing and Presenting Environmental Quality Indices to the Public," in *Proceedings of the International Conference on Environmental Sensing and Assessment*, Las Vegas, NV. IEEE No. 75-CH 10007-1.

Daly, H. 1987. The Economic Growth Debate: What Some Economists Have Learned But Many Have Not, in *Journal of Environmental Economics and Management*, vol. 14, no. 4, pp. 323–337, December.

Dasgupta, P. and G. Heal 1990. "The Optimal Depletion of Exhaustible Resources." in *Review of Economic Studies*, pp. 3–28.

Dasgupta, P. and K. G. Maler 1990. "The Environment and Emerging Development Issues," in *Proceedings of The World Bank Annual Conference on Developmental Economics*, pp. 101–151.

Desai M. 1994, "Greening of the HDI," a draft paper.

Dorfman, R. 1977. "Towards a Social Index of Environmental Quality," in *Economic Progress, Private Values, and Public Policy*, eds. B. Balassa and R. Nelson. New York: North-Holland. pp. 121–135.

Dorfman, R. and P. P. Rogers eds. 1997. *Science With Human Face*. Harvard University Press. Cambridge, Massachusetts.

Environment Agency of Japan. 1992. *"Activities on Environmental Indicators in Japan."* Background Report for the World Resources Institute.

Fiering, M. B. and C. S. Holling 1974. "Management and Standards for Perturbed Ecosystems; Agro-Ecosystems 1.

Fiering, M. B. 1992. "Environmental Indices," A Working Paper from Harvard University, Division of Applied Sciences, Pierce Hall, Cambridge MA 02138.

Foy, G. and H. Daly 1989. "Allocation, Distribution and Scale as Determinants of Environmental Degradation: Case Studies of Haiti, El Salvador and Costa Rica." Working Paper No. 19, Washington DC: World Bank, Environment Department.

Hall, B. and M. Lee Kerr 1991. *Green Index, A State-by-State Guide to the Nation's Environmental Health*, Island Press, Washington DC.

Hammond, A. 1993. "Is There Anything New in the Concept of Sustainable Development." Revised Version of a paper presented at a *Conference on The Environment after Rio*, Courmayeur, Valle d'Aosta, Italy, 10–12 February, pp. 1–17.

Hammond, A., A. Adriaanse, E. Rodenburg, D. Bryant and R. Woodward. 1995. *Environmental Indicators: A Systematic Approach to Measuring and Reporting on Environmental Policy Performance in the Context of Sustainable Development*. World Resources Institute.

Han G. et al. 1993. *Research on the Environmental Protection Objectives in 2020 in China*, China Environmental Science Press, Beijing.

Hartwick, J.M. 1977. "Intergenerational Equity and the Investing of Rents from Exhaustible Resources," in *The American Economic Review*, pp. 972–974, December.

Herfindahl, O.C. and A.V. Kneese, Economic Theory of Natural Resources, Charles Merrill Publishing Co. (1974).

Hettige, H., P. Martin, M. Singh and D. Wheeler. 1994. "IPPS—The Industrial Pollution Projection System." A World Bank Working Paper.

Hueting, R. (1991) "Correcting National Income for Environmental Losses: A Practical Solution for a Theoretical Dilemma" in R. Costanza (ed.) Ecological Economics: The Science and Management of Sustainability, New York: Columbia University Press.

Inhaber, H. 1976 Environmental Indices, John Wiley and Sons: Toronto, Ontario.

Jalal, K. F. 1996. Environmental Diamond, a paper presented at the Workshop on Measuring Environmental Quality in Asia. Asian Development Bank, Manila, the Philippines.

James M. Montgomery, Consulting Engineers, Inc. (JMM, Inc.) in Association with Dames & Moore, Philnor Consultants and Planners, Inc. and Total Consultancy Services, Inc. 1992. Republic of the Philippines, Department of Environment and Natural Resources, Department of Trade and Industry. *Industrial Efficiency and Pollution Control Program: Final Report*. World Bank, Japan Grant Fund.

Krutilla, J. V. and A. C. Fisher 1975. *The Economics of Natural Environments: Studies in the Valuation of Commodity and Amenity Resources*, Washington DC: Resources for the Future.

Leontief, W., "Environmental Repercussions and the Economic Structure: An Input-Output Approach," The Review of Economics and Statistics, 52(3), 262–71, 1970.

Lohani B. N. and G. Todino 1984. "Water quality index for Chao Phraya River" in Journal of Environmental Engineering, 110(6), 1163–1176.

Lohani, B. N. 1980. "An air pollution index based on factor analysis" in Journal of the IPHE, 3, 31–34, India.

Lohani, B. N. and N. Mustapha. 1982. "Indices for water quality assessment in rivers: A case study of the Linggi River in Malaysia" in Water Supply and Management, 6(6), 545–555.

Lutz, E. (ed.) 1993. Toward Improved Accounting for the Environment, An UNSTAT-World Bank Symposium, The World Bank.

Mäler, Karl-Göran, National Accounts and Environmental Resources, *Environmental and Resource Economics*, Vol. 1, pp. 1–15, 1991.

Markandya, A., and J. Richardson 1993. The Economics of the Environment: An Introduction, in Environmental Economics: A Reader, A. Markandya and J. Richardson (Eds.), St. Martin's Press, New York.

Meadows, D. H, D. L. Meadows and J. Randers 1992. Beyond The Limits, Chelsea Green Publishing Co., Post Mills, VT.

Meadows, D. H., et al. 1972, The Limits to Growth: A Report for the Club of Rome's Project on the Predicament of Mankind, Universe Books, New York.

Munasinghe, M. 1993 Environmental Economics and Sustainable Development, World Bank Environment Paper, No. 3.

Murray, F. E. S. and N. Harshadeep 1994. "Project Selection for Sustainable Development: The Use of Environmental Indices," Working Paper No. 6, Harvard University, Environmental Systems Program.

National Center for Economic Alternatives (NCFEA) 1995. Index of Environmental Trends, An Assessment of Twenty-One Key Environmental Indicators in Nine Industrialized Countries over the Past Two Decades, 2040 S Street, NW, Washington, DC 20009.

National Environmental Protection Agency (NEPA) 1996. *The National Ninth Five-Year Plan for Environmental Protection and the Long-Term Targets for the Year 2010*, Beijing, PRC.

Nordhaus, W. D. 1992. Lethal Model 2: The Limits to Growth Revisited, *Brookings Papers on Economic Activity*, No. 2, pp.1–59.

O'Connor, J. 1994. Personal Communication. *Minutes of Harvard University/Asian Development Bank Brainstorming Meeting on Environmental Indices*. Working paper no. 2. Harvard University, Environmental Systems Program.

Orbeta, E. M. and A. Indab. 1994. *Valuation of Direct Environmental Waste Disposal Services: Refinement of 1988 estimates and 1992 update*. Environmental and Natural Resources Accounting Project, Phase III, Manila, Philippines.

Ott, W. (1978) Environmental Indices, Theory and Practice, Ann Arbor Science Publishers, Inc.

Owens, G.M., ed. 1994. Financing Environmentally Sound Development, Asian Development Bank, Manila, Philippines.

Panayotou, T. 1992. Green Markets: The Economics of Sustainable Development, ICS Press for the International Center for Economic Growth, San Francisco.

Pearce, D., E. Barbier, and A. Markandya (eds.) 1990. Sustainable Development: Economics and Environment in the Third World, Edward Elgar Publishing Co.

Pearce, D. W. and Atkinson 1993. "Capital Theory and the Measurement of Weak Sustainability: A Comment." *Ecological Economics*, 8 103–108.

Pezzey, J. 1992. Sustainability Development Concepts: An Economic Analysis, World Bank Environment Paper No. 2.

Pfliegner, K. 1995. "Sustainable Development: Greening of the Human Development Index," United Nations Development Programme, New York, presented at the SCOPE Scientific Workshop on Indicators of Sustainable Development November 17–17, Wupperrtal Institute, Germany.

Repetto, R. 1986 World Enough and Time, Yale University Press, New Haven, CT.

Repetto, R., W. Magrath, M. Wells, C. Beer, and F. Rossini 1989.Wasting Assets: Natural Resources in the National Income Accounts, World Resources Institute, Washington D.C.

Ridker, R. G. 1967. Economic Costs of Air Pollution; Studies in Measurement, F.A. Praeger, New York.

Rogers, P. and Kazi F. Jalal. 1994. "Used Cars, Used Environment: How to Choose One?" Working Paper No. 8, Harvard University, Environmental Systems Program.

Solow, R. M. 1974. Intergenerational Equity and Exhaustible Resources, Review of Economic Studies, 41, Symposium on the Economics of Exhaustible Resources, pp. 29–45.

Solow, R. M. 1991. Sustainability: An Economist's Perspective, *The Eighteenth J. Seward Johnson Lecture*, Marine Policy Center, Woods Hole Oceanographic Institution, Woods Hole, Massachusetts.

Stavins, R. 1992. Comments and Discussion on Lethal Model 2: The Limits to Growth Revisited, by W.D. Nordhaus, *Brookings Papers on Economic Activity*, No. 2, pp.1–59.

Thomas, W. A. 1972. *Indicators of Environmental Quality*. New York: Plenum Press.

Train, R. E. 1973. *"Management for the Future."* Paper presented at the National Conference on Managing the Environment, Washington, DC.

Tschirley, J. B. 1992. The Use of Indicators for Sustainable Agriculture and Rural Development, background materials for the World Resources Institute Workshop on Global Environmental Indicators, World Resources Institute: Washington, D.C.

Tunstall, D. B. 1992. *"The Growing Importance of Scientific Rules of Thumb in Developing Indicators of Resource Sustainability: Draft."* World Resources Institute.

Tunstall, D. B., A. Hammond and N. Henninger. 1992. "Developing Environmental Indicators: Draft." World Resources Institute.

United Nations Development Programme (UNDP) 1992. Human Development Report, Oxford University Press, New York, Oxford.

United Nations Environment Programme (UNEP). 1989/1990 *Environmental Data Report*, Oxford University Press, New York and Oxford.

United States Environmental Protection Agency (USEPA). 1995. *A Conceptual Framework to Support Development and Use of Environmental Information in Decision-Making*. EPA 230-R-95-012. USEPA. Environmental Statistics and Information Division, Office of Policy, Planning and Evaluation.

Vincent, J. R. 1990. Rent Capture and the Feasibility of Tropical Forest Management, Land Economics, Vol. 66, No. 2, pp. 212–223.

Weitzman, M. L. 1992. Comments and Discussion on Lethal Model 2: The Limits to Growth Revisited, by W.D. Nordhaus, *Brookings Papers on Economic Activity*, No. 2, pp.1–59.

World Bank (1991a) *World Tables*. The John Hopkins University Press, Baltmore and London.

World Bank (1991b) *World Development Report 1991, The Challenge of Development*. World Development Indicators: Oxford University Press, New York and Oxford.

World Bank 1994. "Social Indicators of Development" A World Bank Report, Washington, D.C.

World Bank 1995. "Monitoring Environmental Progress," A World in Progress, Washington, D.C.

World Bank 1997. "Expanding the Measure of Wealth: Indicators of Environmentally Sustainable Development," Rio+5 Edition, Draft for Discussion, Washington, D.C.

Yu, C.C. 1994. *Waste-Economy of Industrial-Commercial-Institutional (ICI) Establishments in the Metropolitan Toronto Area, An Integrated Methodology*. Ph.D. thesis, Graduate Department of Geography, University of Toronto.

Yu, C. C., J. Quinn, C. Dufournaud and J. Harrington, P. P. Rogers and B. N. Lohani 1997. Effective Dimensionality of Environmental Indicators: A Bootstrapping Principal Component Analysis, *submitted to Journal of Environmental Management.*

Yu, C. C., C. Dufournaud and P. Rogers 1995. "How Many Indices Do We Need? A Multivariate Analysis of Existing Environment-Related Indicators," Working Paper No. 12, Harvard University, Environmental Systems Program.

Yu, X. and P. Rogers 1995. "Pursuing Sustainable Development: An Index of Performance," A Working Paper, Harvard University, Environmental Systems Program.

APPENDICES

APPENDIX 1

Compiling Emission Factors for DMCs: A Method for
Rapid Assessment Using Secondary Data .173

APPENDIX 2

Cost of Remediation 219

APPENDIX 3

A Review of Environmental Indices 311

APPENDIX 4

Some Theoretical and Technical Issues Regarding
Environmental Elasticity and Environmental Diamonds 369

Appendix I

Compiling Emission Factors for DMCs: A Methodology for Rapid Assessment Using Secondary Data

Measuring Environmental Quality in Asia

Chang-Ching Yu

1. Introduction

The cost-of-remediation (COR) approach, derived by this study, attempts to estimate the costs of reducing environmental emissions or other environmental externalities from a current level "A" to a more desirable level "B." While different environmental standards and targets can be used as proxies for B, one must determine the current level A in order to determine by how much the amount of emissions needs to be reduced to achieve B. The cost-of-remediation approach then computes the cost of moving from A to B. The levels can be expressed as pressure variables (emissions and other measures of environmental assault) or state variables (ambient quality) that can be linked to pressure variables such as emissions, through some spatial modeling techniques (diffusion models).

The purpose of this study is twofold. One is to discuss some of the conceptual and theoretical issues concerning estimating environmental emissions. The other is to derive a rapid-assessment methodology for estimating the environmental emissions of developing countries using secondary data, particularly US data. This will be done by comparing the US emission factors with those of some developing countries for which data are available. Ideally, such comparisons will lead to a quantitative assessment of the differences of pollution intensities among these countries so that certain adjustment factors can be obtained. Since the US possesses perhaps the world's most comprehensive database on environmental emissions, one can adjust the US data to estimate environmental emissions for developing countries, when local data are not available or are incomplete.

From a long-term standpoint, the development of a rapid-assessment methodology is equally important as the actual estimation of the emission factors for the Asian countries that participate in this study. Many countries are evolving rapidly in terms of technologies employed in their production and adoption of pollution abatement measures. The emission levels for these countries on a unit economic-activity basis are also expected to decline, sometimes very rapidly. For example, between 1985 and 1992, the pollution intensities of PRC industries based on employment and output decreased 10–90 percent for some pollutants, the most notable being total suspended particulate (TSP) (Bi 1995). When emission levels change so much in such a short period of time, a methodology that allows quick capture of such changes at minimum cost becomes essential.

2. Some Conceptual Issues Related to Environmental Emissions

Pollution or environmental emission is defined as "the introduction by man into the environment of substances or energy liable to cause hazards to human health, harm to living resources, and ecological systems, damage to structure or amenity, or interference with legitimate uses of the environment." (Holdgate 1979; cited in Orbeta and Indab 1994).

The above definition of pollution includes only anthropogenic emissions. By definition, natural emissions are produced to some extent by natural processes, e.g. volcanic eruptions, forest fires. Anthropogenic emissions are related to human activities. In some cases (e.g. industrial pollution), emissions are generated almost entirely by human activities. In other cases, the distinctions between natural and anthropogenic emissions may be less clear.

Anthropogenic emissions can be further classified according to type of source: area, mobile, and stationary sources, or, alternatively, industrial, agricultural, and domestic sources. An area source is any source of emissions that, by itself is not significant, but when taken collectively with other similar sources distributed on an areal basis, becomes significant. For example, methane emissions from paddy rice fields, runoff pesticides, fertilizers and soil nutrients from cultivated land, and emissions from residential wood combustion fall into the category of areal source. Vehicular emissions from cars, trucks, motorcycles, and airplanes are mobile sources. Stationary sources refer to facilities identifiable by name and location that emit any air pollutant, either from fuel combustion or process emissions (Orbeta and Indab, 1994). Industrial sources are generally stationary while agricultural and domestic sources are often areal.

Figure 1.1 provides a framework for classifying emissions. It will form the basis for compiling emission factors in this study. The sources of emissions are classified as stationary, mobile, and area, and by economic sectors: manufacturing, transportation, energy transformation, agriculture, households, etc. The pollutants generated by different sources are classified by chemical content, by scale of impact (i.e. global—greenhouse gases and acid rain gases—or local), and by the media materials into which they are first released.

Several important points regarding Figure 1.1 need to be stressed. First, the emphasis of this study is on those pollutants that have major impacts on local environment, not because global pollutants such as CO_2 are not important, but rather because local pollutants reflect the immediate environmental concerns of developing countries. As discussed in Chapter 6 of this volume, despite the pressure from developed countries on reducing greenhouse gas (GHG) emissions such as CO_2 and CFC, developing countries continue to place greater priority on those pollutants that have impacts on the immediate environment. Second, there is a considerable amount of overlap among different sources of

APPENDIX FIGURE 1.1

A Framework for Classifying Information

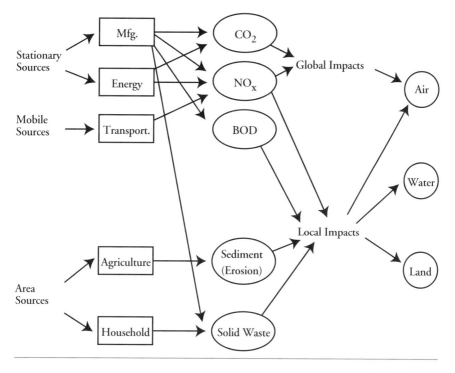

emissions under this classification. For example, manufacturing emissions include emissions from both production processes and energy consumption of manufacturing activities. Similarly, household emissions also include those from heating and cooking stoves. On the other hand, the source category "energy" refers to all the emissions from stationary energy-consumption sources including those from industry, utilities, and households. This brings up a potential possibility of double-counting in computing total emissions of an economy. For example, suppose an economy consists of three sectors: manufacturing, utilities, and households. The total energy consumption of the economy is 10 Gj, including 3 Gj for manufacturing, which operate their own boilers; 4 Gj for the utility sector; and 3 Gj for households; which use their own boilers or stoves. We assume that the emission factor of CO is 100 gram/Gj for all types of boilers and stoves. For manufacturing, we also assume the emission factor of CO is 50 gram/\$ and the total annual output of manufacturing is \$20. The total annual CO emission of the economy, therefore, should be

$$50 \text{ gram/\$} \times \$20 + 100 \text{ gram/Gj} \times (10\text{-}3) \text{ Gj} = 1700 \text{ gram}.$$

Note that the energy uses by the manufacturing sector, i.e. 3 Gj, has been deducted from the total energy consumption of the economy (10 Gj) in the above calculation because the emission factor for manufacturing, i.e. 50 gram/\$, implicitly includes emissions from its energy uses.

Third, under this classification, various land degradation problems such as soil erosion and salinization are considered as "emissions" from agricultural and forestry activities. In terms of erosion, sediments and nutrients are removed from one location and released into water bodies or onto other land areas. Fourth, we are concerned about the initial releases of emissions because the eventual destinations of emissions tend to be more uncertain, due to the movements of pollutants within the environment. For example, in developed countries, solid waste is considered primarily disposed of into land through landfill and partially into air through incineration, despite the fact that some of the heavy-metal-rich leachate generated at landfill sites may eventually find its way to the underground water. In developing countries, however, the practices are very different. For example, it has been estimated that in some river basins in the Philippines, 20 percent of the Biological Oxygen Demand (or BOD[1]) loads are from solid wastes disposed of in the river system (JMMCE, 1992).

3. Pollution Intensities (Emission Factors)
3.1 Definition
Environmental emissions are by-products of economic (productive and consumptive) activities. Given a type of economic activity, the level of emissions generally increases as the level of economic activity increases. As a measure of

pollution intensities caused by economic activities, an emission factor generally takes the form of a ratio between total pollutant quantity and total economic activity, or,

$$\text{Emission Factor (F)} = \frac{\text{Total Emission Quantity (Q)}}{\text{Total Economic Activity (E)}} \qquad (1.1)$$

Given the emission factor F for a region, the total emission Q is,

$$Q = F\ E. \qquad (1.2)$$

The numerator, total waste, or pollutant quantity, may be measured in weight, or volume or, sometimes, multiplied by a health risk factor (toxicity index) of the pollutant. The denominator, total economic activity, can be measured in value added, shipments/outputs, or employment, etc. The advantages of deriving such emission factors are as follows:

1. With these emission factors, pollution intensities of the same economic activities or sectors but in different economies may be compared in order to assess potential for pollution reduction. This is illustrated later in this appendix.

2. With the emission factors derived based on relatively few data points or based on data collected from one region, one can predict the total environmental pollution levels for the entire economy or for another region once the total level of economic activities of the relevant economy or region is known or prescribed. This is particularly useful for estimating emissions of developing countries with data for developed countries, which are generally broader-based and more reliable.

3. Other types of indicators for environmental stress such as ambient pollutant concentrations which is a pollution density per square kilometer, can subsequently be estimated using the emission factors and other geographic and economic data.

3.2 Choices and Classifications of Denominator—Economic Activity

We need to consider several criteria when selecting an appropriate economic variable as the denominator in computing emission factors. First, the economic variable chosen should have a positive relationship with total pollutant quantity. This will ensure statistical precision when using such emission factors to estimate total pollutant emissions using equation (1.2). Second, the information on the economic variable should be widely available. Third, the option should ensure that the emission factors calculated using the economic variable are comparable with those constructed for other regions or countries.

For manufacturing sectors, Hettige et al. (1994) considered several variables for such a purpose:

- physical volume of output

- shipment value

- value added

- employment

The more appealing choice is physical volume of output since it is free from impacts of price variations from one country to another. However, because of the wide diversities of the products produced by any given economic sector, it is difficult to aggregate data of individual facilities to compile interfacility emission factors.

The other three variables—total shipment value (output), value added, and employment—are amenable to interfacility and intersector on aggregation. They are, however, subject to impacts of crosscountry price variations and other undesirable properties that are discussed in more detail below. These three variables were used by Hettige et al. to derive emission factors for the US manufacturing sector.

A common practice of compiling emission factors is by economic activities or sectors. This is because emission generation is generally specific to production processes in that different economic activities generate different types and quantities of pollutants. When predicting total emissions using emission factors multiplied by a total level of economic activity, statistical precision can only be achieved at a relatively disaggregated level of classification of economic sectors so as to ensure homogeneous production processes within each sector.

At the most disaggregated level, USEPA has compiled emission factors for specific production processes, i.e., the air CHIEF database, which will be discussed in Section 4. Such specialized emission factors are difficult to generalize to characterize emission levels of an economic sector that often employs multiple production technologies to produce different products.

Hettige et al. (1994) constructed pollution intensities for the US manufacturing industries at the four-digit level of the International Standard Industrial Classification (ISIC), i.e., 78 sectors. This was in part made possible by the availability of detailed databases at the facility level for the study. Hettige et al. also believe that "pollution projections should always be done with the most disaggregated data available," and that "the resulting gains in accuracy are often quite striking." This conclusion is based on their discovery so-called iron law of pollution intensity: Sectoral pollution intensities are always exponentially distributed, with a few highly intensive sectors and many with very low intensities. High-intensity sectors differ markedly across pollutants, but the exponential pattern persists.

Unfortunately, such detailed emission information may not be available for other countries. Furthermore, what Hettige et al. failed to recognize is that a high disaggregation level is not always desirable due to the fact that the existing economic classifications such as ISIC are mainly designed for economic data reporting and they generally classify the economy by types of economic outputs. However, heterogeneity in economic outputs does not always coincide with heterogeneity in emissions and vice versa. For example, restaurants/hotels and food stores are often classified as two different economic sectors even at very high aggregation levels but they may share the same waste characteristics. The same may also be said about the wood and furniture industries, or the textile and the apparel industries. The gain from increasing disaggregation of economic classification in compiling emission factors may diminish rapidly. On the other hand, high disaggregation leads to increasing scarcity of both economic and environmental data. An "optimal" level of sectoral aggregation should be determined based on both data availability and some level of homogeneity of emission characteristics within the sectors.

For the household sector, we are mainly concerned about two types of emissions—solid waste and emissions from energy consumption. Energy-related air emissions will be considered separately in this appendix. For solid waste, two variables are potential candidates as denominators for computing emission factors:

- number of residents in a household
- annual household income

Both variables have been documented to affect total solid waste generation by households. However, the relationship between a household's waste generation and its income is much less clear than that between waste generation and the number of residents in a household. In North America, some studies have revealed that household income negatively affects household waste generation in that higher-income families generate less waste on a per capita basis (Yu 1994). The justifications provided include the fact that richer families tend to dine out more often than poorer families. In a crosscountry context, however, evidence suggests that countries with higher income generally produce more waste on a per capita basis. By comparison, most existing studies indicate that there is a strong positive relationship between total waste generation and the number of residents in a household (Richardson and Havlicek 1978). We use the number of people as the denominator in estimating the emission factors for household solid waste generation. To account for the impacts of income, we compiled such emission factors by the income levels of different countries.

Vehicular emissions are closely related to kilometers traveled and different types of vehicles. Emission factors are usually expressed in terms of pollutant emissions per kilometer by different vehicle types.

Although erosion is generally considered to be caused by agricultural and forestry activities, there is no clearly established relationship between total amount of erosion and scale of agricultural and forestry activities. In this study, we use the percentage of a country's land areas subject to different levels of erosion as a surrogate for "emission factors."

3.3 Choices and Classifications of Numerator—Types of Pollutants

Emission factors can be constructed for each single pollutant, regardless of the medium materials into which it is released. This type of emission factor is referred to as "all-media" and is useful in identifying those most-polluting economic sectors and individual establishments. For those pollutants such as sediments and solid wastes that are emitted into multiple media, it is desirable to construct medium-specific emission factors for air, water, and land releases separately. Medium-specific emission factors are "particularly useful in analyzing the extent to which intermedium substitution of waste disposal is possible," (Martin et al. 1991). An example of this is the practice of solid waste incineration to trade off air quality for more land space. For the countries considered in this study, the information on the percentage of different pollutants released into air, water, and land is generally unavailable. This, however, should not pose a major concern because most of the pollutants being considered such as SO_2 and BOD are predominantly released into a known medium, i.e. air or water.

A much larger concern stems from the fact that there are literally hundreds of chemical species that can be called pollutants, the majority of which are toxic and hazardous (Rubin 1984). It is necessary to decide on a more workable aggregation scheme for classifying and reporting emissions. Emissions may be classified by chemical composition or species, i.e., SO_2, CH_4, CO_2, NH_3, Cr, etc.; or by potential impacts on the environment and biosphere, i.e., toxic or conventional, greenhouse gases, ozone-depleting gases, or acid-rain gases. At the most disaggregated level is the classification by chemical composition. The information obtained at this level would allow researchers maximum flexibility to manipulate the data into any required formats and, thus, would be the most desirable.

Appendix Table 1.1 contains the commonly-used pollutant categories and their measurement units in a cross-tabular form by toxicity and dominant medium of initial release. Conventional pollutants include those substances that do not have known significant toxic properties (to human beings and the other fauna and/or flora) and can generally be treated by conventional methods such as biological treatment, e.g., organic wastewater from a food processing plant. Toxic and hazardous substances include those that are harmful to

Aggregation and Measurements of Emissions

	Air	Water	Land
Conventional	CO_2 (kg or tonne) CH_4 (kg or tonne) Other Hydrocarbon Gases (kg or tonne) Volatile Organic Compounds (VOC) (kg or tonne) Suspended Particulate Matter (PM10)[a] (kg or tonne) Total Suspended Particulate (TSP)[b] (kg or tonne) CFC (kg or tonne)	Total Wastewater Discharge (m^3 or tonne) Five-Day Biochemical Oxygen Demand (BOD) Loads (kg or tonne) Chemical Oxygen Demand (COD) Loads (kg or tonne) Suspended Solid (SS) (kg or tonne)	Solid wastes (paper, paperboard, glass, ferrous and non-ferrous metal, plastics, rubber, leather textiles, food, sludge, wood, vegetation, construction wastes, mining wastes, others (kg or tonne)
Toxic and Hazardous	SO_2 (kg or tonne) NO_x (kg or tonne) N_2O (kg or tonne) NH_3 (kg or tonne) CO (kg or tonne)	Acid and Alkali Wastes (pH) Heavy Metals (kg or tonne) Solvents and Hydrocarbons Liquids (kg or tonne) Oils and Grease (kg or tonne)	Infectious Wastes (kg or tonne) Intractable Wastes (kg or tonne)

a. Particulate matter in air that is smaller than ten micron in aerodynamic diameter.

b. Total suspended particles in air that are smaller than 100 micron in aerodynamic diameter.

humans or to the environment by virtue of their corrosivity, toxicity, reactivity, or ignitability. The classification of some pollutants are straightforward such as BOD as conventional and acid wastes as toxic and hazardous. Classification of others such as fecal coliforms is less so. Although generally considered "conventional," fecal coliforms are quite hazardous to human health.

Major types of toxic and hazardous wastes include the following listed according to treatment methods (JMMCE 1992):

- acid and alkali wastes, which are treated by neutralization;

- heavy metals, which can be chemically treated and physically separated, then placed in a secure landfill;

- solvents and hydrocarbon liquids such as dioxane ($C_4H_8O_2$), which can be recovered and reused or incinerated;

- oils and grease, which can be incinerated to both destroy the waste and recover energy;

- infectious waste, which can be treated by disinfection, incineration, and/or landfilling;

- intractable wastes, which require highly specialized destruction techniques, or for which there is no treatment method. Examples include organochlorins, e.g. hydrocarbon pesticides containing chlorine such as DDT, or persistent organic compounds, e.g. PCBs, dioxins, asbestos, and nuclear (radioactive) wastes.

It should be stressed that although the above classification scheme is comprehensive by nature, the compilation of emission factors that follows and the estimation of cost of remediation (discussed in Appendix 2 of this report) focus on a much smaller number of pollutants due to information constraints particularly for the participating countries.

4. Industrial Air and Water Emissions: A Comparison Between the US and PRC

4.1 US Databases on Environmental Emissions

USEPA maintains the world's most comprehensive databases of environmental emissions, most of which are electronically accessible to the general public under the Freedom of Information Act. The following is a brief description of six such databases and systems.

The Toxic Release Inventory (TRI)

TRI was established by Section 313 of the Emergency Planning and Community Right to Know Act (EPCRA) of 1986. Under this law, close to 20,000 manufacturers generating 50,000 pounds or more of toxic chemicals must report on an annual basis the amounts of more than 300 toxic chemicals, including those in 20 chemical categories, that they release directly to the air, water, or land, or that they inject underground. The database also includes information on amounts transferred to off-site locations for treatment or disposal, amounts recycled on- and offsite, amounts used for energy recovery on- and offsite, amounts treated on-site, and amounts released due to nonpro-duction-related events (e.g. accidental spills). No nontoxic substances or other environmental parameters, such as chemical or biochemical oxygen demand (COD/BOD), are recorded.

Aerometric Information Retrieval System (AIRS)
AIRS is the national repository for information about airborne pollution in the United States. It contains the emission and compliance data mandated by the Clean Air Act that have been collected at individual facilities monitored by the USEPA and state agencies since 1985. AIRS comprises four subsystems: the Air Quality Subsystem (AQS), the AIRS Facility Subsystem (AFS), the AIRS Area/ Mobile Source Subsystems (AMS), and the Geo-Common Subsystem (GCS). There are seven "criteria pollutants" for which data are stored in AIRS: PM10 (particulate matter less than 10 microns in size), carbon monoxide, sulfur dioxide, nitrogen dioxide, lead, reactive volatile organic compounds (VOC), and ozone. Although there is some overlap with TRI, AIRS includes a number of substances that are not included in TRI, most notably, sulfur and nitrogen compounds, and particulate emissions.

National Pollutant Discharge Elimination System (NPDES)
The NPDES database contains the self-monitoring reports of facilities with NPDES permits for discharges of wastewater. Some 60,000 plants file such reports on monitoring they perform on a monthly basis and more than 2,000 parameters are reported. Some of the more important parameters that are not included in TRI are BOD/COD, pH, and temperature. The database is most complete from 1987 onwards.

Biennial Reporting System (BRS)
BRS is a reporting system, updated every two years, on hazardous and solid waste generation. The information is submitted by the regulated community to states and USEPA regions which then digitize the information to the national system. The 1989 BRS National Oversight Database is available.

Air Clearinghouse for Inventories and Emission Factors (Air CHIEF)
The Air CHIEF CD-ROM was developed by USEPA to provide the public and private sectors with current emission data compiled from existing USEPA reports and databases in a convenient, easily accessible format. The database

includes reports and tabulated data characterizing source emission factors for criteria and toxic air pollutants. The emission factors relate the quantity of a pollutant released to some activity level from a specific source category or process for 24 sources (processes).

The Industrial Pollution Projection System (IPPS)2

The IPPS was developed by the World Bank using existing USEPA databases such as TRI, AIRS, and NPDES (Hettige et al. 1994). The crux of IPPS is the emission factors (pollution intensity) estimated using the pollution and trade (economic) data. The emission factors can then be used to estimate comprehensive profiles of industrial pollution for countries, regions, urban areas, or proposed new projects based on the presumption that similar economic activities generate similar wastes. IPPS adopted shipment value, value added, and employment as the denominators for estimating emission factors. The emission factors for each industry are aggregated through introducing indices of toxicological and carcinogenic potency. Efforts were subsequently made to use the IPPS developed from US data to estimate pollution intensity for Indonesian industries by introducing adjustment factors (see Appendix Table 1.2) (Sabah and Afsah 1994).

It is beyond the scope of this study to provide more detailed information including the actual data of these databases; most, however, are available through an on-line service at a nominal charge. This is not to suggest that the USEPA computer system is easy to use—it is probably the least user-friendly system we have ever accessed. The World Bank's IPPS report summarizes the EPA information in a much more readable form (see Note 2 at the end of this appendix for instructions on obtaining it).

APPENDIX TABLE 1.2

Adjustment Factors Used by the World Bank for Indonesia

Nature of Pollution	Specific Pollutants	Adjustment Factor
Water Pollutants	Biological Oxygen Demand (BOD)	2 x US BOD Intensity
	Suspended Solids (SS)	2 x US SS Intensity
	Chemical Oxygen Demand (COD)	2 x US COD Intensity
Air Pollutants	Sulphur Dioxide (SO_2)	3 x US SO_2 Intensity
	Nitrogen Dioxide (NO_2)	3 x US NO_2 Intensity
	Particulate (PT)	6 x US PT Intensity
	Fine Particulate (PM10)	6 x US PM10 Intensity
	Volatile Organic Compounds (VOC)	3 x US VOC Intensity
	Carbon Monoxide (CO)	3 x US CO Intensity
Toxic	Toxic	2 x US Toxic Intensity
Metals	Metals	2 x US Metal Intensity

Source: Sabah and Afsah, 1994.

4.2 PRC Data

In contrast to the US, most of the Asian countries participating in this study do not possess such detailed information, with the notable exception of PRC. The National Environmental Protection Agency (NEPA) of PRC administers some 3,000 environmental monitoring stations to monitor ambient environmental quality. In addition, NEPA requests that major industries report their self-monitored emission levels on a regular basis and selectively publishes the results. The relatively complete data of the US and PRC make it possible to compare the US emission levels for the same economic sectors on a unit activity basis. The PRC data used in this study were gathered by the National Survey Office of Industrial Pollution Sources (1994).

4.3 Comparative Results

As mentioned earlier, Sabah and Afsah (1994) attempted to adopt US data to estimate emission levels for Indonesia using adjustment factors (Appendix Table 1.2).

Oversimplicity and lack of empirical evidence are obvious drawbacks of this approach. It assumes a universal adjustment factor for a particular pollutant, paying no regard to sectoral variations of pollution generation. The basic assumption of the approach is that the industrial pollution intensities in Indonesia are two to six times those in the US on a unit activity basis measured in monetary values. The discussion below attempts to shed some light on the validity, or lack thereof, of this hypothesis.

As mentioned in Section 4.1, the IPPS developed by the World Bank (Hettige et al. 1994) made use of existing US databases. The system provides three sets of emission factors for 78 manufacturing sectors at four-digit ISIC level, i.e., emission factors with respect to employment, value added, and total output in dollars. The question that arises here is which one of the three is most appropriate to be used in crosscountry comparisons and projections. Hettige et al. made several observations and theoretical speculations. First, they found high correlations across intensity rankings of different sectors based on the three variables. Appendix Table 1.3 shows almost perfect correlations. There-

---

APPENDIX TABLE 1.3

Rank Correlations Between Intensity Measures Using Three Different Scales of Activity

Scale of Activity	Total Value of Shipments	Value Added	Employment
Total Value of Shipments	1.00	0.99	0.98
Value Added	0.99	1.00	0.98
Employment	0.98	0.98	1.00

Source: Hettige *et al.* 1994.

fore, at a purely mechanical level, there is no need to distinguish the three sets of intensity measures as bases for pollution projection because all three measures will usually arrive at the same results of sectoral rankings. In reality, the actual choice of the denominator should be based on information availability.

However, Hettige et al. also suggested that employment-based intensities may be preferable for pollution projection in developing countries. The logic is as follows: (i) effective environmental regulation is thought to be quite income-elastic, although careful empirical work on crosscountry data has yet to be done; (ii) sectoral pollution is thought to be quite responsive to effective environmental regulation in many cases; and (iii) most crosscountry econometrics studies of sectoral labor demand find relatively high wage elasticities; they concluded that both sectoral pollution and sectoral labor demand will rise substantially as one moves from richer (high-wage, high-regulation) to poorer (low-wage, high-regulation) economies.

Appendix Tables 1.4 and 1.5 provide emission factors based on employment and total output measured in US dollars (in 1987 prices and the dollar-yuan exchange rate), respectively, for both US and PRC, in the form of the ratio of US emission factors to PRC emission factors. The value-added-based emission factors are currently not available for PRC and, thus, are excluded from the comparison. The US emission factors were originally compiled at four-digit ISIC level for a total of 78 manufacturing sectors and the PRC data are available for 25 manufacturing sectors. We collapsed the US data into 25 sectors corresponding to the PRC sectors. Ideally, the values for each new US sector should be the weighted means of those of the sub-sectors based on employment or output values. However, due to lack of information on employment and output values for the sub-sectors, simple arithmetic means of the values of the sub-sectors within each sector are used to represent the sector's combined emission factors. Furthermore, due to the poor comparability of the published data, only five pollutants are included in the crosscountry comparison: SO_2, NO_2, CO, TSP, and SS, the first four being air pollutants and the last a water pollutant. The US data also contain BOD emissions and the PRC data contain COD emissions. Unfortunately, the two are not entirely comparable and they cannot be converted at ease. Similarly, although the PRC data contain some information on toxic substances releases, the comparability of such data with those of the US is also poor and so are excluded from the subsequent comparison.

Appendix Table 1.4 indicates that the average per-thousand-employee pollution intensities (second to last row) in the US are larger than those of PRC, the ratio ranging from 1.18 to 6.48 for the five pollutants. Is this result contradictory to the initial hypothesis that the PRC industries are more pollution-intensive than those in the US? The answer is negative. The main reason is that the US industries are more economically productive than the PRC industries is that they produce more economic output and, thus, generate

APPENDIX TABLE 1.4
Emission Factors Based on Employment (kg/1000 Persons) of the US and PRC and Their Ratios (US/PRC)

	ISIC	SO$_2$	NO$_2$	CO	TSP	SS
Food Manufacture	311-312	317994/135778=2.34	181743/52843=3.44	63773/55362=1.15	313817/157118=2.00	65391/357096=0.18
Beverage Manufacture	313	384892/258138=1.49	191719/89132=2.15	21866/114390=0.19	28556/257263=0.11	581015/675125=0.86
Tobacco Manufacture	314	267859/99108=2.70	162100/32841=4.94	21115/66569=0.32	5003/99362=0.05	396/47922=0.01
Textile Industry	321	40350/1077170=0.04	32042/36908=0.87	9586/40250=0.24	16130/71509=0.23	1416/56644=0.03
Wearing Apparel	322	794/62341=0.01	299/16210=0.02	84/34168=0.00	37/62491=0.00	0/11317=0.00
Leather Products	323	31128/107599=0.29	10789/38552=0.28	3624/62689=0.06	12638/117203=0.11	34622/419146=0.08
Timber (bamboo) Prod.	331	46666/166818=0.28	58343/93236=0.63	141620/129516=1.09	100202/248260=0.40	8011/139140=0.06
Furniture Manufacture	332	7617/116794=0.07	5382/41032=0.13	5711/74159=0.08	17146/481079=0.04	1/22444=0.00
Paper and Pulp	341	946203/467394=2.02	519510/179861=2.89	1070606/240305=4.46	184153/478105=0.39	1708526/3021017=0.57
Printing & Publishing	342	1105/17396=0.06	1436/5131=0.28	5530/12563=0.44	594/23445=0.03	95/11231=0.01
Oil Refinery	353	9118030/157306=57.96	5245019/119855=43.76	4736742/312438=15.16	804419/67290=11.95	571935/73498=7.78
Chemical Industry	351-352	484290/387825=1.25	304883/126364=2.41	1192686/528332=2.26	41979/272300=0.15	4677/523420=0.01
Drugs and Medicines	3522	192650/215928=0.89	81752/81286=1.01	9594/105455=0.09	36368/188604=0.19	9701/224000=0.04
Rubber Industry	355	137855/208676=0.66	47719/73872=0.65	5866/100251=0.06	15286/167907=0.09	61062/66471=0.92
Plastics Products	3513, 3560	312250/187615=1.66	808365/58258=13.88	119576/74923=1.60	47906/137857=0.35	41303/32511=1.27
Const. & Nonmetal Prod.	361-369	2486812/645932=3.85	1425114/173272=8.22	216611/349995=0.62	1409076/1254440=1.12	250/130247=0.00
Ferrous Metal Smelting	3710	1293611/200462=6.45	561924/102528=5.48	2015941/2001269=1.01	299729/497313=0.60	88515/463561=0.19
Nonfer. Metal Smelting	3720	3409358/1021742=3.34	111049/77331=1.44	1585950/679552=2.33	286335/250340=1.14	19469/202460=0.10
Metal Products	381	5907/133393=0.04	22965/47585=0.48	27750/291968=0.09	2782/197210=0.01	9989/47692=0.21
Machinery Industry	382	44449/42399=1.05	18578/17163=1.08	43110/80542=0.54	8038/51900=0.15	1457/18143=0.08

APPENDIX TABLE 1.4 (continued)

	ISIC	SO$_2$	NO$_2$	CO	TSP	SS
Transportation Equip.	384	83590/n.a.	35410/n.a.	12553/n.a.	24915/n.a.	521/n.a.
Electric Equipment	3831	130576/n.a.	34362/n.a.	5364/n.a.	2425/n.a.	376/n.a.
Electronic & Commu. Eq.	3832–3839	7671/n.a.	14900/n.a.	29683/n.a.	5180/n.a.	975/n.a.
Apparatus & Instruments	3851	605/n.a.	1051/n.a.	135/n.a.	184/n.a.	35/n.a.
Other Industries	3852–3909	2851/286=9.95	4644/110=42.03	971/180=5.39	1908/339=5.63	7585/105=72.26
Average of the Ratio		4.59	6.48	1.77	1.18	4.03
Std. Deviation of the Ratio		12.47	12.55	3.40	2.77	15.72

APPENDIX TABLE 1.5

Emission Factors Based on Output (kg/$ Million) of the US and PRC and Their Ratios (US/PRC)

	ISIC	SO$_2$	NO$_2$	CO	TSP	SS
Food Manufacture	311–312	797/18563=0.043	535/7225=0.074	201/7569=0.027	714/21481=0.033	n.a./48822
Beverage Manufacture	313	984/39878=0.025	20736/13769=1.506	55/17671=0.003	75/39742=0.002	n.a./104295
Tobacco Manufacture	314	575/4920=0.117	348/1630=0.213	45/3305=0.014	11/4933=0.002	n.a./2379
Textile Industry	321	415/130466=0.003	333/4470=0.075	110/4875=0.023	162/8661=0.019	n.a./6861
Wearing Apparel	322	15/3103=0.005	5/807=0.006	1/1701=0.001	0/3111=0.000	n.a./563
Leather Products	323	338/11758=0.029	88/4213=0.021	27/6850=0.004	145/12807=0.011	273/45802=0.006
Timber (bamboo) Prod.	331	607/31538=0.019	646/17627=0.037	1546/24486=0.063	11974/46936=0.026	73/26306=0.003
Furniture Manufacture	332	110/8958=0.012	78/3147=0.025	83/5688=0.015	249/36897=0.007	0/1721=0.000
Paper and Pulp	341	397/60154=0.007	2265/23148=0.098	770/30927=0.025	770/61533=0.013	7134/388808=0.018
Printing & Publishing	342	12/4232=0.003	15/1248=0.012	59/3056=0.019	6/5704=0.001	1/2732=0.000
Oil Refinery	353	5756/5479=1.051	3311/4174=0.793	2990/10882=0.275	53/2344=0.023	361/2560=0.141
Chemical Industry	351–352	1707/53370=0.032	1105/17389=0.064	5537/72706=0.076	403/37472=0.011	1370/72030=0.019
Drugs and Medicines	3522	830/21951=0.038	352/8263=0.043	41/10720=0.004	157/19173=0.008	6961/22772=0.306
Rubber Industry	355	863/16999=0.051	300/6018=0.050	37/8166=0.005	96/13678=0.007	747/5415=0.138
Plastics Products	3513, 3560	1191/9210=0.129	3066/2860=1.072	454/3678=0.123	184/6767=0.027	158/1596=0.099
Const. & Nonmetal Prod.	361–369	12599/144227=0.087	8846/38689=0.229	1529/78149=0.020	8390/280098=0.030	250/29082=0.009
Ferrous Metal Smelting	3710	8121/23506=0.346	3528/12022=0.294	12656/234669=0.054	1882/58315=0.032	88515/54357=1.628
Nonferrous Metal Smelting	3720	17566/84135=0.209	572/6368=0.090	8171/55957=0.146	1475/20614=0.072	19469/16671=1.168
Metal Products	381	59/10300=0.006	237/3674=0.065	251/22544=0.011	27/15227=0.002	88/3682=0.024
Machinery Industry	382	319/10930=0.029	1601/4424=0.036	319/20762=0.015	56/13379=0.004	15/4677=0.003

	ISIC	SO$_2$	NO$_2$	CO	TSP	SS
Transportation Equip.	384	709/9550=0.074	741/5022=0.148	88/10102=0.009	203/14122=0.014	4/3033=0.001
Electric Equipment	3831	1757/6074=0.289	343/2101=0.163	54/4911=0.011	24/7027=0.003	2/2259=0.001
Electronic & Commun. Eq.	3832–3839	70/2971=0.024	135/1223=0.110	270/1417=0.191	47/2551=0.018	9/763=0.012
Apparatus & Instruments	3851	6/6406=0.001	10/2383=0.004	1/7536=0.000	2/7391=0.000	0/4=0.000
Other Industries	3852–3909	30/25822=0.001	62/9959=0.006	13/16239=0.001	23/30568=0.001	3650/9462=0.386
Average of the Ratio		0.105	0.209	0.045	0.015	0.198
Std. Deviation of the Ratio		0.217	0.368	0.069	0.016	0.431

more pollution on a per-employee basis. This conclusion is further confirmed by Appendix Table 1.5, second to last row, which indicates that on average the US industries only produce between 1.5 and 21 percent of the pollution of the PRC industries on a per-million-dollar-output basis. It should be stressed that the 1985–1988 data are used in this comparison. Evidence shows that the PRC industrial pollution intensities have shown a steady declining trend (Bi, 1995). Between 1985 and 1992, the pollution intensities based on employment and output decreased by approximately 10–90 percent for some pollutants.

There are a number of reasons for the above comparative results. First, they reflect substantial technological gaps that exist between the two countries. The technological superiority of the US industries allows them to produce more economic products and, thus, more pollution with fewer people than their PRC counterparts. This in part explains why the US industries have higher per-employee pollution intensities. The technological superiority also enables the US industries to generate less pollution than PRC industries to produce $1 million worth of output. Apart from technological reasons, the PRC industries also suffer from artificial overstaffing due to the government's policy to maintain a low unemployment rate in order to maintain "social stability." There is at least one third to one half of a labor surplus in most of the state-run factories.

The following factors also contribute to the dramatic differences between the American and the PRC pollution intensities:

■ The US industries have better access to, and are more financially capable of, purchasing pollution abatement equipment than the PRC counterparts. For example, PRC is currently unable to produce NO_x and SO_2 removal equipment, e.g., scrubbers. The foreign-made equipment is far too expensive for small- and medium-sized industries.

■ Environmental regulations are more stringent and better implemented in the US than in PRC.

■ There are significant differences in prices between the two countries. For example, many commodities in PRC, especially raw materials and energy products such as coal and steel, are still subsidized by the government in order to maintain artificially low prices.

■ The dominant fuel type for the US is liquid and gases; for PRC, it is coal which is much more pollution-intensive. The energy intensity of the PRC economy, measured by the ratio between total energy consumption and total GDP, is also known to be very high for PRC, much higher than, for example, India.

In addition to the comparisons of average values for all sectors, Appendix Tables 1.4 and 1.5 also reveal that there are significant variations among sectors, characterized by standard deviation values that are much larger than the means. Some sectors—textile industry, wearing apparel, leather products, timber (including bamboo) products, furniture manufacture, printing and publishing, and metal products—in the US produce much less pollution, in terms of both per-employee and per-dollar output, than their PRC counterparts. Large cross-sectoral variations of the ratios call for caution when using a single adjustment factor to estimate pollution for all sectors, as done by Sabah and Afsah (1994) and shown in Appendix Table 1.2.

There could be several reasons for the large cross-sectoral variations. Possibly, pollution abatement is particularly effective in these industries in the US, though more empirical evidence is needed in this regard. For some sectors such as wearing apparel, the differences in activities between the US and PRC industries are particularly striking. The US industry mainly designs and, to a lesser extent, manufactures high-class, low-material-quantity clothing products whereas PRC mainly produces low-valued-added and high-material-quantity clothing products. In many cases, the products are designed in the US, but all the manufacturing activities take place in a Third World country such as PRC where low-skill labor is much cheaper. This is obvious with a casual tour of American markets where most low-cost clothing and some products of known brands are imported from developing countries. Large differences in terms of technological content and value added in the same category of products manufactured by the two countries also exist in other sectors.

The following is a summary of the comparative results, which bear important implications for using the US data to estimate emissions in a developing country like PRC:

■ There are significant differences in pollution intensities between the US and PRC industries. This means that for any attempt to use the US data to estimate the pollution levels of a developing country with technological and other characteristics similar to PRC, certain adjustments are necessary.

■ The US industries generally produce more pollution than the PRC industries on a per-employee basis. Consequently, to use the US employment-based emission factors to estimate pollution intensities for a developing country like PRC, one needs to multiply an adjustment factor that is less than one. The recommended average adjustment factor ranges from 0.15 to 0.85 (inverse of the second to last row of Appendix Table 1.4).

■ The US industries generally produce less pollution than the PRC industries on a per-dollar-output basis. Consequently, to use the US output-based emission factors to estimate pollution intensities in a developing country like PRC, one needs to multiply an adjustment factor that is larger than one. The recommended average adjustment factor ranges from 5 to 68 (inverse of the second to last row of Appendix Table 1.5).

- There is a large variance in the ratio between the two sets of pollution intensity measured across different sectors. Consequently, a universal adjustment factor for all sectors may not be appropriate. One may vary the adjustment factors based on certain foreknowledge regarding the technological differences between the US and the Asian country sectors.

The analysis conducted in this section supports the speculation made by Hettige et al. (1994) that employment-based pollution intensity measures may be preferable for crosscountry projections because they are relatively stable across different countries. The differences in pollution intensities between the US and PRC appear to be much larger when measured in output-based emission factors than when measured in employment-based emission factors. For example, Appendix Table 1.4 shows that on average the US per-thousand-employee pollution intensities are 1.18 and 6.48 times of those of PRC. By comparison, Appendix Table 1.5 shows that the PRC per-million-dollar pollution intensities are 5 to 68 times (inverse of the average ratios) those of the US. In addition, output-based intensity measures are also more susceptible to the price variations between the US and the Asian countries.

It appears that although the approach of adjusting the US data to estimate emission levels for a developing country is a viable one, the accuracy that can be expected from such estimations may be relatively low, especially when using a single-fixed adjustment factor for all the sectors. Consequently, wherever available, local data should be gathered and used. Another limitation of the above analysis stems from the fact that the comparison was made for only five pollutants, four of which are air pollutants, due to lack of data or poor comparability of the data. Other important pollutants such as BOD, COD, and toxic metals have been excluded. One could, however, assume that the trends of the differences summarized above are also applicable to these pollutants. The World Bank IPPS report contains pollution intensities for these pollutants which potentially can be used as a base for estimating the emissions for developing countries.

5. Vehicular Emissions: A Comparison between the US and the Philippines

On a casual walk in Kathmandu, Manila, Beijing, or Jakarta, one can easily "see" and "feel" the air pollution from automobiles. For most urban centers in these regions, vehicular emissions are the major source of a number of air pollutants, i.e. CO, HC, NO_x, SO_2, TSP and lead (for those countries using leaded fuels). Because of the heavy population densities in cities, the health impacts of vehicular emissions are particularly acute.

Vehicular emissions pertain to many factors: types of vehicles, kilometers traveled, types of fuel used, availability of emission-control devices such as catalytic converters, condition of the vehicles, ambient environment, etc. The emission factors are generally expressed in terms of pollutant quantity per kilometer traveled, computed separately by different types of vehicles and fuels. Average vehicular emission factors for a region are a function of the following variables:

- Basic Exhaust Emission Level (BER)
  BERs are the emission levels in grams per kilometer, assuming the basic test conditions. Different types of vehicles have different BERs. Major vehicle types in the Asian countries include motorcycles (over 100cc), scooters (less than 100cc), light-duty gasoline-power vehicles, and heavy-duty diesel-power vehicles.

- Operating-Mode/Temperature Factor (OMTCF)
  OMTCF provides adjustment for different ambient temperature and the cold start/stabilized/hot start ratio.

- Tampering Offset (OMTTAM)
  OMTTAM is a measure of the effects of tampering (rate of each type of tampering and the associated emission impact should be estimated).

- Speed Correction Factor (SALCHF)
  SALCHF is used to correct emissions at various speeds.

- Travel Weighting Fractions (TF)
  In order to calculate the fraction of annual travel by model year, the fraction of in-use vehicles by model year is weighted on the basis of annual rate of kilometer accumulation.

Engineers have developed complex testing procedures and computerized formulas to derive average emission factors (USEPA 1985). It is beyond the scope of this study to discuss them in detail. However, it should be stressed that different countries often use slightly different testing procedures and, thus, the test results and their emission standards are also different. The discussion that follows compares the average emission factors of the US with those of the Philippines.

In a recent ADB study on vehicular emission control in Metro Manila, Engineering-Science, Inc. (1992) conducted tests of emission levels for major vehicle types. The results are given in Appendix Table 1.6.

The same report also contains the emission factors for the US compiled by USEPA for roughly the same period, although the source did not indicate the specific date the tests were performed (Appendix Table 1.7).

Appendix Table 1.8 provides the ratios of the Philippine vehicular emission factors to those of the US for some selected pollutants contained in Appendix Tables 1.6 and 1.7. Three pollutants—CO, TOC (nonmethane total organic carbons), or HC (nonmethane hydrogen carbons), and NO_x—are included in

Vehicular Emission Factors for Metro Manila (grams/kilometer)

	CO	HC	NOx	Lead	Sulfur*	Particulate
Cars	49.5	6.00	2.7	0.073	0.11	0.10
Gas Utility Veh. (Jeep)	60.0	8.00	3.0	0.092	0.14	0.12
Motor Cycle	26.0	18.60	0.2	0.028	0.04	2.00
Taxi (diesel)	1.9	0.65	2.0	0.000	0.81	0.60
Jeepney (diesel)	2.5	0.70	1.4	0.000	1.21	0.90
Diesel Utility Vehicle	2.5	0.70	1.4	0.000	1.15	0.90
Truck (diesel)	12.4	3.70	12.5	0.000	3.74	1.50

* Through crosschecking with Table 1.9 given later in this section on emission factors per kiloliter fuel, we believe that the original data contain an error of one decimal point (see example given regarding Table 1.9). The values given here are the results of multiplications of the original data by a factor of 10.

Source: Engineering-Science, Inc. 1992.

the comparison as they are. "Sulfur" in Appendix Table 1.6 and "SO$_2$" in Appendix Table 1.7 are not directly comparable. In Appendix Table 1.8, based on the atomic weights of sulfur and oxygen,[3] an adjustment factor of 2 is used to convert "Sulfur" into "SO$_2$." Lead is excluded since it is only included in Appendix Table 1.6 and not in Appendix Table 1.7, and because the US uses unleaded gasoline and the Philippines uses mostly leaded gasoline. Finally, "Particulate" in Appendix Table 1.6 is not comparable to "TSP" in Appendix Table 1.7 because "Particulate" refers to particles smaller than 10 microns in diameter and "TSP" refers to particles smaller than 100 microns. Unfortunately, the two cannot be converted at ease and, therefore, are excluded from Appendix Table 1.8.

Vehicular Emission Factors for the US (grams/kilometer)

	CO	TOC	NO$_X$	SO$_2$	TSP
Petrol					
Cars	33.0	3.04	2.70	0.123	0.33
Utility	33.0	3.04	2.70	0.134	0.33
Truck	117.0	12.20	7.80	0.246	0.68
Mo/Tricycle	17.0	10.10	0.08	0.049	0.21
Diesel					
Cars	1.1	0.29	0.99	0.634	0.45
Utility	1.1	0.30	0.99	1.268	0.45
Truck	17.8	2.90	13.00	3.380	0.93
Buses	13.2	2.90	13.00	2.355	0.93

Source: WHO, 1991, cited in Engineering-Science, Inc., 1992.

Ratios Between the Philippines and US Emission Factors

Phil. Veh. Type	CO(%)	HC/TOC(%)	NO$_x$(%)	2xSul./SO$_2$(%)	US Veh. Type
Cars (gas)	150	197	100	178	Cars (gas)
Gas UV	182	263	111	208	Gas UV
MC	153	184	250	164	Mo/Tricycle
Taxi	172	224	202	256	Cars (diesel)
Diesel UV	227	233	141	182	Diesel UV
Trucks	70	128	96	222	Diesel Trucks
Average	159	205	150	202	Average

Appendix Table 1.8 shows that for all the four air pollutants compared, the vehicular emission factors of the Philippines are on average consistently one and a half to twice those of the US, a result well-expected considering that the US has been much ahead of the Philippines in terms of installing emission controlling devices such as catalytic converters. The vehicle type that exhibits most variability is "Trucks." This could be due to the fact that for the Philippines, "Trucks" (the left-column) includes some petrol trucks while, for the US, "Diesel Trucks" (the right column) comprises only diesel trucks. Despite the minor variations, it appears to be feasible to use the US vehicular emission factors to estimate the emission factors for the other participating countries, assuming these countries have more or less the emission levels of the Philippines. Technically, the recommended adjustment factors for CO, HC, NO$_x$, and SO$_2$ fall into the range between 1.5 and 2. For lead and particulate emissions, one can use the Philippines emission factors contained in Appendix Table 1.7. Again, it should be stressed that such an adjustment approach is only recommended when local data are not available.

Another type of vehicular emission factor is expressed in terms of emissions per unit of fuel consumed. Appendix Table 1.9 provides an example for the Philippines.

The emission factors based on fuel consumption and on kilometers traveled are mutually convertible, given the fuel economy of the vehicles. For example, assuming that the average fuel economy for the gasoline-powered vehicles is 11

Vehicular Emissions Factors with Respect to Fuel Consumption for the Philippines (gram/liter)

Fuel Type	PM	SO$_x$	CO	TOC	NO$_x$
Gasoline	1.8	1.8	324	54.6	18
Diesel	18.0	10.8	9.6	18.0	26.6

Source: Engineering-Science, Inc. 1992.

kilometers per liter, using the emission factor based on fuel consumption, the SO_X emission factor per kilometer traveled can be calculated as

$$1.8g/l \ / \ 11km/l = 0.16 \ g/km.$$

The emission factors based on fuel consumption only provide rough estimates because different types of vehicles generate very different emissions, as shown in both Appendix Tables 1.6 and 1.7. However, when the information on the number of vehicles by type and their annual traveling distances is not available, they can be used to calculate total vehicular emissions given the total amount of fuel consumed by automobiles.

6. Emissions from Energy Consumption by Industries and Households

Emissions from energy-consumption activities by industries and households (stationary sources) are another major source of air emissions. A good example is the city of Beijing where coal forms the main energy source for both industries and households in terms of cooking and heating. The situation gets worse during the winter season when many residential heating stoves are in use. Coupled with air inversions that occur frequently during the winter, the ambient air pollutant concentrations can reach dangerously high levels.

The Intergovernmental Panel on Climate Change (IPCC), (1994) compiled emission factors for different utility and industrial boilers, and residential furnaces and stoves. The following four tables provide the emission factors for some pollutants. Note that TSP and SO_2 are missing from these tables because IPCC is mainly concerned with greenhouse gases. TSP and SO_2 are nonetheless important in local air pollution, especially for coal-burning countries such as PRC.

Given Appendix Tables 1.10 through 1.13, one can calculate total emissions from consuming a particular kind of fuel using a particular device. For example, assume Beijing residents currently consume one million tonnes of coal per year using coal stoves. The annual total CO emission from residential coal burning is (Appendix Tables 1.12 and 1.13)

$$1,000,000 \text{ tonnes/year} \times 22 \text{ Gj/tonne} \times$$
$$3,580 \text{ grams/Gj} = 78,760 \text{ tonnes/year.}$$

Suppose that ADB and the PRC Government are proposing a joint project of centralized residential heating using natural gas boilers. To obtain the same amount of heating values, the annual total natural gas required would be (Appendix Table 1.13),

$$(1,000,000 \text{ tonnes/year} \times 22 \text{ Gj/tonne})/(46 \text{ Gj/tonne}) =$$
$$478,261 \text{ tonnes/year.}$$

Utility Boiler Source Emission Factors (gram/Gj energy input)

Source	CO	CH_4	NO_x
Natural Gas—Boilers	19	0.1	267
Gas Turbine Combined Cycle	32	6.1	187
Gas Turbine Simple Cycle	32	5.9	188
Residual Oil Boilers	15	0.7	201
Distillate Oil Boilers	15	0.03	68
Shale Oil Boilers	15	0.7	201
Municipal Solid Waste Boilers—Mass Feed	98	n/a	140
Coal—Spreader Stoker	121	0.7	326
Coal—Fluidized Bed Combined Cycle	n/a	0.6	n/a
Coal—Fluidized Bed	n/a	0.6	255
Coal—Pulverized Coal	14	0.6	857
Coal—Tangentially Fired	14	0.6	330
Coal—Pulverized Coal Wall Fired	14	0.6	461
Wood-fired Boilers	1,473	18	112

Source: IPCC, 1994.

The annual total CO emission would be (Appendix Table 1.10),

478,261 tonnes/year $\times$ 46 Gj/tonne $\times$ 19 gram/Gj = 418 tonnes/year.

One can see that switching from coal stoves to natural gas boilers will cut Beijing's annual residential CO emission from 78,760 tonnes to 418 tonnes, which will certainly achieve a dramatic improvement of the city's air quality.

Industrial Boilers Emission Factors (gram/Gj energy input)

Source	CO	CH_4	NO_x
Coal-fired Boilers	93	2.4	329
Residual Oil-fired Boilers	15	2.9	161
Natural Gas-fired Boilers	17	1.4	67
Wood-fired Boilers	1,504	15	115
Bagasse/Agricultural Waste-fired Boilers	1,706	n/a	88
Municipal Solid Waste—Mass Burn	96	n/a	140
Municipal Solid Waste—Small Modular	19	n/a	139

Source: IPCC, 1994.

Residential Source Emission Factors (gram/Gj energy input)

Source	CO	CH_4	NO_x
Wood Pits	4,949	200	147
Wood Fireplaces	6,002	n/a	116
Wood Stoves	18,533	74	200
Propane/Butane Furnaces	10	1.1	47
Coal Hot Water Heaters	18	n/a	158
Coal Furnaces	484	n/a	232
Coal Stoves	3,580	n/a	179
Distillate Oil Furnaces	13	5	51
Gas Heaters	10	1	47

Source: IPCC, 1994.

Fuel Properties

Fuel	Heating Value (Gj/tonne)	Carbon %
Gas		
Butane/Propane	45.7	82.0
Coke Oven Gas	36.7	56.1
Methane (pure)	45.0	75.0
Natural Gas	46.0	70.6
Process Gas	48.6	70.6
Liquid		
Crude Shale Oil	40.9	84.5
Diesel/Distillate	42.9	87.2
Gasoline	116.9 Mj/gal	85.7
Jet A	41.0	86.1
Methanol	56.1 Mj/gal	37.5
Residual Oil	40.9	85.6
Solid		
Bagasse/Agriculture	8.6	22.6
Charcoal	27.6	87.0
Coal	22.0	65.0
Municipal Solid Waste	10.7	26.7
Wood	10.1	27.0

Source: IPCC, 1994.

The key to the feasibility of such a project is its costs, including the cost of producing and transporting the 478,261 tonnes of natural gas required and the costs of installing the boilers. Appendix 2 of this report contains cost estimates for switching from coal to natural gases.

Two other major pollutants generated from energy consumption activities are sulfur and TSP. Information on TSP emission factors is at present unavailable. For sulfur emissions, Spiro et al. (1992) compiled the emission factors for different fuels and countries. The results are given in Appendix Tables 1.14 and 1.16.

The emission factors contained in Appendix Table 1.14 are for uncontrolled emissions with no sulphur recovery. They are expressed in terms of the percentage of sulphur content in the fuels given in Appendix Tables 1.15 and 1.16. Appendix Table 1.15 suggests that sulphur contents vary widely with the type and origin of the fuel. Appendix Table 1.16 provides the sulphur contents for different refined petroleum energy products. Note that these are global averages and the percentages are generally much lower than those for the crude petroleum contained in Appendix Table 1.15, because the refinery process removes a significant proportion of sulphur from the crude oil.

To use the above emission factors to calculate the total sulphur emission of a country, one needs to obtain the information, or make certain assumptions, about the average percentage of sulphur already removed through adopting scrubbers or other devices in energy combustion processes. For example, there are virtually no sulphur-removing facilities in operation in PRC due to the fact that the country is currently unable to produce the equipment itself and the imports are prohibitively expensive. As a result, it is reasonable to employ the emission factors and the sulphur contents of fuels contained in Appendix Tables 1.14 through 1.16 to estimate total sulphur emissions of PRC without adjustments. For example, PRC produced and consumed approximately 1.2 billion tonnes of coal in 1994. Assume 60 percent of the total is hard coal,

---

APPENDIX TABLE 1.14

Sulphur Emission Factors from Fuel Combustion

Activity	Emission Factor (% S)
Hard Coal Combustion, Industrial	97.5
Hard Coal Combustion, Residential	77.5
Hard Coal Combustion, Coking	33.0
Lignite Combustion	75.0
Petroleum Uses	
Nonenergy Uses	0.0
Combustion (Kerosene)	15.0
Combustion (Other Petro. Prod.)	100.0

Source: Spiro *et al.* 1992.

Sulphur Contents of Fuels

Fuel Type	Country	% in World Production	Sulphur % (weight)
Hard Coal	Australia	2.7	1.1
	PRC	21.8	1.6
	Germany (west)	3.5	1.1
	India	4.0	2.3
	Poland	7.1	0.8
	South Africa	4.3	0.6
	Former Soviet Union	18.1	1.8
	United Kingdom	4.8	1.4
	United States	26.0	2.5
	Others	6.9	2.4
	World	**100.0**	**1.8**
Lignite	Australia	3.2	2.2
	Bulgaria	2.9	0.7
	Canada	1.5	0.7
	PRC	2.2	0.7
	Czechoslovakia	8.8	1.4
	Germany (east)	29.7	0.9
	Germany (west)	12.6	1.4
	Greece	2.1	1.0
	Hungary	2.2	3.1
	Poland	3.4	1.1
	Romania	2.5	0.7
	Former Soviet Union	15.4	0.7
	Spain	1.4	7.5
	Turkey	1.3	3.3
	United States	3.9	0.7
	Former Yugoslavia	4.3	2.4
	Others	2.6	1.8
	World	**100.0**	**1.3**
Crude Petroleum	Algeria	1.6	0.2
	Canada	2.4	0.5
	PRC	3.6	0.5
	Indonesia	2.6	0.1
	Iran	2.4	1.6
	Iraq	4.4	1.9
	Kuwait	2.8	2.5
	Libya	3.0	0.3
	Mexico	3.4	2.6
	Nigeria	3.5	0.2
	Saudi Arabia	16.6	2.0
	Former Soviet Union	20.2	1.4
	United Arab Emirates	2.8	0.6
	United Kingdom	2.7	0.5
	United States	14.2	0.7
	Venezuela	3.9	2.1
	Others	10.2	0.5
	World	**100.0**	**1.2**

Source: Spiro et al 1992.

Sulphur Contents of Refined Petroleum Energy Products (Global Average)

Product	Sulphur (% by weight)
Aviation Gasoline	0.022
Motor Gasoline	0.036
Gas-Diesel Oils	0.022
Jet Fuel	0.048
Kerosene	0.320
Residual Fuel Oils	1.8
Liquefied Petroleum Gas	0

Source: Spiro *et al.* 1992.

whose sulfur content is 1.6 percent (Appendix Table 1.15) and emission factor is 97.5 percent for industrial uses and 77.5 percent for residential uses (Appendix Table 1.14). Lignite accounted for the remaining 40 percent, whose sulphur content is 0.7 percent (Appendix Table 1.15) and emission factor is 75 percent for all uses (Appendix Table 1.14). For hard coal, assume also 50 percent is for industrial uses and 50 percent is for residential use (heating and cooking). Thus, the average emission factor for hard coal is 87.5 percent. Given the above information and assumptions, PRC's total annual sulphur emission from coal combustion can be calculated as

$$60\% \times 1.2 \text{ billion tonne} \times 1.6\% \times 87.5\% + 40\% \times$$
$$1.2 \text{ billion tonne} \times 0.7\% \times 77.5\% = 12.68 \text{ million tonnes.}$$

7. Emissions from Agricultural and Forestry Activities

Air emissions from agricultural activities mainly include methane (CH_4) and ammonia (NH_3), both greenhouse gases. Water and land emissions from agriculture include runoff pesticides, soil nutrients, etc. As suggested in Section 2, different forms of land degradation including soil erosion, waterlogging, and alkalization are also classified as "emissions" from agriculture and forestry. The following discussion provides some default values and examples on the emission factors related to agricultural activities.

7.1 Methane Emissions (CH4)

Methane emissions from the agricultural activities in the study regions come from two sources: rice cultivation and farming of livestock. For rice cultivation, IPCC (1994) has compiled the emission factors and total rice-cultivated areas for different countries in the world. They are partially given in the following tables.

Given Appendix Tables 1.17 and 1.18, one can calculate total methane emission from rice fields for a country. For example, for Pakistan, assuming the average growing season temperature is 30 degrees, the total methane emission is

$$1000 \times 103 \text{ ha} \times 103 \text{ days} \times 7.03 \text{ kg/ha/day} =$$
$$74{,}581{,}270 \text{ kg} = 74{,}581 \text{ tonnes.}$$

The methane emission from farming of animals comes from two sources: enteric fermentation and manure management. The emission factors for these two sources are given below (Appendix Tables 1.19, 1.20).

The information on animal populations required to calculate total emissions is contained in a series entitled The FAO Production Yearbook, published by the FAO (1991).

7.2 Ammonia Emissions (NH$_3$)
Appendix Table 1.21 provides emission factors for NH$_3$ by different major sources in Asia. It is clear that agricultural activities are the main contributors of ammonia.

7.3 Land Degradation
Under the classification scheme shown in Figure 1.1, land degradation is conceptually a part of the "emissions" generated by agricultural activities. By definition, land degradation broadly refers to soil erosion (water and wind), depletion of soil fertility, salinization, waterlogging, etc. It is characterized by the temporary or permanent lowering of the productive capacity of land (FAO et al., 1994).

As mentioned in Section 3.2, there is no clearly established relationship between a country's total area of land degradation and total agricultural and forestry activities. A proxy measurement of the "emission factors" is used here—total area and percentage of land affected by each type of land degradation. Appendix Table 1.22 is an example for PRC taken from a recent FAO report (1994).

The same FAO report also contains similar land degradation data for four participating countries: Philippines, Pakistan, Nepal, and Indonesia. It should be mentioned that different countries or regions experience different types of land degradation problems. For the Loess Plateau and southwestern PRC, Philippines, and Nepal, soil erosion, particularly water erosion, is a major concern. For northern PRC and Pakistan where most of the arable land is irrigated, salinization, alkalization, and waterlogging are the main factors for lowering land productivity.

8. Solid Waste Generation by Industries and Households
Compared to air and water emissions, solid waste generation and management may have received less attention in developing countries. However, the situation is no better than that of the other two forms of pollution. The

Seasonal Average Emission Factors Corrected for Average Temperature

Growing Season Average Temperature	Emission Factor kg/ha/day	
	Continuously Flooded	Intermittently Flooded
15	2.91	1.75
16	3.09	1.85
17	3.28	1.97
18	3.48	2.09
19	3.68	2.21
20	3.91	2.34
21	4.14	2.94
22	4.39	2.64
23	4.66	2.80
24	4.94	2.97
25	5.24	3.15
26	5.56	3.34
27	5.90	3.54
28	6.25	3.75
29	6.63	3.98
30	7.03	4.22
31	7.46	4.48
32	7.91	4.75
33	8.39	5.03
34	8.90	5.34
35	9.44	5.66

Source: IPCC, 1994.

Rice Cultivation Areas for the Participating DMCs

Country	1990 Area (1000s ha)	Season Length (days)	Continuously Flooded %	Dry %	Intermittently Flooded %
Pakistan	103	103	100	0	0
Nepal	1,440	90	29	4	67
PRC	33,265	115	93	2	5
Indonesia	10,403	110	78	15	7
Philippines	3,413	98	54	12	34

Source: IPCC, 1994.

Enteric Fermentation Emission Factors

| Livestock | Emission Factor kg/head/year or Mg/1000 head/year | |
	Developing Countries	Asian Countries
Buffalo	55	n/a
Sheep	5	n/a
Goats	5	n/a
Camels	46	n/a
Horses	18	n/a
Mules and Asses	10	n/a
Swine	1.0	n/a
Poultry	n/a	n/a
Dairy Cows	n/a	56
Non-Dairy Cows	n/a	44

Source: IPCC, 1994.

Manure Management Emission Factors

| Livestock | Emission Factor kg/head/year for Developing Countries Including Asia | | |
	Cool	Temperate Climate	Warm
Sheep	0.10	0.16	0.21
Goats	0.11	0.17	0.22
Camels	1.3	1.9	2.6
Horses	1.1	1.6	2.2
Mules and Asses	0.60	0.90	1.2
Poultry	0.012	0.018	0.023
Dairy Cows	7	16	27
Non-Dairy Cows	1	1	2
Swine	3	4	6
Buffalo	4	5	5

Source: IPCC, 1994.

Emission Factors of NH_3 from Different Sources in Asia

Category	Emission Factor	Unit
Human Being	0.3	kg NH_3/person/yr
Dairy Cow	28.3	kg NH_3/head/yr
Cow	12.8	kg NH_3/head/yr
Cow *	23.04	kg NH_3/head/yr
Horse	12.5	kg NH_3/head/yr
Pig	5.03	kg NH_3/head/yr
Sheep	2.2	kg NH_3/head/yr
Goat	2.2	kg NH_3/head/yr
Donkey	12.5	kg NH_3/head/yr
Mule	12.5	kg NH_3/head/yr
Camel	12.5	kg NH_3/head/yr
Chicken	0.32	kg NH_3/head/yr
Duck	0.32	kg NH_3/head/yr
Goose	0.32	kg NH_3/head/yr
Turkey	0.32	kg NH_3/head/yr
Nitrogen Fertilizer	6.07	percent
Phosphorous Fertilizer	6.07	percent
Urea	12.14	percent
Compound Fertilizer	6.07	percent
Fertilizer *	6.07	percent
Fertilizer Product	5.8	kg NH_3/t
Ammonia Production	0.8	kg NH_3/t
Coal Combustion	2.51	kg NH_3/tce (coal equiv.)
Oil Combustion	0.183	kg NH_3/tce
Gas Combustion	0.009	kg NH_3/tce

* Used when no data on different species available.

Source: Zhao and Wang, 1994.

infamous "smoky mountain" in Manila, and garbage dumped along major streets in Kathmandu, along the Yangtze River banks in Chongqing, PRC are the results of poor solid-waste management practices. The resulting health effects—methane emission from garbage dumps, disease vectors, underground water pollution—are equally acute as with other forms of pollution. The health impacts could be particularly severe for scavengers who virtually live on garbage.

In North America, the garbage crisis is characterized by diminishing existing landfill capacities and lack of geographically and economically available land for new landfill sites. Garbage incineration as an alternative to landfill is less than ideal because it converts land pollution into air pollution. There has been an increasing emphasis on the so-called three Rs (reuse, recycling, and recovery) as a solution to the crisis. In order to assist the three-R programs, many studies have been conducted to estimate solid-waste generation rates and composition for both industries and households (Yu 1994). Unlike air and water emissions, the estimates derived from developed countries bear little resemblance to those for developing countries in terms of both quantity and composition. In North America, for example, paper, paperboard, plastics, and metal account for a significant portion of both industrial and residential waste streams. In developing countries, such high-value materials are generally recovered before or after they reach garbage bins. Other less valuable materials such as coal ash and organic materials may dominate the waste composition. The differences in waste composition often determine the employment of waste management methods. For example, the abundance of low-energy-content materials undermines the feasibility of adopting garbage incinerators. This in part explains why PRC currently has no functioning incinerators. In contrast, high organic contents in the waste streams make composting more appealing for developing countries.

As suggested in Section 3, we employ per capita waste generation rates as emission factors to estimate domestic waste generation. Appendix Tables 1.23 and 1.24 contain per capita waste generation rates and waste composition, respectively, for some Asian cities (UNESCAP 1990). They are compiled by income levels.

It is clear from both tables that income level is a significant factor in determining waste quantity and composition. Cities in low-income countries tend to generate less wastes than cities in high-income countries. Compostable materials account for most of the waste stream in low-income cities, i.e., 96 percent for Karachi and 78 percent in Calcutta. In contrast, in more developed countries, nonfood materials such as paper, glass, and metals dominate the waste stream. Based on income levels, it can be speculated that Kathmandu may resemble Calcutta and Karachi in waste quantities and compositions.

Compared to municipal wastes, industrial and commercial wastes are generally much more heterogeneous across different economic sectors. Studies have shown that the waste generation rates vary drastically from one sector to another (Yu 1994). For metropolitan Toronto, Canada, Yu (1994) estimated that the food processing sector generated and disposed of 2,379 kg waste per employee in 1990, in which paper accounted for 16 percent and glass accounted for 27 percent. In contrast, the printing and publishing sector produced 807 kg per employee in the same year, 39 percent of which was paper.

Cultivated Land Degradation in Eight Regions of the People's Republic of China (million ha)

Degradation type	1 NE	2 North	3 Loess Pl.	4 NW	5 Tibet Pl.	6 Changjiang	7 Mid-lower	8 South	Total SW
Water Erosion									
Medium [a]	6.54	6.29	7.19	1.47	0.14	3.68	1.44	8.13	34.88
Strong [b]	1.46	0.70	4.09	0.56	0.06	0.94	0.68	2.04	10.53
Subtotal	8.00	6.99	11.28	2.03	0.20	4.62	2.12	10.17	45.41
% [c]	37.38	26.82	71.30	15.38	20.60	17.74	21.92	52.53	34.26
Wind Erosion									
Subtotal [d]	0.61	0.20	1.19	0.45	0.04	0.05	0.00	0.00	2.54
%	2.85	0.77	7.52	3.41	4.12	0.19	0.00	0.00	1.92
Depletion of Soil Fertility									
Shallow (<10cm)	4.26	2.71	6.52	1.48	0.07	3.79	2.13	5.05	26.01
%	19.91	10.40	41.21	11.21	7.22	14.55	22.03	26.06	19.63
OM (<0.6%)	4.26	6.88	3.67	3.91	0.02	3.94	0.95	3.73	27.36
%	19.91	26.40	23.26	29.62	2.06	15.13	9.82	19.27	20.65
Saline									
Medium [e]	0.55	1.59	0.39	0.40	0.01	0.55	0.04	0.00	3.53
Strong [f]	0.08	0.34	0.08	0.10	0.00	0.00	0.15	0.00	0.75
Subtotal	0.63	1.93	0.47	0.50	0.01	0.55	0.19	0.00	4.28
%	2.94	10.35	2.97	3.79	1.03	2.11	1.96	0.00	3.23
Alkaline									
Subtotal [g]	0.43	0.14	0.05	0.04	0.00	0.03	0.00	0.00	0.69
%	2.01	0.53	0.32	0.30	0.00	0.01	0.00	0.00	0.52

Degradation type	1 NE	2 North	3 Loess Pl.	4 NW	5 Tibet Pl.	6 Changjiang	7 Mid-lower	8 South	Total SW
Waterlogging									
Subtotal [h]	1.55	2.09	0.27	0.21	0.01	1.66	0.72	0.61	7.12
%	7.24	8.02	1.71	1.59	1.03	6.38	7.45	3.15	5.37
Pollution									
Subtotal	0.06	0.29	0.00	0.00	0.00	0.09	0.03	0.13	0.60
%	0.28	1.09	0.00	0.00	0.00	0.30	0.35	0.69	0.38

Source: FAO, 1994.

a. Medium > 8,000 t/sq km.
b. Strong > 15,000 t/sq km.
c. Percentage of the subtotal areas in the regional areas.
d. I soil body eroded.
e. Salt content. Medium: 0.4–0.6%.
f. Strong: 0.6–1.0%.
g. Sodium content >1.5, pH>9.0.
h. Underground water table: 0–100 cm.

Municipal Solid Waste Generation Rates in Selected Asian Cities (kg/capita/day)

Income	Cities	Waste Generation Rate
Low-income	Calcutta, Karachi	0.4–0.7
Middle-income	Manila, Bangkok	0.5–1.0
High-income	Tokyo, Singapore	0.8–1.5

Source: UNESCAP, 1990.

By comparison, little is known about industrial and commercial wastes in developing countries.

9. Summary

The estimation of environmental emissions is an important first step in the cost-of-remediation approach. Nevertheless, for most of the six countries included in this study, such data are scarce. This appendix attempts to develop a rapid assessment approach to estimate environmental emissions for these countries using secondary data, particularly the US data. The term rapid is used strictly in the sense that when local data are not available, the secondary data or default values provided in this appendix could be used to arrive at quick and "dirty" estimates with or without the recommended adjustment factors.

Figure 1.2 schematically summarizes the steps for compiling emission factors described in this appendix. First, we need to determine the numerator (Q) and denominator (E) to be used in computing the emission-economy ratio or emission factor ($F=Q/E$; equation 1.1). The choice of numerator (emission) depends on study objectives. As shown in Figure 1.2, if the main concern were local pollution, the types of emission would include CO, TSP, BOD, SS, etc., which have more impact on the immediate environment. Alternatively, if the main concern were global environmental changes, namely, global warming and acid rain, the types of emissions should include CO_2, SO_2, and NO_X. For the denominator, three potential choices are available: total output expressed in monetary terms, total employment, and value added expressed in monetary terms. Although it has been suggested in a World Bank study that all three choices are technically equivalent because the emission factors based on the three variables are highly correlated with each other, this appendix has provided some empirical evidence suggesting that total employment may be preferable to the others because employment-based emission factors tend to be more stable in a crosscountry context.

Once the numerators and denominators have been chosen, an inevitable question arises: Do you have enough data for the variables you have selected? The next few steps to be taken depend on the answer to this question. First, as discussed in Section 3.2, the level of economic sectoral aggregation depends in part on the availability, or lack thereof, of emission information for different

Municipal Solid Waste Composition in Selected Cities (% by Weight)

Material Type	High-income		Middle-income		Low-income	
	Brooklyn, US	London, UK	Manila, Philippines	Jakarta, Indonesia	Karachi, Pakistan	Calcutta, India
Paper	35	37	17	2	<1	3
Glass/Ceramics	9	8	5	<1	<1	8
Metals	13	8	2	4	<1	1
Plastics	10	2	4	3	n/a	1
Leather/Rubber	n/a	n/a	2	n/a	<1	n/a
Textiles	4	2	4	1	1	4
Wood, Bones, Straw	4	n/a	6	4	<1	5
Nonfood Total	74	57	40	15	4	22
Vegetative/putrescible	22	28	43	82	56	36
Misc. Inerts	4	15	17	3	40	42
Compostable Total	26	43	60	85	96	78

Source: UNESCAP, 1990.

Steps for Compiling Emission Factors

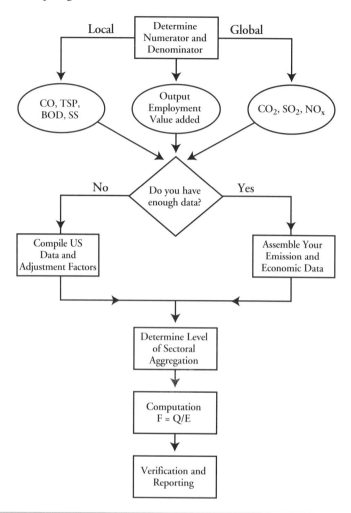

economic sectors. Frequently, developing countries do not possess databases of environmental emissions for a detailed sectoral breakdown, though the economic information such as total employment is generally available in great detail. An ideal sectoral aggregation level should be based on the availability of both environmental and economic information, subject to maximum homogeneity of emission levels within each sector.

For each economic sector, if one finds that there is sufficient economic and environmental data, the next step is simply to assemble the data for the sector and compute the emission-economy ratios (F=Q/E) or the emission factors. However, if there is little information or the information is insufficient, one might consider using the comprehensive US databases on emissions for different economic sectors. As discussed in great detail in much of this manual, when using the US pollution intensities to estimate those of developing countries, certain adjustments are necessary because the pollution intensities of developing countries are generally much higher on a per-employee or per-dollar output basis than those of the US. The estimation of an appropriate adjustment factor requires data or knowledge of the differences in technological and pollution-control levels between the US and the developing countries. Some adjustment factors are provided in this manual for estimating industrial and vehicular emissions for PRC and the Philippines, respectively.

The last step is to verify and report the results. The verification of the estimated emission factors becomes particularly necessary when secondary data have been used to estimate emissions with or without adjustments. Unfortunately, this is only possible when other independent estimates are available, even if such estimates are at different aggregation levels.

Based on our study objectives and information availability, we have included five types of emissions in this manual for detailed discussion: industrial air and water emissions, vehicular emissions, emissions from energy-consumption activities by industries and households, emissions from agricultural and forestry activities, and domestic solid waste generation. These account for most of the environmental emissions in developing countries and characterize most of the environmental problems facing these countries.

Industrial Air and Water Emissions

We compared the pollution intensities of five pollutants generated by the same economic sectors in the US and PRC, including four air pollutants and one water pollutant. The comparison provided some quantitative assessment of the differences in industrial pollution intensities between the two countries. Two types of pollution intensity measures—emission factors based on employment and output measured in dollars—were compared for 25 manufacturing sectors. The results indicate significant differences in pollution intensities between the US and PRC industries. Specifically, on a per-employee basis, the PRC industries on average produce 15 to 85 percent of those of the US. On an unit-dollar-output basis, PRC industries on average produce 5 to 68 times those of the US industries. In addition, there are significant variations in the differences of pollution intensities across different sectors. Finally, in response to an earlier World Bank working paper, the comparison supported the hypothesis that employment-based pollution intensity measures may be preferable for crosscountry projections because they exhibit less variability than output-based pollution intensities.

The comparison suggests that the approach of adjusting US data to estimate emission levels for developing countries is possible when local data are not available. However, the accuracy that can be expected from such estimation may be relatively low, especially when using a single-fixed adjustment factor for all sectors. Consequently, wherever available, local data should be gathered and used.

Vehicular Emissions

We compared vehicular emission factors in the US and the Philippines for four pollutants: CO, HC, NO_x, and SO_2. The results indicate that, on average, the Philippines vehicular emission factors are 50–100 percent higher than those of the US. The main reason for lower vehicular emissions in the US is the regulated use of emission-control devices such as catalytic converters. To estimate a developing country's vehicular emission factors using US data, one may assume that its levels are more or less the same as those of the Philippines. The recommended adjustment factors fall into the range between 1.5 and 2.

Emissions from Energy-Consumption Activities (Stationary Sources)

The IPCC has compiled the emission factors for three greenhouse gases—CO, CH_4 and NO_2—according to energy consumption of different boilers, stoves, and furnaces. The emission factors in the form of emissions per Gj energy consumed were used as an example to demonstrate how to compile and use such emission factors for decision-making. An example was given to show how switching from coal to natural gas may reduce Beijing's air pollution.

Emissions from Agricultural and Forestry Activities (Areal Sources)

The main air emissions generated by agricultural activities are methane and ammonia, mainly from rice cultivation and animal husbandry. The emission factors compiled by IPCC were given as default values for calculating the total emissions in developing countries. Different forms of land degradation including soil erosion, depletion of soil fertility, salinization, alkalinization, and waterlogging were also considered as "emissions" from agricultural activities. The emission factors for land degradation were expressed in terms of total area and relative percentage affected by each type of land degradation. An example was given to show the total areas subject to different types of land degradations in eight regions of PRC.

Solid Waste Generation by Industries and Households

Unlike air and water emissions for which North American data can be used to estimate the emissions for developing countries, there is little resemblance between the solid waste characteristics of North America and those of developing countries, despite the fact that large quantities of solid waste data are available for North America. However, the waste characteristics of countries with similar income levels may be similar, allowing comparable use of data on waste quantities and compositions within these countries. We provided some estimates of waste generation rates and composition of residential wastes for some Third World cities that may be used as default data for developing countries when local data are not available. Unfortunately, no data are currently available on industrial wastes for developing countries. Although such data are available for developed countries, they are not transferable to developing countries due to the dramatic differences of the waste characteristics.

This appendix has not attempted to gather all of the emission factors for all the participating countries. Rather, it attempts to provide a methodology for doing so. Some default emission factors were given as examples to demonstrate how to compute emission factors and total emissions of different sources.

Notes

1 BOD, as used throughout this appendix, always refers to five-day BOD and, thus, the subscript "5" is omitted.

2. The full report for IPPS can be obtained by contacting Mala Hettige at Internet: HHETTIGE@ WORLDBANK.ORG or Fax: (202) 522-3230.

3. The atomic weights of sulfur and oxygen are 32 and 16, respectively. The molecular weight of SO_2 is therefore 64. The factor for adjusting S to SO_2 is 64/32=2.

References

Akimoto, J. and H. Narita. 1994. "Distribution of SO_2, NO_x, and CO_2 Emissions from Fuel Combustion and Industrial Activities in Asia with 1 percent x 1 percent Resolution." in *Atmospheric Environment*, vol.28, no.2, pp. 213–225.

Banerjee, B. D., A. K. Singh, J. Kispotta and B. B. Dhar. 1994. "Trend of Methane Emission to the Atmosphere from Indian Coal Mining." in *Atmospheric Environment*. vol. 28, no.7, pp. 1351–1352.

Bi, J. 1995. "Temporal Variations of Pollution Intensities of Chinese Industries." Paper presented at the Interim Workshop, Asian Development Bank–Harvard Study of Environmental Indicators and Indices, Asian Institute of Technology, Bangkok.

Bouwman, A. F., I, Fung, E. Matthews and J. John. 1993. Global Analysis of the Potential for N_2O Production in Natural Soils, in *Global Biogeochemical Cycles*, vol. 7, no. 3, pp. 557–597.

Break Consultants Limited. 1980. *Environmental Considerations in the Pulp and Paper Industry*. Prepared in cooperation with the World Bank. Vancouver, British Columbia, Canada.

Brosseau, J. and M. Heitz. 1994. "Trace Gas Compound from Municipal Landfill Sanitary Sites", in *Atmospheric Environment*, vol. 28, no.2 pp. 285–293.

Campbell, M. E. and William M. Glenn. 1982. *Profit from Pollution Prevention: A Guide to Industrial Waste Reduction and Recycling*. Toronto, Canada: Pollution Probe Foundation.

Engineering-Science, Inc. in association with Basic Technology and Management Co. 1992. *Vehicular Emission Control Planning in Metro Manila:* Final Report. Asian Development Bank (T.A. No 1414 – PHI). Republic of the Philippines, Environment Management Bureau of the Department of Environment and Natural Resources, Manila. (mimeo.)

FAO. 1991. The FAO Production Yearbook.

FAO, UNDP, and UNEP. 1994. *"Land Degradation in South Asia: Its Severity, Causes and Effects Upon the People."* World Soil Resources Report, Rome.

FAO. 1994. *"The Collection and Analysis of Land Degradation Data."* Report of the expert consultation of the Asian network on problem soils, Regional Office for Asia and the Pacific, Bangkok.

Guenther, A., P. Zimmermann and M. Wildermuth. 1994. "Natural Volatile Organic Compound Emission Rate Estimates for US Woodland Landscapes", in *Atmospheric Environment*, vol. 28, no. 6, pp. 1197–1210.

Hashimoto, Y., Y. Sekine, H. K. Kim, Z. L. Chen and Z. M. Yang. 1994. "Atmospheric Fingerprints of East Asia, 1986–1991. An Urgent Record of Aerosol Analysis by the JACK Network", in *Atmospheric Environment*, vol. 28, no. 8, pp. 1437–1445.

Hettige, H., P. Martin, M. Singh and D. Wheeler. 1994. "IPPS—The Industrial Pollution Projection System." A World Bank Working Paper.

Intergovernmental Panel on Climate Change (IPCC). 1994. *Greenhouse Gas Inventory Reference Manual, First Draft.* IPCC Draft Guidelines for National Greenhouse Gas Inventories, vol. 1, 2, and 3. An IPCC/OECD Joint Program, Bracknell, United Kingdom.

James M. Montgomery, Consulting Engineers, Inc. (JMMCE) in association with Dames & Moore, Philnor Consultants and Planners, Inc., and Total Consultancy Services, Inc. 1992. Republic of the Philippines, Department of Environment and Natural Resources, Department of Trade and Industry Industrial Efficiency and Pollution Control Program, Final Report. The World Bank, Japan Grant Fund

Kato, N. and H. Akimoto. 1992. "Anthropogenic Emissions of SO_2 and NO_x in Asia: Emission Inventories," in *Atmospheric Environment*. vol. 26A, no. 16, pp. 2997–3017.

Kim, Deug-Soo, V. P. Aneja and W. P. Robarge. 1994. "Characterization of Nitrogen Oxide Fluxes from Soil of a Fallow Field in the Central Piedmont of North Carolina", in *Atmospheric Environment*, vol. 28, no. 6, pp. 1129–1137.

Klimont, Z., M. Amann, J. Cofala, F. Gyárfás, D. Klaassen and W. Schöpp. 1994. "An Emission Inventory for the Central European Initiative 1988", in *Atmospheric Environment*, vol. 28, no. 2, pp. 235–246.

Little, J. C., A. T. Hodgson and A. J. Gadgil. 1994. "Modelling Emissions of Volatile Organic Compounds from New Carpets", in *Atmospheric Environment*, vol. 28, no. 2, pp. 227–234.

Lowenthal, D. H., B. Zielinska, J. C. Chow and J. W. Watson. 1994. "Characterization of Heavy-Duty Diesel Vehicle Emissions", in *Atmospheric Environment*, vol. 28, no. 4, pp. 731–743.

Martin, P., M. Hettige, D. Wheeler, and R. Stengren. 1991. *The Industrial Pollution Projection System: Concept, Initial Development, and Critical Assessment*. World Bank (ENVAP and IENIN) internal draft document, dated October 23, 1991.

Middleton, P. and H. Lansford (eds.). 1994. *Fourth International Workshop on Global Emissions Inventories: Summary Report*. Boulder, Colorado, November 30–December 2, 1993. Data Management and Information Exchange Center, Global Emissions Inventory Activity, Boulder, Colorado.

National Survey Office of Industrial Pollution Sources (NSOIPS). 1994. *Country-Wide Survey of Industrial Sources: Assessment and Research*. Beijing: Chinese Environmental Sciences Publisher.

Orbeta, E. M. and A. Indab. 1994. Valuation of Direct Environmental Waste Disposal Services, Refinement of 1988 Estimates and 1992 Update, Environmental and Natural Resources Accounting Project (ENRAP III), Manila, the Philippines.

Richardson R. A. and J. Havlicek, Jr. 1978. "Economic Analysis of the Composition of Household Wastes." *Journal of Environmental Economics and Management*, 5:103–111.

Rubin, K. I. 1984. *US Industrial Hazardous Waste: A System Analysis of Generation, Management and Opportunities for Waste Reduction*. Thesis submitted to the Division of Applied Sciences, Harvard University.

Russell, C. S. and W. J. Vaughan. 1976. *Steel Production: Processes, Products, and Residuals*. Baltimore and London: Johns Hopkins University Press, for Resources for the Future.

Radian Corporation. 1992. *Air CHIEF CD-ROM User's Manual, Version 2.0 Beta*. EPA–450/4–92–015, US Environmental Protection Agency, Office of Air and Radiation, Office of Air Quality Planning and Standards, Research Triangle Park, North Carolina.

Romo-Kröger, C. M., J. R. Morales, M. I. Dinator and F. Llona. 1994. "Heavy Metals in the Atmosphere Coming from a Smelter in Chile," in *Atmospheric Environment*, vol. 28, no. 4, pp. 705–711.

Sabah, F. and S. Afsah. 1994. *Application of Industrial Pollution Projection System (IPPS) to Identify Industrial Pollution Control: Priorities Under REPELITA VI*. World Bank (PUSDATA and PRDEI) internal draft document, dated January 28, 1994.

Spiro, P. A., D. J. Jacob and J. A. Logan. 1992. "Global Inventory of Sulfur Emissions with 1% x 1% Resolution." *Journal of Geophysical Research*, vol. 97, no. D5, pp. 6023–6036.

UNESCAP. 1990. *State of the Environment in Asia and the Pacific*.

United Nations. 1988. *Final Draft of the Revised International Standard Industrial Classification of All Economic Activities (ISIC), Rev. 3*. Provisional, ST/ESA/STAT/SER.M/4/Rev.3/Add.1. October 14, 1988, 88–25546 0499 (E).

United States Environmental Protection Agency (USEPA). 1985. *Compilation of Air Pollutant Emission Factors*. Vol 2: Mobile Sources. 4th ed.

Yu, C.C. 1994. *Waste-Economy of Industrial-Commercial-Institutional (ICI) Establishments in the Metropolitan Toronto Area, An Integrated Methodology*. Ph.D.thesis, Graduate Department of Geography, University of Toronto.

Zhao, D. W. and A. P. Wang. 1994. "Estimation of Anthropogenic Ammonia Emissions in Asia," in *Atmospheric Environment*, vol. 28, no. 4, pp. 689–694.

Zelenka, M. P., W. E. Wilson, J. C. Chow and P. J. Lloy. 1994. "A Combined TTFA/CMB Receptor Modelling Approach and Its Application to Air Pollution Sources in China," in *Atmospheric Environment*, vol. 28, no. 8, pp. 1425–1435.

Appendix II

Cost of Remediation

Measuring Environmental Quality in Asia

Nagaraja Harshadeep
Fiona Murray
Xiang Yu
Chang-Ching Yu
Martha Crawford
Annette Huber

1. Introduction

The Cost of Remediation (COR) is defined as the total investment required to go from the existing state of the environment to a desired one as measured by a standard or set of standards. The computation of a COR involves determining the level of pollution, estimating how far the pollution is from a suitable standard, and estimating the lowest cost of controlling the pollution to meet the standard for those outputs of the environment characterized as "brown." On the other hand, "green" issues such as biodiversity usually deal with preserving the current level of an environmental good (such as trees) or achieving some level (perhaps that of an earlier year) by a certain time; the goals could also be an arresting of the rate of decline of the good. The computation of the COR in this case is more difficult and surrogate measures such as the cost of constructing and maintaining national parks can be specified. Appendix 1 of this report deals with the computation of emission factors that help determine the level of the pollution. This appendix discusses cost functions and the computation of COR for a variety of cases. Appendix Figure 2.1 depicts a schematic of the development and use of the cost-of-remediation index. We compute the costs of remediation for four components of the environment—air, water, land, and ecosystem. This appendix also illustrates the use of the COR index for a variety of purposes, such as for comparison, ranking, and investment decisions at various levels.

One of the most important issues to be considered before embarking upon a computation of the COR is the level of aggregation desired. The scale of aggregation would dictate and be dictated by the amount of disaggregated data on emissions, standards, and costs available and the intended purpose of the COR index. The COR could be computed on a facility level or at the level of nations. Also, for any reasonable interpretation of the COR, it is necessary to set standards in a consistent and rational manner. The emissions and costs should also be computed in a consistent manner.

2. Cost Functions
In order to compute a cost of remediation, it is necessary to estimate the costs per unit of environmental enhancement desired.

2.1 Types of Cost Functions
Cost functions for environmental remediation can be of many types—linear, quadratic, exponential, hyperbolic, or other nonlinear forms. A popular form of cost function is to use a single-term power function such as:

APPENDIX FIGURE 2.1

Development and Use of Cost-of-Remedation Index

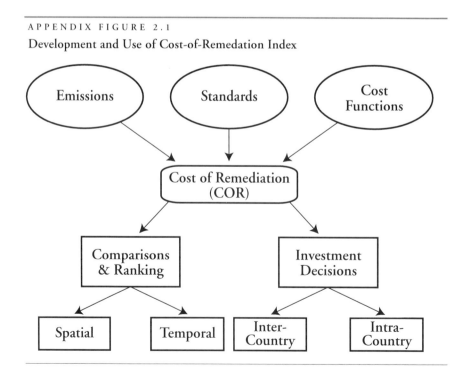

$$C = \alpha X^\beta \tag{2.1}$$

where:

C = cost of treatment
X = variable controlling costs
α = cost coefficient, and
β = elasticity of cost with respect to the variable X

If more than one variable controls the costs, the same power formulation could be used as follows:

$$C = \alpha X_1^{\beta_1}\, \alpha X_2^{\beta_2}\, \alpha X_3^{\beta_3} \tag{2.2}$$

In developing the cost functions for this study, we have often used some variation of a power formulation or constant elasticity function. However, where appropriate, we have departed from this standard and have used other forms. For example, we use linear forms in cases where we have only average costs.

APPENDIX TABLE 2.1
Factors Affecting Costs of Control

Component	Type	Factors Affecting Cost of Control
Air	*Stationary*	Quantity of effluent, concentration and type of pollutants, type and availability of control technology, retrofit or new control, existing level of control, input and process changes possible, climate
	Mobile	Number, type and age of vehicles, fuel quality, alternative fuels, type and availability of control technology, retrofit or new control, extent of control, climate
Water	*Point*	Quantity of wastewater, type and concentration of pollutants, type and availability of control technology, land costs, effluent and sludge disposal costs
	Non-point	Source area, slope, soil type, type and availability of control technology
Land	*Erosion*	Source area, slope, soil type, type and availability of control technology
	Solid & Hazardous Wastes	Type and concentration of pollutants, location, ease of extraction, soil type, type, availability and efficiency of treatment options, disposal costs
Ecosystem	*Forests*	Area of site, whether preserving existing forests or creating new ones, type of trees, climate, soils, location
	National Parks/ Biosphere Reserves	Area of site, whether maintaining existing reserve or creating new ones, sensitivity of species, costs of relocation, alternative sources of forest products, location

2.2 Components of Cost Functions

The exact construction of cost functions depends on their proposed use and the level of detail required. It is important at the outset to determine the factors that may influence the costs of control. Typically, one would have a set of estimates of costs for particular projects along with some characteristics of each project. A regression (usually nonlinear) is performed on these numbers to yield estimates of costs as a function of one or more of the characteristics of the environmental assault being remediated. It must be borne in mind that only the variables that yield significant coefficients need be used in the final cost functions developed. Also, it must be remembered that the cost functions are valid only in the range for which they were developed.

Appendix Table 2.1 lists variables that could be important in determining the control costs for a variety of environmental components.

2.3. Issues in Computation

It is important to note the year of the cost data as these data change very quickly, being functions of rapidly changing technologies, policy issues, and differential inflation. There are a variety of engineering and other indices that are available for indexing costs by year. It is imperative that costs be compared for the same year in order to allow for a proper evaluation of alternatives. It is also necessary to separate capital and operation and maintenance (O&M) costs (and also foreign exchange requirements where possible) in order to more fully appreciate the intertemporal financial aspects of the control technologies. In discounting for future costs or in the annualizing of capital costs, we also encounter the usual intertemporal economic problem of what discount rate to use. The discount rate itself is not very important (a value between five percent and 10 percent is usually used)—what is more important is that the same discount rate be used to compute costs for various alternatives.

3. Cost Functions—Air

3.1 Stationary Sources

3.1.1 Sources for Cost Functions

US Sources

The Cost Digest (DeWolf et al. 1984) includes data for a range of pollution control technologies on total capital investment (including 40 cost elements: direct costs, indirect engineering and construction and field costs, contingency, contractors' fees, retrofit increments, interest during construction, start-up, and land costs, working capital, etc.). Net annual operating expenses are also given and unit annualized costs calculated from the annualized cost divided by the annual capacity of the process to give a cost per unit of capacity.[1]

Costs are given for March 1980, and may be adjusted using one of the engineering cost indices. They are based on total treatment systems rather than on individual system components to give an idea of typical pollution control system costs and are given as they would be applied to a new system rather than a retrofit. Retrofit costs can be calculated by adding a penalty that can be as much as 70 percent of the new investment costs. Cost estimate accuracy is considered to be +/– 50 percent. Reported costs often vary because of some site-specific factors such as waste-source characteristics, contractor competition, variations in local material and labor costs, timing of construction, variation in construction practices, and architectural features.

The OAQPS Control Cost Manual (Vatavuk 1990) includes data that have been gathered by USEPA for cost estimates of pollution control systems, specifically for air pollution control. The data are at a level of accuracy of ± 30 percent, defined by Perry's Chemical Engineers' Handbook as "used to estimate the economic feasibility of a project before expending significant funds," (Perry 1984).

The total capital investment costs include purchased equipment costs based on vendor data. In a retrofit situation costs will be higher due to extra duct work, handling and erection problems, piping, site preparation, offsite facilities, and lost production. Total capital investment figures include all costs related to equipment (purchased equipment costs), labor, installation materials, site preparation, buildings (direct and indirect installation costs), cost of land, working capital, and offsite facilities. Contingency is also included. Working capital and land are both included as nondepreciable investments (working capital is used to cover the initial cost of fuel, chemicals, utilities, and maintenance) and are generally small (except for the land portion). Only the depreciable portion of the capital can be used toward income tax credits and depreciation allowances. No salvage value is assumed.[2]

The Chemical Marketing Reporter is used for materials data, while labor is size-dependent and related to capacity via the expression

$$L(2)/L(1) = (\text{capacity } 1)/(\text{capacity } 2)^{0.2–0.25}$$

where:

    $L(1)$ = labor associated with capacity 1
    $L(2)$ = labor associated with capacity 2.

In this study, the capital investment that is made at the start of a project can be annualized with the help of the capital recovery factor (CRF).[3]

Like the previous cost digests, the Integrated Air Pollution Control System (IAPCS) was developed for the USEPA Air and Energy Engineering Research Laboratory to estimate costs and performance for emission control systems (Kaplan 1994). Unlike the others, it is a computer-based digest that can be applied specifically to coal-fired boilers by specifying a range of system parameters. It incorporates a broader range of pollution control equipment than the other cost databases and includes NO_x controls, physical coal

cleaning, coal switching and blending, integrated gasification, and pulveriza-
tion. Capital cost functions are provided in the technical manuals of IAPCS for
several of the technologies, based on a range of different studies. They are a
function of several utility boiler parameters including boiler size, boiler heat
input, etc. Indirect capital costs are calculated by the so-called EPRI method,
which estimates general facilities, engineering office, process contingency, and
project contingency as a percentage of the process capital direct costs. Annual
cost equations are also given. A retrofit factor is included for different
technologies so that retrofit costs can be calculated.

Sources from Developing Countries
These include data from Meier, World Bank reports on PRC, ADB/INET
studies, and the INET comparison of coal and nuclear power. ADB, in a study
of the energy sector in several developing countries (ADB 1992b), included a
detailed set of appendices that covered the costs and performance characteristics of conventional technologies, nonconventional technologies, and emer-
gent technologies. Capital and levelized annual cost estimates are provided, but
there is also "no attempt to reflect financial cost levels in the DMCs," and the
data are mainly from studies from Western Europe, the US, and Japan. There
is "no attempt at a comprehensive treatment of the relationship between size
and capital cost…[rather] costs for a typical installation size [are given] and size
is [mentioned]." Accurate definitions of capital costs and levelized annual costs
are available only through primary sources.

Tavroulareas and Charpentier (1995) also gathered data on the performance, costs, and suitability of use of clean coal technologies in developing
countries. They include precombustion, in situ, and post-combustion technologies for pollution control (as well as new process technologies such as
fluidized bed combustion, etc.). Capital costs again reflect costs in Europe and
the US, but according to the authors, "provide a good budgetary estimate for
developing countries" (p. 5). Data for both new and retrofit plants are included.

3.1.2 Cost Functions for Pollutant Abatement
Classification for Air Pollution Control Cost Functions
The literature on the US costs of air pollution abatement has been developed
by the Environmental Protection Agency (EPA) mainly in response to increasingly stringent environmental regulations, in order to better predict the costs
of proposed regulations or the effectiveness of proposed pollution charges and
fines. Like that on power plants themselves, the data include detailed empirical
studies and cost digests for engineering approximations. Country- , region- ,
and project-specific costs are available for PRC and other developing countries
on a limited basis. Pollution control technologies can be grouped into three
categories: particulate control, sulfur dioxide control, and nitrogen oxide

control technologies. They are further subdivided into precombustion, in situ, and postcombustion approaches to pollution control.

Precombustion Technologies

The most basic precombustion coal treatment is screening. The coal is separated by size and blended to improve its quality and consistency. The coal is crushed and screened using gravity separation. Many of the ash and sulfur-related minerals are dense and can be separated from the organic (carbon containing) material by cyclone systems, jigs, dense-medium baths or froth flotation—all physical methods. These physical methods are most effective in reducing the ash content (often up to 60 percent) and some of the mineral sulfur (usually in the form of pyrites, FeS_2).

Coal-washing is more effective than screening; it involves the physical and/or chemical cleaning of coal. Coal-washing is the most effective precombustion technology to decrease fuel use, improve fuel quality, increase plant efficiency, and reduce emissions. In PRC about 20 percent of the coal is washed, and only about 50 percent of this coal finds its way to utility boilers (World Bank 1990; Sinton 1992). Coal-washing can be used to remove a significant fraction of both the ash and sulfur in coal and when washed coal is targeted for utility boiler use, emissions can be reduced dramatically, primarily from small, old boilers that use high-ash or high-sulfur coal.

Advanced coal-washing involves advanced physical cleaning processes (advanced froth flotation, electrostatic precipitation, and heavy liquid cycloning), aqueous phase treatment (ion exchange and bio-processing), or organic phase treatment (depolymerization, alkylization, solvent swelling, and organic sulfur removal) (Tavroulareas and Charpentier 1995). The most significant advantage of these methods over conventional coal-washing lies in their ability to remove a much larger proportion of the sulfur from high-sulfur coals.

Costs

According to the IAPCS manual, cost functions can be derived for coal switching from bituminous to subbituminous coals (of 33 percent lower heating value) in the following manner:

coal handling	cost	=	$155,000 \, MW^{0.45}$
pulverizers	cost	=	$1,422,000 \, MW^{0.40}$
steam gen.	cost	=	$218,000 \, MW^{0.6}$
fuel cost[4] cost		=	$(8,760 \, CF \, Q \, 10^6 / (HHV \, 2,000))$
			(new coal cost – old coal cost)

where:
CF = the capacity factor
Q = the boiler heat input (10^6 Btu/hr)
HHV = the higher heat value of the existing coal.

Capital Costs of Coal Screening and Coal-washing

	US Capital Costs ($/tonne annual capacity)	PRC Capital Costs ($/tonne annual capacity)
Coal-Screening	1.75–2.25	1.60 (Y8)
Coal-washing (New Plant)	4.00–8.00	10.00 (Y53)
Coal-washing (Retrofitting)		4.00–6.00 (Y20–Y30)
Coal-washing (Unused Capacity)		1.00 (Y5)
Coal-washing Operating Costs		0.80/t (Y4/t)

There is limited information available on the costs of the actual cleaning in the IAPCS or other pollution control cost manuals. The annual costs for coal screening estimated by the World Bank are US$1.75–$2.25 per ton. Coal screening can recover approximately 2.5 percent of the coal (by weight). Empirical data for US coal suggest that the total annual costs of physical coal cleaning are US$3.70–$4.57 per ton, with (annualized) capital costs accounting for approximately 30 percent of the costs (Kaplan 1994).

An economic analysis of coal-washing performed by the World Bank illustrated that for PRC, at an economic price of coal of Y150/ton (in 1990), screening investments showed a rate of return on investment of 23 percent (assuming a coal recovery rate of 2.5 percent). However at state-controlled prices, the return fell to 0 percent. The World Bank (1990) also highlighted that physical coal-washing costs about 17 percent more on a heat value basis per ton. However, in any economic analysis of coal-washing, additional economic benefits of reducing transportation, minimizing ash disposal, reducing boiler maintenance due to better coal quality, and increasing boiler availability should be incorporated. The costs of screening and coal-washing are summarized in Appendix Table 2.2.

In Situ Combustion Pollution Control Technologies
In situ pollution control methods can be used to control both sulfur and nitrogen emissions. Sulfur emissions can be reduced by lime or limestone injection into the furnace (or into the air ducts). At high boiler temperatures, SO_2 reacts with lime to form calcium sulfate, which is trapped together with the fly ash and any remaining lime (or limestone) by the electrostatic precipitator or bag filter.[5] Sulfur dioxide removal rates of 30–60 percent can be achieved through the addition of limestone. However, the injection technology is still being demonstrated in the US and is not widely available.

In contrast, in situ methods of NO_X control are well demonstrated. NO_X abatement occurs by changing the combustion process through modifying the temperature and restricting the air in different parts of the boiler. Low-NO_X

Capital Costs and SO$_2$ Reduction Efficiency of Lime Addition

Source	Unit Size (MW)	SO$_2$ Reduction Efficiency (%)	Capital Cost ($/KW)	Net Annual Operating Cost (c/W)	Unit Annualized Cost (c/MW)
Tavroulareas and Charpentier (1995)		30–60	$70–$120	0.03–0.07	

burners (LNB) restrict air early in the combustion process and allow full air-mixing later in the cycle. Used alone, some decrease in combustion efficiency is experienced. Therefore overfire air (OFA) systems are introduced to increase combustion later in the cycle. Reburning creates three combustion zones: the first in which NO$_X$ is created, the second where it is converted to elemental nitrogen, and the third which provides overfire air to burn the remaining combustion gases.

Costs
Although the capital costs of lime addition are low as is illustrated in Appendix Table 2.3, since removal efficiencies are also low, it has not been widely disseminated in the US or Europe. Demonstration projects are underway for plants whose size range from 33MW to 104 MW (Tavroulareas and Charpentier 1995). However, it is a potentially cost-effective technology for the retrofitting of old burners where lower removal rates are acceptable (DOE 1994).

Similarly, NO$_X$ boilers can be incorporated into new boilers with an increase in capital costs of only 1–3 percent for a 30–55 percent reduction in NO$_X$ emissions, shown in Appendix Table 2.4.

Capital Costs and NO$_X$ Reduction Efficiency of Burner Adaptation

Source	Burner Adaptation	NO$_X$ Reduction Efficiency (%)	Capital Cost ($/W)	Net Annual Operating Costs (c/W)	Unit Annualized Cost (c/MW)
Tavroulareas and Charpentier (1995)	LNB	30–55	1–3	—	—
	LNB + OFA	40–60	3–10	—	—
	Reburning	50–70	10–30	0.01–0.04	—
Rossiter and Kumana (1994)	Low excess air	15	15	1% fuel saving	—
	Staged burners	55	15	—	—
	Flue gas recirc.	75	27	—	—
EPRI (1993)	LNB + OFA	40	10	0.01c/kWh	0.03 c/kWh

Postcombustion Pollution Control Technologies Particulate Control

Between 1976 and 1982, about 50 percent of US air pollution expenditures were for particulate removal equipment. The efficiency of particulate removal depends on particulate size distribution (particulate size varies from about 1 to 200 micron in diameter), the chemical composition of the material, the concentration in the outlet flow, and the nature of the removal process. Particulate control technologies include cyclones, electrostatic precipitators, and fabric filters. These technologies have different particle removal efficiencies.

Cyclones are mechanical dust collectors that remove particulates by spinning the inlet gases and causing the particulate matter to be propelled (by centrifugal forces) toward the walls where they are trapped and fall into hoppers whence they are transferred for storage and disposal. Collection efficiency ranges from 50–90 percent but typical efficiencies reported in the OECD are about 90 percent (OECD 1993). Efficiency values are, however, only an overall measure of removal rates, and it should be noted that cyclones are inefficient for collecting particulates of less than 5 microns. Cyclones are rarely found on large utility units although in PRC they are found on older, smaller power stations (World Bank 1990).

Advanced particulate controls, notably electrostatic precipitators (ESPs), are more commonly found than cyclones on power plants in PRC, and elsewhere. Their application ranges from coal-fired power stations to aluminum smelting, sulfuric acid recovery, pulp and paper manufacturing, and iron and steel production. ESP efficiency is related to particulate size and resistivity.[6]

Particles moving through an ESP are charged by an electric field. The charging takes place via the interception of the particulates by ions generated in the electric field. The larger particles pick up a much larger number of charged ions and consequently are more easily removed by the electric forces running through the precipitation device. The charged particles migrate to the collecting electrode and are dislodged and collected in hoppers for disposal. Inefficiencies in the removal system arise because, once entrapped, the particulates must be dislodged into a hopper. Generally, some portion get reentrapped in the outlet gas during the dislodging (trapping) process. Typical removal efficiencies for ESPs are 95–99.9 percent. However, as the desired efficiency increases, the required surface area (and consequently the cost) of the collecting plate increases. In PRC ESPs are currently only found on units of over 200MW, but they are typically suitable for units larger than 35MW.

Fabric filters (FFs) are used for dry particulate removal in a wide range of applications, and are increasingly used on coal-fired boilers. Removal relies on the physical process of particulate entrainment by a sieving mechanism consisting of a number of filtering elements (bags) and a bag cleaning system. The dust accumulates in the bag, which is then cleaned and the solids collected for disposal. Cleaning of the filter is accomplished by shaking (oscillation by a motor), reverse air cleaning, and pulse jet (air) cleaning. Efficiency depends

Capital Costs and Efficiency of Cyclones

Source	Unit Size (MW)	Cyclone Efficiency (%)	Coal-S Content (%)	Capital Cost ($/kW)	Net Annual Operating Costs (c/kWh)	Unit Annualized Cost (c/MW)
Cost Digest	10	85	n/a	25	0.12	
(1984)	100	85	n/a	15	0.08	
ADB (1992)	n/a	90	n/a	10–20% of ESP costs	n/a	n/a

on the fabric used and the particulate size distribution and is greatest for small particulates. Since FFs can reach efficiencies of up to 99.9 percent and remove particulates of less than one micron, they are considered to be the best alternative to ESPs for power plants. ESPs are less efficient than fabric filters at small particulate diameters but can remove them up to 0.01 microns.

Costs
In general, the major variables that influence the cost of particulate collection are gas flow rate, inlet concentrations, particulate size distribution, and desired removal efficiency.

For cyclones the cost of the cyclone tubes represents less than one half of the capital investment, while fans, motors, and ducting account for a significant fraction. Ash removal and storage costs vary between 19 and 60 percent of the costs. If waste material can be recovered or disposal costs minimized, then the overall costs can be significantly lower. Appendix Table 2.5 presents a range of cyclone costs taken from several different sources, and normalized to 1993 US$ amounts.[7]

The major cost variable for electrostatic precipitators is the size of the collection plate and the cost of the ash removal systems. The costs given here are for inlet particulate loadings typical of coal-fired boilers and lime kilns. Ash reuse can significantly reduce the overall costs.

According to Komanoff (1981), the efficiency of ESPs improved from 97 to 99.5 percent over the 1970s, with average costs of approximately US$40/kW. These costs have risen from $20/kW (97 percent efficiency) in 1971, to $35/kW (99.5 percent efficiency) in 1978 for high-S coal, and $85/kW for low-S coal (with an average of $60/kW). In general, Komanoff found that costs increased by 10 percent for lower S coal, 10 percent for greater reliability, and 130 percent for efficiency improvements for a given coal type. An increase in efficiency to 99.9 percent is predicted to cause a 100 percent cost increase using ESP technology (Komanoff 1981). In general, price comparisons between 1980 and 1990 suggest that there has been a minimal increase in the selling price for ESP units because of more effective designs, increasing competition from European suppliers, and a shrinking US utility market.

The IAPCS manual documents a cost function for ESPs which assumes a cold-side insulated ESP unit with a maximum efficiency of 99.9 percent (Kaplan 1994).

Capital cost (million $) = (8.17 SCA Q/1000 + 232,349)$^{2.17}$

where:
SCA = specific collection area (ft^2/1,000 acfm)
Q = flue gas inflow rate (acfm).

Ash-handling is included in the costs and includes collection hoppers, piping and storage. Maintenance costs are about 1 percent direct capital investment cost and the fuel requirements for ESPs are about 1.94*10^–3*plate area (ft^2)*operating hours (Kaplan 1994).

These and other data are given in Appendix Table 2.6, assuming a SCA of 500 for high-S coal and 1000 for low-S coal where applicable.

For fabric filters the major variable costs are the type of cleaning system that is chosen. Typically a pulse jet system is used which has annual operating costs almost 15 percent lower than those of reverse air systems. However, with a low air-to-cloth ratio and reverse air cleaning, capital costs can be 45 percent greater and operating costs 40 percent higher. Komanoff, using data from the US in the 1970s, reports that baghouses cost $54/kW for low-S coal and US$48/kW for high-S coal. However, as they are not proven for large plants, he adds a 25 to 50 percent cost increase contingency (EPA reference, Komanoff p. 194). The IAPCS uses a cost function for capital costs that, like the function for ESPs, is related to the flue gas flow rate and, in this case, to the air-to-cloth ratio:

Capital cost ($) = (215,416 + 7.29 Q/AC) 2.02

where:
Q = flue gas flow rate in acfm
AC = air-to-cloth ratio in acfm/ft^2.

A typical AC ratio is about 2.0 acfm/ft2, which is appropriate for fly ash and also for a series of lime containing SO$_2$-removing particulate systems. Process capital costs are a function of total cloth area, determined by inflow rate/(AC). Maintenance is four percent of the total plant costs (Kaplan 1994). Data based on this cost function and further data are included in Appendix Table 2.7.

Sulfur dioxide control
The most widely used SO$_2$-removal technology is a chemical process known as flue gas desulfurization (FGD) which "scrubs" SO$_2$ from the flue gases through a dry- or water-based chemical absorption process.

APPENDIX TABLE 2.6
Capital Costs and Efficiency of ESPs

Source	Unit Size (MW)	ESP Efficiency (%)	Coal S Content (% S)	Capital Cost ($/kW)	Net Annual Operating Costs (c/kWh)	Unit Annualized Cost (c/MW)
Cost Digest (1984)	10	99.9	Low-S	180		
		95	Low-S	102		
		99.9	High-S	90		
		95	High-S	60		
	100	99.9	Low-S	90		
		95	Low-S	70		
		99.9	High-S	50		
		95	High-S	35		
Komanoff (1981)		99.5	High-S	35		
			Low-S	85		
		99.9	High-S	65		
			Low-S	160		
IAPCS (1994)	100	99.5	High-S	3.34		
			Low-S	6.18		
	600	99.5	High-S	17.5		
			Low-S	34.5		
ADB (1992)	500	99.5	Med-high-S	4% plant costs	5-8% plant costs	
Anderson (1993)		99.9				0.4c/kWh
Tavroulareas and Charpentier (1995)		99.5		40-60		
		99.9		100		
World Bank (1990)		98		20-40		
EPRI (1993)	500	99.5	High-S	65	0.15 c/kWh	0.25 c/kWh

Capital Costs and Efficiency of Fabric Filters

Source	Unit Size (MW)	FF Efficiency (%)	Coal S Content (% S)	Capital Cost ($/kW)	Net Annual Operating Costs (c/kWh)	Unit Annualized Cost (c/MW)
Cost Digest (1984)	10	99.9		65	0.22	
	100	99.9		45	0.16	
Komanoff (1981)			High	48		
			Low	54		
IAPCS (1994)	100	99.7		30		
	500	99.7		24		
EPRI (1993)	500	99.9	All	50–70	0.17–0.2	0.3 c/kWh
ADB (1992)		99.5		<4% plant costs		
Tavroulareas and		99.0		50		0.035 c/kWh
Charpentier (1995)		99.5		70		0.045 c/kWh

Wet scrubbers are the most common FGD technology. Removal efficiency (without additives) is 80–90 percent. It requires four major steps: preparation of the slurry, contact between the gas and the slurry, reaction of the lime with the SO_2 and solid waste removal. Preparation involves crushing the limestone and forming a liquid/slurry that is fed into the scrubbing loop: an absorber (spray tower) and reaction tank. In the spray tower, SO_2 is removed through the reaction of dissolved SO_2 with the slurry to form calcium sulfite and sulfate. Additives such as adipic acids, dibasic organic acids, or magnesium can be used to improve removal. The calcium-sulfur compounds are dewatered to a 50 percent solids mixture and waste disposal is accomplished through thickeners, vacuum filters, and piping for landfill/ponding (Kaplan 1994). The whole FGD process is very energy intensive and uses at least two percent of the plant's power generation for operation.

Alternatives to lime or limestone wet FGD include dual-alkali, magnesium-oxide, and Wellman-Lord systems. Their major differences lie in the chemical used to scrub the SO_2 and the product of the scrubbing reactions. Lime/limestone-scrubbing uses a calcium hydroxide or calcium carbonate slurry that creates calcium sulphite and sulphate waste products; when limestone is used, carbon dioxide is formed as a by-product in large quantities directly proportional to the amount of SO_2 scrubbed.

Limestone: $CaCO3 + SO_2 \rightarrow CaSO_3 + CaSO_4 + CO_2$

Lime: $Ca(OH)_2 + SO_2 \rightarrow CaSO_3 + CaSO_4 + H_2O$

In contrast, the dual-alkali process uses a sodium alkali (usually soda ash or sodium hydroxide), which is soluble. SO_2 reacts to form sodium sulfite and bisulfite, and some limited amount of sodium sulfate. This is then reacted with lime to form calcium sulfite and sulfate, which precipitates while the sodium alkali is regenerated and recycled.

Dual-alkali: $Na_2CO_3 + SO_2 \rightarrow NaSO_3 + NaHSO_3 + Na_2SO_4 + CO_2$

$Na SO_3 + NaHSO_3 + Na_2SO_4 + Ca(OH)_2 \rightarrow CaSO_3 + CaSO_4 + NaOH$

The slurry used in the magnesium-oxide process is magnesium oxide (MgO), which forms magnesium hydroxide, which (after a pretreatment step designed to minimize chlorine in the waste stream) absorbs the SO_2. Magnesium sulfite and sulfate are formed and precipitated, separated, thickened, and then regenerated as magnesium oxide by a two-stage process that requires drying and then calcining to reconvert the sulfates to oxides, with the formation of a concentrated stream of SO_2 that can be used as a precursor to sulfuric acid production.

Magnesium-oxide: $MgO + H_2O \rightarrow Mg(OH)_2$

$$Mg(OH)_2 + SO_2 \rightarrow MgSO_3 + MgSO_4$$

$$MgSO_3 + MgSO_4 \rightarrow MgO + SO_2$$
(concentrated)

The Wellman-Lord system also produces a concentrated stream of SO_2, this time with sodium sulfite. On reaction with SO_2 and air, sodium sulfate is formed. This is sent to a crystallizer for the formation of a sodium sulfate slurry that is dried and disposed of as solid waste. The remaining liquid is regenerated by converting bisulfate to sulfite through heating. Sodium sulfite crystals are then formed, regenerated in solution, and returned to the scrubber.

An alternative to all the forms of wet FGD is the use of dry scrubbers. This is a dry SO_2-capture process in which SO_2 is dissolved or absorbed onto a sorbent sprayed into the flue gas. The contact process occurs through an atomized lime slurry in a spray drying tower. Any water in the slurry evaporates and calcium hydroxide reacts with the SO_2 to form calcium sulfite and some sulfate. No CO_2 production takes place due to the use of lime in this process. The calcium is almost dry (due to the process heat) and the solid and fly ash are collected in a fabric filter or ESP and then landfilled. Wastes from the spray dryer are reslurried and fed into the spray dryer again. The system is generally more effective in low-S systems and with low-sulfur coals removal efficiencies reach 70–90 percent. It can be used for retrofit if there is sufficient land area available.

Costs
The costs of wet scrubbers are high at 10–20 percent of new plant costs (and can reach 30 percent of PRC plant costs), and 15–30 percent for retrofitting. The variation in the capital and operating costs of FGD systems in utility boilers is large, due to the design bases including the efficiency of SO_2 removal (85–90 percent), the S content of the fuel, sludge disposal techniques, and redundancy in process equipment (i.e., scrubber modules), which enhances reliability. The sulfur content of the fuel also affects the materials-related operating costs. Komanoff again reports from US empirical experience, that the first generation of scrubbers with removal efficiencies of 75 percent cost $120/kW (1981). Costs rose to $175/kW for 1978 with an efficiency of 90 percent. These estimates are in line with EPA estimates for 1979, but 35 percent lower than cost estimates by Bechtel made in a study of scrubber costs for the Electric Power Research Institute (EPRI 1977). The IAPCS provides estimates on cost function for FGD costs based on the TVA Shawnee model, which is

APPENDIX TABLE 2.8
Capital Costs and Efficiency of Different FGD Technologies

Source	Unit Size (MW)	FGD Efficiency (%)	Coal S Content (% S)	Capital Cost ($/kW)	Net Annual Operating Costs (c/kWh)	Unit Annualized Cost (c/MW)
Cost Digest (1984)	150	90	3.5	267 (240)	1.07	
	500	(80)		200 (180)	0.90	
cost factors	lime			*0.9	*0.9	*0.9
	dual alkali			*1.0	*1.0	*1.0
	MgO			*1.1	*1.2	*1.2
	W-L			*1.0	*1.0	*1.0
Komanoff (1981)		75		120		
		90		175		
IAPCS (1994)		95	1	110		
ADB (1992)	l'stone	95		81–170		
	W-L			120–255		0.33–0.64 c/kWh
Tavroulareas and Charpentier (1995)		90		120–210	0.074–0.13	
EPRI (1993)	l'stone 500M	95–98	High-S	120–200	0.28	0.48–0.61c/kWh
Anderson (1993)		90				1.5c/kWh
World Bank (1990)		90		150		
OECD (1993)	1009	5	<3.5	385		
	600			186		

based on research at the TVA's Alkali-Scrubbing Test Facility where experimental tests were used to develop a computer model to estimate costs of lime/limestone scrubbers. Ten years of plant data in 1988 dollars have also been added to update the model (Sudhoff and Torstrick 1985). The cost function is as follows:

Direct capital cost (\$) = 763,900 (boiler size in MW)0.69.

The IAPCS equation assumes that the system is new, not retrofit, burning one percent–S coal, with an operating capacity factor of 65 percent, a 35-year plant life, and credit for sulfuric acid production where appropriate. Other cost data are given in Appendix Table 2.8.

The costs of dry scrubbers are given in Appendix Table 2.9, but are sensitive to coal S content, the choice of particulate collection device, and the fuel heat value and its ash content. One important advantage of the technology is its lower capital cost especially for lower removal requirements than wet FGD (Tavroulareas and Charpentier 1995).

Again, a simple, generic cost function for lime spray-drying is given by IAPCS (Kaplan 1994):

Capital cost (\$ '000) = 9,186.2 + (39.05 size(MW)).

Cost adjustments
S content: Capital cost = base cost (0.81 + (0.097 S percent))
Removal efficiency: Capital cost = base cost* $(0.778e^{0.003}$ (SO2 percent removal))

Nitrogen Oxides Control
Both Selective Catalytic Reduction (SCR) and Selective Non-Catalytic Reduction (SNCR) are highly efficient removal systems for NOX, but to date they have not been widely used in the US (particularly SNCR).

For SCR, NO_X removal occurs through a series of redox reactions catalyzed at 600 percent F by vanadium pentoxide and titanium dioxide in the presence of ammonia.

SCR: $4NH_3 + 6\ NO \rightarrow 5\ N_2 + 6\ H_2O$

$8NH_3 + 6\ NO_2 \rightarrow 7\ N_2 + 12\ H_2O$

$4NH_3 + 4\ NO + O_2 \rightarrow 5\ N_2 + 6\ H_2O$

$4NH_3 + 2\ NO_2 + O_2 \rightarrow 3\ N_2 + 6\ H_2O$

For SNCR, NOX removal occurs through the conversion of the emissions to nitrogen by injecting a nitrogen chemical (generally ammonia or urea) into the

Capital Costs and Efficiency of Lime Spray-Drying

Source	Unit Size (MW)	LSD Efficiency (%)	Coal S Content (% S)	Capital Cost ($/kW)	Net Annual Operating Costs (c/kWh)	Unit Annualized Cost (c/MW)
	200	90	3.5	225	0.9	1.00
	500			150	0.8	0.95
	200	70	0.7	150	0.2	0.75
	500			115	0.3	0.60
IAPCS (1994)	100	90	2	130		
	600			55		
OECD (1993)	100	70–90		320		
	600			160		
EPRI 19(93)	500	80–90	Low S	100–150	0.16	0.35–0.40
ADB (1992)		65–95		136		
Tavroulareas and Charpentier (1995)		70–90		110–165	0.074–0.11	
URBAIR (1994)				20–100		

/ is less widely demonstrated than SCR but has lower catalyst, which is a large cost component in SCR, is

$$CH_2CONH_2 + HO_2 \rightarrow 2N_2 + CO_2 + 2H_2O$$

$$.\ NH_3 + O_2 + H_2O + (H_2) \rightarrow N_2 + H_2O$$

Cost
Some limited cost data for SCR and SNCR are provided in Appendix Table 2.10. Annual costs are dominated by the catalyst replacement costs, ammonia handling and storage, and electricity requirements.

Cost Functions for Pollution Control Technologies
Cost Function Formulation

For each pollutant, there is a limited range of abatement technologies. Furthermore, each technology is generally only effective over small removal efficiency ranges. Each technology, therefore, provides only a point (or small range) on a function of pollutant abatement versus cost. The costs are dependent on several variables, specifically the size of the source (generally given in MW of installed capacity), the sulfur and ash content of the fuel, and whether or not the pollution control equipment is being used in a new plant or as a retrofit technology. Cost functions can therefore be developed for each technology for a limited range of removal efficiency. These functions could then be aggregated into functions of least-cost pollutant removal over a removal range. Parameters such as unit size and fuel type can be incorporated into these more general functions using additional parameters. In order to gather together all the data from cost digests and empirical studies, and include in the cost functions some notion of the impact of parameters such as unit size, efficiency, and S coal content, a standardized form was selected for the cost functions. Based on the literature for engineering cost estimates for wastewater treatment technology, the form of a single term power function was chosen. The function form is as follows:[8]

$$C = \alpha X^\beta \tag{2.3}$$

where:

C = cost in million $ (1993)
α = constant
X = size of plant installation in MW
β = economy-of-scale parameter.

Using data and cost functions (in other functional forms) from cost digests, different single-term power functions were developed for each data source.

Capital Costs and Efficiency for SCR and SNCR Technologies

Source	Unit Size (MW)	SCR/SNCR Efficiency (%)	Capital Cost ($/kW)	Net Annual Operating Costs (c/kWh)	Unit Annualized Cost (c/MW)
ADB (1992)		SCR 60–90	53–102	catalyst is 65% levelized costs	0.34–0.66
	300–350	SNCR 30–50	11–53		0.02–0.06
Tavroulareas and Charpentier (1995)		SCR	50–150	0.04–0.08	
		SNCR	10–20	0.01–0.02	
Anderson (1993)		SCR			0.5
OECD (1993)		SCR 70–90	150–190		
		SNCR 30–60	15–35		
EPRI (1993)		SCR 40–80	70–90	0.28	0.41–0.45
			SNCR 60–80%	$5–10	0.1c/kWh 0.11–0.12
Rossiter and Kumana (1994)		SCR 85	230	$1,100/t NO_x	
		SNCR 70	10	$800/t NO_x	

This was done using simple regression analysis based on the log-log transformation of the cost function into a linear form:

$$C = \alpha X^\beta \qquad (2.4)$$

$$\log C = \log \alpha + \beta \, \log X \qquad (2.5)$$

These were then standardized to reflect 1993 US$ costs (using a 4.6 percent annual rate of inflation). This form was augmented where appropriate with additional terms to represent fuel S content (in percent S) and technology removal efficiency (percentage removal). However, this form was chosen to be the most tractable (Tihansky 1974).

Adjustment for Retrofit Versus New
For most pollution control technologies, particularly end-of-pipe controls, the cost of retrofitting is considerably higher than the cost to install technologies into a new, "green" field site. Therefore, an adjustment factor needs to be added to any capital cost functions that are developed and applied to existing facilities. Appendix Table 2.11 provides some retrofit factors derived from a range of literature sources.

Cost Functions for Pollution Abatement (See Appendix Table 2.12)
3.1.3 Transforming cost functions
PRC-specific Adjustments to Cost Functions
The costs and cost functions described above are based on data from the United States, Europe, and Japan. There are very few empirical data available on the costs of pollution control technology for developing nations, probably because the experience with pollution abatement is limited, and also because systematic reporting is less well developed. In order to apply costs and cost functions

APPENDIX TABLE 2.11
Retrofit Factors for Different Pollution Control Technologies

Technology	Retrofit Factor	Comments
Low-NO$_X$ burners	3–5	Tavroulareas and Charpentier (1995)
LNB + OFA	2–3	Tavroulareas and Charpentier (1995) & EPRI (1993)
Reburning	2	Tavroulareas and Charpentier (1995)
Cyclones		no information available
ESP	1.3–1.5	IAPCS (1994) & EPRI (1993)
Fabric Filters	1.2–1.3	EPRI (1993)
Wet FGD	1.25	Tavroulareas and Charpentier (1995) & EPRI (1993)
Spray Dryers	1.27–1.33	Tavroulareas and Charpentier (1995) & EPRI (1993)
SCR	1.15	EPRI (1993)
SNCR	2	Tavroulareas and Charpentier (1995) & EPRI (1993)

APPENDIX TABLE 2.12

Cost Functions for Pollution Abatement Using Different Pollution Control Technologies

Source	Assumptions	Cost Functions $C = aX^b$	Cost Functions $C = aX^b$
Electrostatic Precipitators			
IAPCS (1994)	Functional form $C = (8.17 \text{ SCA } Q/1000+232349)\ 2.2$ $\text{SCA} = 500$ (low res) $= 1000$ (high res) $Q = X\ 3200$	$C = 0.07\ X^{0.93}$ 99.5% removal High-S (low resistivity)	$C = 0.012\ X^{0.96}$ 99.5% removal Low-S (high resistivity)
Cost Digest (1984)	Lifetime of 20 years Operating factor 70% Specifically for coal-fired boilers	$C = 0.31\ X^{0.71}/$ $C = 0.19\ X^{0.74}$ 99.9–95.0% removal high-S (low resistivity)	$C = 0.64\ X^{0.69}/$ $C = 0.37\ X^{0.71}$ Low-S (high resistivity) 99.9–95.0% removal
Cyclones			
Cost Digest (1984)	Lifetime of 20 years Operating factor 70% Overall removal efficiency 85%	$C = 0.11\ X^{0.63}$	
Fabric Filters			
IAPCS (1994)	Functional form $C = (215416 + 7.29\ Q/AC)\ 2.02$ $AC = 2$ $Q = X\ 3200$ Efficiency 99.5%	$C = 0.18\ X^{0.73}$	

Source	Assumptions	Cost Functions C = aX^b	Cost Functions C = aX^b
(Fabric Filters)			
Cost Digest (1984)	Lifetime of 20 years Operating factor 70% Bag lifetime 2 years AC = 2	$C = 0.18\ X^{0.80}$	
Flue Gas Desulfurization			
IAPCS (1994)	Efficiency 99.5% S content 1% 1988 costs Range 100–1300 MW	$C = 0.92\ X^{0.69}$	
Cost Digest (1984)	Lifetime of 20 years Operating factor 70%	S content 3.5% Limestone $C = 1.55\ X^{0.76}$ Lime $C = 1.40\ X^{0.76}$ Dual-alk $C = 1.55\ X^{0.76}$ Mag-ox $C = 1.70\ X^{0.76}$ Well-L $C = 1.55\ X^{0.76}$	S content 0.7% Limestone $C = 1.33\ X^{0.76}$ Lime $C = 1.20\ X^{0.76}$
OECD (1993)	Limestone FGD	$C = 2.56\ X^{0.59}$	
URBAIR (1994)	Limestone FGD Cost function = (12/X + 0.11) 1000 (0.6 FGV/3250 + 0.4 S O2em/0.01 S%/1.5%) FGV = 4000	S content 3.5% $C = 5.94\ X^{0.60}$	S content 1.5% $C = 1.68\ X^{0.60}$

APPENDIX TABLE 2.12 *(continued)*

Source	Assumptions	Cost Functions C = aX^b	Cost Functions C = aX^b
Lime Spray-Drying			
IAPCS (1994)	Functional form C = 9.19 + 0.039 X	C = 1.52 X$^{0.508}$ S content 2%	
	C (function S%) = C (0.81 + 0.097 S%)	Generic function C = (0.983 + 0.118 S%) X$^{0.508}$	
	Efficiency 90%		

Comparison of Efficiencies of Typical PRC and
OECD Manufactured Cyclones and ESPs

Technology PRC	Typical Average Efficiency (%)	OECD Cost Differential Efficiency (%)	PRC Capital (% higher than OECD)
Dry Cyclone	80–85	90	2–20
Wet Venturi Cyclone	85–90	97	5–15
ESP	95–98	>99	25–30

(presented above) successfully to developing country problems, specifically to PRC, adjustments should be made, where possible, to reflect local cost differentials. With regard to pollution control technologies, it might be expected that since PRC has no domestic capability to manufacture SO_2 control devices, the costs, if such technologies were used, would reflect importation costs. However, for particulate controls there are limited data to support the notion that PRC-made particulate controls cost less, but are of lower efficiency (World Bank 1990).

For example, cyclones commonly found in OECD countries have an efficiency of 90 percent while those in PRC are often only 80 percent efficient. The average efficiency of PRC manufactured ESPs is also low at 98 percent probably due to poor operation. Capital costs of ESPs in PRC are quoted as being only 6–8 $/kW, compared to 20–40 $/kW in the United States; however this may be in part due to their lower efficiency (World Bank 1990). There is only a limited capability to manufacture fabric filters in PRC and the PRC product has an average filter life of only a year compared to five years for an equivalent OECD product. The fabric manufacturing process seems to be the main limitation to their longevity (Appendix Table 2.13).

In contrast to particulate controls, that are widespread in PRC, at least on plants of capacity of over 200MW, S controls are rare. Only five scrubber systems have been constructed or were under construction in PRC as of 1994. All these were installed using technology from Japan (Evans 1995). Average costs are quoted as approximately $100/kW for Asia, which has decreased from $ 150/kW over the last few years (Evans 1995). These are highlighted in Appendix Table 2.14, but no costs of installation are currently available.

3.2 Mobile Sources

3.2.1 Introduction

Motor vehicles emit pollutants as the result of combustion of fuel, whether the fuel used is gasoline, diesel, alcohol (e.g. ethanol, methanol), or natural gas. Commonly emitted pollutants of concern include hydrocarbons, carbon monoxide, nitrogen oxides, sulfur oxides, particles, and lead compounds. This

APPENDIX TABLE 2.14

Efficiencies of FGD Technologies in Some Plants in PRC

Source	Technology	Efficiency SO_2 Removal (%)	Location & Plant Size	Manufacturer
Evans (1995)	Wet FGD	95	Luohuang, Chong Ching, 360MW x 2	Mitsubishi
	Semi-dry FGD	70	Huangdao, Shangdong 210MW	Mitsubishi
	Limestone injection	60–70	Nanjing City, Jiangshu	Mitsubishi
	Simplified wet FGD	80	Taiyuan, Shanxi	Babcock-Hitachi
Meier (1994)	FGD (3% S)	80, $257/kW	Mawella 150MW	
	FGD (3% S)	80, $163/kW	Trinco 300MW	

section has been organized to introduce the technological means that can be used to control their emission, and to present data useful for COR calculations. Readers who already have a conceptual understanding of mobile source air pollution will probably find the data tables of most interest.

3.2.2 Technological Control of Mobile Source Air Pollution

A range of control technologies exist, each with associated efficiency and cost. The simultaneous implementation of multiple control technologies may result in interactions that are: (1) synergistic—where controlling for one pollutant also involves reducing another; (2) antagonistic—where controlling for one pollutant involves the increase in emissions of another; and (3) exclusive—where controlling for one pollutant precludes controlling for another. Thus, it is impossible to develop "cost curves" in the traditional sense, where the control of a single pollutant is considered. In mobile source air pollution control, it is necessary to consider "packages" of control technologies, with control of one pollutant contingent on control, or noncontrol, of another.

To review available control technologies, we will consider the three major motor vehicle engine types in use today. These are: (1) spark-ignited gasoline engine (most passenger cars); (2) compression-ignited diesel engine (most utility vehicles and hauling trucks); and (3) two-stroke gasoline-plus-oil fueled motorcycle engine (most scooters and motorcycles). For the sake of simplification, we do not address the use of engines using alternate fuels (e.g., LPG, or alcohols), or other types of engines (e.g., Brayton, Rankine, or hybrid) here.

The primary pollutants of concern, when trying to control emissions from a spark-ignited gasoline engine, are hydrocarbons, carbon monoxide, and oxides of nitrogen. According to Faiz et al. (1994), emissions of all three pollutant categories can be reduced by 50 percent or more (from uncontrolled levels), through engine modifications, at a cost of about $130, per car. Using three-way catalysts and electronic engine control systems, hydrocarbon and carbon monoxide can be reduced by 90–95 percent, and nitrogen oxides by 80–90 percent, for a cost approximately $600 to $800, per car. Although some of these measures may incur slight penalties in fuel economy, the use of "lean burn" technology, combined with an oxidation catalytic converter, can achieve roughly comparable results (HC and CO reduced by 90–95 percent, and NO_x reduced by 60–75 percent), while achieving slight gains (10–15 percent) in fuel economy.

For diesel engines, the principle pollutants of concern are nitrogen oxides, hydrocarbons, and particulates (PM_{10}). Compared with gasoline-fueled vehicles of the same size, light-duty diesel-fueled vehicles emit considerably less HC (about 90 percent less), CO (about 90 percent less), and NO_x (about 50–70 percent less). Emission of particulates, however, is quite high—six to ten times higher than that from gasoline engines. Because of the relatively high sulfur content of diesel fuels, sulfur oxides are often associated with the emitted particles, making them much more dangerous from a public health point of view. Large diesel trucks emit 90–95 percent less hydrocarbons, and about 98 percent less carbon monoxide, than large gasoline-fueled trucks. The trade-off is that they emit 50–100 percent more NO_x. Normally, diesel engines are considerably more fuel efficient than gasoline-powered engines (for light-duty vehicles, 15–40 percent improvement in fuel economy; for heavy-duty vehicles, up to 100 percent greater fuel economy). Control measures for diesel vehicles include engine design changes, fuel injection systems, turbo charging, and charge-air cooling. Although these measures have associated costs, they also improve fuel economy. Emissions of hydrocarbons and particulates can be further reduced through the use of low-sulfur fuel and an oxidation catalytic converter.

Motorcycles and three-wheelers, especially common in developing countries, use two-stroke engines, which are fueled by a mixture of gasoline and oil. Due to the relatively low temperature of combustion, a sizeable portion of the fuel mixture enters the exhaust unburned. Thus, hydrocarbon emissions are quite high. Furthermore, particulate emissions are notoriously high. This is due to the mixing of oil with the gasoline. In the exhaust, unburned oil recondenses into oil particles, appearing as white smoke trailing the vehicle. Faiz et al. (1994) report that hydrocarbon emissions from one two-stroke motorcycle can exceed the combined hydrocarbon emissions of three passenger cars, while the particulate emissions can exceed those from a heavy-duty diesel truck. For a cost of $60 to $80 per motorcycle, these emissions can be substantially controlled by converting to an advanced two-stroke design that uses fuel injection. This change also improves fuel economy by as much as 40 percent.

Technologies for the Control of Emissions from Spark-Ignited
Gasoline Engines

The majority of passenger cars are powered by spark-ignited gasoline engines, also known as "Otto cycle" engines. Some heavy-duty trucks and utility vehicles also have this type of engine. In recent years, some Otto cycle engines have been altered to run on natural gas, liquefied petroleum gas, alcohols, and hydrogen. But the control technologies discussed here are specifically oriented toward gasoline-fueled engines. Spark-ignited engines can be either two-stroke or four-stroke in design. The technologies discussed here are for the control of emissions from four-stroke engines, which are used by most commercially available passenger vehicles today. At each "stroke" (180° of crankshaft rotation) of the piston, one of four steps of engine operation occurs: (1) intake— intake valve allows air and fuel to enter intake manifold; (2) compression— upward movement of piston compresses the mixture into the combustion chamber and the spark ignites it; (3) power—pressure of burning gases produces power by pressing the piston down and turning the crankshaft; or (4) exhaust—piston moves upward, exhausting the spent gases. Each of the technologies described aims to control emissions of one or more of three types of pollutants—hydrocarbons, carbon monoxide, and nitrogen oxides.

Positive Crankcase Ventilation Systems

Automobile engines must be ventilated if the engine is to work properly. "Blowby" gases, those that are forced past the piston rings whenever a high pressure condition is present in the combustion chamber (i.e., during the compression stroke and the power stroke), must be exhausted. At high speeds, more air and fuel are being drawn into the combustion chamber and the number of engine strokes peaks. Therefore, the volume of blowby gas is highest when the vehicle is operating at high speeds.

Composition of the blowby gases usually includes unburned hydrocarbons, corrosive acids, and water vapor. If allowed to remain in the crankcase, they would cause engine corrosion, oil dilution, and slurry deposits. The earliest models of cars (1950s) removed blowby gases via a "road draft tube," a simple tube, connected at one end to the crankcase and open at the other end, that serves as a conduit to the airstream behind the vehicle. A slight vacuum developed in the tube as the vehicle moved at speeds over 25 miles per hour. About 20 percent of hydrocarbon emissions originated from the crankcase under these conditions (USEPA 1977).

Positive crankcase ventilation (PCV) systems collect the blowby gases and return them to be burned by the engine, by circulating a stream of fresh air through the crankcase before injection into the intake manifold. Thereby, blowby gases are drawn into the combustion chamber and burned with the air/ fuel mixture. Air is always circulated through the crankcase whenever the engine is running. The PCV valve plunger prevents blowby gases from escaping during engine backfire or stalling conditions.

Thermostatic Air Cleaner Systems

Thermostatic (heat-activated) air cleaners (TACs) provide heated air to the carburetor during the engine warm-up period. Without the TAC, the carburetor would need to be "choked" (momentarily flooded with a rich air/fuel mixture) during engine warm-up to facilitate burning. When the engine is warm, the fuel injected into the carburetor atomizes to form a relatively homogeneous vapor that burns readily in contact with air. During cold start-up, the TAC allows better atomization, by warming the air stream and regulating its temperature, prior to its entering the carburetor. Air is heated by the exhaust manifold before entering the carburetor.

The air/fuel ratio has a very important effect on emissions, as well as on engine power and efficiency. A stoichiometric air/fuel ratio exists when there is exactly enough air to burn the fuel, with neither air nor fuel leftover (numerically equal to 14.7:1). A lean air/fuel ratio exists when there is more air than required, and a rich air/fuel ratio exists when there is less air than what is required to completely burn the fuel. For several reasons, engines are more efficient when the air/fuel mixture is lean, rather than stoichiometric. At lean ratios, heat loss is reduced, higher compression ratios are achieved (less likely to have engine "knock"), and throttling losses are lessened. So-called "lean-burn" engines are those specifically designed to run on very lean mixtures (numeric air/fuel ratio of 17.6:1).

The TAC system is important, for it allows the air/fuel ratio to be set as "lean," thus reducing emissions of hydrocarbons and carbon monoxide during normal driving conditions. Also, by obviating the need for "choking" the engine, it eliminates much of the hydrocarbon and carbon monoxide emissions usually formed during cold start-up. It also helps to ensure smooth driving conditions and to prevent carburetor icing (when frozen air is injected) when the engine is cold. During normal driving conditions, engine compartment air is supplied to the carburetor, and the TAC is disengaged.

Air Injection Systems

The air injection system supplies additional oxygen (air) to the exhaust manifold, thereby extending the combustion process into the exhaust system. This decreases emissions of hydrocarbons (HC) and carbon monoxide (CO), since they are oxidized to form H_2O and CO_2 prior to emission. Since the air injection system operates on the exhaust stream after combustion, it does not limit the specifications a manufacturer may choose for carburetion or ignition timing.

During normal driving conditions, an air pump shunts air to the diverter valve, which supplies the air to the air nozzles, which inject it into the exhaust manifold. The hot exhaust gases already in the manifold mix with the fresh oxygen supply (the injected air) and undergo further combustion. During deceleration, the air injection system must be disengaged, because there is a high intake manifold vacuum, and an excessively rich air/fuel mixture. Injection of air into the exhaust stream during deceleration would result in re-ignition and engine backfire. To prevent this, a diverter valve senses the high intake manifold vacuum (during deceleration), and vents the air from the pump to the exterior, rather than injecting it into the exhaust manifold.

Fuel Evaporation Control Systems
According to USEPA (1977), nearly 20 percent of all hydrocarbon emissions were caused by fuel evaporation, prior to the installation of fuel evaporation control systems. Such systems capture fuel vapors from the fuel tank and the carburetor, the two main sources of volatilized fuel emissions. Since the evaporation rate increases with increasing heat, most evaporation from the carburetor occurs after the vehicle is turned off. When the vehicle is no longer moving, air is no longer rapidly circulating through the engine compartment. Therefore, the temperature of the engine increases, and the fuel in the carburetor and gas tank will start to evaporate.

Fuel evaporation control systems are simply constructed, designed to trap the gasoline vapors in the fuel system, and to inject them into the combustion chamber during engine operation. The fuel tank and carburetor are completely sealed to the environment, so that any hydrocarbon vapors formed in the system (while the engine is off) are contained. When the engine is started up, the captured vapors are drawn into the combustion chamber and burned.

Exhaust Gas Recirculation Systems
Exhaust gas recirculation (EGR) systems are designed to limit emissions of NOX. The system provides a means of recirculating (returning to the intake manifold) a portion of the exhaust gas, thereby lowering and regulating the temperature of combustion to a range that produces minimal NO_x emissions. The exhaust gas recirculated is basically inert—nearly 99 percent of the oxygen and fuel has been burned. Thus, when the recirculated exhaust gas mixes with the air/fuel mixture in the intake manifold, it dilutes it, lowering the peak flame temperature of combustion and reducing the rate of formation of NO_x.

An EGR valve, activated by a manifold vacuum condition, is integral to the operation of the EGR system. The vacuum can be sensed at driving conditions between idle and full throttle. At idle speed, there is no real need for the EGR system, as NO_x production is characteristically negligible. At full throttle, presumably high (and immediate) speed is required, so the EGR system is disengaged to ensure that full power is reached. When operational, the EGR system regulates the amount of exhaust gas that is recirculated, to ensure a certain range of combustion temperatures is maintained.

Spark Control Systems

The spark control system reduces NO_X emissions, while also limiting hydrocarbon emissions. The highest concentration of NO_X is emitted by a vehicle when it is under heavy load (e.g., when it is accelerating, climbing a mountain, or towing a trailer). Under these conditions, a rich air/fuel mixture will enter the carburetor, and hydrocarbon emissions will increase. With the throttle plates almost completely open (fully loaded conditions), oxygen supply is plentiful, and the rich air/fuel mixture will ensure that high combustion temperatures are achieved.

The spark control system controls the ignition timing of the engine, so that the spark plug fires later in the compression stroke. Under these conditions, not as much heat energy is transferred to the piston. Instead, the excess heat energy is released into the exhaust manifold during the engine stroke, where it burns any remaining hydrocarbons in the exhaust. In the combustion chamber, the lower temperature of combustion precludes the formation of high concentrations of NO_X. Thus, the spark control system reduces emissions of NO_X.

Catalytic Converter Systems

Two types of catalytic converters are in wide use today: the "two-way," or "oxidation," catalyst and the "three-way," or "oxidation-reduction," catalyst. An oxidation catalyst is designed to reduce emissions of hydrocarbons and carbon monoxide, while an oxidation-reduction catalyst is designed to reduce these two pollutants, plus nitrogen oxides. Catalytic converters reduce emissions by providing an additional site for the oxidation of HC and CO, or the reduction of NO. Resembling a muffler in appearance, the catalytic converter is usually located in the exhaust system anterior to the muffler, and fairly close to the exhaust manifold. Unlike a muffler, the exterior of the catalytic converter is constructed of stainless steel (because it is a rather expensive component, and should therefore be durable and corrosion-resistant).

Platinum and palladium are the catalysts that are the functional core of a catalytic converter. Oxidation converters use about 70 percent platinum and 30 percent palladium. Although platinum is the more efficient catalyst, it is also very expensive, whereas the reverse is true for palladium. The use of both catalysts allows the construction of a catalytic converter with the desired efficiency at least cost. Both catalysts work to accelerate the oxidization of HC and CO to H_2O and CO_2. Burning takes place in the converter, usually at temperatures about 200°F hotter than exhaust gas temperatures. The converter, which will only start to operate when exhaust temperatures reach 500°F, will usually have internal temperatures of about 1400°F, and outer shell temperatures of about 700° F. If the internal temperature reaches 2500° F, the catalytic elements will be irreversibly damaged.

Three-way catalytic converters use rhodium in addition to platinum and palladium. Palladium and rhodium promote the reduction of NO to N and O, while platinum continues to promote the oxidation of HC and CO to water and carbon dioxide. Reduction of NO is most efficient when rich or stoichiometric air/fuel ratios are used. There is only a narrow range of air/fuel ratios that are allowable, if a three-way catalyst is to work properly. Usually, to maintain the precise air/fuel ratio, vehicles must be outfitted with exhaust, or oxidation, sensors. These sensors are linked with electronic control systems, as described below.

A third type of catalytic converter, not yet in wide use, is the lean nitrogen-oxide catalytic converter. Because three-way converters do not function well at lean air/fuel ratios, lean-burn engines have not been widely produced, even though their high fuel efficiency and low CO emissions are attractive. Recently, a zeolite catalyst has been developed, which uses unburned hydrocarbons in the exhaust to reduce NO. As the NO_x catalytic converter is only about 50 percent effective, it is not widely produced. Future technological advances may make its production more feasible.

Catalyst protection systems protect the converter from overheating, using several different means. One is that the air injection system can be designed to inject air into the converter to ensure that the proper combustion conditions are maintained. Another means is by establishing a system whereby the throttle closes during driving conditions likely to result in rich air/fuel ratios. Alternatively, the converter may simply be bypassed, during driving conditions likely to result in a rich air/fuel mixture (e.g., deceleration, overheated engine operation).

There are two basic internal designs of catalytic converters: the monolith and the pellet. Inside the stainless steel shell of the former type is a stainless steel mesh, a flow diffuser, and a ceramic honeycomb monolith. When the exhaust gases enter the converter, they first encounter the flow diffuser, which spread the gas stream evenly through the honeycomb passages of the monolith element, which are coated with a thin layer of platinum and palladium. The stainless steel mesh cradles the monolith element against road shocks.

The pellet type converter contains baffles, baffle plates, insulation, and aluminum oxide pellets. When the exhaust gas stream enters the converter, it encounters a baffle that directs the gases upward. The gases then pass through holes in the baffle plate and down into a bed of aluminum oxide pellets, before exiting the converter through another baffle. The pellets are cradled in a shell of insulation inside the stainless steel skin, which serves to keep the heat inside the converter. The pellets are coated with platinum and palladium that catalyze the reaction of HC and CO.

For both converter designs, the use of leaded fuel is strictly prohibited. Leaded fuel destroys catalyst effectiveness by coating the catalyst. Special fuel tank filler necks may be installed at gas station pumps, during periods of transition from leaded to unleaded fuel, to disallow the addition of leaded fuel.

Electronic Control Systems

The 1980s introduction of three-way catalysts (discussed above) which have stringent air/fuel ratio requirements, fostered the development of sophisticated electronic control systems that regulate and maintain the air/fuel ratio. Since 1981, virtually all engine emission control systems used in the US feature computerized control of the air/fuel ratio. These systems constantly monitor the exhaust and adjust the air/fuel ratio to maintain stoichiometric conditions. Advanced systems electronically control spark timing, exhaust gas recirculation systems, idle speed, evaporative canister purging, and air injection systems.

Technologies for the Control of Emissions from Diesel Vehicles

Unlike spark-ignited engines, diesel engines do not premix fuel and air before injection into the combustion chamber. Instead, ignition is achieved by injecting pressurized fuel near the top of the compression stroke. Upon contact with the compressed air (about 700–900°C, due to the heat of compression) the fuel ignites, eliminating the need for a spark-ignition system. Most heavy-duty trucks and buses, and some passenger cars (about 20 percent of the European fleet) are powered by diesel engines. Principal pollutants of concern from diesel engines are particulates and sulfur oxides. The technologies discussed here are specifically oriented toward the control of the emissions from diesel engines.

Technologies for the Control of Emissions from Two-Stroke Engines

Compared to four-stroke engines, two-stroke engines are cheaper, lighter, and more efficient (in terms of power output per unit displacement), but they are also greater polluters. This is primarily because they emit as much as 30 percent of their fuel, unburned, in the exhaust. Oil must be mixed with the fuel when refueling, so that, when the air-fuel mixture is pumped through the engine by the crankcase, the oil can lubricate the bearings and the pistons. Instead of four strokes (intake, compression, power, and exhaust), these engines only have two strokes—compression and power. The missing two strokes, intake and exhaust, occur simultaneously, as the engine operates. As the piston makes its downward movement during the power stroke, first exhaust ports, and then intake ports, are exposed in the cylinder wall. Since the burning gases are under high pressure (thanks to the preceding compression stroke), as the piston moves down and exposes the exhaust ports, the burned gases are forced out from the cylinder. Even so, since the intake ports open soon after, there is some mixing of the fresh charge and the exhaust. Two-stroke engines are widely used in small motor-cycles, outboard motors, and lawn-mowers.

Automaker Estimates of Cost of Emission Control Technologies for Spark-Ignited Gasoline Engines

Control Technology	Fuel Consumption Change (%)	Increase in Engine Cost (%)
Lean-Burn Engine with Carburetor and Conventional Ignition	-2	1.0
Pulse Air and Exhaust Gas Recirculation	3	4.5
Lean-Burn Engine with Carburetor and Programmed Ignition	1	2.0
Recalibrated Conventional Engine with Electronic Fuel Injection	2	8.0
Lean-Burn Engine with Electronic Fuel Injection	-7	9.0
Lean-Burn Engine with Oxidation Catalyst	-3	4.5
Open Loop, Three-Way Catalytic Converter	2	4.1
Lean-Burn Engine, Closed Loop, Electronic Fuel Injection, Variable Intake Oxidation Catalyst	-7	15.0
Closed Loop, Electronic Fuel Injection, Three-Way Catalyst	3	13.0

Note: Baseline is a small vehicle (1.4 liter engine) with conventional carburetor engine, meeting ECE 15/04 standard.

Source: ECMT, 1990.

3.2.3 Efficiency and Cost of Control Options

Spark-Ignited Gasoline Engines (See Appendix Tables 2.15 and 2.16)
Compression-Ignited Diesel Engines (See Appendix Tables 2.17–2.19)
Two-Stroke Engines (See Appendix Table 2.20)
Appendix Table 2.21 lists common mobile source air pollutants and average costs of control.

Costs and Efficiencies of Several Control Technology Packages for Spark-Ignited Gasoline Engines

Policy Option	Controls Implemented	Pollutants Emitted	Emissions (g/km)	Control Efficiency	Fuel Consumption Change (%)	Cost Per Vehicle ($)
BASELN	Business as Usual	Pb:		0	0	0
Baseline Scenario		HC:		0		
		NO$_X$:		0		
		CO:		0		
		Benzene:		0		
NONCAT	Ignition Timing	Pb:		0	- 5	130
Non-Catalyst Controls	Air-Fuel Ratio	HC:	1.5	66		
	Air Injection	NO$_X$:	1.9	11		
	Exhaust Gas	CO:	15.0	63		
	Recirculation	Benzene:				
OXYCAT	Oxidation Catalyst	Pb:	0	100	- 5	380
Oxidation Catalyst	Ignition Timing	HC:	0.5	89		
	Exhaust Gas	NO$_X$:	1.3	39		
	Recirculation	CO:	7.0	83		
		Benzene:				
TRICAT	Three-way Catalyst	Pb:	0	100	± 5	630
Three-Way Catalyst	Closed-Loop	HC:	0.25	94		
	Carburetor or	NO$_X$:	0.63	71		
	Electronic Fuel Injection	CO:	2.1	95		
		Benzene:				

APPENDIX TABLE 2.16 *(continued)*

Policy Option	Controls Implemented	Pollutants Emitted	Emissions (g/km)	Control Efficiency	Fuel Consumption Change (%)	Cost Per Vehicle ($)
LNBURN						
Lean-Burn Engine	Oxidation Catalyst	Pb:	0	100	+15	630
	Electronic Fuel Injection	HC:	0.25	94		
	Fast-Burn Combustion Chamber	NO$_x$:	0.63	71		
		CO:	1.0	98		
		Benzene:				
USTIER						
US Tier 1	Three-way Catalyst	Pb:	0	100	+5	800
	Electronic Fuel Injection	HC:	0.16	96		
	Exhaust Gas Recirculation	NO$_x$:	0.25	88		
		CO:	1.3	97		
		Benzene:				
CALOWE						
California Low-Emission	Electric Three-Way Catalyst	Pb:	0	100	Unknown	>1,000
Vehicle Standard	Electronic Fuel Injection	HC:	0.047	99		
	Exhaust Gas Recirculation	NO$_x$:	0.13	94		
		CO:	0.6	99		
		Benzene:				

Source: ECMT, 1990.

Estimated Cost of Technologies for the Control of Emissions from Diesel Vehicles

Control Technology	Increase in Engine Cost (%)
No Emission Control (BAU)	0
Injection Timing Retard	0
Low Sac Volume and Valve Covering Nozzle	Negligible
Turbo-Charging	3-5
Charge Cooling	5-7
Improved Fuel Injection	13-15
High Pressure Fuel Injection with Electronic Control	14-16
Variable Geometry Turbo-Charging	1-3
Particulate Trap	4-25

Source: ECMT, 1990,

Estimated Costs and Efficiencies of Options for the Control of Emissions from Heavy-Duty Diesel Vehicles

Policy Option	Emission Factor (g/W)	Fuel Consumption Change (%)	Estimated Cost Per Engine ($)
NOCONTL	NO_X: 12.0 to 21.0		
No controls	PM: 1.0 to 5.0	0	0
MINCONT	NO_X: 11.0	-3–0	0–200
Injection Timing	PM: 0.7 to 1.0		
Smoke Limiter			
MODCONT	NO_X: 8.0	-5–0	0–1,500
Injection Timing	PM: 0.7		
Combustion Optimization			
1991 USSD	NO_X: 7.0	-5–5	1,000–3,000
Variable Injection Timing	PM: 0.15 to 0.34		
High-Pressure Fuel Injection			
LOWSSD	NO_X: 2.7 to 5.5	-10–0	2,000–6,000
Electronic Fuel Injection	PM: 0.07 to 0.13		
Charge-Air Cooling			
Combustion Optimization			
Exhaust Gas Recirculation			
Catalytic Converter or			
Particulate Trap			

Policy Option	Emission Factor (g/W)	Fuel Consumption Change (%)	Estimated Cost Per Engine ($)
ALTFUEL	NO$_x$: < 2.7	-30–0	0–5,000
Gasoline/3-Way Catalyst	PM: < 0.07		
Natural Gas Lean-Burn			
Natural Gas/3-Way Catalyst			
Methanol-Diesel			

Source: Weaver, 1990.

APPENDIX TABLE 2.19

Estimated Cost and Efficiency of Options for Control of Emissions from Light Diesel Vehicles

Policy Option	Emissions Factor (g/km)	Percent Reduction	Fuel Consumption Change (%)	Estimated Cost Per Engine ($)
UNCONT	NO$_x$: 1.0 to 1.5	0	0	0
No Controls	PM: 0.6 to 1.0	0	0	
MODCONT	NO$_x$: 0.6	40	-5–0	0–500
Injection Timing	PM: 0.4	33		
Combustion Optimization				
1988 USSD	NO$_x$: 0.6	40	-5–0	100–200
Variable Injection Timing	PM: 0.4	78		
Combustion Optimization				
Exhaust Gas Recirculation				
ADVTECH	NO$_x$: 0.5	40	-10–0	200–500
Electronic Fuel Injection	PM: 0.05 to 0.08	92		
Combustion Optimization				
Exhaust Gas Recirculation				
Catalytic Converter or Particulate Trap				

Source: Weaver, 1990.

Estimated Cost of Emission Control Measures for Two-Stroke Engines

Policy Option	Emissions Factor (g/km)	Percent Reduction	Fuel Consumption Change (%)	Estimated Cost Per Engine ($)
ELIMTWO	HC: 5.0	66	30–40	60–80
4-Stroke Engine or	CO: 12.0	50		
Advanced 2-Stroke	NO$_X$: NR			
PM: 0.15	50-95			
NONCATL	HC: 1.0	90	0	80–100
4-Stroke or 2-Stroke with Catalyst	CO: 12.0	50		
Ignition Timing	NO$_X$: 0.5	200		
A/F Ratio Control	PM: 0.15	50–90		
OXITECH	HC: 0.5	98	-5	80–100
4-Stroke or Advanced 2-Stroke	CO: 2.0	80		
Ignition Timing	NO$_X$: 0.5	200		
A/F Ratio Control	PM: 0.05	85		
Catalytic Converter or Electronic Fuel Injection				

Source: Weaver and Chan, 1993.

Overall Costs of Control

Pollutant	Costs [a]
Lead	4 ¢/gallon
Nitrogen Oxides	—
Carbon Monoxide	12 ¢/gallon
Volatile Organic Compounds	—
Particulate Matter (diesels)	4 ¢/gallon
Sulfur (diesels)	8 ¢/gallon
All Fossil Fuels	—
CO$_2$ (electricity)	2–4 ¢/kWh
CO$_2$ (nonelectricity markets)	50–100 ¢/gallon

[a] Abatement to various levels.

4. Cost Functions—Water

4.1 Point Sources

4.1.1 Introduction

The primary approach used in this report to estimate the cost functions for pollutant control in point sources of water pollution is based upon statistical generalization across a wide range of data. With sufficient data, we can derive cost functions for individual industrial sectors, unit treatment processes, or the overall industry of a country. The paper by Yu et. al. (1995) on the cost functions for PRC industrial wastewater treatment provides various functions based on such statistical analysis.

If cost data are not sufficient to establish functional relationships, it may still be possible to estimate the cost functions by analogy or inference. One such analogy is the single-term power cost function (aQ^b). For example, if the exponent b has been well established from sufficient data elsewhere and has been widely acknowledged, only a few sample points can lead to a good estimate for the other constant, a. In this appendix, we use data derived from the US and PRC to determine the value of parameter b, and to deduce cost functions for other Asian countries using samples from the countries concerned.

4.1.2 Nature of Current Literature on Cost Functions for Water and Wastewater Treatment

Volume four of USEPA's Treatability Manual (1980) is a handbook of wastewater treatment cost estimation. The manual covers 54 unit processes and their variations, from grit removal to deep-well injection. For each treatment unit process, the manual first produces a detailed description of the technology and equipment, then presents design criteria and operating characteristics to provide the operating conditions under which costs are incurred. Both total capital investment and annual operating cost depend on flowrate. The results are cost curves on a logarithm-logarithm coordinate system. The Treatability Manual is a very good reference of treatment technology and cost estimation for a specific treatment process.

The cost functions in *Generalization and Summarization of the Cost Functions of Chinese Industrial Wastewater Treatment* (Yu et al. 1995) were developed by a research project sponsored by the National Environmental Protection Agency of PRC and are grouped according to treatment processes and industrial sectors (Wang et al. 1992). Among the total 414 cost functions, 191 are construction cost or capital investment functions, 149 are operation cost functions (electricity costs are excluded from the operation cost), and 74 are electricity usage functions. All costs are related to flowrates. The normal ranges of the influent concentration of COD, removal rate, and flow are provided. Statistical significance and sampling size are also given for each function.

Based on those 414 cost functions, Yu et al. made generalizations by using the figures calculated from the cost functions as data for further statistical analysis. Various forms of cost functions were explored in the process of generalization. They determined three forms of cost functions to be appropriate for different situations: the single term power function, the Shah-Reid cost function, and the Smeers-Tyteca cost function. These three kinds of cost functions established for PRC industrial wastewater treatment are presented below. We will also use the exponents in these functions to derive cost functions for other Asian countries.

The USEPA report, *Estimating Costs for Water Treatment as a Function of Size and Treatment Efficiency* (Gumerman et al. 1978) deals with cost estimation of various water treatment facilities. The costs are given in tables and cost curves. Some design and operating parameters are also provided. Both capital and maintenance costs are related to flow and treatment facility size.

The Cost Digest: Cost Summaries of Selected Environmental Control Technologies (DeWolf et al. 1984) is a brief report on the costs of a wide range of environmental control technologies, from an ozonation system in drinking water treatment to flue gas desulfurization processes. In its water treatment section, only costs incurred by treatment technologies are considered. This report indicates that, "on a historical basis, the cost of the treatment step is approximately 11 percent of the total cost of supplying drinking water." A breakdown of the costs excerpted from the report is shown in Appendix Table 2.22.

We use this report to determine the exponents in our water treatment cost functions. Some other papers (Clark 1982; Qasim et al. 1992) report cost functions in more complicated forms and consider more factors affecting the costs. If high accuracy is required and detailed information about a specific treatment facility is available, those cost functions could be useful.

APPENDIX TABLE 2.22

Charge Rate Profile for Typical Total Drinking Water System Costs Based on Survey Data

System Component	Percentage of the Total Costs	
	Large System (85 mgd)	Small System (5 mgd)
Support Services	24.4	17.6
Acquisition	13.4	15.1
Treatment	11.8	10.3
Distribution	29.0	41.9
Interest on Debt	21.4	15.1

Source: DeWolf *et al.* 1984.

4.1.3 Wastewater Treatment Cost Functions

As industrial and municipal effluents contribute most to water pollution, and data are limited on commercial wastewater, we focus our analysis on industrial wastewater and municipal sewage treatment.

The cost of wastewater treatment is affected by many factors, with principal elements being flowrate of influent, concentration of pollutants, and removal rate. Although specific site characteristics such as constituents of pollutants, geological conditions of the site, and technological details may also play significant roles in determining costs, cost functions are usually generalized as a function of flowrate, influent concentration, and removal rate. Three forms of cost functions are frequently used:

1. Single-term power function (Tihansky 1974):

$$C = aQ^b \qquad (2.6)$$

where:

$$
\begin{aligned}
C &= \text{cost;} \\
Q &= \text{flowrate, m}^3/\text{day;} \\
a, b &= \text{constants.}
\end{aligned}
$$

2. Shah-Reid cost function (Shah and Reid 1970):

$$C = aQ^b r^c \qquad (2.7)$$

where:

$$
\begin{aligned}
C &= \text{cost;} \\
Q &= \text{flowrate, m}^3/\text{day;} \\
r &= \text{removal rate;} \\
a, b, c &= \text{constants.}
\end{aligned}
$$

3. Smeers-Tyteca cost function (Smeers and Tyteca 1984):

$$C = aQ^b(1-r)^c S^{b+c} = aQ^b R^c S^{b+c} \qquad (2.8)$$

where:

$$
\begin{aligned}
C &= \text{cost;} \\
Q &= \text{flowrate, m3/day;} \\
r &= \text{removal rate;} \\
S &= \text{influent concentration of pollutants such as} \\
&\quad\ \text{BOD}_5, \text{mg/l;} \\
a, b, c &= \text{constants;} \\
R &= \text{residual rate, equal to } 1-r.
\end{aligned}
$$

The three forms of cost function above have been calculated based on the data for PRC industrial wastewater treatment facilities. Cost functions are developed for various treatment processes and industrial sectors, and then the generalized functions for the overall industry are established using the three models above.

We propose a revision of the single-term power function. The function is still written as a single term power function:

$$C = aM^b \qquad (2.9)$$

M does not represent the fluid flowrate, however. Rather, M is the amount of BOD_5 removed from a treatment facility per day, with the unit of kg BOD_5/ day. The relationship between M and other parameters is

$$M = rQS \times 10^{-3} \qquad (2.10)$$

where:

M	=	BOD_5 removed in a day, kg/day;
Q	=	flowrate, m^3/day;
r	=	removal rate;
S	=	influent concentration of BOD_5, mg/l.

For a country or a region, the amount of BOD_5 discharged by an industrial sector can be related to the gross production or other economic indicators of that sector. After building the relationship between the discharge and production, we can use this single term function, equation (2.9) to find out the cost of remediation for different removed amounts of BOD_5 from the economic production levels or other selected economic indicators, which are usually more readily available.

Knowing the total amount of discharge, we may choose different levels of removal to determine how much BOD_5 we wish to reduce and then use equation (2.9) to calculate the required abatement costs. But only removal rates between 30 percent and 85 percent are appropriate for such a calculation. For removal rates higher than 85 percent, we recommend using the Smeers-Tyteca model.

It appears that a large database would be necessary for constructing such cost functions. With sufficient data on costs and mass flowrate of BOD_5, we would employ regression methods to find out parameters a and b. For PRC, this has been done. But the scarcity of data hinders us from doing the same thing for other countries. Fortunately, we have some knowledge about parameter b, which simplifies the procedure of finding cost functions. Parameter b is called the elasticity. It is the constant ratio of percentage increase in cost and percentage increase in capacity. Industrial experiences show that the same technology has similar economies of scale, even for different countries. For some mature and old industries, this parameter has standard values; for example, it is often assumed to be around two thirds for the chemical industry.

For some young and growing industries, this parameter usually becomes smaller over time until it evolves into a stable constant.

We find this parameter has a mean of 0.72 for the wastewater treatment facilities of the US (DeWolf et al. 1984), and 0.76 for PRC (Yu et al. 1995). We believe that the difference between the US and PRC is due to their different stages of development in wastewater treatment. Older American wastewater treatment plants have more significant economies-of-scale effect than their PRC counterparts. Developing countries in the Asian region should have a story similar to PRC. We expect their parameter b to be comparable to that of PRC. By setting the value of parameter b, the value of parameter a—and thus the cost function—can be found using only one or a few cost samples. For a specific industrial sector, such a sampling point can be typical flowrate and the corresponding cost, or typical flowrate and the corresponding marginal cost.

Based on the PRC and US experiences, we determine the exponents in the preceding four cost functions of industrial wastewater treatment for countries in the Asian region as follows:

1. Single-term power function (Tihansky, 1974):

$$C = aQ^{0.76} \qquad (2.11)$$

where:

C = cost;
Q = flowrate, m^3/day;
a = constant.

2. Shah-Reid cost function (Shah and Reid, 1970):

$$C = aQ^{0.8035}r^{1.5736} \qquad (2.12)$$

where:

C = cost;
Q = flowrate, m^3/day;
r = removal rate;
a = constant.

3. Smeers-Tyteca cost function (Smeers and Tyteca, 1984):

$$C = aQ^{0.81}(1-r)^{-0.84}S^{-0.03} = aQ^{0.81}R^{-0.84}S^{-0.03} = aQ^{0.81}(SR)^{-0.84} \qquad (2.13)$$

where:

C = cost;
Q = flowrate, m^3/day;
r = removal rate;
S = influent concentration, mg/l;
a = constant;
R = residual rate, equal to $1 - r$.

4. Revised single term power function:

$$C = aM^{0.76} \qquad\qquad (2.14)$$

where:

C = cost;
M = BOD$_5$ removed in a day, kg/day;
a = constant.

Attention should be paid to the implications of the cost functions established in this paper. Since the flowrate and the amount of BOD$_5$ removed are defined as variables of single treatment facilities, using total flow of an industrial sector or a region as the flow variable in the cost functions to calculate the pollution abatement cost would be wrong. As all the cost functions are developed for individual treatment facilities, Q must be the influent flow of a facility and M must be the amount of BOD$_5$ removed from an individual plant in a day. If the total discharge of a sector or of a region is known, we recommend using average flow of plants (or average removal amount) in the sector or in the region to find the typical cost of a single facility and then multiplying the typical cost of a single facility by the number of facilities in that sector or region to find the total cost; that is:

Step 1: Cost of remediation for a single treatment plant (if Smeers-Tyteca cost function is used):

$$C = aQ^{0.81}(1-r)^{-0.84}S^{-0.03} = aQ^{0.81}R^{-0.84}S^{-0.03} = aQ^{0.81}(SR)^{-0.84} \qquad (2.15)$$

where:

C = cost;
Q = flowrate, m^3/day;
r = removal rate;
S = influent concentration, mg/l;
a = constant;
R = residual rate, equal to $1 - r$.

Step 2: Cost of remediation for an industrial sector or a region:

$$TC = Cn \qquad\qquad (2.16)$$

where:

TC = total cost of remediation for a sector or a region,
C = typical cost for an individual treatment facility,
n = the number of treatment facilities in the sector or the region.

Such a procedure indicates that some knowledge about the average capacity of treatment plants would be necessary in finding the total cost of remediation for an industrial sector or a region.

The following section details wastewater treatment cost functions for PRC, Philippines, and Indonesia.

PRC

For PRC, we prepared a working paper entitled "Generalization of Cost Functions for Chinese Industrial Wastewater Treatment" (Yu et al. 1995), in which we have derived:

- single-term power cost functions for different treatment processes in different industrial sectors with fluid flowrate as the variable;

- generalized cost functions for individual industrial sectors, in three forms of cost functions (equations (2.6), (2.7), and (2.8));

- summarized cost functions for the overall industry, in three forms mentioned above.

Single-term power functions were developed to relate the treatment costs to different processes. As the focus was on biochemical pollution of industrial wastewater, only treatment processes that can reduce BOD_5 were under consideration. The cost functions for six processes were established based on 1987 data. The unit of the cost was 10^4 yuan (1987), and the unit of flowrate was m^3/day. Only the construction or capital cost was included in the following functions:

Activated sludge process:

$$C = 0.2302Q^{0.7609} \qquad (2.17)$$

Contact stabilization process:

$$C = 0.2249Q^{0.7609} \qquad (2.18)$$

Trickling filter process:

$$C = 0.2401Q^{0.7609} \qquad (2.19)$$

Biological rotating contactors:

$$C = 0.3646Q^{0.7609} \qquad (2.20)$$

Gas flotation process:

$$C = 0.2147Q^{0.7609} \qquad (2.21)$$

Coagulation plus sedimentation:

$$C = 0.1902Q^{0.7609} \qquad (2.22)$$

Cost functions for different levels of treatment were also developed. For primary treatment process, a generalized cost function is:

$$C = 0.2021Q^{0.7609} \qquad (2.23)$$

For secondary treatment, the cost is higher:

$$C = 0.2594Q^{0.7609} \qquad (2.24)$$

An average cost function for all processes would also be appropriate in a general cost estimation:

$$C = 0.2387Q^{0.7609} \qquad (2.25)$$

By forcing the exponents of flow to be the same, we obtain the cost functions with the same power above. It is reasonable to wonder how much variation has been eliminated in doing so. For this, please refer to the paper by Yu et al. (1995). One may find that the loss of variation is quite small.

The Shah-Reid and Smeers-Tyteca cost functions are established for five industrial sectors that are major BOD_5 dischargers: the textile, chemical, petroleum, tannery, and pharmaceutical industries. The cost functions are presented in Appendix Table 2.23.

For all the industrial sectors as a whole, the Shah-Reid model is found as follows:

$$C = 0.2852Q^{0.8035}r^{1.5736} \qquad (2.26)$$

Cost functions for PRC presented here are only for the construction or capital costs. For an example of constructing a function for total cost, please refer to Yu et al.(1995).

For municipal sewage treatment, the cost functions are (Wang et al. 1992): Capital investment:

$$C1 = 1.03Q^{0.7878} + 3.29Q^{0.7878} + r^{1.234} \qquad (2.27)$$

APPENDIX TABLE 2.23

Shah-Reid and Smeers-Tyteca Cost Functions for
PRC Industrial Wastewater Treatment

	Shah-Reid	Smeers-Tyteca
Textile	$0.1609Q^{0.8035}r^{1.5736}$	$3.50 \times 10^{-2}(QS)^{0.807}(SR)^{-0.842}$
Chemical	$0.3072Q^{0.8035}r^{1.5736}$	$6.94 \times 10^{-2}(QS)^{0.807}$
Petroleum	$0.3416Q^{0.8035}r^{1.5736}$	$7.67 \times 10{-2}(QS)^{0.807}$
Tannery	$0.2709Q^{0.8035}r^{1.5736}$	$6.03 \times 10{-2}(QS)^{0.807}$
Pharmaceutical	$0.4202Q^{0.8035}r^{1.5736}$	$9.62 \times 10{-2}(QS)^{0.807}$

Source: Yu et al., 1995.

Annual operation cost:

$$C2 = 56.16Q^{0.801} \qquad (2.28)$$

where:

Q = influent flow, m^3/day;

C1, C2 = costs in 10^4 yuan;

r = removal rate of BOD$_5$, usually 30 percent to 85 percent.

Philippines

From the World Bank's Environmental Sector Study of the Philippines (World Bank 1993), we find typical mass flowrates, typical marginal costs, and typical removal rates of wastewater treatment for ten industrial sectors. We have derived single-term power cost functions, Shah-Reid models, Smeers-Tyteca models, and typical costs for these sectors, which are:

Beverages
Laundry
Textiles
Food Processing
Tanneries
Metal Finishing
Chemicals
Pharmaceuticals
Pulp and Paper
Slaughterhouses

The results, derived from 1992 data, are presented in Appendix Table 2.24. The cost functions give costs in pesos. As at June 8, 1992, the exchange rate between the peso and US dollar was 26.695 pesos per US dollar.

An overall cost function has also been established from the weighted average of the Smeers-Tyteca cost functions for individual sectors. Mass flow of each industrial sector has been used as the weight:

$$C = 40.11 \, (QS)^{0.81} \, (SR)^{-0.84} \qquad (2.29)$$

As the treatment cost data are obtained from the top 100 polluting firms located within the Metropolitan Manila area, we can use those cost functions to determine the pollution abatement cost for different removal levels. Since the plants represent the principal pollution sources within that area, their costs would be a good indicator of total regional cost of abatement.

The calculations can be described in five steps: (1) Choose a common removal rate for all plants, say, 30 percent or 85 percent; (2) For a plant in a specific industrial sector, introduce the average flowrate and typical onsite BOD$_5$ concentration of that sector to the Smeers-Tyteca cost function for that

Cost Functions for the Industrial Wastewater Treatment Facilities in the Philippines

	Beverages	Laundry	Textiles	Food Proc.	Tanneries	Metal Fin.	Chemicals	Pharm.	P. & Paper	Slghtrhse
Smeers–Tyteca Model	$37.8(QS)^{0.81}$	$73.8(QS)^{0.81}$	$27.1(QS)^{0.81}$	$36.4(QS)^{0.81}$	$28.6(QS)^{0.81}$	$62.1(QS)^{0.81}$	$15.7(QS)^{0.81}$	$52.3(QS)^{0.81}$	$10.3(QS)^{0.81}$	$53.0(QS)^{0.81}$
Single-Term Power (M)	$66.2M0.76$	$43.3M^{0.76}$	$68.1M^{0.76}$	$56.4M^{0.76}$	$36.9M^{0.76}$	$76.1M^{0.76}$	$48.0M^{0.76}$	$130.8M^{0.76}$	$122.9M^{0.76}$	$39.1M^{0.76}$
Single-Term Power (Q)	$99.4Q^{0.76}$	$96.2Q^{0.76}$	$47.5Q^{0.76}$	$74.6Q^{0.76}$	$42.2Q^{0.76}$	$107.1Q^{0.76}$	$25.6Q^{0.76}$	$344.4Q^{0.76}$	$21.4Q^{0.76}$	$82.6Q^{0.76}$
Daily Removed BOD$_5$ (M: kgBOD/d)	4,100	620	1,430	1560	1667	423	657	2360	350	2463
Typical Fluid Flow (Q: m³/d)	2,400	230	2,300	1080	1400	270	1500	660	3500	920
Typical Inflow Concentr. (S: mgBOD/l)	2,750	9,830	1,210	2815	4135	3445	1360	4045	230	7500
Typical Removal Rate(r)(%)	62.1	27.4	51.5	51.4	28.8	45.5	33.2	88.4	43.8	35.7
Typical Residual Rate(R)(%)	37.9	72.6	48.5	48.6	71.2	54.5	66.8	11.6	56.2	64.3
Typical Cost per Facility (C: 10³ pesos/d)	36.8	6.0	17.0	15.1	10.4	7.5	6.6	47.9	10.5	14.8
Typical Average Cost (pesos/m³)	15.4	26.1	7.4	14.0	7.4	27.9	4.4	72.5	3.0	16.1
Typical Average Cost (pesos/kg removed BOD)	9.0	9.7	11.9	9.7	6.2	17.8	10.1	20.3	30.1	6.0
Typical Marginal Cost (pesos/m³)	11.7	19.8	5.6	10.6	5.6	21.2	3.4	55.1	2.3	12.2
Typical Marginal Cost (pesos/kg removed BOD)	6.8	7.4	9.1	7.3	4.7	13.6	7.7	15.4	22.9	4.6

For the form of the cost functions, please refer to the paper by Yu et al. 1995.

sector to find out the abatement cost for an average plant; (3) Obtain total cost of an industrial sector by multiplying the number of plants in that sector and cost per plant; (4) Aggregate the costs of all sectors to get the final total cost; and (5) Choose another removal rate and repeat the calculation to determine the abatement cost at other treatment levels.

In Appendix Table 2.25, we choose two removal rates, 30 percent and 85 percent, to represent two situations: complete primary treatment in all plants and complete secondary treatment in all plants. The word complete here means no direct discharge of wastewater occurs and all wastewater is treated. As the cost function for the electronics sector (in which there is only one plant) is not available, the calculated cost does not include that plant. The costs are present values in 1992 pesos/day.

When the removal rate is 30 percent across the industrial sectors, the pollution abatement cost is 1.15×10^6 pesos/day for the 99 plants. If the removal requirement is increased to 85 percent, the cost will go up to 1.06×10^7 pesos/day. Appendix Table 2.26 gives the cost of remediation and corresponding removal rate.

Indonesia
From the World Bank's Industrial Pollution Projection System (Afsah et al. 1994), we find the average abatement costs of BOD_5 for ten industrial sectors. Assuming the daily amount of BOD_5 removed from a single treatment facilty in a specific industrial sector is comparable to its Philippines counterpart, we have constructed single-term power cost functions for nine industrial sectors. Typical costs for these sectors have also been obtained. These sectors are:
   Food Products
   Beverages
   Pulp and Paper
   Metal Products
   Iron and Steel
   Textiles
   Pharmaceuticals Chemicals
   Agricultural Chemicals

Please refer to Appendix Table 2.27 for the Indonesian wastewater treatment cost functions, which are based on 1990 data.

The most polluting nine industrial sectors discharge 96.5 percent of total BOD_5 pollution. Using a weighted average, we may find an overall cost function for the whole industry. The weight for a sector is its percentage contribution to the total discharge. The single-term power cost functions for the overall industry are as follows:

$$C = 4.37M^{0.76} \qquad (2.30)$$

APPENDIX TABLE 2.25

Top 100 Polluting Firms in Metropolitan Manila (Costs are present values in 1992 pesos/day)

	Number of Plants	Flowrate per Plant (m3/day)	BOD$_5$ Concentr. (mg/l)	Cost per Plant if 30% Removal	Cost per Plant if 85% Pemoval	Cost of the Sector (r=30%)	Cost of the Sector (r=85%)
Beverages	8	2,400	2,750	2.20×10^4	8.03×10^4	1.76×10^5	6.42×10^5
Laundry	2	230	9,830	6.18×10^3	2.25×10^4	1.24×10^4	4.51×10^4
Textiles	13	2,300	1,210	1.25×10^4	4.56×10^4	1.63×10^5	5.93×10^5
Electronics	1	240		n/a	n/a	n/a	n/a
Food	44	1,080	2,815	1.11×10^4	4.04×10^4	4.88×10^5	1.78×10^6
Tanneries	2	1,400	4,135	1.06×10^4	3.88×10^4	2.13×10^4	7.76×10^4
Metal Finishing	4	270	3,445	6.11×10^3	2.23×10^4	2.44×10^4	8.92×10^4
Chemicals	9	1,500	1,360	6.39×10^3	2.33×10^4	5.75×10^4	2.10×10^5
Pharmaceuticals	3	660	4,045	1.06×10^4	3.86×10^4	3.17×10^4	1.16×10^5
Pulp and Paper	3	3,500	230	8.77×10^3	3.20×10^4	2.63×10^4	9.60×10^4
Slaughterhouse	11	920	7,500	1.38×10^4	5.02×10^4	1.51×10^5	5.52×10^5

Cost of Remediation for Top 99 Polluting Firms in Metropolitan Manila

Removal Rate (%)	30	45	60	75	85	95
Cost of Remediation (pesos/day)	1.15×10^6	1.41×10^6	1.84×10^6	2.73×10^6	4.20×10^6	1.06×10^7

Using the total mass flowrate of a region as the M variable in the functions above and in Appendix Table 2.27 to find the total cost for a region or a sector would be wrong. To do so would lead to biased estimation of the cost due to two causes: one involves the construction of those cost functions, which is based on costs of individual plants; the other involves the definition of the M variable. On one hand, the M variable should be the average capacity of the treatment facilities since the function can only be used to find the abatement cost of a single treatment facility. In case there are many facilities, one should use the average M for a single plant to obtain a cost figure for an average facility and then multiply the number of facilities by the cost per facility. For Indonesia, the average capacity of a wastewater treatment facility is removing 960 kg BOD_5 per day. On the other hand, M is not defined as influent mass flow of an individual facility, but rather, as the amount of BOD_5 removed in a day by a plant.

Marshall Islands, Nepal, and Pakistan

As wastewater treatment facilities have not been widely used in the Marshall Islands and Nepal, no cost functions have been estimated using data from the concerned countries. We suggest that cost functions from neighboring countries be used to make estimates. Data from Pakistan on this topic are unfortunately limited, so that no cost functions have been established at this stage.

4.1.4 Water Treatment Cost Functions

The Asian Development Bank's Water Utilities Data Book (ADB 1993) compiles data from 38 water utilities in 23 developing countries. All information in the book is derived from questionnaires designed by the ADB and completed by the utilities. The book provides cost figures in 1990 or 1991. Three kinds of costs are presented: annual operation and maintenance costs, annual collection costs and annual capital investment.

We have developed single-term power cost functions for annual capital investment and annual operation and maintenance costs. Whenever possible, groundwater and surface water systems are broken down and separate cost functions are reported. The exponents of the functions are determined based on US data as follows:

Cost Functions for the Industrial Wastewater Treatment Facilities of Indonesia

	Food	Beverages	Pulp & Paper	Metals	Iron & Steel	Textiles	Pharm.	Chemicals	Agricul. Chemicals
Contribution to Total Emission (%)	26	1	24	6.5	8	1.5	7	16.5	6
Single-Term Power (M)	$2.01M^{0.76}$	$2.56M^{0.76}$	$1.49M^{0.76}$	$1.62M^{0.76}$	$2.23M^{0.76}$	$3.28M^{0.76}$	$8.02M^{0.76}$	$7.41M^{0.76}$	$19.81M^{0.76}$
Typical Amount of BOD$_5$ Removed per Plant per Day (M: kgBOD/d)	1,560	4,100	350	423	423	1,430	2,360	657	657
Typical Cost per Facility (C: US$/d)	538.2	1,426.8	128.1	160.7	220.8	819.4	2,935.8	1,026.2	2,743.6
Typical Average Cost ($/kg Removed BOD)	0.345	0.348	0.366	0.380	0.522	0.573	1.244	1.562	4.176
Typical Marginal Cost ($/kg Removed BOD)	0.262	0.264	0.278	0.289	0.397	0.435	0.945	1.187	3.174

Overall Cost Function: Cost = $4.37M^{0.76}$ which is obtained by weighted average of cost functions for different industrial sectors. The contribution of each sector to the total emission of the overall industry is used as the weight. M in the overall cost function is the average or typical treatment ability of plants, expressed in the amount of BOD$_5$ removed per day by a single facility. Its typical value for Indonesia is 960 kg BOD$_5$ per day per treatment facility.

Groundwater system, annual capital investment:

$$C = aQ^{0.55} \qquad (2.31)$$

Groundwater system, annual operation and maintenance costs:

$$C = bQ^{0.62} \qquad (2.32)$$

Surface water system, annual capital investment:

$$C = cQ^{0.62} \qquad (2.33)$$

Surface water system, annual operation and maintenance costs:

$$C = dQ^{0.65} \qquad (2.34)$$

Overall water treatment cost functions for both systems:
Annual capital investment:

$$C = eQ^{0.59} \qquad (2.35)$$

Annual operation and maintenance costs:

$$C = fQ^{0.64} \qquad (2.36)$$

where:

a, b, c, d, e and f = constants,
e = the average of a and c; f is the average of b and d.

For the following functions, all cost are in US dollars. The unit of flow is m3/day.

PRC
The data are from Beijing, Shanghai, Guangzhou, and Tianjin. The functions are:

Groundwater system, annual capital investment:

$$C = 4412Q^{0.55} \qquad (2.37)$$

Groundwater system, annual operation and maintenance costs:

$$C = 2178Q^{0.62} \qquad (2.38)$$

Surface water system, annual capital investment:

$$C = 2349Q^{0.62} \qquad (2.39)$$

Surface water system, annual operation and maintenance costs:

$$C = 1333Q^{0.65} \qquad (2.40)$$

Philippines

The data are from Cebu and Metropolitan Manila. The functions are:

Groundwater system, annual capital investment:

$$C = 21812Q^{0.55} \qquad (2.41)$$

Groundwater system, annual operation and maintenance costs:

$$C = 5504Q^{0.62} \qquad (2.42)$$

Surface water system, annual capital investment:

$$C = 3835Q^{0.62} \qquad (2.43)$$

Surface water system, annual operation and maintenance costs:

$$C = 3335Q^{0.65} \qquad (2.44)$$

Indonesia

The data are from Bandung, Jakarta, and Medan.

Annual capital investment:

$$C = 7705Q^{0.59} \qquad (2.45)$$

Annual operation and maintenance costs:

$$C = 3279Q^{0.64} \qquad (2.46)$$

Pakistan

The data are from Karachi and Lahore.

Groundwater system, annual capital investment: not available.

Groundwater system, annual operation and maintenance costs (no treatment plant):

$$C = 1745Q^{0.62} \qquad (2.47)$$

Surface water system, annual capital investment:

$$C = 2147Q^{0.62} \qquad (2.48)$$

Surface water system, annual operation and maintenance costs:

$$C = 1990Q^{0.65} \qquad (2.49)$$

Nepal

The data are from Kathmandu.

Annual capital investment:

$$C = 3101Q^{0.59} \qquad (2.50)$$

Annual operation and maintenance costs:

$$C = 2350Q^{0.64} \qquad\qquad (2.51)$$

Marshall Islands
No data are available.

In addition to the overall cost functions we have derived, there are detailed cost breakdowns for the components in the treatment processes. These costs vary widely by country and region. A breakdown of US treatment costs is presented in Appendix Table 2.28. Collection costs are even more variable by region and type of soil, and labor costs and can be very high if the sewerage system is to be introduced or modified into an already developed area. A breakdown of collection costs is listed in Appendix Table 2.29.

4.1.5 Combined Sewer Overflows
Many cities have combined drainage systems for wastewater and street runoff disposal. During storms, the flows overwhelm the capacity of treatment plants and are usually discharged directly into the receiving bodies of water with little or no treatment, leading to substantial degradation in water quality. These combined sewer overflows (CSOs) are actually point source discharges, but are sometimes classified as nonpoint sources. Presented in Appendix Table 2.30 is a comparison of the capital costs for various alternative solutions to managing this problem.

4.2 Nonpoint Sources
Nonpoint source pollution is caused by runoff from agricultural land, feedlots, etc. Nonpoint sources often receive less attention than point sources, although they cause comparable levels of water pollution. Nonpoint sources deliver pulses of pollutant loadings associated with storm events, unlike the more constant point source discharges. The type and intensity of pollutant loading depends on locational factors, type and level of human activity, drainage and runoff characteristics of the land, and the intensity, duration and frequency of storms. Nonpoint source pollution is primarily nitrogen in different forms, phosphorus and other nutrients, soil loss, and BOD (from animal lots, etc.). The nutrient shock loadings often lead to eutrophic conditions in the receiving waters. Control of nonpoint sources of water pollution primarily involve best management practices for conservation in agriculture. The costs of these measures vary widely by region, crop, country, climate, scale of farming, and access to technology. Urban nonpoint sources may be a result of traffic, litter, atmospheric deposition, plant debris, lawn chemicals, deciding chemicals, erosion, septic systems, crossconnections, and illicit discharges into storm sewers and combined sewer overflows (that are sometimes classified as point

Cost of Sewage Treatment (Design Flow = 1 mgd)

Process	Initial Capital Cost ($)	Annual Costs			Unit Cost (¢/1000gal)
		Capital[a]	Operation & Maintenance	Total	
Imhoff Tank	380,000	41,720	15,500	57,270	15.7
Rotating Biological Disks	800,000	87,832	57,680	145,512	39.9
Trickling Filters	900,000	98,811	58,480	157,291	43.1
Activated Sludge	1,000,000 (ext.digestion)	109,790	74,410	184,200	50.5
	500,000 (int. digestion)	54,895	48,800	103,695	28.4
Stabilization Pond	250,000	27,447	23,680	51,127	14.0
Land Disposal	340,000 (basic)	37,328	41,540	78,869	21.6
(irrigation and	940,000 (primary)	103,302	81,540	184,742	50.6
overland flow)	1,240,000 (secondary)	136,139	115,950	252,089	69.1
Land Disposal	200,000 (basic)	21,958	25,100	47,058	12.9
(infiltration-percolation)	800,000 (primary)	87,832	65,100	152,932	41.9
	1,000,000 (secondary)	109,790	99,510	209,300	57.3

[a] Capital Recovery Factor = 0.10979 (15 years at 7%)

APPENDIX TABLE 2.29

Typical Sewage Charges

Item	Cost[a] (1990 $)
Manhole (4' dia; precast; 10')	1400 ea.
Drop Inside Manhole (8" sewer; 10' ABS or PVC pipe)	30 per ft.
Y-Branch	50
6" House Service Pipe	20
8" Sewer (10'; ductile iron pipe)	35 per ft.
Rock Excavation	70 per yd^3 (blasting)
	30 per yd^3 (soft rock)
	320 per yd^3 (air hammer)
Restoration	9 per yd^2 (gravel and shoulder pavement)
	85 per tonne (asphalt-concrete pavement)
Topsoil and Seeding	10 per yd^3
Pumping Station (1 mgd; underground)	175,000 (1mgd, underground)
	480,000 (above ground)
	35,000 (small submersible)

[a] Note that these cost estimates are for unencumbered land—they would be substantially higher for introducing sewerage systems in built-up areas.

APPENDIX TABLE 2.30

Comparison of Capital Costs for Various Alternative Solutions for CSOs

CSO Control Type	Control Option	Capital Costs ($ per acre)
Source Controls	Catchbasin Cleaning	—
	Street Sweeping	—
	Sewer Flushing	100–500
Flow System Optimization	Enhanced Flow Regulation and Static Inline Control	100–500
	Dynamic Inline Storage	500–1,000
	Real Time Control	500–1,000
System Flow Reduction	Conventional Full Separation	50,000–100,000
	Conventional Partial Separation	10,000–50,000
	Flow Slipping	5,000–10,000
High Rate Satellite Treatment	Screening	2,000–5,000
	Vortex Solids Separators	2,000–5,000
	Vortex Separators and Storage Combination	5,000–10,000
Off–Line Storage	Upstream Stormwater Hybrid	10,000–50,000
	Near-Surface Contaminated Upstream Storage	5,000–10,000
	Near-Surface Contaminated Downstream Storage	5,000–10,000
	Decentralized Deep Storage	10,000–50,000
	Consolidated Deep Storage	10,000–50,000

Source: National Research Council, 1993.

sources and are discussed in the previous section). Control options are intended primarily to reduce runoff (increase infiltration, decrease impervious areas), detain runoff (detention ponds, artificial wetlands), reduce pollution sources (minimize spills, dumping and chemical applications, control erosion), and provide some treatment (structural controls), although cost data for these options is extremely difficult to come by (NRC 1993).

Walker et al. (1993) have compared various alternative best management practices (BMPs) in terms of their cost effectiveness. Although BMP costs to control agricultural erosion tend to be highly variable, the costs reported in this study are presented in Appendix Table 2.31 as typical values.

It can easily be seen that if all the options are available to an unlimited extent, some options will completely dominate others. Cost changes with scale of operation (such as economies or diseconomies of scale) can be incorporated if marginal cost, not average cost, data can be constructed.

5. Cost Functions—Land

5.1 Erosion

Erosion is usually measured by some form of the Universal Soil Loss Equation. In this section we present general cost functions for soil erosion control that yield a rough estimate of control costs using readily available data. We have also mentioned some control methods and costs under the section on nonpoint sources of water pollution. Attempts to derive regional cost functions or

APPENDIX TABLE 2.31

Best Management Practice Costs to Control Agricultural Erosion

BMP	Costs of Control		Sediment Reduction (Mt/ha)
	$ per hectare (ha)	$ per metric tonne (Mt) of sediment reduction	
Wheat Filter Strips	-1.24	-0.20	6.32
Mini-Basins	6.23	0.83	7.49
Buried Drains	19.52	2.47	7.91
Sediment Basins	26.91	3.13	8.58
I-Slot	21.74	3.59	6.05
Gravity-Improved Management	27.50	4.24	6.48
Tailwater Pumpback	61.75	6.12	10.08
Side-Roll Sprinkler	65.68	6.51	10.08
Semi-Automated Grated Pipe	120.83	18.21	6.64

average costs for soil erosion control over an entire country are rare, as regions differ by soil and crop type, and countless numbers of crop rotations exist. For the 1985 US Resources Conservation Act, however, several studies attempted to assess the cost per acre per year for erosion control on highly erodible soil in different regions in the US.

In particular, Barbarika and Dicks (1988) devised two cost functions using data from representative high-erosion regions in the US. The two cost-of-compliance functions estimate the cost per acre per year for farmers to implement conservation plans, reducing the erosion to the T level (allowable erosion in tonnes per acre for that soil type), as dictated by the US Soil Conservation Service now under the auspices of the National Resources Conservation Service. The acceptable level of erosion rate, or the T level, is specified as 1 t/ha/year or 0.40 t/acre/year (used by the US Soil Conservation Service). Farmers have the option to comply and receive benefits, or continue farming as before and lose the benefits.

The cost functions were estimated using ordinary least-squares regression of data collected by CRES (Conservation Reporting and Evaluation System). The data were subject to six criteria:

1. erosion control was the primary purpose of assistance;

2. land is cropland;

3. erosion rate before treatment exceeded a given T;

4. sheet, rill, or wind erosion was reduced;

5. costs did not decline with a shift from conventional to conservation tillage;

6. cost-sharing with Agricultural Conservation Program (ACP) or Rural Clean Water Program (RCWP) was provided.

The annual per acre cost of treatment was assumed to be a function of current erosion rate (instead of an erodibility index), the level of treatment in tonnes saved per acre, the type of erosion, the size of the field, and the regional location. The first function was derived for cases in which conventional tillage was used in 1982; the second was derived for cases in which conservation tillage was used in 1982. The treatment methods and costs were derived for each region by the Soil Conservation Service. The equations also do not take into account the effect of crop rotations or types of crops on erosion in the estimation of erosion reduction and cost. This is because there are an unlimited number of ways of rotating and combining crops; producers generally select crops in response to prices and demand, not conservation considerations; and the current linear programming models that do take crop rotations into account only consider the most popular rotations, not necessarily the ones derived to specifically mitigate erosion. Costs of technical assistance are taken into account, however.

The functions are as follows:

$$CAY = Ir + 3.07 \; TYPE + 0.551 \; SAVED + 0.0133$$
$$SAVED2 - 0.0141 \; SAVED \; RATE + Dr \; IACRES \qquad (2.52)$$

$$CAY = Ir + 4.24 \; TYPE + 0.662 \; SAVED + 0.0160$$
$$SAVED2 - 0.0170 \; SAVED \; RATE + Dr \; IACRES \qquad (2.53)$$

where:

CAY	=	annualized treatment cost/acre
Ir	=	intercept for farm production region r (r = 1, 2,…10)
TYPE	=	dummy variable that changes the intercept
TYPE	=	0 if erosion is sheet, rill, and wind
TYPE	=	1 if erosion is sheet and rill only
SAVED	=	reduction in erosion (tons/acre/year) due to treatment
RATE	=	erosion rate in tonnes/acre/year
IACRES	=	inverse of acres affected by treatment
Dr	=	coefficient associated with IACRES for region r.

This study found that reducing erosion to T level on the most highly erodible farmlands in the US costs $667 million per year, or $15 per acre.

This method may not give the least cost of T-level compliance, as it omits crop rotation and changes in land use (like putting a permanent vegetative cover on the land); also, as stated before, the equations are derived based on the costs of methods that are suggested for certain areas by the SCS. Presumably the SCS has done studies to determine the least costly method of erosion control for each area and has made suggestions accordingly. One may be able to use these equations for a different country, assuming that the farmland of that country can be classified into one of the categories covered by the equations.

The equations (and their study) do not estimate the benefits of soil conservation, or the costs of soil erosion; they also do not estimate yields (annual income of the farmer). Whether it is profitable for a given farmer to adopt conservation measures would strongly depend on such considerations as his income, cost-sharing programs, and erosion control benefits.

Barbarika and Dicks make reference to the CARD linear programming model, which has been used by other researchers (English and Frohberg 1987) to estimate the costs of compliance with the 1985 Food Security Act. Quite different estimates were produced by this study; differences in model inputs and scope account for the discrepancies.

5.2 Solid and Hazardous Wastes

5.2.1 Description of Solid Waste Generation-Collection-Management System

The system of solid waste management of a city generally consists of three parts: (1) waste generation sources including household wastes, public littering, and industrial wastes; (2) waste collection and transportation including transfer stations; and (3) waste management facilities including sanitary landfill, incineration, composting, recovery (materials or fuels), etc. (Figure 2.2). The waste generation rates for the DMCs have been discussed in Appendix 1. This section estimates the costs of running such a solid waste management system. The costs are incurred mainly by the two categories of waste collection and transportation, and waste management facilities or disposal. In most developing countries, about 95 percent of the solid waste management costs are attributable to collection and public cleansing, as compared with about 60 percent (Cointreau-Levine 1994). In this section, the cost estimation will also be conducted in two parts: transportation and facility costs. The two types of costs will then be aggregated into one single cost function.

5.2.2 Transportation Costs

The total cost of transportation of wastes from the sources to intermediate facilities such as transfer stations or landfills, and from intermediate facilities to landfills depend on the distance traveled; the amount of waste transported; type of transportation used; compactors or trailer trucks; frequency of collection; routing of the trucks; and pay scales of the workers, among other factors

---

APPENDIX FIGURE 2.2

Waste Management System

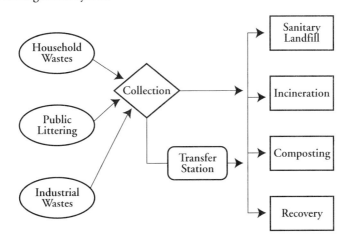

(Gottinger 1991). The nature of the current study renders it neither possible nor necessary to model all of these factors in our cost estimation. Instead, we take a simple approach of using the average price of tipping for different countries as the cost function for transportation expressed in terms of dollars per tonne of wastes transported. By taking this approach, one does not preclude the significance of other factors but rather assumes that these factors are either constant or implicitly included in the tipping price.

As an example, travel distance is obviously an important factor in determining the total transportation costs. The optimal routing in waste collection systems falls into the domain of a larger mathematical programming problem, best known as the PRC postman problem. It is defined as the finding of the minimum distance continuous tour through a network that travels all arcs at least once (Gottinger 1991). Thus the PRC postman problem is an arc-covering problem while another type of programming problem known as the traveling salesman problem is a node-covering problem. Much mathematical modeling work has been done on optimization of waste collection routing (Gottinger 1991). The estimation in this section does not intend to get into these issues but assumes the cost figures derived from existing sources are optimal.

Clearly the costs of these various items will vary from country to country. Cointreau-Levine (1994) suggests that the costs of waste transportation are closely associated with income of a country or a region. For the costs of different types of trucks, we made the following estimations:

■ *Collection in low-income areas:*
Characterized by narrow, or steeply-graded roads, accessible only by small vehicles of two-ton payload making two trips per day (for a total of four T/day), or container vehicles with three-tonne payloads making five trips a day (15 T/day). Assuming a waste generation rate of 0.35 kg/c/day, one vehicle may serve 10,000 to 40,000 residents respectively.
Price of vehicle: $70,000–90,000

■ *Collection in high-income areas:*
Characterized by roads of moderate width and grade, accessed by compaction vehicles with six-tonne payloads, two daily trips (12 T/day). Assuming a waste generation rate of 0.60 kg/c/day, 1 vehicle may serve 20,000 residents.
Price of vehicle: $60,000–130,000

Another factor that pertains to income level is the wages paid to the truck crews. It is likely that the wages are higher in high-income countries and vice versa.

Based on 17-year experiences working in the field, Cointreau-Levine (1994) estimated collection and transportation costs for countries of different income levels. Appendix Table 2.32 shows that in low-income countries, the capital cost of equipment such as trucks, and O&M costs account for 85 percent of the total, while labor only accounts for 15 percent. The reverse is true for high-income countries for which labor alone accounts for 70 percent of the total cost.

Pakistan, PRC, and Nepal fall into the low-income category and Philippines and Indonesia fall into the middle-income category. According to their income levels, we estimate that the collection costs for these five countries are $25/tonne for Pakistan, $25/tonne for PRC, $20/tonne for Nepal, and $40/tonne for both Philippines and Indonesia.

Another type of waste collection expense is public cleansing costs. When citizens litter indiscriminately and collection service is inadequate, waste accumulates in streets and on open lots. Cointreau-Levine (1994) estimated that a well-run city in a developing country would have no more than ten percent of its total waste quantity collected through public cleansing, whereas a well-run city in an industrialized country would have no more than five percent of its total wastes collected this way. The author also estimated the public cleansing costs shown in Appendix Table 2.33.

By comparing Appendix Tables 2.32 and 2.33, one can see that public cleansing is primarily assumed to be twice as expensive as curbside waste collection on a per tonne basis. For low- and middle-income countries, the percentage of labor costs in the total increase significantly due to the extra amount of work in collecting litters. Based on these discussions, we estimate that the public cleansing costs for these five countries are $50/tonne for Pakistan, $50/tonne for PRC, $40/tonne for Nepal, and $80/tonne for both Philippines and Indonesia. Additionally, we assume that 10 percent of the total municipal wastes are collected through public cleansing for all the five countries.

As shown in Figure 2.2, wastes collected are not necessarily all sent to transfer stations before being sent to disposal facilities. Nonetheless, when waste generation sources are sporadically located far from waste disposal facilities, transfer stations help cut down the total costs of transportation by employing long-distance hauling vehicles. The costs of running transfer stations are estimated by Cointreau-Levine (1994) as shown in Appendix Table 2.34.

Cost of Waste Management Facilities
Once wastes are collected, they are sent to certain waste management facilities for disposal or other treatment. In industrialized countries, the two most commonly found waste disposal facilities are sanitary landfilling and incineration with energy recovery. Nonetheless, incineration as an option is limited in developing countries whose waste streams are often characterized by low energy content and high moisture and, thus, are not suited for incineration. In order for incineration to be technically feasible, the waste stream that comes to the

Waste Collection Costs

	Low-Income Country	Middle-Income Country	High-Income Country
Collection Costs ($/tonne)	15–30	30–70	70–120
Capital (%)	40	30	10
Labor (%)	15	40	70
O&M (%)	45	30	20
Collection Costs ($/c/year)	3–6	9–21	42–72

Source: Cointreau-Levine, 1994.

Public Cleansing Costs

	Low-Income Country	Middle-Income Country	High-Income Country
Public Cleansing Costs ($/tonne)	30–60	60–140	140–240
Capital (%)	30	20	20
Labor (%)	50	70	65
O&M (%)	20	10	10
Public Cleansing Costs ($/c/year)	0.6–1.2	1.8–4.2	4.2–7.2

Source: Cointreau-Levine, 1994.

Transfer Costs

	Low-Income Country	Middle-Income Country	High-Income Country
Transfer Costs ($/tonne)	3–5	5–15	15–20
Capital (%)	65	50	35
Labor (%)	10	25	45
O&M (%)	25	25	20
Transfer Costs ($/c/year)	0.6–1.2	1.8–4.2	4.2–7.2

Source: Cointreau-Levine, 1994.

incinerator must have both a low moisture content (< 45 percent) and a high calorific content (> 1300 kcal/kg). In developing countries, the waste streams often have high moisture content (generally 45–85 percent) and low calorific content (900–1200 kcal/kg) of the solid waste generated. On the other hand, the average composition of the waste stream in developing countries appears to be well-suited to composting, since often more than 40 percent is compostable material. The problem is that in actuality, the supply of material is sporadic, and much is never properly collected. Improving the existing waste collection system is the important first step in waste management.

Cost data for solid waste disposal are highly variable depending on the kind of disposal technique, the level of efficiency and local factors (Appendix Table 2.35).

The cost function of running a single waste-management facility is conceptually shown by Appendix Figure 2.3. The costs consist of two parts: fixed cost, denoted by F, and process cost, denoted by P. Cost functions of this sort are of little use due to the aggregated nature of this study. Gottinger (1991) cited the estimates made by the Midwest Research Institute in 1973 on the costs and

APPENDIX TABLE 2.35

Sample Cost Data for Solid Waste Disposal for Different Disposal Methods

Purpose	Equipment Type	Capacity	Cost (1991 $)
General	Storage Containers	35 yd³	3,000
	Collection Vehicles	30 yd³	100,000
	Recycling and Transfer Equipment	3,400 lb	30,000
	Transport Equipment	300 hp	70,000
	Compacting and Densifying	100 tonne/hr	415,000
	Conveying Equipment	10 tonne/hr	0.7/lin.ft.
	Shredders	400 hp	270,000
	Screens	20 tonne/hr	70,000
	Magnets	20 tonne/hr	60,000
Landfilling	Compactors	45,000 gross weight	220,000
	Road graders	30,000 gross weight	175,000
	Tractor scraper	23 yd³	415,000
	Track loader	40,000 gross weight	215,000
	Rubber-tired loader	270 hp	320,000
	Track loader	100,000 hp	480,000
	Backhoe	60,000 gross weight	235,000
	Dump trucks	30 tonnes	315,000
	Water truck	2000 gal	50,000
Materials Recovery	Low-end system		15,000/ton/day[a]
	High-end system		20,000/ton/day[a]
Composting	Low-end system		15,000 /ton/day[a]
	High-end system		40,000/ton/day[a]
	Waste to energy		100,000/ton/day[a]

[a] Typical capital costs

Source: Tchobanoglous et al. 1993.

Summary of Resource Process Economics of Waste Management Approaches (in 1973 prices)[a]

Process	Sub-Process	Investment ($'000)	Total Annual Cost ($'000)	Resource Value ($'000)	Net Annual Cost ($'000)	Net Cost Per Input Tonne($)
Incineration	Only	9,299	2,303	0	2,303	7.68
	Residue recovery	10,676	2,689	535	2,154	7.18
	Steam recovery	11,607	3,116	1,000	2,116	6.57
	Steam & resid. rec'y	12,784	3,508	1,535	1,973	6.57
	Elect. energy recovery	17,717	3,892	1,200	2,682	8.97
Pyrolysis		12,334	3,287	1,661	1,626	5.42
Composting	Mechanical	17,100	2,987	1,103	1,884	6.28
Recovery	Materials	11,568	2,759	1,328	1,431	4.77
	Fuel	7,577	1,731	920	811	2.70
Sanitary Landfill	Close-in	2,472	770	0	770	2.57
	Remote	2,817	1,781	0	1,781	5.94

Based on municipality-owned 1000-TPD (tonne per day) plant with 20 year-economic life, operating 300 days/year.

[a] To convert the 1973 costs into 1995 costs, the multiplier is 2.93, assuming a five percent annual inflation rate.

Source: Midwest Research Institute, 1973, as cited in Gottinger, 1991.

Cost Function of an Existing Capacity

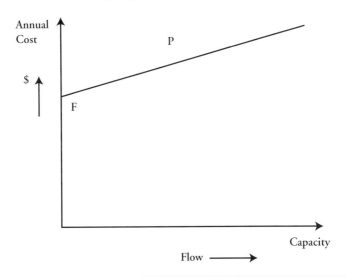

resource values incurred by different waste-management facilities on a per tonne basis (Appendix Table 2.36), while Cointreau-Levine (1994) estimated the average costs of running a sanitary landfill facility in countries of different income levels (Appendix Table 2.37).

The cost values in both Appendix Tables 2.36 and 2.37 are expressed in terms of dollar per tonne of waste input and, thus, much more useful than the cost function illustrated by Appendix Figure 2.2. To compare the two tables, the estimated cost of close-in sanitary landfill in Appendix Table 2.36 was $2.57 in 1973. Multiplied by the inflation adjustment factor of 2.93 between 1973 and 1995, the cost in 1995 is approximately $7.53 per tonne, falling into the middle-income range in Appendix Table 2.37. Appendix Table 2.37 is a more recent, perhaps more accurate, estimate, and we therefore recommend

APPENDIX TABLE 2.37
Sanitary Landfill Costs

	Low-Income Country	Middle-Income Country	High-Income Country
Disposal costs ($/tonne)	1–3	3–10	15–50
Capital (%)	55	50	40
Labor (%)	10	20	35
O&M (%)	35	30	25
Disposal Costs ($/c/year)	0.2–0.6	0.9–3.3	9.0–30.0

using it rather than Appendix Table 2.36 for landfill costs. For other waste management facilities such as incineration and composting, we will use Appendix Table 2.36 because Appendix Table 2.37 does not contain the required cost estimates. We estimate the costs of sanitary landfill for the five countries being $2 per tonne for Pakistan, Nepal, and PRC, and $4 per tonne for Philippines and Indonesia.

5.2.3 Aggregated Cost Functions for Solid Waste Management

The cost functions for solid waste management, COSTwm, can be derived by aggregating the costs of waste collection, COSTcol, and waste disposal, COSTdisp, or

$$COST_{wm} = COST_{col} + COST_{disp} \qquad (2.54)$$

The values of $COST_{col}$ and $COST_{disp}$ are determined as follows:

$$COST_{col} = MSW\ (0.90p_h + 0.10p_l + t\ p_t) \qquad (2.55)$$

$$COST_{disp} = c_i\ MSW \qquad (2.56)$$

where:

MSW = the quantity of municipal solid wastes (not including industrial wastes)

p_h = the cost of collecting one tonne of household waste (Appendix Table 2.32);

p_l = the cost of public cleansing per tonne (Appendix Table 2.33);

p_t = the cost of transferring one tonne of wastes at transfer stations (Appendix Table 2.34);

t = the percentage of total MSW sent for disposal via transfer stations

c_i = the cost of waste disposal per tonne (Appendix Tables 2.36 and 2.37),

where:

i = sanitary landfilling, incineration, composting, recovery, or pyrolysis.

The two parameters in equation (2.55), 0.9 and 0.1, are the estimated proportion of total MSW collected through curbside collection and public cleansing, respectively, for the DMCs (Cointreau-Levine 1994).

Perhaps an example will best illustrate how to use equations (2.54), (2.55) and (2.56) in estimating the costs of solid waste management. Suppose that the city of Kathmandu generates 100,000 tonnes of MSW annually. We estimated earlier that, for Nepal, the cost of collecting and transporting one tonne of MSW from curbside (p_h) = $20/tonne, the cost of collecting one tonne of wastes from public cleansing (p_l) = $40/tonne; and the cost of disposing of one tonne of MSW through sanitary landfill (c_i, i = sanitary landfill) = $2. We assume no transfer station is needed in Kathmandu (or t = 0). The total annualized solid waste management cost through sanitary landfill for Kathmandu would be:

$$COST = 100,000 \text{ tonnes } (0.9 \times \$20/\text{tonne} + 0.1 \times \$40/\text{tonne} + \$2/\text{tonne}) = \$2,400,000.$$

5.2.4 Remarks

The cost function developed in this section for solid waste management is linear. It is, thus, unable to account for any potential economies-of-scale effects. Such effects, however, have been shown to be very limited in the solid waste management sector (Cointreau-Levine 1994). In addition, industrial wastes account for a significant proportion in most of the urban centers in the participating DMCs. Although the cost function developed in this section is mostly based upon municipal wastes, it is also applicable to industrial wastes, with the exception of toxic and hazardous wastes, when the industrial waste quantities are known. It should be noted that industrial wastes are generally collected and managed by the private sector and municipal wastes are generally managed by governments.

Hazardous wastes have costs that are dictated primarily by legislation. Much of hazardous waste legislation mandates the type of technology to be used. These costs tend to be very specific to each case. There is also great debate as regards the standards to be set in these cases. For example, in the multibillion-dollar US Superfund program to clean up hazardous waste sites on a national priority list, the standards set have often been too stringent, and the resulting costs have been very high. In these cases, legal costs are often much higher than actual cleanup costs. Critics have suggested that the money might be better utilized for other projects that may reduce health risks more cost-effectively. It has also been argued that disturbing the wastes during cleanup sometimes poses more of a health risk than would be present without the cleanup. Innovative methodologies are being developed intensively and costs are usually difficult to estimate without large-scale field trials.

Presented in Appendix Table 2.38 is a compendium of average prices and costs for common hazardous waste disposal options.

6. Cost Functions—Ecosystems

6.1 Introduction

In this section, we use the cost of managing protected areas as an approximation of the cost of conserving the ecosystem. This implies an assumption that the protected areas represent the biodiversity of the country, and so protecting these areas would ensure the conservation of the ecosystem. This may not be true. There are other factors involved, which we discuss below. Habitat

Average Prices and Costs for Common Hazardous Waste Disposal Options

Disposal Type	Case	Price Range (1985 $/tonne)
Incineration	Average (on-site)	40–475
	Liquid organic waste	300–425 (low BTU; onsite)
		100–175 (high BTU; onsite)
		250–725 (low BTU; offsite)
		50–250 (high BTU; offsite)
	PCBs	350–450 (conc < 500ppm)
		850–1350 (conc >25,000 ppm)
	Fluidized Bed	45–300 (onsite)
		375 (offsite)
	Dioxin Contaminated Soils	600
Landfill	Drums (local facility)	25–250
	Bulk (local facility)	30–100
	Regional Facility (Germany)	20–75
	High-Hazard Waste (local facility)	100–300
	Low-Hazard Waste (shipped + 300 mi)	100–300
Other	Landfarming (35 tpd)	10–50
	Deep-Well Injection (toxic wastewater)	125–275
	Regional Facility	100
	Warehouse Tank Farm (20 yr. facility life)	450–1000

Source: Freeman, 1989.

preservation in protected areas, is however, the most effective and efficient mechanism for the conservation of biodiversity and the ecosystem (McNeely et al., 1990), and as such, the costs involved could provide a useful way of estimating the costs of conserving the ecosystem.

A precise estimation of costs would require detailed study of individual protected areas. Such estimates are probably available for at least one site in each country. In the absence of detailed studies of most protected areas, rough estimates of costs could be made by taking into account the degree of similarity or difference between the site for which detailed cost estimates are available and for which they are not.

As part of the post-UNCED commitment of countries to the provisions of the Convention on Biological Diversity, various countries have conducted studies on the costs of preserving biodiversity. Indonesia is one such country. The Indonesian study (MSPE 1993) provides estimates of some cost figures, which we use.

6.2 Costs of Conserving Biodiversity

The two main types of costs associated with conservation of biodiversity are those for in situ and ex situ conservation. The former is mainly the cost of protecting wild habitats, while the latter deals with the costs of off-site activities such as botanical and zoological gardens, seed banks, etc.

6.2.1 Costs of In Situ Conservation

The three main types of costs associated with establishing and maintaining protected areas are (Swanson and Barbier 1992; Dixon and Sherman 1990):

1. Direct Costs
   - land acquisition
   - relocation of people
   - zone developments
   - management facilities
   - wildlife and habitat management
   - law and regulation enforcement
   - training and education
   - research and training
   - routine management activities
   - integrated conservation and development projects (ICDPs) for people living inside, and in the vicinity of, the areas.

2. Indirect Costs
   - damages indirectly caused by the existence of the protected area (e.g., crops and property damaged by wildlife outside the protected area).

3. Opportunity Costs
   - the loss of potential benefits associated with protecting an area rather than harvesting its resources.

6.2.2 Costs of Ex Situ Conservation

Ex situ measures of promoting conservation of biodiversity include the following:
   - botanical gardens
   - captive breeding in zoos
   - gene banks
   - collection, documentation, and storage of specimens
   - systematic taxonomic inventory of fauna
   - research and training
   - public awareness and education.

6.3 Economic Valuation of Ecosystems

The preservation of ecosystems yields several tangible and intangible benefits as outlined in Appendix Table 2.39. While few people dispute the desirability of protecting selected natural areas, the costs of establishing and managing protected areas, especially in developing countries, appear formidable (Dixon and Sherman, 1990). Faced with acute shortages of funds, governments are

Classification of Total Economic Value for Wildlife and Wildlands

Use Values			Non-Use Values
1. Direct Value	2. Indirect Value	3. Option Value	Existence Value
Sustainably Harvested Products (meat/fish, timber, plants, etc.)	Ecological Functions/Roles	Future uses as per 12	Biodiversity
Recreation	Protection Functions		Culture, heritage
Tourism	Waste Assimilation		
Genetic Material	Microclimate Functions		
Education	Carbon Store		
Human Habitat			
Other Services (water transportation supply)			

Source: Dixon and Sherman, 1990.

reluctant to make the investments needed to provide effective protection. It is thus necessary to value the benefits of protected areas to justify the costs. However, many of the benefits that result from establishing and maintaining protected areas, subjected to market imperfections, are not easily valued in financial terms. Appendix Table 2.40 presents estimates of these values for some developing countries.

6.4 Cost Functions

Compared to other types of environmental problems discussed earlier, the costs of ecosystem and biodiversity protection are more uncertain and subject to more controversy. This is largely because of the complexity of the ecosystem itself. For example, no one can say with confidence which species should be protected and which should not, based on the "values" (to humans) of the species and the economic conditions of a particular country. There are also many uncertainties regarding the protection of species. Different approaches imply different degrees of protection and, thus, costs. Despite the difficulties, below we will make some preliminary efforts in developing some simple cost functions for building and running national parks via the Indonesia example.

As of 1993, the total protected area (IUCN categories I–V) in Indonesia was 19.3 million hectares, accounting for 10.2 percent of its total land area. The current expenditure on protected areas is $0.75/ha/yr, which was deemed inadequate. The official goal is to increase the total protected area by 68.7 million hectares by the year 2000. This has been deemed necessary from a sustainability viewpoint.

APPENDIX TABLE 2.40

Some Recent Wildlife and Wildlands Valuation Estimates for Developing Countries ($)

Direct-Use Values	
Fruit and latex forest harvesting, Peru	$6,330/ha
Sustainable timber harvesting, Peru	$490/ha
Buffalo range ranching, Zimbabwe	$3.5–$4.5/ha
Wetlands fish and fuelwood, Nigeria	$38–$59/ha
Viewing value of elephants, Kenya	$25 million/year
Ecotourism, Costa Rica	$1250/ha
Tourism, Thailand	$385–$860,000/year
Research/education, Thailand	$38–$77,000/year
Tourism, Cameroon	$19/ha
Genetic value, Cameroon	$7/ha
Sustainable harvesting of medicinal plants, Belize	$3,327/ha
Forest production, Malaysia	$2,455/ha
Opportunity cost of protected forests, Kenya	$34/ha
Marine/Coastal systems, Galapagos	$53/ha
Indirect-Use Values	
Watershed protection of fisheries, Cameroon	$54/ha
Control of flooding, Cameroon	$23/ha
Soil fertility maintenance, Cameroon	$8/ha
Carbon storage, tropical forests	$1,300/ha/year
Option/Existence Values	
Elephants and other species, Khao Yai National Park, Thailand	$4.7 million/year
Total Economic Value	
Annual non-market benefits of 51.5 m ha of Mexican forest	$4,214.8 million

Source: Brown et al. 1993.

The costs of biodiversity and ecosystem protection consist mainly of two parts: in situ conservation, and ex situ conservation. In situ costs can be further divided into two categories: (1) costs of protected area management, including those associated with managing the land area (land acquisition, zone development, management facilities, etc.); and (2) costs of integrated conservation and development projects (ICDPs), including the costs of managing the people affected (relocation, training, education, etc.). Ex situ costs include such items as inventory of plants, inventory of animals, gene banks, and research and training. Consequently, a linear generic cost function for building and running national parks can be constructed as follows:

$$COST_{bio} = COST_{InSitu} + COST_{ExSitu} \qquad (2.57)$$

$$COST_{InSitu} = a\ AREA + b\ PEOPLE \qquad (2.58)$$

$$COST_{ExSitu} = COST_{InvPla} + COST_{InvAni} + COST_{Res} + COST_{Othe} \qquad (2.59)$$

The subscripts of the symbols used in equations (2.57) through (2.59) are self-explanatory. In particular, AREA refers to the total protected area and PEOPLE refers to the number of people affected. The main parameters that need to be estimated empirically are (a) area management costs per ha of land protected; and (b) ICDP costs per capita. The following example illustrates the values of (a) and (b) and other terms in the equations for Indonesia.

Appendix Tables 2.41, 2.42, and 2.43 provide detailed cost estimates for the next ten-year period.

The value of a falls in a range between $0.50 and $5 per hectare per year depending on the type of reserves, with higher degree of protection generally incurring higher costs. The parameter b has a value range between $7.50 and $30 per capita per year. The cost values are not proportional to either AREA or LAND and, thus, no ratio cost figures are given. Note that the total costs are all calculated as the net cost for ten years, rather than the annualized costs as expressed by equations (2.57) through (2.59). The total ten-year net cost for realizing the government's goal by the year 2000 is 1030 + 900 + 1033 = $2,963 million.

7. Full-Cost Accounting

It has often been suggested that there should be fuller cost accounting of human activities that impact the environment. The problem with this approach is that although it is conceptually an excellent idea, it is practically an impossible task to fully account for the impacts of all the activities on the environment and to estimate the costs of these damages. COR can serve as a reasonable surrogate for more detailed analysis by estimating what difference a particular level of activity makes on the cost of remediating to a particular overall standard. The difference of the CORs with and without the activity would yield the marginal cost contribution of the activity to the degradation of the environment. This can then be incorporated into a more complete assessment of the real cost of the activity.

8. Use of COR for Investment Decisions

An important application of the COR approach is to use the numbers developed to aid in decision-making. For example, governments can use these kinds of indicators to prioritize investment in environmental sectors. These indicators can also be used to update traditional methods of project appraisal by means of one of two applications. The first is to choose among a set of environmental mitigation projects, given the relative costs and benefits of each

In Situ Measures: Protected Area Management

Type of Protected Area	Area (mn/ha)	a ($/ha/yr)	Duration (yrs)	Net Cost ($ mn)
Key Top Priority Reserves	12.5	5	10	625
Other Top Priority Reserves	6.2	2.5	10	155
Proposed Marine Reserves	17.4	0.5	10	87
Hydrological Protection Forests	30.3	0.5	10	151.5
Other Reserves	2.3	0.5	10	11.5
Total	68.7			1030

In Situ Measures: ICDP

Intensity of Input	People (mn)	b ($/c/yr)	Duration (yrs)	Net Cost (mn)
Most	1	30	10	300
Medium	2	15	10	300
Least	4	7.5	10	300
Total	7			900

Ex Situ Measures

Measures	Year 1 Cost ($ mn/yr)	Year 2–10 Cost ($ mn/yr)	Net Cost 1–10 ($ mn)
Inventory of Plants	75	50	525
Inventory of Animals	154	26	388
Gene Banks, Research & Training	12	12	120
Total	241	88	1033

project, and how they affect COR. Another is to evaluate traditional projects by keeping track of how much each affects COR even though the intent of the project may be solely economic. This would underscore the fact that many economic projects do have environmental consequences (and probably vice versa). An interesting spin-off of this approach would be to adapt the multiobjective programming approach used by Murray and Harshadeep (1994) to evaluate all projects, whether economic or environmental, in a consistent manner by trading off these two components which are not always incompatible. This would help to decide on mitigation projects if any component of the environment is too damaged by any chosen project.

The COR approach does not answer the question of where multilateral financial institutions such as ADB should invest; to do so would require an estimation of the benefits of the investment, which are subject to much controversy. Rather, COR strives to determine how much is needed if a regional development bank decides to invest in a particular country and a particular sector. Past efforts to estimate the costs of abatement, notably Weatherly's estimates (Owens 1994), lacked sophistication in many of their underlying assumptions. The cost functions developed in this study are, it is hoped, an overall improvement over the cost-effectiveness ratios used by Weatherly. Although these cost functions are generic and generally developed in the US, we have made use of local data wherever possible.

8.1 Environmental Investments
8.1.1 Intracountry
Most developing countries usually have severe budgetary restrictions for environmental protection. It is inevitable in any comprehensive approach to environmental problems that a triage situation develops where the decision-makers have to decide into which problems they should invest their resources. Environmental problems span various media (air, water, land, ecosystem) and are heterogeneously distributed over a region. With knowledge of the severity of the problem, unit costs of remediation, and sensibly set standards, COR could be computed. An approach such as COR helps government agencies reduce environmental problems into terms that can be used for cost-effective decision-making. This is possible by computing COR with and without certain environmental projects and then using the difference as another input into cost-benefit analysis to determine an optimal environmental project portfolio.

8.1.2 Intercountry
Multilateral financial institutions (MFIs), such as the World Bank and ADB, may also benefit similarly from the use of COR in a similar manner. Just as countries have to make decisions about which provinces within the country they have to invest in, MFIs have to do the same between countries. A similar approach could be used, but here the crosscountry and global effects of environmental problems should also be considered by examining the local, regional, and global components of COR.

8.2 Use in Project Appraisal
In the long term, COR and other environmental indices can be used not only to help choose among a set of environmental projects, but also to help incorporate environmental concerns into regular project selection. All over the world, the integration of environmental concerns into development strategies has become a high priority. Accomplishing economic development, especially in developing countries, in a fashion that is compatible with environmental

quality is a key component in the push toward "sustainable development." This phrase has attracted much attention since it was brought into the limelight by the Stockholm Conference on Environment and Development in 1972. World leaders and NGOs alike have warmly embraced this rather vague concept; however, there is little consensus on either a definition of sustainability—over 50 definitions were cited in a recent paper by Pezzy (1992)—or on the tools needed to operationalize sustainable development.

The primary problem in addressing environmental concerns has been that the situation has been misrepresented as a black-and-white case—a choice between economic benefits and environmental quality improvements. The truth, rather, is a shade of gray, where it is possible to have varying degrees of both. Although the lack of an operational definition of sustainability has led to its initial widespread acceptance, the real questions have been avoided: what tradeoffs, if any, do we have to make between economic development and the environment? What really is "the environment" and how do we make trade-offs among its different components? Such complex questions are the reasons decision-makers pursue only piecemeal attempts at sustainable development without any overall coherent structure.

So, how does one operationalize sustainable development? First, we have to look at who makes or significantly influences major development decisions—these are MFIs, other international organizations, multilateral agencies, and country, state, and local governments. Although these organizations and the environmental problems with which they deal vary in scale from global to regional and national to local, the decisions made are mostly in two categories: (1) "softer" issues such as structural adjustment, restructuring, institutional infrastructure, pricing, etc.; and (2) more obvious major projects such as dams, canals, power plants, and transportation infrastructure. In this appendix, we will concentrate on this latter category and focus on how their environmental impacts could be incorporated into the selection process of such projects—in particular on how to evaluate investments in a sustainability context.

Cost-benefit analysis is generally the tool of choice for lending institutions addressing project portfolio management. MFIs routinely conduct cost-benefit-based project assessments to determine the economic viability of projects and usually initiate environmental impact assessments to determine the environmental impacts in selected projects. These assessments are some-times used to make minor changes in project design that might then render the project neither environmentally nor economically optimal (compared with other initial project alternatives). The structure of MFIs exemplifies this behavior—they generally have a separate "end-of-the-pipe" environment division that reviews the projects that the institution is considering financing to assess their potential environmental impact and suggest improvements, but that rarely participates in the initial project selection process. This is probably not a satisfactory method to properly include and act upon the environmental impacts of projects—for example, few projects financed by official assistance have been rejected purely on environmental grounds. However, these institutions have recently felt the need to integrate externalities such as environmental concerns into their project selection process. Turning to environmental economists for guidance, the overwhelming advice has been to promote valuation methods.

At the heart of the economic approach to integrating environmental externalities into cost-benefit analysis is the valuation of environmental benefits and environmental damage. Although the field of valuation has advanced considerably in the last few years, the limited acceptability of the results of these techniques, the controversial nature of some analyses involved, and the exorbitant costs involved in conducting such analyses on a routine basis for all potential projects, limit the widespread applicability of valuation methods to sustainable development at the project or sectoral lending level. Valuation techniques, while gaining more widespread acceptance for the evaluation of environmental damages to be assigned in legal proceedings (e.g., the case of the Exxon Valdez oil spill), are unlikely to be widely applied in project selection and portfolio investment due to time and resource constraints, and the geographic and project specificity of the results. There is an increasing need for routine, quick evaluations of projects in a flexible and customizable framework.

Ideally, proposed projects would be considered in the context of their incremental impact on the environment, whether positive or negative, and in particular, of their impact on the sustainability of the affected area. As discussed above, this has been a difficult task to date. However, COR approach bypasses the issues of environmental valuation and gives an estimate of the investment necessary to achieve sustainability as defined through the selection of environmental standards. In other words, COR is a measure of the distance from sustainability, and once calculated for a region or nation, projects can be evaluated from the standpoint of their effect on the regional COR. Regional plans can be developed that reduce total COR (environmental impacts) while supporting economic development.

9. Commentary on the COR Index

9.1 What Do the Costs Mean?

COR is one of the most important contributions of this research project. Its value rests, first, principally on the fact it is a cardinal measure of the cost of maintaining sustainability. Therefore, the values can be readily added to derive an overall estimate without having to choose, or motivate, arbitrary weights. Second, its value derives from the fact that it is expressed in monetary units. Its interpretation as the welfare that must be given up to restore the environment is obvious. COR tells us how much excess consumption a society is enjoying today at the expense of future generations. Third, the COR can be adjusted to reflect increments of human capital. Fourth, the cost of repair focuses specifically on the types of environmental damage known to be substantive problems in the countries in the Asian region. A fifth major advantage of COR is that it is a cost measure that links pressure both to impacts and to possible responses. The simplest example could be the conclusion that for a specific country, water pollution has a much higher COR than air pollution. This implies that the investments needed to improve water quality to meet standards must be higher than that required for air pollution. This could lead to a policy response of pushing public investments into water quality infrastructure improvements at the expense of similar government programs to alleviate air pollution.

The significant contribution this set of indicators makes is to determine the amount of current well-being that must be given up to restore the environment to its pristine state, or to some other acceptable state. COR is a measure of the increase in defensive expenditures that a society must undertake in order to leave to future generations environmental assets equivalent in quality to the ones the current generation received. These expenditures are indicative and we are not arguing that they all need to be made now. Whether they are made or not, however, they are an indicator of the magnitude of resources that would have to be committed once a political decision has been made to restore or improve the environment.

It is essential to realize that the emissions, standards, and costs of control do not necessarily dictate a particular solution to be used in computing COR. COR implicitly assumes a least-cost solution to meet the given standard. For example, in reducing the SO_2 concentration to a standard, we may have many options; we have to choose if, and at what level, each of these reduction strategies is adopted so as to minimize the total cost. It should be noted that there may be many "near-optimal" solutions that could then be reselected from, depending on other factors that we had not included in the analyses. In water pollution cases, some of the optimal waste load allocation concepts could be utilized to determine the most cost-effective set of effluent treatments while meeting in-stream standards.

9.2 Advantages of the COR Approach

One of the advantages of using a COR measure is that it avoids the more intractable issues of benefit or damage valuation of environmental degradation. This brief review of the application of COR reveals precisely how difficult it is to estimate even the costs of control. As shown in Chapters 4 and 6, the actual computation of the costs involved a variety of assumptions and priorities. This points to the fact that a proper computation of COR to enable cross-country comparisons should include a list of priority pollutants, the level of spatial and sectoral disaggregation, control technologies available, and a guide to which kinds of pollution should be included in each of the four COR types (air, water, land, and ecosystem). Consistency in the setting of the level and type (ambient, loading, performance) of standards is essential before comparisons can be made. The COR approach also requires consistency in the evaluation of emission factors and cost function development and the interest rates used. Such standardization is necessary before the CORs can be used either for comparison (e.g., ranking) or other decision-making (e.g., investment prioritization) purposes. However, the computation of COR illustrates the power of using such an index. The components should help decision-makers determine not only how much achieving a particular standard would cost, but also what the effect of different standards are and how much clean-up one could expect for a particular investment. The organization of the data on emissions, technologies, standards, and costs is by itself a great asset in providing the decision-makers with a synoptic view of the environmental problems that a country faces in identifying priority regions, sectors, pollutants, and media in approaching the problem of environmental degradation.

In summary, we believe that the approaches used in this study would significantly augment the literature on environmental indicators due to the following reasons:

- COR enables comparison of environmental changes with economic changes on the same monetary terms.

- It enables comparison among various media (e.g., air, water, land, biodiversity). We can determine how much money theoretically is needed to bring each of the different pollution sources to a certain set of standards.

- It estimates an upper bound of the cost of remediation for comparison with more innovative approaches (the COR approach requires the use of the cheapest alternative to meet standards—source changes, process redesign, end-of-pipe treatment or remediation to estimate costs; however, if better ways to achieve compliance to well-set standards are considered, e.g., tradeable permits, this could be reflected in subsequent estimations of the COR).

- It avoids the weighting problem that plagues most EQIs.

- COR subcomponents would help determine environmental investment strategies by helping to maximize the environmental improvement (determined by COR subcomponent costs) that could be achieved for a given amount of investment.

- An interesting spinoff effect would be the setting of more realistic standards by countries. These standards could vary spatially and temporally, be set by pollutant and sector or source, and be based on emission, ambient, or performance criteria to reflect the impact of the different kinds of pollution and the inherent triage in environmental control in various media and with economic development. The standards would be set primarily to incorporate health risks or the risks to ecosystems. Note that these standards could be set at different levels of conceptual aggregation (e.g., project level, sectoral level, national level).

■ It would enable spatial and dynamic comparisons—across countries or among various spatial regions (or sectors) within a country (or economy), and also over time. This would reflect any change in the environment, standards, economy, or technological or policy innovations that affects the ease of compliance. This would enable the use of these indicators for ranking or prioritization purposes.

■ These new indicators could be used for decision-making purposes such as environmental portfolio management, prioritization of pollution types, identification of target sectors and "win-win" or other costless or low-cost solutions, assessment of the utility of existing technological and policy options, and identification of the need for future developments in these areas.

■ By focusing on the costs of control, we have made the computation of COR much easier than other EQIs that usually require much more extensive monitoring, modeling, weighting, or controversial damage/benefit valuation. Well-set standards would reflect the environmental benefits or losses by dictating the degree of cleanup required.

■ The COR attempts to capture the environmental pressures, states, and responses in a unitary measure.

■ Depending on use, these indices could be developed at different levels of accuracy—from back-of-the-envelope computations for getting rough estimates for prioritization to more detailed analyses for project appraisal.

■ Its use would be enhanced by any rational set of traditional EQIs.

■ The integrating nature of the COR indices is ideally suited to put a more concrete handle on the fuzzy concept of sustainable development.

9.3 Limitations
9.3.1 Applicability
The comparability of COR across countries, sectors and regions over time should be viewed carefully. Emission factors, standards, and cost data cannot be directly transferred from one country to another. It is necessary to estimate the data as best as possible on a local basis. However, this is not always possible; in such cases, one should use data from another country with appropriate corrections. It is also a good idea when faced with such uncertainties to try a few sensitivity analyses to get a feel for the magnitudes of differences caused by the uncertainty.

9.3.2 Data Issues

An actual application of the COR concept would require the collection and organization of vast quantities of data, especially if important investment decisions are to be made using the COR as an input. These data may be patchy, inconsistent, unavailable, or of uncertain quality or source. An important point that this study brings to light is the need to collect, organize, and analyze data in a systematic manner. Improvements in data quality are essential before such indices can be used for real decision-making. An advantage of constructing indices with available data is that one can then determine how sensitive the COR will be to changes in the parameters assumed. This would indicate which data should be examined in more detail to construct better estimates. We have found during the course of this study a substantial amount of sketchy data for countries, provinces, and sectors; these data should be utilized to their fullest, with the aim of identifying important parameters and collecting spatially-disaggregated time-series data. Geographic information systems (GIS) may be invaluable for their ability to collate, analyze, update, and display data from different data sources and scales.

It is inevitable that any routine computation of COR would involve a significant amount of computer effort to manage the data; this may involve a restructuring or coordination of institutions that have traditionally handled the data. It is important to realize that we now have the opportunity to do the kinds of analyses that one could not even imagine just a few years ago. Computers would certainly play a pivotal role in any integrated strategy for comprehensive environmental management.

9.3.3 Interactive Effects

One of the complicating factors in estimating COR is keeping track of the interactive effects of controlling one environmental problem on the state of another. For example, technologies to control SO_2 may affect the level of CO_2 or NO_X discharged. These cross-pollutant control effects must be considered before an overall COR for air can be determined.

9.3.4 Missing Components

There are a whole set of issues that have not been included in the CORs as proposed in this study. These may be important in the case of individual countries or sectors. Some of these could be other local concerns, cultural factors, value differences, political views, gender issues, religious perceptions both across countries and regions that would play an important part in any investment or other decisions relating to the environment. These issues tend to be subjective and not easily incorporated into any quantitative or systematic framework. That is why COR is proposed as a systematic approach to act as one of the major inputs into rational decision making and does not preclude the consideration of other factors.

9.3.5 Poverty

Indira Gandhi once remarked that "poverty is the greatest polluter." In reality, many developing countries, environmental concerns are often sidelined in the face of more pressing basic economic problems. The concept of the Kuznet's Curves also propose an income threshold above which environmental problems become less severe in some cases, presumably due both to public concern about the environment and access to more efficient and less polluting technology. There is also a belief that environmental problems exist only in the minds of the rich, as environment is a "luxury good." However, this could not be further from the truth. Most environmental problems disproportionately adversely affect the life style of the poor. Environmental and economic problems are intertwined and cannot be considered in isolation of each other.

9.3.6 Technology Transfer

The computation of COR is strongly affected by the level of control technology. COR would be extremely high if we restricted ourselves to existing control technologies in many developing countries. But there is also a problem in using US costs, as technologies may not be available in the developing countries considered, due to intellectual property rights, patent laws, tariffs, subsidies, and other concerns regarding the importation of technology.

9.3.7 Benefit Valuation

The COR approach reports on the costs of achieving standards. It does not deal with the issue of which environmental component is more important than another. The valuation of environmental damages and benefits is not a very well developed science, and it involves many assumptions that may be harder to justify than those involved in computing COR alone. Approaches to estimating environmental damages and benefits include market and nonmarket methods such as hedonic pricing, travel cost methods, contingent valuation, etc. and these have limited applicability for some specific purposes. It is necessary, however, to derive estimates of the damages in order to choose between environmental projects if the standards do not fully reflect the comparison of CORs across media.

9.4 A Final Note

In spite of the various problems with the cost-of-remediation approach, we feel that it is a practical one. The computation of COR makes decision-makers grapple with the most important issues—what the level of the pollution is, what level would be acceptable, and what the most cost-effective set of solutions would be to help us go from one to the other. We have listed a variety of cost functions that have been derived from the vast but scattered literature on the subject. This appendix also addresses the question of how to adapt common functions to particular regions. However, it must be stressed that any local data that are available must be used to the fullest. The cost functions must be constructed in a manner that best utilizes the available data without becoming extremely data-demanding. Appropriate smoothing functions, adjustment factors and the like may be employed where required, while keeping in mind the accuracy needed for the purpose to which COR would be put. In fact, it is this purpose that would dictate the level and type of analyses that one would perform to obtain a COR.

A focus on cost-effectiveness yields an index that is not only useful but also avoids the more controversial damage valuations. The examples that have been outlined in this appendix regarding the use of the COR demonstrate the utility of this versatile index. It is suggested that an economic approach to addressing environmental problems should use some version of the COR index as a component.

The most important advantage of such an approach is that it compares environmental damage of several different kinds in several different regions using a common metric. This, combined with the fact that the index is scalable depending on data available and intended purpose, is invaluable for comparison and decision-making both from the point of view of a country and international institutions. We feel that the COR is a practical tool that should be adopted as soon as possible as part of the quest for managing the environment in a comprehensive manner.

Notes

1   This cost includes net annual operating expenses, depreciation, cost of financing, and allowance for income taxes (i.e., the minimum revenue requirement for the project).

2   Total Annual Costs = DC + IC – RC
    where:
      DC = direct costs
      IC = indirect costs
      RC = recovery credits on an annual basis.

3   CRF = i(1+i)n/{(1+i)n-1}
    where:
      n = the control system life (generally 10–20 years)
      i = a pretax marginal rate of return on private investment of ten percent.

4   A premium is associated with the use of a lower sulfur coal, assuming that coal has the same HHV.

5   The calcium sulfate and lime particulates have different properties from the fly ash and can reduce the effectiveness of particulate removal by the electrostatic precipitator unless other measures are taken.

6   Resistivity is a function of the chemical composition and size of the particulates and their temperature. The source of the particles is the determining factor for chemical composition, for example, particles from coal-burning utilities are large compared to cement, glass, Kraft, or metal particles (generally 10–20 micron in diameter as compared to about 1).

7   Costs are normalized by assuming a 4.6 percent annual inflation rate from the date of the cost data to 1993, following World Bank documents on pollution abatement costs (Wheeler et al. 1994).

8   In the wastewater treatment literature, X is replaced by the flow rate Q in cubic meters per day.

9   In order to cut down the costs, transfer stations play an intermediate role by collecting incoming wastes from surrounding areas and channeling them to landfill sites or incinerators.

References

Afsah, S., Martin, P. and Wheeler, D. 1994. *Industrial Pollution Projection System.* World Bank, PRDEI, Washington, DC.

Anderson, D. 1993. "Energy-Efficiency and the Economics of Pollution Abatement," in *Annual Review of Energy and the Environment*, vol. 18, pp. 291–318.

Asian Development Bank (ADB). 1992a. Vehicular Emissions Control Planning in Manila. Department of Environment and Natural Resources. Manila.

ADB 1992b. Environmental Considerations in Energy Development. Manila.

ADB 1993. *Water Utilities Data Book—Asian and Pacific Region.* Manila.

Bagchi, A. 1994. *Design, Construction, and Monitoring of Landfills.* 2nd ed., chapter 12: Economic Analysis. New York: John Wiley & Sons.

Bao Q. and J. Z. Chen, eds. 1993. *The Quantification of Environmental Protection Strategic Objectives for the Year of 2000.* China Environmental Sciences Press.

Barbarika, A. Jr. and M. R. Dicks. 1988. "Estimating the Costs of Conservation Compliance," in *Journal of Agricultural Economics Research.* Summer 1988, vol. 40, no 3, pp. 12–20, Summer, 1988.

Bi, J., S. Zhang, Q. G. Cai, and Y. J. Tang. 1995. "Assessing the Feasibility of Developing New Environmental Indices in the People's Republic of China." Working paper no. 11. Harvard University, Division of Applied Sciences.

Brown, K. et al. 1993. "Economics and the Conservation of Global Biological Diversity." Working paper no 2. Global Environment Facility.

Chan, L. and C. Weaver. 1994. "Motorcycle Emission Standards and Emission Control Technology." Working paper series no. 7. Washington, DC: World Bank, Asia Technical Department.

Clark, Robert M. 1982. "Cost Estimating for Conventional Water Treatment." in *Journal of the Environmental Engineering Division.* Proceedings of the American Society of Civil Engineers, vol. 108, no. EE5, pp. 819–34. October, 1982.

Cointreau-Levine, S. J. 1994. "Private sector participation in municipal solid waste services in developing countries." The Formal Sector. Vol. 1 Urban Management Programme Discussion Paper No. 13. Washington, DC: World Bank.

Companhia de Tecnologia de Saneamento Ambiental (CETESB). 1994. *Relatorio de Qualidade do ar no Estado de Sao Paulo 1993.* CETESB Sao Paulo, Brasil.

CONCAWE. 1992. *Motor Vehicle Emission Regulations and Fuel Specifications: 1992 Update. Report 2/92.* Brussels: Oil Companies' European Organization for Environmental Protection and Health.

De Wolf, G., P. Murin, J. Jarvis and M. Kelly. 1984. *The Cost Digest: Cost Summaries of Selected Environmental Control Technologies.* Austin: USEPA-600/8–84–010, October. Radian Corporation.

Department of Trade and Industry 1993. *Clean Coal Technology: Options for the Future.* Produced in the UK for the Organisation for Economic Cooperation and Development and the International Energy Agency. France.

Department of Energy (DOE) 1994. *Foreign Markets for US Clean Coal Technologies.* Report to the US Congress by the USDOE, May 2.

DeWolf, G., Murin, P., Jarvis, J. and Kelly, M. *The Cost Digest: Cost Summaries of Selected Environmental Control Technologies.* Austin: US EPA- 600/8–84–010, 1984. EPA Contract Number: 86–02–3171.

Dhrymes, P. and M. Kurz. 1964. "Technology and Scale in Electricity Generation," in *Econometrica,* vol. 32, no. 3, July, pp. 287–315.

Dickinson, H. 1958 "The Steam Engine to 1830," in *The Oxford History of Science and Technology,* vol. 4, chapter 6. Oxford: Oxford University Press.

Dixon, J. A. and P. B. Sherman. 1990. *Economics of Protected Areas: A New Look at Benefits and Costs.* Washington, DC: Island Press.

Electric Power Research Institute (EPRI) 1977. *Coal-Fired Power Plant Capital Cost Estimates.* Produced for EPRI by Bechtel Power Corporation. EPRI AF–342. Palo Alto, California: 1977.

EPRI. 1993. *Technical Assessment Guide, TR102276,* September. Palo Alto, California.

Elsom, D. 1992. Atmospheric Pollution: *A Global Problem.* 2nd ed. Oxford: Blackwell Publishers.

English and Frohberg. 1987. "Executive Report on the T-Study." Unpublished Report. Center for Agricultural and Rural Development, Iowa State University.

Eskeland, G. 1994. "A Presumptive Pigovian Tax: Complementing Regulation to Mimic an Emissions Fee." *The World Bank Economic Review.* (ECMT) 8(3) pp. 373–394.

European Conference of Ministers of Transport. 1990. *Transport Policy and the Environment.* Organisation for Economic Cooperation and Development. Paris: OECD.

Evans, P. 1995. "Clean Coal Technologies in Asia," in *Independent Energy.* April, 1995. pp. 28–34.

Faiz, A. and S. Gautam. 1994. "Motorization, Urbanization, and Air Pollution." Draft document. Transportation, Water, and Urban Development Department, Transport Division. World Bank, Washington, DC.

Freeman, H. M. ed. 1989. *Standard Handbook of Hazardous Waste Treatment and Disposal.* McGraw-Hill.

General Electric Capital Company. 1995. Personal correspondence on cost functions for power plant installations, January.

Gottinger, Hans-Werner. 1991. *Economic Models and Applications of Solid Waste Management*. New York: Gordon and Breach Science Publishers.

Grant E., W. Ireson and R. Leavenworth. 1976. *Principles of Engineering Economy*. 6th ed. New York: John Wiley.

Gumerman, R. C., Culp, R. L. and Hansen, S. P. 1978. *Estimating Costs for Water Treatment as a Function of Size and Treatment Efficiency*, USEPA–600/2–78–182, August. EPA Contract Number: CI–76–0288.

Hellman, R. and C. Hellman.1983. *The competitive economics of nuclear and Coal Power*. Lexington: Lexington Books.

Kaplan, N. 1994. *Integrated Air Pollution Control System, Version 4.0*, vol. 2, Technical Documentation Manual. PB91-133520. Radian Corporation, Research Triangle Park, North Carolina. M. Maibodi, A. Blackard, and R. Page, EPA Norman Kaplan, EPA 68–02–4286.

Karmokolias, Y. 1990. "Automotive Industry: Trends and Prospects for Investment in Developing Countries." IFC Discussion Paper No. 7. Washington, DC: World Bank.

Komanoff, C. 1981. *Power Plant Cost Escalation: Nuclear and Coal Capital Costs, Regulation, and Economics*. New York: Van Nostrand Reinhold Company.

Komanoff, C. 1976. *Power Plant Performance: Nuclear and Coal Capacity Factors and Economics*. Council on Economic Priorities Studies from the Council on Economic Priorities. New York.

Krupnick, A. 1992. "Measuring the Effects of Urban Transportation Policies on the Environment: A Survey of Models." Policy Research Working Papers Series 1030. Country Economics Department, World Bank. Washington, DC.

Manins, P. 1991. "Model for Air Pollution Planning." Report of WHO Consultant to Environmental Management Bureau. Manila, Philippines.

McNeely, J. A. et al. 1990. Conserving the World's Biological Diversity. IUCN, WRI, CI, WWF-US and World Bank. Gland, Switzerland and Washington, DC.

Meier, P. and M. Munasinghe. 1994. "Incorporating Environmental Concerns into Power Sector Decision-Making." March. World Bank Environment Paper No. 6, World Bank, Washington DC.

Michaelis, L. 1991. "Air Pollution from Motor Vehicles." Draft Position Paper. World Bank. Washington, DC.

Midgley, P. 1994. "Urban Transport in Asia: An Operational Agenda for the 1990s." World Bank Technical Paper No. 224. Asia Technical Department Series. Washington, DC.

Ministry of State for Population and Environment (MSFE). 1993. *Indonesian Country Study on Biological Diversity*. Jakarta.

Murray, F. and N. Harshadeep, "Project Selection for Sustainable Development: The Use of Environmental Indices," Working Paper #6, The Asian Development Bank Environmental Indices Project, Environmental Systems Program, Division of Applied Sciences, Harvard University, May, 1994.

Motor Vehicle Manufacturer's Association (MVMA). 1992. *World Motor Vehicle Data*. Washington, DC.

MVMA. 1990. *World Motor Vehicle Data*. Washington, DC.

MVMA. 1989. *World Motor Vehicle Data*. Washington, D.C.

National Research Council (NRC). 1993. *Managing Wastewater in Coastal Urban Areas*. Washington, DC: National Academic Press.

NRC. 1982. "Diesel Cars: Benefits, Risks, and Public Policy." Final Report of the Diesel Impacts Study Council, Assembly of Engineering, National Research Council, Washington, DC.

Nerveril, R., J. Price and K. Engdahl. 1978. "Capital and Operating Costs of Selected Air Pollution Control Systems I," in *Control Technology News*, August.

OECD. 1993. *Advanced Emission Controls for Power Plants*. OCED: Paris.

Ottinger, R., D. Wooley, N. Robinson, D. Hodas, S. Babb et al. 1991. *Environmental Costs of Electricity*. Pace University Center for Environmental Legal Studies. New York: Oceana Publications Inc.

Owens, G. M., ed. 1994. Financing Environmentally Sound Development, Asian Development Bank, Manila, Philippines

Perry, R. H. ed. 1984. *Chemical Engineers' Handbook*. 6th edition. New York: McGraw-Hill.

Pezzey, J. 1992. Sustainability Development Concepts: An Economic Analysis, World Bank Environment Paper No. 2.

Princiotta, F. 1989. "Pollution Control for Utility Power Generation, 1990 to 2020," in *Energy for the Twenty-First Century*. MIT.

Qasim, S. R., Lim, S. W. (Daniel), Motley, E. M. and Heung Kim G. 1992. "Estimating Costs for Treatment Plant Construction," in *Journal American Water Works Association*. August, pp. 56–62.

Rossiter, A. and J. Kumana. 1994. "Rank Pollution Prevention and Control Options." in *Chemical Engineering Progress*. February.

Shah, K. L. and Reid, G. W. 1970. "Techniques for Estimating Construction Costs of Waste Treatment Plants," in *Journal of the Water Pollution Control Federation*, vol. 42, p. 776.

Shudhoff, F. and R. Torstrick. 1985. *Shawnee Flue Gas Desulfurization Computer Model Users Manual*. EPA–600/8–85–006.USEPA Research Triangle Park. North Carolina.

Siegel, J. and J. Temchin. 1989. "Role of Clean Coal Technology in Electric Power Generation in the 21st Century," in *Energy in the Twenty-First Century*, MIT.

Sinton, J. E. ed. 1992. *China Energy Databook*. Energy Analysis Program, Lawrence Berkeley Laboratory. University of California, Berkeley.

Smeers, Y. and Tyteca, D. 1984. "A Geometric Programming Model for the Optimal Design of Wastewater Treatment Plants," in *Operations Research*, vol. 32, no. 2, pp. 314–342.

Swanson, T. M. and E. B. Barbier. 1992. *Economics for the Wilds: Wildlife, Diversity and Development.* Washington DC: Island Press.

Tavroulareas S. and J. P. Charpentier. 1995. "Clean Coal Technologies for Developing Countries." World Bank Technical Paper, Energy Series. Washington, DC.

Tchobanoglous, G., H. Theisen and S. A. Vigil. 1993. *Integrated Solid Waste Management: Engineering Principles and Management Issues.* New York: McGraw-Hill.

Tihansky, D. 1974. "Historical Development of Water Pollution Control Cost Functions," in *Journal of the Water Pollution Control Federation,* vol. 46, no. 5. May, pp. 813–833.

US Department of Energy, 1995, Energy Production Technology Database, Department of Energy (personal communication with Dr. Larry Nelson).

US Department of Energy, 1994, IGCC: Integrated Gasification Combined Cycle, Morgantown Energy Technology Center. West Virginia.

UNEP. 1992. *Air Pollution in Megacities of the World.*

UNESCAP. 1990. *State of the Environment in Asia and the Pacific.* Bangkok.

USEPA. 1979. *Cost Analysis of Lime-Based Flue Gas Desulfurization Systems for New 500 MW Utility Boilers.* Prepared for USEPA by PEDCo Environmental, Inc.

USEPA (Office of Research and Development). *Treatability Manual, Volume IV. Cost Estimating.* EPA-600/8–80–042d, July 1980.

USEPA. 1977. *Motor Vehicle Emissions Control: A Seven Book Series.* USEPA, Office of Air and Waste Management, Office of Air Quality Planning and Standards, Research Triangle Park, North Carolina.

Vatavuk, W. 1990. OAQPS Control Cost Manual, 4th ed., January 1990, EPA 450/3–90–006, (ed. William Vatavuk).

Walker, D. J., B. L. Calkins and J. R. Hamilton, Marginal Cost Effectivensss Analysis for Agricultural Nonpoint Source Water Quality Control, *Journal of Soil and Water Conservation,* pp. 368–372, July–August, 1993.

Walker, D. J., B. L. Calkins, and J. R. Hamilton. 1993. "Marginal Cost Effectiveness Analysis for Agricultural Nonpoint Source Water Quality Control." Journal of Soil and Water Conservation. July–August, 1993, vol. 28, no. 4, 368–372.

Wang, F. K., Wang, S. G., and Li, X. P. *A Technological and Economic Manual of Industrial Wastewater and Municipal Sewage,* in Chinese, Tsinghua University Press, Beijing, 1992.

Weaver, C., Chan, L., and D. McGregor. 1995. *Thailand: Emissions Standards and Emission Control Technology for Diesel Vehicles.* Report to the Royal Thai Ministry of Science, Technology, and Environment, and the World Bank. Automotive Emissions Control, International, Inc. Sacramento, CA.

World Bank. 1990. China: Efficiency and Environmental Impact of Coal Use. vol. 1. Main Report. Industry and Energy Division. China Department, Asia Region. World Bank. Washington, D.C.

World Bank (Industry and Energy Division, Country Department I, East Asia and Pacific Region). *Philippines—Environmental Sectors Study: Towards Improved Management of Environmental Impacts.* May 1993.

Yeager, K. 1989. "Powering the Second Electrical Century," in *Energy for the Twenty First Century.* MIT.

Yu, X., J. J. Harrington, P. P. Rogers, and C. C. Yu. "Generalization of Cost Functions for Chinese Industrial Wastewater Treatment." *the Working Papers of the Study of Environmental Indicators and Indices.* Division of Applied Sciences, Harvard University, May, 1995.

APPENDIX III

A Review of Environmental Indices

Measuring Environmental Quality in Asia

Fiona Murray
Chris Legget

1. Introduction

This appendix begins with a critical review of the historical development of environmental indicators. It then describes current activities in both the national and international community to develop comprehensive environmental indicators in response to the need for indicators of sustainable development. Much of the information on current indicator development was gathered at brainstorming meetings, held at Harvard University in January, 1994 and May, 1995, and at the SCOPE Scientific Workshop on Indicators of Sustainable Development held in November, 1995 at the Wuppertal Institute, Germany.

The organization of this appendix is as follows: we start with a broad overview of both the historical and current rationale for indicator development. Then the early work on indices and indicators is described, including the work of Ott, Ridker, and Dorfman. The increasing interest in comprehensive indicators of sustainable development is described in the context of the UNCED meeting and a growing awareness on the part of international and national organizations that environmental considerations must be incorporated into the decision-making process and that this, in turn, requires measures of progress. This appendix ends with an extensive discussion of current activities by the following: a number of international institutions, such as the World Bank, Organisation for Economic Cooperation and Development (OECD), United Nations Environment Programme (UNEP), Earth Council, and the Food and Agriculture Organization of the United Nations (FAO); NGOs, such as the World Resources Institute; and some national institutions such as the Netherlands Ministry of Housing, Physical Planning and the Environment, the US Environmental Protection Agency (USEPA), the Environment Agency of Japan, and the International Development Research Center (IDRC) in Canada.

2. Rationale for Environmental Indicator Development

The original work on environmental indicators started in the early 1970s, as attention became increasingly focussed on the state of the environment in both the United States and Europe. With the creation in the United States of the President's Council on Environmental Quality, systems of measuring progress toward environmental goals and pollution control targets were in demand. The work that followed was compiled in an extensive book by Wayne Ott (1978), then a senior engineer in the monitoring technology division of USEPA. He brought together indices on air and water pollution, and described more broadly defined indexing approaches such as quality of life and environmental damage functions. It is clear from this work that environmental indicators, as conceived in the 1970s, were tools to describe the level of environmental quality in a particular media for a particular region, facilitating interregional comparisons, but not intermedia comparisons. As the 1970s progressed, attention in the environmental area was increasingly focused on regulation, and there was a surprising and significant lull in the literature regarding indicators.

The United Nations Conference on Sustainable Development in 1992 and Agenda 21 focused interest once again on defining environmental indicators. These indicators are fundamentally different from those conceived in the 1970s. They are focussed on decision-making and on sustainability. What followed was a concerted attempt to find comprehensive indices rather than media-specific indicators. Work in this area is currently being led by international institutions such as the World Bank, OECD, and UNSTAT, in conjunction with active NGOs such as the World Resources Institute. National environmental institutions have varied in their commitment to the formulation of environmental indicators, and the Netherlands Ministry of the Environment has been a major force in this work.

3. Early Development of Media-Specific Indicators

The basic purpose of many of the early indicators was to facilitate the objective and precise determination of the state of the environment and humanity's impact on the environment. The fundamental assumptions underlying much of the past work on indicators have been those of simplification. An environmental indicator was seen as a means of reducing the number of environmental variables to a single number or set of numbers which retained the meaning of the larger set. Traditionally, environmental indicators were closely linked to environmental monitoring, with the intent that they give insight into environmental conditions and provide a yardstick with which to judge the effectiveness of environmental regulatory programs. The role of indicators as described by Train in 1973 is still appropriate today:

> For top management and public policy development, monitoring data must be shaped into easy-to-understand indices that aggregate data into understandable forms. Much more effort must be placed on the development of ... indices than we have in the past. Failure to do so will result in sub-optimum achievement of goals at much greater expense. (Train 1973)

At this time, the National Academy of Sciences (NAS) in the United States was playing a central role in promoting environmental indicators. A 1975 NAS report concluded that:

> Despite strong statements of need from all three branches of government, progress toward the development and use of methods for evaluating environmental quality has not been satisfactory. (NAS 1975)

Recommendations on improving environmental indicators focused on their role in six major areas: financial resource allocation, ranking of locations, enforcement of standards, trend analysis, public information, and scientific research. But this wide range of potential audiences required different indices, and the role of the user in formulating indicators was already viewed as a critical issue:

> It is absolutely necessary that the user be identified. The scientist, administrator, elected official, and general public cannot usually be satisfied by the same environmental measure. The administrator needs to see the resource allocation implications and the scientist needs to see the cause and effect implications. Who the user is will also affect the geographic or political aggregation of data and the decision to highlight or obscure inter-jurisdictional comparisons. (Coates and Mason 1975)

During this period of intense activity in indicator development, their uses were generally confined to public information (e.g., daily reports of air pollution in a local newspaper), and very few of the indicators developed in the scientific literature found their way into routine use by pollution control agencies. There is little or no literature that describes the application of indicators to real problem-solving, either in the US or elsewhere. This was probably because the modeling and simulation techniques required to develop scenarios of future environmental quality under a set of possible policy choices was not sufficiently developed.

Two general index forms were identified by Ott, those in which the index numbers increase with increasing environmental pollution and those in which the numbers decrease. He identified two steps in developing indicators, calculation of subindices for the pollutant variables and the aggregation of these subindices into an overall index. The formulation of different indices within this framework relied on the almost infinite capacity to generate different mathematical functions for both subindex and index formulation (Ott 1978). Indicator calculations used a range of different aggregation methods and mathematical functions. Subindices required the generation of a mathematical function by which to move from a set of data points to a subindex. Aggregation could be accomplished through addition, multiplication, power series or a range of other methods. Most of the indices generated in the 1970s were based on US environmental statistics. The President's Council on Environmental Quality published a set of environmental indices each year, and different groups, from state agencies to local newspapers, calculated their own environmental quality indices. However, it is the methodology of index formulation rather than the actual value of the indices that provides us with valuable insights into the work of a whole generation of environmental scientists and policy-makers.

4. A Modern Interpretation of Environmental Indicators

Most of the recent work on environmental indicators, and more broadly, on indicators of sustainable development, has arisen in response to UNCED and Agenda 21, specifically:

> Commonly used indicators such as GNP and measures of individual resource and pollution flows do not provide adequate indications of sustainability. Methods for assessing interactions between different sectoral environmental, demographic, social, and developmental parameters are not sufficiently developed or applied. Indicators of sustainable development need to be developed to provide solid bases for decision-making at all levels and to contribute to a self-regulating sustainability of integrated environment and development systems. (Chapter 40.4)

> Relevant organs and organizations of the UN system, in cooperation with other international governments...should use a suitable set of sustainable development indicators and indicators related to areas outside of national jurisdiction, such as the high seas, the upper atmosphere, and outer space. The organs and organizations of the UN system...could provide recommendations for harmonized development of indicators at the national, regional, and global

levels, and for incorporation of a suitable set of these indicators in common, regularly updated, and widely accessible reports and databases, for use at the international level. (Chapter 40.7)

At the same time as the declaration of Agenda 21, confidence has risen in our ability to predict the incremental affects of environmental policies and technologies. Further, institutions are concerned with making rational choices between environmental policies and investments, given budget constraints and other limits to our environmental management activities. Therefore, most of the agencies involved in indicator development in the 1990s focus on the fact that indicators should be useful for making decisions and setting objectives.

OECD has set out the following criteria for an indicator, stating that it must:

1. be relevant i.e., serve a clearly defined purpose;

2. be reliable i.e., have a sound scientific basis; and

3. be realizable i.e., be measured using available data.

The World Bank suggests that an indicator must also be tolerant to inconsistencies that arise from aggregation and valuation and, more stringently, keep all the implications of the original information while decreasing the amount of information. The World Bank suggests that indicators be empirically based and driven by operational interests, but stresses that indicators be agreed upon so that their compilation and the necessary data gathering is undertaken to the fullest extent possible by all agencies. The theme of understandability is developed by the USEPA, which suggests that indicators be simple enough to provide a vehicle for public debate in the setting and meeting of goals.

On a more practical note, IDRC suggests that indicators should also:

1. be sensitive to interventions;

2. demonstrate change over time;

3. be reliably and reproducibly measured with limited resources;

4. permit examination of ethical and equity considerations through disaggregation.

In general, the current debate suggests that indicators must have utility, efficiency, and effectiveness. It is also acknowledged that a solid database and information foundation is a major prerequisite for indicator development. The frameworks developed today are more elaborate and reflect the growing concern to integrate the environment with a range of socioeconomic issues, as is well illustrated in Appendix Table 3.1, taken from Ruitenbeek (1991) which highlights the differences between traditional and new approaches to indicator formulation.

In highlighting how indicators can be formulated to introduce these refinements, Ruitenbeek (1991) includes an illustrative example from water quality indicators, as shown in Appendix Table 3.2.

There are many different formulations for indicator development, some of which follow the traditional aggregation of indices approach, as exemplified by Ott (1978). Others focus on the integration of a wider range of data and on incorporating both quantitative and qualitative material. Modern indicators more closely focus on the interaction between the natural environment and socioeconomic decision-making. According to the World Bank, an indicator is intended to be harmonized with socioeconomic indicators and be oriented toward the specified aims of the institution. They hope to use indicators in a "bold effort to squeeze more policy-relevance from the data that exist" (O'Connor 1994), with the objective of improving current practices in the analysis of traditional projects, public expenditures, and investment reviews. The indicators should also set the context for economic-sector work as well as sectoral and structural adjustment operations. The indicators will then be used in identifying the environmental impacts of national economic policies, in the choice of policy instruments for environmental protection, and the evaluation of environmental and economic impacts of projects.

At the national scale, the function of indices lies in the coordination of data collection and assessment of progress toward environmental goals (national and international). For example, USEPA considers indices to be a means of characterizing the environment and environmental goals and of facilitating data-gathering. The Netherlands Government has taken these ideas a step further with the intention of creating policy-oriented indices that can be used in decision-making and in presenting yearly trends and progress. They have set goals based on policy relevance, analytical soundness, and measurability, and are using indices to help Parliament assess progress. Indices provide a means of defining and communicating progress toward environmental goals and facilitating public participation in environmental management. The user is the decision-maker in the environmental agency on the one hand, and the national government on the other. Therefore at a national level, indices at the project, sectoral, national, and international scale are all necessary to make strategic choices about environmental management. At OECD, the predominant focus is also on indices for the use of the policy-maker at the national level. However, communicability is also an important consideration (probably through inclusion in state-of-the-environment reporting) and OECD acknowledges the importance of environmental policy objectives and sectoral environmental policies in implementing national-level environmental improvements.

Changing Perspective on Information: Description, Projection and Prediction

Information Class	Application	Illustrative "Economic" Examples	Illustrative "Environmental" Examples
Descriptive Indicators	"Bottom-line" description of past or current conditions.	Energy Demand = 340,000PJ Energy Price = $4/GJ	Energy Demand = 340,000PJ Mean Global Temperature = 13°C
Indicators with Projective Applications	Analytical description of past conditions.	Elasticity of: Energy Demand to Price = −0.8	Elasticity of: Mean Global Temperature to Energy use = 0.005. (Example only)
Projective Indicators	Projection of future conditions based on explicitly stated scenario.	"Energy Demand will fall 8% over the long term if a 10% end-use tax is applied."	"Global temperatures will be 0.1°C less than they would otherwise be if a 10% energy end-use tax is applied." (example only)
Predictive Indicators	"Bottom-line" unconditional prediction of future conditions.	"Energy prices will increase 2% per year in real terms over the long term."	"The globe will warm by 1°C as a result of past greenhouse gas emissions." (example only)

Source: Ruitenbeek, 1991.

General Augmentation of a Sample Indicator—Water Quality

Reference Point	Water Quality Characteristic Important to Human Health (Qh)
Broader Scope	Water Quality Characteristic Important to Ecosystem Health (Qe)
Explicit Distributive Elements	Average Water Quality Consumed by Lowest and Highest Income Quintile (y) of Population (Qh;y = 1; Qh;y = 5)
Applications as a Projective Tool	Impact Elasticity between Population (P) and Water Quality $$\varepsilon = \frac{\%\Delta Qh}{\%\Delta P}$$
Reflect Explicit Linkages	Water Quality Characteristic Important to Ecosystem Health $$\varepsilon = \frac{\%\Delta Qe; t = 2010}{\%\Delta Pt = 1990}$$
Reflect Inherent Uncertainty	Range of Probable Critical Levels of Water Quality Characteristic (Qe) $$\frac{\text{Projected Range } \{Qe;low : Qe;high\}}{\text{Critical Range } \{Q^*e;low : Q^*e;high\}}$$

Source: Ruitenbeek, 1991.

5. Summary of Traditional Indices

What follows is a detailed account of a large number of different environmental indices. Many of these have been taken from the literature of the late 1960s, 1970s, and early 1980s. Most are concerned with providing a measure of pollution in one medium—for example, in air, water, or soil. Accordingly, there has been little written on detailed composite indicators.

5.1 Air Quality Indices

Ridker's Air Pollution Cost Index (Ridker 1967)

This index attempts to describe economic damages as a function of air pollution intensity. It divides damages into several categories, each corresponding to a different type of air pollution effect. The total costs of each type of damage are calculated by multiplying the damage per unit by the number of units affected and by the monetary cost per damaged unit. Total air pollution costs are then obtained by summing over all damage types as follows:

$$TC = \sum_{i=1}^{n} C_i \, Q_i \, F_i(S) \qquad (3.1)$$

where:

TC	=	total air pollution costs
C_i	=	cost per unit of damage type i
Q_i	=	number of units affected by damage type i
F(S)	=	function describing how per unit damage of type i varies with air pollution level.

Sereda's Corrosiveness Index (from Ridker 1967)

Sereda developed an index to measure the corrosive effects of air pollution. The index predicts the amount of deterioration that various uncoated materials will undergo when exposed to polluted air.

$$Y = 0.131X + 0.0180Z + 0.787 \qquad (3.2)$$

where:

Y	=	log of the corrosion rate (mg per square meter per day of wetness)
X	=	SO_2 pollution rate (mg sulfur dioxide per square meter per day)
Z	=	temperature in Fahrenheit (monthly average during time of wetness).

Green's Index (Ott 1978)

Green's Index, proposed by Marvin Green in 1966, was one of the earliest air pollution indices. It measured air pollution by means of only two variables, sulfur dioxide and coefficient of haze.

$$I = \frac{(84X^{0.431} + 26.6Y^{0.576})}{2} \qquad (3.3)$$

where:

I = index of air quality
X = concentration of sulfur dioxide in ppm
Y = coefficient of haze.

Green's Index was designed for use as a system for triggering governmental control action during air pollution episodes. Along with the index, one of three descriptors was supposed to be reported: desired level, alert level, or extreme level.

Combustion Products Index (Ott 1978)

Rich recommended a source-based index as an aid to determining the potential severity of air pollution within a fixed geographic area. The index would have the advantage of requiring few actual measurements of air quality, relying instead on the assumption that the severity of pollution is (1) directly related to the quantity of fossil fuel burned and (2) inversely related to the atmospheric mixing volume overhead.

$$CPI = \frac{F}{V} \qquad (3.4)$$

where:

CPI = combustion products index of air pollution severity
F = quantity of fuel burned in the area
(obtained by inventorying fuel deliveries)
V = volume of air in which the combustion products are mixed.

$$V = u\,w\,h \qquad (3.5)$$

where:

u = average wind speed
w = width of the city
h = atmospheric mixing height.

Measure of Undesirable Respirable Contaminants (Ott 1978)
Conceived in 1968, this index was used routinely in Detroit to report air quality data to the public. It uses only the coefficient of haze as an air pollution variable.

$$MURC = 70X^{0.7} \qquad (3.6)$$

where:
MURC = measure of undesirable respirable contaminants
X = coefficient of haze.

Five descriptors were assigned to various MURC ranges and were reported along with the numerical MURC:

MURC Range Descriptor
0 – 30 extremely light contamination
31 – 60 light contamination
61 – 90 medium contamination
91 – 120 heavy contamination
> 121 extremely heavy contamination.

Air Quality Index (Ott 1978)
This index used emission data on carbon monoxide, particulates, and sulfur dioxide to evaluate the air quality of 29 metropolitan areas in the United States. An overall index is calculated based on a weighted sum of the subindices assigned to each of the three pollutants,

$$AQI = \sum_{i=1}^{3} w_i I_i \qquad (3.7)$$

where:
AQI = air quality index of the metropolitan area
I_1 = estimated CO subindex
I_2 = estimated TSP subindex
I_3 = estimated SO_2 subindex
w_i = weight assigned to pollution type i.

The AQI, since it relies on emission data, has the advantage of being applicable in cities where less air quality data are available. It is, however, limited by the assumptions of the atmospheric diffusion model, which are:
1. The urban area is square with the wind always parallel to one of its sides.
2. The sources emit continuously and are evenly distributed over the urban area.
3. Meteorological conditions remain at a constant stability throughout the year.

MITRE Air Quality Index (Ott 1978)

MAQI makes use of National Ambient Air Quality Standards (NAAQS) for five different pollutants to create an overall air quality index. A subindex is determined for each pollutant by using standards for several different averaging times. These subindices are then aggregated in the following manner:

$$MAQI = \sqrt{\sum_{i=1}^{5} I_i^2}$$

(3.8)

where:

MAQI = MITRE air quality index
I_i = air quality subindex for pollutant i.

The subindices for the MITRE air quality index are determined as follows:

I_1: carbon monoxide

$$I_1 = \sqrt{\left(\frac{X_8}{S_8}\right)^2 + \delta \left(\frac{X_1}{S_1}\right)^2}$$

(3.9)

where:

I_1 = carbon monoxide subindex
X_8 = concentration of CO (maximum 8-hr value)
S_8 = 8-hr NAAQS ($S_8 = 9$ppm)
X_1 = concentration of CO (maximum 1-hr value)
S_1 = 1-hr NAAQS ($S_1 = 35$ppm)
d = 1 if $X_1 > = S_1$, 0 otherwise.

X_1, for example, is the single highest hourly value for the entire year. It is the maximum of 8760 hourly values. d is a factor which gives added emphasis to a violation of NAAQS.

I_2: nitrogen dioxide

$$I_2 = \frac{X_a}{S_a}$$

(3.10)

where:

I_2 = nitrogen dioxide subindex
X_a = annual arithmetic mean of the nitrogen dioxide concentration
S_a = annual mean NAAQS ($S_a = 0.05$ppm).

I_3: photochemical oxidants

$$I_3 = \frac{X_1}{S_1} \tag{3.11}$$

where:

I_3 = photochemical oxidants subindex
X_1 = oxidant concentration (maximum 1-hr value)
S_1 = 1-hr NAAQS (S_1 = 0.08ppm).

I_4: TSP

$$I_4 = \sqrt{(\frac{X_a}{S_a})^2 + (\frac{X_{24}}{S_{24}})^2} \tag{3.12}$$

where:

X_a = TSP concentration (annual geometric mean)
S_a = secondary annual NAAQS for TSP (S_a = 60mg/m^3)
X_{24} = TSP concentration (maximum 24-hr value)
S_{24} = 24-hr secondary NAAQS for TSP (S_{24} = 150mg/m^3).

I_5: sulfur dioxide

$$I_5 = \sqrt{(\frac{X_a}{S_a})^2 + \delta_1 (\frac{X_{24}}{S_{24}})^2 + \delta_2 (\frac{X_3}{S_3})^2} \tag{3.13}$$

where:

X_a = sulfur dioxide concentration (annual arithmetic mean)
S_a = annual NAAQS for sulfur dioxide (S_a = 0.03ppm)
X_{24} = sulfur dioxide concentration (maximum 24-hr value)
S_{24} = 24-hr NAAQS (S_{24} = 0.14ppm)
X_3 = sulfur dioxide concentration (maximum 3-hr value)
S_3 = 3-hr NAAQS (S_3 = 0.5ppm)
d_1 = 1 if X_{24} S_{24}, 0 otherwise
d_2 = 1 if X_3 S_3, 0 otherwise.

Extreme Value Index (Ott 1978)
To circumvent MAQI's dependence on extreme values, its developers produced a second index, EVI, that was intended to reflect the frequency of air pollution events rather than the maximum values. EVI used "accumulated extreme" values by summing all periods when the concentrations exceeded their NAAQS. The subindex for CO, for example, is calculated as follows:

$$I_1 = \sqrt{(\frac{A_8}{S_8})^2 + (\frac{A_1}{S_1})^2} \tag{3.14}$$

where:

A_8 = sum of observed 8-hr CO concentrations that exceed NAAQS

S_8 = 8-hr NAAQS (S_8 = 9 ppm)

A_1 = sum of observed 1-hr CO concentrations that exceed NAAQS

S_1 = 1-hr NAAQS (S_1 = 35 ppm).

The other subindices were calculated in a similar manner, with accumulated extremes substituting for maximum concentrations in the MAQI subindex equations. The EVI included only four of the five MAQI pollutants, and the indices for these pollutants were combined using a root-sum-square function.

$$EVI = \sqrt{I_1^2 + I_2^2 + I_3^2 + I_4^2} \qquad (3.15)$$

where:

EVI = extreme value index

I_1 = CO subindex

I_2 = photochemical oxidants subindex

I_3 = TSP subindex

I_4 = SO_2 subindex.

Pollutant Standards Index (Ott 1978)

In 1976 USEPA developed PSI to serve as a nationally uniform air pollution index. The index includes five pollutants—CO, NO_2, oxidants (O_3), TSP, and SO_2. A sixth subindex is calculated as TSP* SO_2. Each subindex is derived from a segmented linear function of averaged-time concentrations. PSI is calculated by entering the observed concentrations on the horizontal axis of each of the graphs and reading the appropriate subindex off of the vertical axis. PSI is then reported as the maximum of the six subindices.

$$y = max(I_1, I_2, \ldots, I_6) \qquad (3.16)$$

where:

y = Pollutant Standards Index

I_{1-6} = subindices for each pollutant.

The pollutant responsible for the maximum subindex is called the "critical pollutant" and is reported along with the index. The structure of PSI allows for easy incorporation of additional pollutant subindices in the future if desired.

Oak Ridge Air Quality Index (Ott 1978)
Developed in 1971, ORAQI is based on the 24-hour average concentrations of five air pollutants: carbon dioxide, nitrogen dioxide, photochemical oxidants, particulate matter, and sulphur dioxide.

Each subindex is calculated as the ratio of the observed pollutant concentration to its respective standard:

$$I_i = (X/X_s)_i \qquad (3.17)$$

The ORAQI aggregation function is nonlinear:

$$ORAQI = [5.7 \sum_{i=1}^{5} I_i]^{1.37} \qquad (3.18)$$

Ontario Air Pollution Index (Ott 1978)
In 1970, the government of Ontario, Canada developed an air pollution index (API) that was intended both to provide the public with daily information about air quality levels and to trigger control actions during air pollution episodes.

The Ontario API included two pollutant variables, COH and SO_2, and used linear subindex functions:

$$COH \ I_1 = 30.5 \ X_1 \qquad (3.19)$$

$$SO_2 \ (ppm)I_2 = 126 \ X_2 \qquad (3.20)$$

The pollutant variables X_1 and X_2 were both 24-hour running average concentrations. The aggregate function was:

$$API = 0.2(I_1 + I_2)1.35 \qquad (3.21)$$

An API value less than 32 was considered "acceptable" air quality. A value of greater than 50 called for curtailment of some air pollution sources.

Inhaber's Air Quality Index for Canada (Parker 1991)
This air quality index was composed of three subindices: a specific pollutants index (SPI), interurban air quality (IAQ), and industrial air emissions (IAE). The five indicators for the SPI were: sulphur dioxide (SO_2), particulates (P), haze (H), carbon monoxide (CO), ozone (O_3), and nitrogen oxides (NO_x). The SPI was calculated by the following formula:

$$SPI = \{[(SO_2)^2 + 0.5(P)^2 + 0.5(H)^2 + (CO)^2 + (O_3)^2 + (NO_2)^2]/5\}^H \qquad (3.22)$$

The IAE subindex was calculated by the following formula:

$$IAE = (E_c/P_c)/(E_t/P_t) \qquad (3.23)$$

where:

E_c = weight of the industrial emissions in a given county
P_c = population of that county
E_t = total nationwide weight of the emission
P_t = the national population.

The IAQ subindex was based on visibility readings at airports. A national IAQ was computed by weighting each value of the index, according to the urban population near the airport.

The overall air quality index for Canada was calculated by:

$$I_{air} = \{[5(SPI)^2 + 3(IAQ)^2 + 2(IAE)_2]/10\}^H \qquad (3.24)$$

5.2 Water Quality Indices
Horton's Water Quality Index (Ott 1978)
In 1965, Horton developed an index that he hoped would standardize methods for reporting on stream water quality. Eight subindices were calculated for dissolved oxygen, sewage treatment, pH, coliforms, specific conductance, carbon chloroform extract, alkalinity, and chloride. (Specific conductance was used as a proxy for total dissolved solids, and carbon chloroform extract was used to measure the influence of organic matter. Horton excluded toxic substances, for he felt that streams under no circumstances should contain material hazardous to human or aquatic life.) Subindex values were determined using staircase step functions, and overall water quality was a weighted linear sum of the subindices, multiplied by temperature and "obvious pollution" factors.

$$QI = \frac{\sum\limits_{i=1}^{n} w_i I_i}{\sum\limits_{i=1}^{n} w_i} \, M_1 M_2 \qquad (3.25)$$

where:

QI = Horton's Water Quality Index
w_i = weight assigned to pollution variable i
I_i = subindex calculated for pollution variable i
M_1 = 1 if water temperature is below a specific value; 0.5 otherwise
M_2 = 1 if there is no "obvious pollution"; 0.5 otherwise.

"Obvious pollution" can include sludge deposits, oil, debris, foam, scum, odor, colored water, etc. M_1 and M_2 are designed to be tailored to fit individual situations.

National Sanitation Foundation Water Quality Index (Ott 1978)

The NSFWQI, developed in 1970 "as a means for communicating water quality information to the lay public and to legislative decision-makers," is widely used in water quality indices in the US. In an attempt to combine the opinions of water experts throughout the country, the index was developed empirically through the use of questionnaires. It was thought that by involving a large number of water experts in a variety of geographic areas, biases toward any single professional viewpoint or local situation would be avoided.

The panel of experts was first asked to choose variables which should be included in an index and the weight that they felt should be assigned to each of these variables. From the responses, eleven variables were selected: dissolved oxygen, fecal coliforms, pH, five-day biochemical oxygen demand (BOD_5), nitrates, phosphates, temperature, turbidity, total solids, toxic substances and pesticides. Then, for the first nine variables, the panel members were asked to draw curves showing how they felt that subindices should vary with various levels of the pollutants. These curves were averaged to establish implicit nonlinear subindex functions. For toxic substances and pesticides, upper limits were established which could drive the NSFWQI to zero. The overall NSFWQI was then calculated by summing the products of subindices and their corresponding weights.

$$NSFWQI_a = \sum_{i=1}^{n} w_1 \, I_i \qquad (3.26)$$

where:

$NSFWQI_a$ = additive National Sanitation Foundation Water Quality Index

w_1 = weight assigned to pollutant variable i

I_i = subindex for pollutant variable i.

An alternative multiplicative form of the NSF WQI has been proposed to avoid the eclipsing that occurs when a single pollutant variable shows extremely poor water quality:

$$NSFWQI_m = \prod_{i=1}^{n} I_i^{w_i} \qquad (3.27)$$

where:

$NSFWQI_m$ = multiplicative National Sanitation Foundation Water Quality Index.

Prati's Implicit Index of Pollution (Ott 1978)

Prati proposed an index for surface water pollution in 1971 based on water quality classification systems already adopted in seven western countries. The index was intended to be used as a tool for comparisons of water quality over time; it was not intended for use in determining the degree of pollution or siting of treatment efforts. For each of 13 pollution variables, the investigators used the countries' classification systems to establish four pollution level categories. Subindices of 1, 2, 4, and 8 were assigned to pollution levels deemed "excellent," "acceptable," "slightly polluted," or "heavily polluted." Next, based on their own judgments of the severity of pollution effects within each category, the investigators created explicit mathematical functions for each subindex. Linear, segmented linear, and nonlinear functions were employed. Finally, an overall index was calculated as the arithmetic mean of the subindices.

$$I = \frac{1}{13} \sum_{i=1}^{13} I_i \qquad\qquad (3.28)$$

where:

I = Prati's Implicit Index of Pollution
I_i = subindex for pollution variable i.

The pollution variables included were pH, dissolved oxygen, five-day biochemical oxygen demand, chemical oxygen demand, suspended solids, ammonia, nitrates, chlorides, iron, manganese, alkyl benzene sulfonates, and carbon chloroform extract. The investigators excluded toxic substances, for they felt that toxic concentrations above a particular threshold level should automatically drive the index to "heavily polluted."

Deininger and Landwehr's PWS Index (Ott 1978)

This index is similar to the NSFWQI index but emphasizes use of water as a public water supply (PWS). Twelve members of the WQI panel were selected, and the questionnaires asked them when choosing variables and weights to keep in the back of their minds "a free-flowing stream which will serve as a source of raw water for a public water supply." The PWS index was based on the following parameters: pH, dissolved oxygen, five-day biochemical oxygen demand, dissolved solids, nitrates, fluorides, iron, fecal coliforms, temperature, turbidity, phenols, color, and hardness.

Walski and Parker's Index (Ott, 1978)

Walski and Parker developed a water quality index in 1974 that was specifically geared toward recreational uses. For twelve pollution variables (dissolved oxygen, pH, total coliforms, temperature, phosphates, nitrates, suspended solids, turbidity, color, grease, odor, and secchi disk transparency), they established nonlinear and segmented nonlinear explicit functions for subindex determination. The subindex functions were based on the investigators' judgment and on their review of the literature. To aggregate the subindices, the investigators chose a geometric mean, which they felt would avoid the problem of eclipsing associated with an arithmetic mean. No information was provided for the weights.

$$I = \left[\prod_{i=1}^{12} I_i^{w_i} \right]^{\frac{1}{12}}$$

(3.29)

where:

I = Walski and Parker's Index
I_i = subindex for pollutant variable i
w_i = weight assigned to pollutant variable i.

Stoner's Index (Ott 1978)

Stoner proposed a single aggregation function that selected from two sets of recommended limits and subindex equations. Type I variables were toxic and their subindices could take on values of either 0 or –100, depending on whether or not the recommended limit had been exceeded. Type II variables affected health or aesthetic characteristics, and their subindices were determined using explicit mathematical functions (linear, parabolic, or a combination of the two), with 100 being the ideal value and 0 being the recommended limit. An overall water quality index was computed by combining the unweighted Type I subindices with weighted Type II subindices.

$$I = \sum_{i=1}^{n} T_i + \sum_{j=1}^{m} I_j$$

(3.30)

where:

I = Stoner's Water Quality Index
T_i = i^{th} Type I pollutant subindex
w_j = weight for the jth Type II subindex
I_j = j^{th} Type II pollutant subindex.

Nemerow and Sumitono's Specific Use Index (Ott 1978)

This water quality index is similar to those mentioned previously, with two important differences. First, the index is divided into three subindices based on the extent of human use of the water. Human contact use is given the highest weight, followed by indirect contact use and remote contact use. We assume (although it wasn't explicitly stated) that different variables are involved in calculating each of these use-based subindices. The subindices are aggregated in the typical manner:

$$I = \sum_{i=1}^{3} w_i I_i$$

(3.31)

Second, each subindex is calculated in a manner which reflects both the most extreme pollution variable and the average of all of the variables:

$$I_j = \sqrt{\frac{[\max I_{ij}]^2 + [\frac{1}{n}\sum I_{ij}]^2}{2}}$$ (3.32)

where:
I_j = water quality index for use j
I_{ij} = subindex for use j and pollutant variable i.

Prevalence Duration Intensity (PDI) (Ott 1978)
Developed jointly by the USEPA and the MITRE Corporation, this index is designed to reflect the effects of water pollution on the environment:

$$PDI = \frac{P \; D \; I}{M}$$ (3.33)

where:
PDI = Prevalence Duration Intensity index
P = prevalence: number of stream miles in violation of recommended limits within an area
D = duration: number of quarter-year periods during which violations occur. This can range from 0 to 1, depending on the fraction of the year limits were exceeded.
I = intensity: severity of the effects of violations. This is calculated as the sum of three other subindices: ecological effects, utilitarian effects, and aesthetic effects.
M = total stream miles.

The PDI index was then used in the calculation of the National Planning Priorities Index.

National Planning Priorities Index (Ott 1978)
The NPPI, also developed by MITRE, was intended for use in prioritizing waste treatment projects in order to achieve cost-effectiveness. NPPI was calculated as a weighted sum of ten subindices: current area population, downstream affected population, investment in FY 1972/73, Investment in FY 1973/74, Investment in FY 1975/76, controllability (a measure of the difficulty of controlling the water pollution sources in the area), required planning level, delta planning level, PDI index, and per capita planning cost. Each subindex was computed using a segmented linear function. The subindex receiving the greatest weight was that based on the PDI index.

Priority Action Index (PAI)

This index, also intended to assist decision-makers in allocating funds for wastewater treatment facilities, is a simplified NPPI. It includes only four subindices: current area population, downtown area population, controllability, and the PDI index.

Dee's Environmental Evaluation System (Ott 1978)

Dee's evaluation system was intended for use in evaluating the environmental impact of large-scale water projects. The environmental impact was calculated as the difference between the index value with the project and the index value without the project. Seventy-eight weighted subindices were used, all of which were related to ecology, environmental protection, aesthetics, or human interest.

$$EI = \sum_{i=1}^{78} w_i I_i \text{ [with]} - \sum_{i=1}^{78} w_i I_i \text{ [without]} \qquad (3.34)$$

where:

EI = environmental impact of project (from 0 to 1000)
I_i = subindex i (from 0 to 1)
w_i = weight assigned to subindex i.

Zoeteman's Pollution Potential Index (Ott 1978)

This pollution potential index relies on indirect factors which are assumed to be responsible for pollution. This very simple index uses GNP and river discharge to determine the potential for water pollution in a region. It does not, however, take into account the impact of abatement activities used for reducing pollution levels.

$$PPI = \frac{N\ G}{Q}\ 10^{-6} \qquad (3.35)$$

where:

PPI = Pollution Potential Index
N = number of people living in a drainage area
G = average per capita GNP
Q = yearly average flow rate (cubic meters per second).

Using historical records, Zoeteman found that his index correlated well with measures of ambient quality.

Smith's Minimum Operator Index (Smith 1990)

Smith designed an index for use in New Zealand using methods similar to those used in the development of the NSFWQI. Smith's index differed in two ways. First, the index was based on water uses rather than ambient conditions.

Subindices were calculated for fish spawning, water supply, bathing, and general uses. Second, the subindices were aggregated using the minimum operator method because "a water's suitability-for-use is largely governed by the poorest characteristic."

$$I = \min (I_1, I_2, I_n)\qquad(3.36)$$

where:
I = water quality index
I_n = subindex rating score.

Use-Based WQI (House and Ellis 1987)
House and Ellis developed an index based on the intended use of water. For a single river, each pollutant would be scored from 10 to 100 for each potential use. The score would reflect the water's suitability for a specific use at the given pollution level.

Chao Phraya River and Factor Analysis (Lohani and Todino 1984)
The researchers applied factor analysis to the calculation of a water quality index for the Chao Phraya river in Thailand. Factor loadings were used in determining the weight of each pollutant variable in the overall index calculation.

Factor Analysis and Opinion Polling (Lohani and Mustapha 1982)
Lohani and Mustapha compare two different methods for the calculation of water indices: opinion polling and factor analysis. These methods are applied to data from the Linggi River in Malaysia.

North Sea Sustainability Index (SINS) (James, Fernandes, Koudstaal, Rijsberman, and Wijffels 1993)
A sustainability index is developed for the North Sea based on a hierarchy of indicators, where the lowest level refers to specific physical characteristics of the sea, and the highest level refers to SINS, which is intended for use in policy decisions. Just below SINS is a level of indicators which represents the five main areas of policy focus identified by the Netherlands Government: economic development, ecological integrity, spatial efficiency, sociocultural values, and administrative/international feasibility.

The researchers comment that the selection and weighting of indicators form the most difficult step in the process, and it is somewhat arbitrary. They recommend the use of multi-criteria-analysis for the scaling and weighting necessary to aggregate values for the ultimate indicators to higher levels in the indicator hierarchy. The report is only a proposal, and no calculations were carried out.

5.3 Soil and Irrigation Indices
Universal Soil Loss Equation (Wischmeier 1976)

This widely-used empirical equation relates soil loss in a field (A) to rainfall (R), soil erodibility (K), length of slope (L), slope steepness (S), cropping system (C), and the support practice factor (P), which takes into account farming methods that reduce erosion:

$$A = R \ K \ L \ S \ C \ P \qquad (3.37)$$

The length of slope (L) is calculated by determining the shortest distance, measured perpendicular to all contours, from the location under study to a drainage basin divide. The equation can be modified to determine soil quality indices for different pollutants/nutrients (i.e., nitrogen). In using the universal soil loss equation, it is important to keep in mind that it was developed only to measure soil loss on farms with slopes ranging from zero to seven degrees, and it was to be applied only in the eastern and central United States. Stretching the model to account for different circumstances requires extreme caution. Because the equation is empirical, new applications will require field calibration. Wischmeier cautions against the misguided application of the soil loss equation. In particular, he cautions against applying the model to a large watershed by using average slopes (which tends to increase L and decrease S), failing to subtract deposition of soils in depressions, and failing to add streamed erosion. Furthermore, if the model is used to determine cumulative soil loss over time, one must adjust for the variability in K due to the temporal distribution of rainfall. Many more caveats can be found in the above source.

WEPP Surface Runoff (Sababi 1994)

USDA's Water Erosion Prediction Project (WEPP) is a deterministic model that predicts water-induced erosion. Input to the model consists of climate, soil, slope, and land management data. The climate data are very detailed and include day-by-day reports on precipitation, storm intensity, temperature, and wind speed. Soil data include parameters such as soil albedo, initial soil water content, soil texture, bulk density, saturated hydraulic conductivity, percent rocks, percent organic matter in soil, and soil cation exchange capacity. Slope data include slope length, slope steepness, and aspects. Land management data require specification of land use: agriculture, range, or forest.

The Sababi paper includes a description of the methods for calculating surface runoff, but it does not describe the routine that links erosion with runoff. Surface runoff is calculated as the difference between rainfall and infiltration. Infiltration is determined using the following relations:

$$f_t = K_e \ (1 + \frac{N_s}{F}) \qquad (3.38)$$

$$N_s = (h_e - \theta)\Psi \qquad (3.39)$$

where:

f_t = infiltration rate for time period t
K_e = effective saturated hydraulic conductivity
N_s = effective metric potential
F = cumulative infiltration depth
h_e = effective porosity of 0–20 cm of soil
q = volumetric soil water content of 0–20 cm of soil
(provided by a water balance routine)
Y = average wetting-front capillary potential.

Once surface runoff is calculated, the overland flow hydrograph is estimated using the kinematic wave method. The application of WEPP to large regions would be extremely difficult due to the detailed data requirements.

WEPP Erosion (Eckstein & Zaporazec 1993)
The authors use USDA's WEPP model to attempt to predict changes in soil erosion rates due to climate fluctuations. The steady-state sediment continuity equation is used as a basis for erosion computations. Soil detachment is broken down into two components: rill detachment and interrill detachment.

$$D_r = K_r(S_f - S_c) \qquad (3.40)$$

where:

D_r = rill detachment capacity, $kgs^{-1}m^{-2}$
K_r = rill soil erodibility parameter, sm^{-1}
S_f = shear stress of the flow, Pa
S_c = critical shear stress of the flow necessary to initiate soil detachment, Pa.

$$D_i = K_i I^2 \qquad (3.41)$$

where:

D_i = interrill detachment rate, $kgs^{-1}m^{-2}$
K_i = interrill soil erodibility, $kgs^{-1}m^{-4}$
I = rainfall intensity, ms^{-1}.

Detachment in the rills occurs if the hydraulic shear stress is greater than the critical shear and the flow is at less then transport capacity. Hydraulic shear stress is determined in a surface runoff routine. Adjustments are made to incorporate effects of canopy, ground cover, and buried residue. Details of these adjustments are not provided.

Chemical Runoff and Erosion from Agricultural Management Systems
(de Roo 1993)

The CREAMS model, developed by Foster in 1972, is one of the most popular physically-based erosion models. It was designed to compare the erosion effects of several different types of field management systems. The model consists of three main components: hydrology, erosion/sedimentation, and chemistry. The hydrology component estimates storm runoff from daily rainfall data. A modification of the universal soil loss equation determines the soil detachment resulting from a single storm event. Yalin's sediment movement model is then used to derive the transport capacity of the overland and channel flow. Unfortunately, CREAMS is limited to qualitative assessments and comparisons; it cannot be used to quantify erosion rates. In addition, CREAMS was designed as a field-scale model and cannot be applied to entire basins.

Areal Nonpoint Source Watershed Environment Response Simulation
(de Roo 1993)

Another popular physically-based model, ANSWERS was designed to simulate runoff and erosion in entire catchments which have agriculture as their primary land research use. The hydrologic part of the model is derived from USDA. Kinematic wave equations are used to route overland and channel flow, and separate equations are used for detachment and transport on overland flow areas. ANSWERS was designed only to model single rainfall events, but some authors have nonetheless been optimistic about its potential applicability to long-term erosion assessments.

Recently, a few attempts have been made to model erosion with geographic information systems (GIS). These systems, which allow for the spatial referencing of data, have several advantages over traditional erosion models when undertaking regional assessments. Perhaps most important is their ability to work with raster data from remote sensing images. This facilitates data input as well as long-term monitoring. In addition, the mapping abilities of GIS software make displaying and interpreting results fairly simple.

Pilesjo's GIS Erosion Model (Pilesjo 1992)

Pilesjo linked the universal soil loss equation to a GIS to assess erosion rates in Ethiopia and Sudan. Remote sensing images were utilized as data input for most of the parameters in the equation. Vegetation cover was measured as a percentage of vegetation per unit area, and it was field-checked using ground observations. Estimates of rainfall erosivity were developed from contour maps of mean annual rainfall. Slope steepness and length were calculated from contour maps, and soil erodibility was determined using government soil maps. The support factor was determined using both land-cover remote sensing data and subjective visual interpretation. GIS raster layers of each of these variables were then combined according to the mathematical relationships in the universal soil loss equation.

Two problems arose from Pilesjo's study. First, the final result was strongly dependent on the scale of the data, since smaller scales tended to decrease gradients and increase slope lengths. Second, the results were not calibrated to field observations, so only qualitative analyses could be undertaken.

de Roo's GIS/ANSWERS Erosion Model (de Roo 1993)

de Roo used GIS for a more limited erosion analysis. He linked the physically-based ANSWERS erosion model to a GIS and applied it to two small catchments. 137-Cs was used as a tracer to field-test the model's results. Although the predictions were good, the de Roo model required detailed information about the catchments, and it only predicted erosion from single rainfall events.

Relative Water Supply (Rao 1993)

This index is defined as the ratio of water supply to water demand. Two forms of the RWS have been found to be useful: the Theoretical Relative Water Supply (RWST) and the Actual Relative Water Supply (RWSA). RWST is defined as the ratio of water supply at the location of interest to the water demand associated with maximum production of the optimal crop or cropping pattern grown with appropriate cultural practices on the total irrigatable area designed or intended to be served from that location. RWSA is defined as the ratio of water supply to the water demand associated with the crops actually grown, with the cultural practices actually used, and for the actual irrigated area. It is computed by the following expression:

$$RWSA = \frac{IR + RN}{ET + SP} \tag{3.42}$$

where:

IR	=	irrigation water supply
RN	=	rainfall
ET	=	evapotranspiration
SP	=	seepage and percolation.

Christiansen's coefficient (Rao, 1993) is used to measure the spatial uniformity of irrigation water distribution. Its generalized form can be expressed as:

$$UCC = 1 - \frac{\sum_{1} (|X_i - \overline{X}| \, a_i)}{(\sum_{1}^{n} a_i)\overline{X}} \tag{3.43}$$

where:
X_i = depth of irrigation delivered to incremental area a_i
n = number of incremental areas
X = mean depth of irrigation water.

5.4 Biodiversity Indices

Article 2 of the Convention on Biological Diversity defines biological diversity as:

> the variability among living organisms from all sources including, inter alia, terrestrial, marine, and other aquatic systems and the ecological complexes of which they are part; this includes diversity within species, between species and of ecosystems. (UNEP 1992).

WRI Biodiversity Indicators (World Resources Institute 1992)

The authors present three different types of biodiversity indicators: (1) Indicators of Wild Species and Genetic Diversity; (2) Indicators of Community Diversity; and (3) Indicators of Domesticated Species.

■ Indicators of Wild Species and Genetic Diversity

1. Species richness—number of species per unit area or number of species per habitat type. Since there are inadequate data on the total number of species, better-known taxa such as plants and vertebrates can be used as proxies. The heavy emphasis on plants and vertebrates is justified, according to the researchers, because they tend to be important to humanity, they are good indicators of species richness in other groups, and data for them are easily obtainable.

2. Number or percent of species threatened with extinction or extirpation—extirpation is the removal of a species from a local area, but not worldwide.

3. Number or percent of endemic species—an endemic species is found only in the local area.

4. Number or percent of endemic species threatened with extinction.

5. Species risk index—this index combines information on endemic species and on the status of the community in which they live.

$$SRI = e \cdot s \qquad (3.44)$$

where:
SRI = the Species risk index
e = the number of endemic species per unit area
s = the status of the community (the percentage area of the biogeographic unit that has been lost due to conversion).

6. Number or percent of species with stable or increasing populations.

7. Number or percent of species with decreasing populations—this index allows the status of species to be analyzed well before they are threatened. The high costs involved in obtaining the requisite information can be avoided through the use of indicator species.

8. Number or percent of threatened (or endemic) species in protected areas—this index takes account of the fact that species are safer from extinction if they are located in protected areas such as national parks.

9. Number or percent of threatened species maintained in ex situ collections—this index weights surviving species in the wild higher than surviving species in ex situ breeding collections.

10. Number or percent of species used by local residents—where local residents utilize a variety of wild species for food, medicine, etc., the local economic benefits of maintaining biodiversity will be high.

■ Indicators of Community Diversity

11. Percentage of area dominated by nondomesticated species—this indicator gives less weight to controlled ecosystems such as agricultural land or timber plantations and more weight to natural, more diverse ecosystems such as forests or wetlands.

12. Rate of change from dominance of nondomesticated species to domesticated species.

13. Percentage of area dominated by nondomesticated species occurring in patches larger than 1,000 sq km—this indicator accounts for the fact that the fragmentation of a community has a significant influence on the numbers and types of species that can be supported.

14. Percentage of area in strictly protected status.

■ Indicators of domesticated species diversity

15. Crops (livestock) grown in an ecoregion as a percentage of the number grown 30 years previously—the status of diversity in fields has a direct bearing on the vulnerability to disease and pests, as well as on the vulnerability of the local economy to market or environmental changes.

16. Varieties of each crop (livestock) grown in an ecoregion as a percentage of the number grown 30 years previously.

17. Coefficient of kinship or parentage of crops—this index takes accounts of the fact that several varieties descending from a common parent do not represent a high degree of genetic diversity.

Diversity Indices (Harmsworth 1994)

List of terms:

S = the number of species in either a sample or a population
K = number of taxa in either a sample or a population
N = the number of individuals in a population or community
N_i = the number of individuals in species i of population or community
n = the number of individuals in a sample from a population
n_i = the number of individuals in species i of a sample from a population
P_i = n_i/n = the fraction of a sample of individuals belonging to species i.

Species Richness Indices

If the study area can be successfully delimited in space and time, and the constituent species enumerated and identified, species richness provides an extremely useful measure of diversity. It has been categorized into two types. Species density, which is the number of species per specified collection area, is the most commonly used measure of species richness, and is specifically favored by botanists. Numerical species richness, which is the number of species per specified number of individuals or biomass, although on the whole less frequently adopted, tends to be popular in aquatic studies. Odum's species per thousand individuals, proposed in 1962, is an example of a numerical species richness index. Homer (1976), for example, used Odum's index to investigate the effect of coastal power plants on fish in a salt-marsh tidal creek. The number of species invariably increases with sample size and sampling effort. To cope with this problem, a technique called rarefaction has been developed. The formula given below calculates the number of species expected in each sample if all samples were of a standard size:

$$E(s) = \sum 1 - [\left(\frac{N - N_i}{N} \right) / \left(\frac{N}{n} \right)] \qquad (3.45)$$

where:

E(s) = expected number of species
n = standardized sample size
N = total number of individuals
N_i = number of individuals in the ith species.

A number of simple indices have been developed using some combination of S and N. These include:

Margalef's Index: Proposed in 1958, it is based on the presumed linear relation between the number of species and the logarithm of the area or the number of individuals.

$$D = \frac{S-1}{\ln N} \qquad (3.46)$$

Menhinick's Index: Menhinick suggested this in 1964 to replace Margalef's index. No rational relation to the biological world is proposed.

$$D = \frac{S}{\sqrt{N}} \qquad (3.47)$$

Although ease of calculation is one great advantage of Margalef's and Menhinick's indices, they do not seem to be in common use.

Species Abundance Models

These describe the distribution of species abundances. Species abundance models range from those which represent situations where there is high evenness to those which characterize cases where the abundances of species are very unequal. The diversity of a community may therefore be described by referring to the model that provides the closest fit to the observed pattern of species abundances. If a single diversity index is required, a parameter of an appropriate distribution can be used.

Geometric Series: This method was first applied by Motomura in 1932. It is most commonly applied to species-poor assemblages. The basic assumption is that the dominant species will use proportion k of some limiting resource, the second most dominant species will take proportion k of the remainder, and so on until all species have been accounted for. The abundance of each species is assumed to be equivalent to the proportion of the resource it uses. In a geometric series the species abundances, ranked from most abundant to least abundant, are therefore

$$n_i = NC_k k(1-k)^{i-1} \qquad (3.48)$$

where:

k = the proportion of the available niche space or resource that each species occupies

n_i = the number of individuals

N = the total number of individuals

C_k = $[1-(1-k)^s]^{-1}$, and is a constant which ensures that $\sum n_i = N$.

When abundances are calculated for each species, the observed and expected values can be compared using a c_2 goodness-of-fit test; or a rank abundance plot may be made and examined to see whether all points lie on a straight line. Field data have shown that the geometric series pattern of species abundance is found primarily in species-poor (and often harsh) environments or in the very early stages of a succession. Very few people seem to have used the geometric progression.

Log Normal Distribution: This was first applied to species abundance data by Preston in 1948. The majority of communities studied by ecologists display a log-normal pattern of species abundance. The distribution is usually written in the form:

$$S(R) = S_0 \exp(-a^2 R^2) \qquad (3.49)$$

where:

$S(R)$	=	the number of species in the Rth octave (i.e., class) to the left of the symmetrical curve
S_0	=	the number of species in the modal octave
a	=	$(2s2)^H$ = the inverse width of the distribution
R	=	number of octaves.

Empirical studies have shown that a is usually = 0.2. One further parameter of the log-normal (g) is also conventionally defined. When a curve of the total number of individuals in each octave (the individuals curve) is superimposed on the species curve of the log-normal, g, is a measure of the relationship between the mode of the individuals curve and the upper limit of the species curve. Explicitly it is an estimate of the number of species at the octave where the individuals curve reaches its crest.

$$\gamma = R_N / R_{max} = \frac{\ln 2}{2a(\ln S_0)^{\frac{1}{2}}} \qquad (3.50)$$

where:

R_N	=	the modal octave of the individual curve
R_{max}	=	the octave in the species curve containing the most abundant species.

In many cases the crest of the individuals curve coincides with the upper tail of the species curve to give g=1. Such distributions are described as canonical. Species-rich communities—those with 200 or more species—are most likely to be canonical. The log-normal distribution is a symmetrical "normal" bell-shaped curve. If, however, the data to which the curve is to be fitted derive from a finite sample, the left hand portion of the curve (representing the rare and consequently unsampled species) will be obscured. The truncation point is called the veil line. Methods have been devised for fitting a truncated log normal.

It is noted that stable, equilibrium communities often follow a log-normal pattern of species abundance. When a mature community becomes polluted, its species abundance shifts backward through succession to take up the shape of the less equitable log or geometric series. Preston's log normal has been used to study stressed communities, both terrestrial and aquatic. Patrick (1973), for example, showed the effect of organic pollution on the diversity of diatom community. The Park Grass experiment forms another excellent example. In this experiment, the effect of a continuous heavy application of nitrogen on pasture was investigated (Kempton 1979). Cairns (1977), however, states that biologists have moved away from the use of Preston's log normal because it is not sufficiently applicable to all types of biological assemblages and very large amounts of data are needed.

Broken Stick Model: This model was proposed by MacArthur in 1957. It reflects a much more equitable state of affairs than those suggested by the log normal, log series, and geometric series. It is the biologically realistic expression of a uniform distribution. It is conventionally written in terms of rank order abundance and the number of individuals in the ith most abundant of S species.

$$N_i = \frac{N}{S \sum_{n=1}^{s} \frac{1}{N}} \qquad (3.51)$$

where:
  N = total number of individuals
  S = total number of species

$$S(n) = [\frac{S(S-1)}{N}](1 - \frac{n}{N})^{S-2} \qquad (3.52)$$

where,
  S(n) = the number of species in the abundance class with n individuals.

A goodness-of-fit test is used to compare the observed and expected frequencies in abundance classes. No diversity index has been derived from the distribution since it represents a highly equitable state of affairs. S (species richness) is an adequate measure of diversity. This model has been used successfully in a few studies, for example passerine birds (MacArthur 1960), and minnows and gastropods (King 1964).

The Q Statistic: This method takes into account the distribution of species abundance but does not actually entail fitting a model. This index is a measure of the interquartile slope of the cumulative species abundance curve and provides an indication of the diversity of the community, with no weighting either toward very abundant or vary rare species. Estimated from empirical data,

$$Q = \frac{\frac{1}{2} n_{R1} + \sum_{R^1+1}^{R^2-1} n_r + \frac{1}{2} n_{R2}}{\log(R^2/R^1)} \qquad (3.53)$$

where:

n_r = the total number of species with abundance r

S = the total number of species in the sample

R_1, R_2 = the 25 percent and 75 percent quartiles

n_{R1} = the number of individuals in the class where R_1 falls

n_{R2} = the number of individuals in the class where R_2 falls.

The quartiles are chosen so that:

$$\sum_1^{R^1-1} n_r < \frac{1}{4} S \leq \sum_1^{R^1} n_r, \sum_1^{R^2-1} n_r < \frac{3}{4} S \leq \sum_1^{R^2} n_r \qquad (3.54)$$

Although Q may be biased in small samples, this bias is low if >50 percent of all species present are included in the sample.

Indices Based on the Proportional Abundances of Species

These indices provide an alternative approach to the measurement of diversity. They take both evenness and species richness into account.

Shanon's H': Proposed in 1949, this index assumes that individuals are randomly sampled from an indefinitely large population. It also assumes that all species are represented in the sample. It is calculated from the equation:

$$H' = -\sum_{i=1}^{s} p_i \ln p_i \qquad (3.55)$$

The variance of H' can be calculated as

$$VarH' = \frac{\sum p_i (\ln p_i)^2 - (\sum p_i (\ln p_i)^2}{N} + \frac{S-1}{2N^2} \qquad (3.56)$$

Shanon's index is widely used in pollution monitoring. Bechtel and Copeland (1970) showed that the diversity of fish in Galveston Bay, Texas, increased with increasing distance from Baytown, the site of considerable effluent discharge. Egloff and Brakel (1973) used Shanon's index to monitor the change in the diversity of benthic macroinvertebrates along an Ohio stream.

Brillouin Index: First proposed by Brillouin in 1951, this information index is the appropriate form when the randomness of a sample cannot be guaranteed, or if the community is completely censused with every individual accounted for. It is calculated using the formula:

$$H = \frac{\ln N! - \sum \ln n_i!}{N} \qquad (3.57)$$

Tomascik and Sander (1987) measured the effects of eutrophication on reef building corals in Barbados, West Indies using Brillouin's index. In general, ecologists have tended to shy away from it because of its sample size dependency and because it can only be used on a population.

Redundancy: This index was described by Patten in 1962. Redundancy depends on the intensity of the internal correlations in the system and this is an index of organization. It is stated that redundancy is a good index of diversity since it depends on the way individuals are distributed into species. It ranges from 0 at high evenness (many codominant species) to 1 at low evenness.

$$H'_{max} = \log N! - S\log \left(\frac{N}{S}\right)! \qquad (3.58)$$

Patten's redundancy index has been used on aquatic ecosystems by Wilhm and Dorris (1966). Very few others have used it as a diversity index.

Simpson's D: In 1949, Simpson gave the probability of any two individuals drawn at random from an infinitely large community belonging to the same species as:

$$H'_{min} = \log N! - \log(n - (S-1))! \qquad (3.59)$$

As D increases, diversity decreases. Simpson's index is therefore usually expressed as 1–D or 1/D. Simpson's index is heavily weighted towards the most abundant species in the sample while being less sensitive to species richness. It has been applied by Wilhm (1967) to populations of benthic macroinvertebrates in a stream receiving organic wastes.

McIntosh's Index: McIntosh proposed this index in 1967. It ranges from 0 to 1 and could be looked at as a measure of evenness.

$$M = \frac{n - \sqrt{\sum_{i=1}^{s} n_i^2}}{n - \sqrt{n}} \qquad (3.60)$$

It appears to be seldom used.

Berger-Parker Index: This index was proposed by Berger and Parker in 1970. It expresses the proportional importance of the most abundant species as:

$$M = \frac{n_{max}}{n} \qquad (3.61)$$

where:

n_{max} = the number of individuals in the most abundant species.

As with Simpson's index the reciprocal form is usually adopted.

Hurlbert's PIE: Hurlbert proposed this index in 1971. He states that the interest in diversity stemmed from its proposed relationship to community stability, and that stability is related to the number of links in a food web. As such, he says, links imply interspecific encounter and thus the probabilities of such encounters are of interest. Probability of interspecific encounters is given by:

$$PIE = (\frac{N}{N-1})(1 - \sum p_i^2) \qquad (3.62)$$

This index is not extensively used.

ß of Differentiation Diversity

ß diversity is essentially a measure of how different (or similar) a range of habitats or samples are in terms of the variety (and sometimes the abundances) of species found in them.

Whittaker's measure ßW (1960):

$$ß_W = \frac{S}{\alpha} - 1 \qquad (3.63)$$

where:

S = the total number of species recorded in the system

a = the average sample diversity where each sample is a standard size and diversity is measured as species richness.

Cody's Measure ß (1975): This index is a good intuitive measure of species turnover. It simply adds the number of new species encountered along a transect to the number of species which are lost.

$$ß_C = \frac{g(H) + l(H)}{2} \qquad (3.64)$$

where:

g(H) = the number of species gained along the habitat transect

l(H) = the number of species lost over the same transect.

Routledge's Measures R, I, and E (1977): The first measure, R_R, takes overall species richness and the degree of species overlap into consideration.

$$ß_R = \frac{S^2}{(2r + S)} \tag{3.65}$$

where:

S = the total number of species in all samples

r = the number of species pairs with overlapping distributions.

$ß_I$, the second index, stems from information theory and has been simplified for qualitative data and equal sample size.

$$ß_I = \log(T) - [(1/T)Se_i\log(e_i)] - [(1/T)Sa_j\log(a_j)] \tag{3.66}$$

where:

e_i = the number of samples along the transect in which species i is present

a_j = the species richness of sample j

T = _ei =_j.

The third index, $ß_E$ is simply the exponential form of $ß_I$:

$$ß_I = \exp(ß_I) - 1 \tag{3.67}$$

Similarity Indices

The easiest way to measure the diversity pairs of sites is by the use of similarity indices.

Jaccard's Index: Proposed by Jaccard in 1908, this is the oldest and simplest similarity index. It is calculated using the equation:

$$C_J = \frac{j}{a + b - j} \tag{3.68}$$

where:

j = the number of species common to both sites

a = the number of species in site A

b = the number of species in site B.

Jaccard's index has been used for terrestrial systems by plant ecologists and for marine comparisons on coral reefs (Tolbat, et al. 1978).

Sorenson's Index: This index is similar to the Jaccard's index and uses identical variables.

$$C_S = \frac{2j}{a + b} \qquad (3.69)$$

Bray Curtis Index: This is a version of Sorenson's index proposed by Bray and Curtis in 1957. The formula is:

$$C = \frac{2_{jN}}{a_N + b_N} \qquad (3.70)$$

where:

a_N = the number of individuals in site A
b_N = the number of individuals in site B
j_N = the sum of the lower of the two abundances of species that occur in the two sites.

Percentage Similarity (PSC): This index was first discussed by Whittaker in 1952. It compares both species number and the relative abundance of species.

$$PSC = 100 - 0.5 \sum_{i=1}^{K} |a - b| \qquad (3.71)$$

where, a and b are, for a given species, percentages of the total samples A and B which that species represents. It has been used by Whittaker and Fairbanks (1958) to compare copepod communities of small lakes and ponds.

Pinkham and Pearson's Index: Pinkham and Pearson first discussed this index in 1976. They define $X_i a$ and $X_i b$ as the numbers of individuals in the i_{th} taxon for stations a and b, respectively. They state that the species composition of two stations may be compared by determining the average $X_i a\, X_i b$ for them. The similarity index is given as:

$$B = -\sum_{i=1}^{K} \frac{\min(X_{ia}, X_{ib})}{\max(X_{ia}, X_{ib})} \qquad (3.72)$$

Index of Threatened Mammals and Birds (MacGillivary, 1993): This index, which excludes fish, reptiles, amphibians, invertebrates, and flora because of patchy data, attempts to measure the state of mammal and bird species in 21 OECD countries. Threatened, in this case, refers to endangered or vulnerable species.

$$I = \frac{Thr_{m+b}}{Tot_{m+b}} \qquad (3.73)$$

where:

I = percent of threatened mammal and bird species
Thr_{m+b} = number of threatened mammal and bird species
Tot_{m+b} = total mammal and bird species.

World Bank Biodiversity Criteria (World Bank 1992): The World Bank report suggests that biodiversity indicators be capable of reflecting diversity at the regional landscape level, the community or ecosystem level, and the species or population level. The authors also emphasize that if researchers are using individual plant or animal species as indicators, they should be careful to select those species which are more important than others in helping to maintain ecological processes (e.g., major herbivores, top carnivores, fruiting trees, seed dispersers). An explicit presentation of a biodiversity index is avoided.

Hierarchical Biodiversity Indicators (Reed Noss 1990): The author adds to Jerry Franklin's notion of three primary attributes of biodiversity: composition, structure, and function. Composition has to do with the identity of the species, structure involves the habitat complexity within communities and patchiness at the landscape level, and function deals with ecological and evolutionary processes such as gene flow and nutrient cycling. Noss adds further complexity to Franklin's framework by dividing composition, structure, and function into four additional levels: regional landscape, community-ecosystem, species-population, and genetic. The presentation is entirely theoretical, and no explicit calculations of biodiversity are attempted.

Biodiversity Strategy (WRI 1992): Without explicitly mentioning biodiversity indices, the authors imply two alternative strategies for measuring a country's progress with regard to biodiversity. Either the current amount of biodiversity or the mechanisms for loss of biodiversity could be measured and used as indicators. The current amount of biodiversity has three levels: genes, species, and ecosystems. Genetic diversity refers to the variation of genes within a species or population. Species diversity covers the variety of species within a region. This could involve either a simple measure of the number of species or it could include a taxonomic diversity factor, which would give greater weight to less closely related species. Ecosystem diversity refers to the number and distribution of ecosystems within a region. In addition to these three levels of biodiversity, other factors such as the relative abundance of species, the age structure of populations, the pattern of communities in a region, and the changes in community composition and structure over time could be considered.

Mechanisms for biodiversity loss which could be quantified include habitat loss and fragmentation, introduction of foreign species, exploitation of plant and animal species, environmental pollution, climate change, and industrial agriculture/forestry. Evaluation of the monetary costs of biodiversity would need to include the current benefits of biodiversity.

Shannon's Index (Batten 1976): Batten recorded bird species richness and abundance in a number of native woodlands and conifer plantations in Killarney, Ireland. The aim of the study was partly to determine whether conifer plantations are impoverished relative to the endemic woodlands. In this example the diversity of two of the woodlands—Derrycunihy oakwood (area

10.75 ha) and a Norway spruce plot (area 11 ha)—is estimated using Shannon's index. A test is used to test for differences in the diversity of the two sites.

Hierarchical Richness Index (HRI): This procedure of measuring diversity and richness was proposed by French in 1993. He claims that it is conceptually simple and easily calculated, and should therefore be of practical use in a wide variety of situations. It is computed as follows:

1. Define mutually exclusive groups and assign items (e.g., individuals, species, cover scores) to groups (e.g., species, typical habitats, vegetation layers).

2. Calculate a total score for items within each group (e.g., number of individuals, number of species, total cover in layer).

3. Rank groups in descending order of within-group score (highest score ranks 1, next highest 2, etc.). Equal scores are ranked, as in most ranking procedures, as the average of the ranks they would have occupied if different.

4. Multiply within-group scores by group ranks to get group scores.

5. Sum group scores to get final HRI.

$$\text{HRI} = \sum_{i=1}^{g} (s_i \ i) \qquad (3.74)$$

where:
  g = the number of different groups
  i = group ranks
  s_i = within-group scores such that $s_i >= s_i + 1$.

This calculation requires mutually exclusive groups; i.e., every item must be able to be assigned unambiguously to one and only one group. The grouping can be done on any suitable criteria. Individuals might be grouped by species; species might be grouped by genera or by habitat-indicator classes, or in functional groups (herbivores, carnivores, detritivores, etc.), or in any other way that seems reasonable. Similarly, for a habitat classification, vegetation cover in a forest might be grouped by layers (canopy, tall shrub, etc.), or one might assess the richness of a landscape by measuring or scoring the amounts of different landtypes within it. It also requires some kind of quantitative measure within groups. Again, this can be any suitable consistent measure; e.g., counts of individuals, cover scores, areas, weights, etc.

Appendix Table 3.3 provides a summary of the performance and characteristics of a range of diversity indices.

Summary: Performance and Characteristics of a Range of Diversity Indices

	Discriminant Ability	Sensitivity to Sample Size	Richness (R) or Dominance (D)	Widely Used?
a(log series)	Good	Low	R	Yes
l(log normal)	Good	Moderate	R	No
Q statistics	Good	Low	R	No
S(species richness)	Good	High	R	Yes
Margalef's	Good	High	R	No
Shannon's	Moderate	Moderate	R	Yes
Brillouin's	Moderate	Moderate	R	No
McIntosh's	Poor	Moderate	D	No
Simpson's	Moderate	Low	D	Yes
Berger-Parker's	Poor	Low	D	No

5.5 Other Indices

Urgency Index (Thomas 1972)

Reiquam's urgency index attempted to establish a hierarchy among environmental stresses by comparing their relative urgencies.

$$U_i = P_i \, R_i \, C_i \qquad (3.75)$$

where:

U_i = importance of stress i

P_i = persistence of stress i (0 P_i 5; days = 1, months = 2, years = 3, decades = 4, centuries = 5)

R_i = geographical extent of stress i (0 R_i 5; local = 1, regional = 2, continental = 3, intercontinental = 4, global = 5)

C_i = complexity of stress i (determined by counting the number of components of the environment that are affected by the stress).

Odor Sensation Index of Air Pollution (Thomas 1972)

Engen developed an index of air pollution based on olfactory annoyance.

$$R = k(S - S_0)^n \qquad (3.76)$$

where:

R = perceived or subjective intensity

S = physical intensity or concentration

S_0 = estimate of threshold concentration or intensity

$$k \quad = \quad \text{constant}$$

n = parameter indicating rate of growth of perceived intensity with increases in physical concentrations (n varies from approximately 0.15 to 0.75).

Recreational Resource Index (Thomas 1972)

This index provides a measure of the amount of outdoor recreational opportunity available to the residents of a particular city or region. The area surrounding a city is divided up into j different (approximately concentric) sectors, each sector corresponding to a particular level of access from the city. The index is then derived by summing the recreational areas in each sector and weighting the result by the sector's distance from the city.

$$R_m = \sum_P w_{pm} \sum_P S_{jm} \qquad (3.77)$$

where:

R_m = recreational resources available to city m

S_{jm} = area of site j in sector m

w_{pm} = weight assigned to sector p (varies inversely with travel time from m).

An aggregate recreation index for an entire region would then be defined as:

$$R = \sum_m w_m R_m \qquad (3.78)$$

where:

R = aggregate recreation index for region

w_m = population weight for city m, equal to ratio of population of m to population of region

R_m = recreational resources available to city m.

Statistical Approaches (Ott 1978)

Some researchers, such as Shoji Yamamoto; Nakamura; Joung et al. and Coughlin et al., have used statistical approaches such as factor analysis and principal components to reduce the number of variables involved in calculating water quality indices. Interrelationships among all variables are examined, and combinations of variables which best explain the variance but which have low correlations with one another are chosen for use in index calculations. B. N. Lohani demonstrated the use of factor analysis in evaluating air quality data from Taipei, China ("An Air Pollution Index Based on Factor Analysis." 1980).

Liu's Quality of Life Index (Ott 1978)

Liu attempted to rate metropolitan areas in the United States by their quality of life. One component of his quality of life index was an environmental quality subindex. This environmental component was represented by 17 variables that were grouped into seven categories (chosen, in part, based on data availability): air pollution, visual pollution, noise, solid waste, water pollution, climate, and recreational areas and facilities. The data for each variable were transformed into standard normal scores based on the mean and standard deviation of all metropolitan areas. These scores were then aggregated for each location using arbitrarily chosen weights:

$$I = \sum_{i=1}^{n} w_i \, z_i \qquad (3.79)$$

where:

I = environmental quality subindex of quality of life index for the metropolitan area

w_i = weight assigned to i^{th} pollutant variable

z_i = normal score of the ith pollutant variable for the metropolitan area.

6. Institutions Engaged in Index Studies

6.1 World Bank

The World Bank describes an indicator as a performance measure that aggregates information into a usable form. However, issues of valuation, inter-temporal variations, and uncertainty are highlighted as being unresolved in their definitions and motivations of indicators. There have been a number of different World Bank activities related to indicator development, including the development diamonds as discussed in Chapter 2 of this volume, the greening of national accounts (see Section 6.6 below), and the most recent Wealth of Nations report. Another simple approach for comparative assessment of environmental performance of countries may be adopted from the World Bank's 1994 report on the social indicators of development, which defines a "development diamond" for a given country constructed from four indicators: GNP per capita, life expectancy, gross primary enrollment, and access to safe water. This approach is not without its shortcomings.[1] One of the first steps taken by the World Bank was the development of the Environmental Sustainable Development triangular framework, which requires that proposals be found to be sustainable in economic, environmental, and social terms. In terms of indicator development, the Wealth of Nations is the most recent attempt to develop a comprehensive environmental index at the World Bank. It is based on a new measure of a country's wealth. According to its proponents, a nation's wealth conceptually contains four ingredients: natural capital (such as soil, atmosphere, forests, water, wetland, minerals), human capital (people, their education, their health and capacity levels), social capital (institutions, cultural cohesion, collective information, knowledge), and manmade capital (houses, roads, factories, ships). Therefore, the total wealth of a nation at any given time is the sum of all four kinds of capital measured in an unified unit, i.e., dollars. To attach monetary values to each kind of capital, the Bank adopted the following methods.

- Tradable natural capital including forest, oil, minerals, and coal was estimated by multiplying the total known reserves by 50 percent of the prevailing international prices. Water was valued at 1 US cent per gallon of freshwater available for human use.

- The value of nontradable (immobile) natural capital, i.e., land of different uses was assumed to be proportional to per capita income of a country, e.g., the weightings given to one hectare of cropland, forest, pasture, and other land are 2, 1.75, 0.75, and 0.25 times per capita income, respectively.

- Manmade capital was estimated using perpetual inventory models (PIMs) that accumulate annual estimates of fixed capital formation while retiring some fraction of produced assets that came into the PIMs in previous years, based on assumptions about the useful life of broad categories of such assets.

- The weighting of human capital was assumed to be the expected lifetime earnings of today's population—computed as the residual of per capita gross national income after deducting the parts accounted for by manmade assets and by natural capital multiplied by the average years of life remaining in the current population. When the residual is negative (as occurred for 19 of 192 nations) a minimum value of one third of the value of produced assets and land is assigned.

- Social capital was "excluded" from this accounting process due to difficulties of quantification.

6.2 OECD

OECD has set out a framework for indicator development that has been followed, or is at least being considered, by a number of other institutions. They base indicators on a pressure-state-response (PSR) framework that assumes that the state of the environment is linked to the state of the economy and that human activities impose pressures on the environment but also depend on it for natural resource inputs. The response in the PSR model is the response of humans to the state of the environment, which occurs as a result of feedback mechanisms. Within this framework, OECD envisages the integration of sectoral-level data to link economics and the environment in key sectors. The environmental pressures of the seven themes were expressed in theme equivalents, weighted, and aggregated into a single index. The seven themes were change of climate, ozone depletion, acidification, eutrophication, dispersion of toxic substances, disposal of solid waste, and disturbance (noise and odor). The weighting was realized by dividing the given values, expressed in theme equivalents, by the corresponding target values for a certain year, or by sustainability values. This rendered a dimensionless parameter that expressed the distance to target for each theme. The dimensionless parameters that were obtained were summarized into one single yearly environmental indicator that represented the total environmental pressure.

6.3 European Union

■ The Eurostat Pressure Index Project develops an environmental pressure index that includes ten subindices: climate change, ozone layer depletion, loss of biodiversity, resource depletion, dispersion of toxins, waste, air pollution, marine environment and coastal zones, water pollution and water resources, and urban problems, noise and odors. This list varies from the fourteen items included by OECD in their state-of-the-environment work, but the list is more tailored to the needs of environmental policy in the EU member states, and is more suitable for aggregation.

The initial work is directed at a pressure index for each problem, rather than a single index. The aggregation of these indices is seen only as occurring at a much later stage in the project development. Any weights used would be calculated by valuing the impact of the policy fields with various methods, e.g., expert assessments, willingness-to-pay or policy goals. This is in contrast to the approach of the UNEP/SCOPE project, which aims to aggregate on the basis of common goals and distance to goals, an approach also followed by Adriaanse and the Netherlands group. The second-order weighting coefficients would be calculated on the basis of natural science, where possible, or with expert assessments.

■ In a study to develop an index framework for the sustainability performance of European cities Mega (1994), inspired by the Dutch system (Adriaanse, 1993), suggests a set of 14 urban indicators, expressed as theme unit equivalents. A weighting by contribution to sustainability levels is proposed, before aggregating to form an Index of Urban Sustainability Performance.

The urban indicators are:

1. Global climate indicator: indicates the contribution of cities to the change of the global climate.

2. Acidification indicator: indicates the deposition of acidic components.

3. Ecosystem toxification indicator: indicates the emissions of toxic substances.

4. Urban mobility indicator or clean transportation indicator: it indicates the use of environment-friendly transport means, especially for enforced mobility, defined as mobility for commuting and basic needs.

5. Waste management indicator: indicates the total amount of the dumped waste.

6. Energy consumption indicator: indicates the total amount of the consumed energy.

7. Water consumption indicator: indicates the total amount of the consumed water.

8. Disturbance indicator: indicates the disturbance of the population from noise, odor or visual pollution.

9. Social justice indicator: indicates the degree of social sustainability of a city.

10. Urban safety indicator: expresses the degree to which people suffer from lack of urban safety.

11. Economic urban sustainability indicator: expresses the viability of the urban economy.

12. Quality of green and public space indicator: expresses the improvements needed for the upgrading of public and monumental space.

13. Citizens' participation indicator: expresses the degree to which the local population participates in the decision-making and improvement of the local quality of life.

14. Unique sustainability indicator: this indicator, defined by each city, should represent the degree to which unique factors or events lead to urban sustainability with its environmental, social, and economic dimensions.

6.4 United Nations Environment Programme

The UNEP/SCOPE project envisages four indices—net resource depletion, composite pollution, ecosystem risk, and human welfare impact. It is global in its coverage, and the proposed method of aggregation is on the basis of "common goals which are widely accepted."

6.5 Food and Agriculture Organization

The major source of primary date and information about land and natural resources in developing countries is the Food and Agriculture Organization of the United Nations (FAO). FAO, focusing on agricultural indicators, highlights the importance of the linkages between the environment and other variables and suggests a framework in which macro- , middle- , and micro-economics levels of agriculture are encompassed, including the feedback mechanisms between them. FAO suggests linking data and indicators so that they provide clear and valuable signals of changes.

As an indication of its wealth in data and information systems, FAO reported on the World Agricultural Information Centre (WAICENT). This is supported by two distinct components: FAOSTAT, which contains time-series statistics from 210 countries and territories, and FAOINT, composed of text files. In addition to these, FAO supports AGROSTAT-PC which provides statistics collected since 1961, updated annually, on population, land use, production, agricultural inputs, trade-food balances, and forest products. Every ten years FAO coordinates the World Census of Agriculture. Several other databases, such as the Africa Real-Time Environmental Monitoring System (ARTEMIS) and the Global Early Warning System (GIEWS) are also supported.

6.6 UNSTAT

In order to integrate environmental costs and benefits into national accounts, UNSTAT is developing national indicators of the environment of green GNPs. The World Bank is working in collaboration to develop case studies (Costa Rica, Indonesia and Mexico), traditional SNA short-cut methods, and potential cost or defensive expenditures. This approach concentrates largely on the cost side and is linked to the smaller-scale issues of project environment-economic relationships by cost-benefit analysis as a means of better assessing environmental impacts. Models are being used to find creative solutions to valuation and aggregation at all scales. Valuation attempts are highlighting the cost side, using full-cost pricing.

The development of a System of Environmental and Economic Accounts (SEEA) and the Framework for Indicators of Sustainable Development (FISD) "succeed in linking different data systems and indicator frameworks." But they do not overcome the dichotomy of monetary accounting versus physical indicator development (see Appendix Figure 3.1).

The SEEA, developed under the auspices of the United Nations, aims to integrate environmental and economic accounts by costing fixed and natural capital consumption and by introducing broader concepts of capital and capital accumulation. However, this method only allows for the integration of those aspects of natural capital which can be valued and ignores many of the environmental indicators incorporated in the FISD. However, with the development of many different methods by which to evaluate natural resources and environment, this problem may diminish (See Appendix Figure 3.2).

6.7 United Nations Development Programme

The main activity in indicator development at UNDP is the integration of environmental considerations into the Human Development Index (HDI).

Sustainability Concepts and Measures

Legend

Arrows indicate flow of goods,
services and amenities.

Acronyms

CC   Carrying Capacity
EDP   Environmentally-adjusted net
       Domestic Product
ENI   Environmentally-adjusted
       National Income
EI   Environmental Indicators
ES   Environment Statistics
GPI   Genuine Progress Indicator
HDI   Human Development Index
ISEW Index of Sustainable Economic Welfare
NDP   Net Domestic Product
NEW   Net Economic Welfare
NI   National Income
NRA   Natural Resource Accounts (aggregates)
QOL   Quality of Life (indicators)
SDP   Sustainable net Domestic Product
SI   Social Indicators

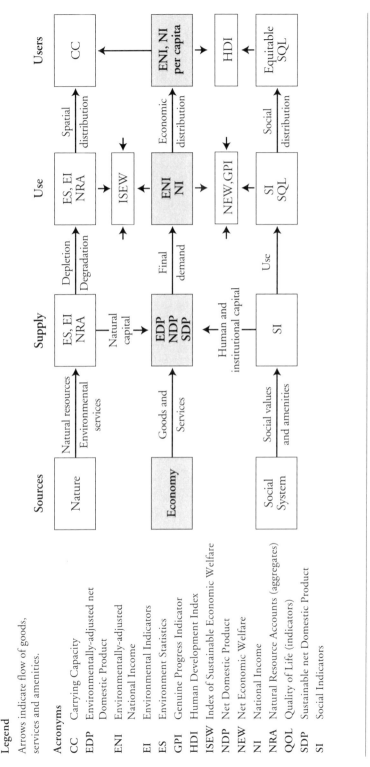

Incorporating Indicators in Accounting

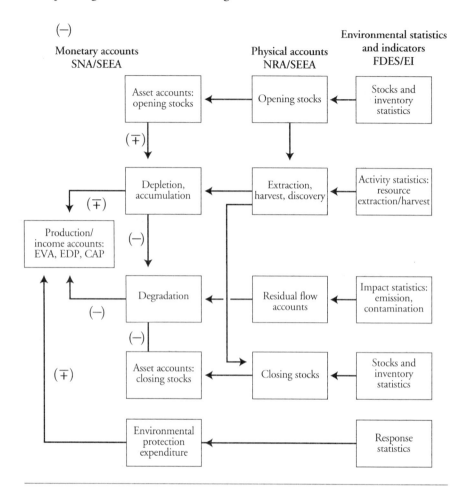

HDI measures a country's ability to meet certain economic and social needs of its people, and integrates the following measures:

- average life expectancy at birth
- educational level
- per capita income.

Intercountry comparisons are made by comparing HDI for a given nation to the maximum and minimum levels of the indicator within three income groups—high, medium, and low. This index could be greened by including a fourth environmental dimension, which itself is an aggregate environmental indicator. Alternatively, all three of the HDI components could be greened by adjusting income for natural resource depletion and health by environment pollution. As a third alternative, Pfliegner (1995) has proposed that a green index be created and compared to HDI. This Index of Intensity of Environmental Exploitation is represented by three components:

■ water withdrawal as a percentage of the annual internal renewable water resources;

■ greenhouse gas emissions per capita;

■ energy consumption per constant $ of GDP.

These three components are combined through either an ordinal or cardinal ranking. The ordinal index is based on the average rank of a nation after ranking nations on each of the three components. The cardinal index aggregates the components according to the variance from the minimum, and then creates an average. Another conceptual approach being considered by UNDP to supplementing HDI is to calculate a Materials Inputs per unit of Services (MIPS), based on a lifecycle approach. It measures the environmental costs of human development in terms of waste production, emissions, and the use of resources. However, there are severe data limitations to generating these indices.

UNDP suggests that future research should focus on the interlinkage between other environmental indicators (including energy consumption) and HDI, and the construction of several green indices for comparison with the HDI, rather than the "greening" of HDI itself.

6.8 World Health Organization
The main area in which WHO is working on indicator development is that of environmental health indices. The Scientific Committee on Problems of the Environment (SCOPE) recommended that sustainability indices include such indicators and WHO is taking a leading role in this regard. WHO's programs include Healthy Cities and the European Health for All. WHO defines environmental health indicators as an expression of the link between environment and health, targeted at an issue of specific policy or management concern and presented in a form which facilitates effective decision-making. The DPSEEA framework developed for the indicators can be seen in Appendix Figure 3.3.

The final goal in the use of this framework is to develop core sets of environmental indicators for policy support and to provide a basis for comparison among different areas over time. One limiting factor of this work is the uncertain nature of the environment-health linkages on which the indicators are based. However, these obstacles are being overcome.

DPSEEA: A Conceptual Framework for the Development and Identification of Environmental Health Indicators

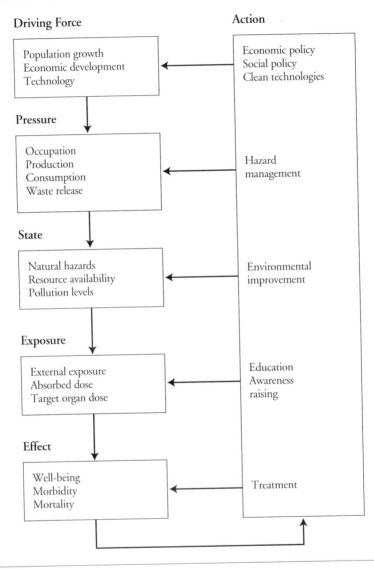

6.9 National Institutions

Netherlands

The Netherlands Ministry of Housing, Physical Planning, and the Environment has developed a set of indicators for environmental themes by gathering emissions data and weighing it according to scientific principles. By confining the data to specific themes, they limit the environmental issues. The target sectors are evaluated for their economic activity and environmental pollution pattern relative to each of the themes, determining an indicator for each sector with respect to each theme. However, there is no weighting system with which to generate one indicator per sector, or define both normative and descriptive indicators: descriptive indicators present a certain state of the world, while normative indicators enable valuation by comparing a descriptive indicator with a standard, acting as a norm, or so-called (environmental) performance. Accordingly, an indicator is not simply a measure of a state variable, but rather a measure of progress to show change. However, a number of institutions caution that an indicator gives a limited picture of change rather than the underlying complex realities. They allow that because of such complexities, not all indicators will be quantitative; some will be qualitative.

The Netherlands Ministry of Housing, Physical Planning, and the Environment has elaborated a framework centered on the PSR model and based on an approach to problem-solving that provides an internally integrated (within the environment) and externally integrated (with other policy areas) model, to avoid isolated solutions that overlook interconnections. They state that clearly specified goals are required so that performance indicators as value judgments can be determined. They then use PSR framework as a means of identifying the range of possible indicators, with performance-based goals pertaining to resource use, pollution patterns and the state of the environment. Disaggregation then follows, using a theme approach—environmental themes with specified goals provide the key environmental indicators. These are linked to performance indicators such as the impact on the economic sector. Sectors are themselves disaggregated to assess the pollution pattern caused by each and to find their contribution to the environmental theme indicators.

Japan

The Japanese approach has been to develop indicators at a local level before moving to a larger scale. They have done a series of case studies to determine physical measures of the environment and are trying to find a means of monetization. In their framework, they build up their indicators sequentially. They focus first on the natural environment, then on intergenerational equity, poverty, and quality of life, and finally on level of (monetized) welfare. In Japan, sector-based studies are being used to illustrate the principles of indicator calculation, but are being broadened to a national scale to consider the possible incorporation of the environment into economic indicators through the cost of pollution. The Japanese have also generated some simple indicators of performance based on compliance rates, emissions, treatment capacity, and budgets. The notion of environmental satellite accounts is also being explored, through calculation on a sectoral basis.

United States

In its study entitled "Gold and Green," the Institute for Southern Studies in Durham, North Carolina, uses two separate lists of indicators to evaluate each state's economic performance and the stresses on its natural environment. The following environmental indicators were used:

1. Hazardous waste generated: Pounds per capita of RCRA-regulated hazardous waste produced in-state during 1991.

2. Toxic chemical discharges: Pounds per capita of toxic chemicals released into the environment or transferred offsite by reporting manufacturing facilities during 1992.

3. Cancer-causing toxins: Pounds per capita of toxic chemicals released into the environment in 1991 that are classified as positive or suspected human or animal carcinogens by the International Agency for Research on Cancer.

4. Solid waste generated: Pounds per capita of municipal solid waste produced in 1993.

5. Solid waste recycled: Estimates by the state of percent of solid waste that is recycled, average of 1992 and 1993 figures.

6. Pesticides: Estimated total pounds of active ingredients in herbicides, fungicides, and insecticides applied per 1987 acre of harvested cropland.

7. Fertilizer use: Pounds per capita of single-nutrient fertilizer used in 1993.

8. Total water use: Gallons per day per capita of surface and groundwater for all offstream purposes, 1990.

9. Hazardous spills: Gallons of unauthorized releases of oil and hazardous substances, totaled for 1990, 1991, and 1992.

10. Global warming gases: Tons per capita of gases from human sources contributing to global warming (carbon dioxide, carbon monoxide, volatile organic compounds, nitrogen oxides, methane, and chlorofluorocarbons).

11. Air quality: Score based on degree to which residents live in areas that exceed national ambient air quality standards for ozone and/or carbon monoxide, 1992–1993.

12. Gasoline use: Average miles traveled by car, truck, or bus per gallon of gas consumed, 1992.

13. Miles driven: Thousands of miles driven in 1992 by cars, trucks, or buses, per square mile of land in-state.

14. Energy consumption: Millions of British thermal units (BTUs) consumed per capita from all energy sources, 1992.

15. Change in energy consumption: Percent change in per capita energy consumption from 1973 to 1992.

16. State spending on environment: Total spending in fiscal 1991 for state programs addressing environmental and natural resource protection. Includes state, federal, and other funds (fines, licenses, etc.) that pass through the state budgetary process. Excludes funds raised and spent by local governments.

17. Portion of state budget for environment: State spending for environmental and natural resource protection as a percent of state's total budget for fiscal 1991.

18. Environmental policy record: Score based on 67 policy indicators (from recycling programs to groundwater protection) measuring state initiatives to protect the environment.

19. Pollution subsidy versus investment: Score based on capital expenditures from pollution abatement made by a state's industries compared to national average for industries with similar chemical emissions. The higher the number, the greater the eventual subsidy required from public to pay for industries' poor pollution prevention strategies; a negative number means industries invest more than national average on pollution abatement equipment.

20. Emission-to-job ratio: Pounds of toxic chemical emissions per manufacturing job for 1991.

In an attempt to measure the effectiveness of the actions the world's major economic power has taken to protect the environment, the US National Center for Economic Alternatives (NCFEA) has developed a composite, aggregated index of environmental quality, known as the Index of Environmental Trends (IETs). The index is an aggregate of 21 environmental-change indicators for air,

APPENDIX TABLE 3.4

Indicators Used by NCFEA

Air	Water	Chemical	Waste	Land	Causal
CO_2	DO	Fertilizers	Municipal	Grasslands	Automobiles
NO_x	Nitrates	Pesticides	Nuclear	Woods	Energy
SO_x	Phosphorous	Ind. Chemical			
CO	Ammonium				
Particulate	Metals				
VOC or HC	Withdrawal				

land, and water quality; chemical and waste generation; and energy use since the 1970s summarized in Appendix Table 3.4.

The index was compiled for four time periods: 1970–1975, 1970–1980, 1970–1985 and 1970–1990. For each time period, the percentage change of each indicator was calculated. The sign of the percentage change is determined by the nature of the indicators. For example, if CO_2 emission increases by 20 percent during a time period, the value of the indicator takes a negative sign, i.e., –20 percent, and vice versa since the increase of CO_2 causes adverse environmental impacts. Conversely, if the total forest area increases by 20 percent during the time period, the value takes a positive sign because the increase is considered an environmental plus. The aggregate index for each sector and for the overall environmental quality is a simple mean of all the indicators in each category, assuming an equal weight for all. NCFEA computed the index for each of the six sectors separately and for all the sectors combined for the four time periods. This allows decision-makers and the general public to examine, for any given country, environmental progress in air, water, or land, and the overall environmental quality for different time periods.

Canada

First developed by Inhaber in 1976 the National Index for Canada was a composite index based on four sectoral indices: air, water, land, and a miscellaneous category (pesticides and radiation), which were in turn made up of 33 indicators. Indicators, sectoral indices, and the composite index were expressed as unit-free numbers. These ranged from 0, for the best possible environmental conditions, to higher numbers for progressively worse environmental quality. A value of 1 meant that an objective (or standard) was being achieved; a value above 1 indicated cause for warning.

Inhaber assigned a system of weights on the advice of experts. The overall environmental quality index (I_{eqi}) for Canada was calculated by:

$$I_{eqi} = \{[0.3(I_{air})^2 + 0.3(I_{water})^2 + 0.3(I_{land})^2 + 0.1(I_{misc.})^2]\}H \qquad (3.80)$$

where:
I_{air}, I_{water}, I_{land}, and $I_{misc.}$ = the sectoral indices for air, water, land, and the miscellaneous categories.

In his doctoral dissertation (1991), Parker used 15 environmental indicators to construct composite indices for France, Italy, and UK Environmental indicators were placed into three categories: (1) air-nitrogen oxide, sulphur dioxide, low-level ozone, carbon dioxide, and particulates; (2) bathing-water quality, oil spills, river quality, fertilizer use, and pesticide use; and (3) landscape-population change, new dwellings, tourism, road traffic volume, and wastes.

Weights were derived from public opinion polls. Each indicator was normalized by dividing its value in each year by its value for the year for which it was first available. Individual indicator weights were also normalized by dividing each one by the total of the index weights for the indicators that were available in that year. Each normalized weight was then multiplied by the corresponding normalized environmental indicator, and the results summed across all available indicators to produce a composite index for each year.

If an environmental indicator was missing from any index, or it started or finished during the period for which the index was being calculated, then the weight for that indicator was not applied in that year. In this way, the normalized weights in any year always added up to 1.

Ruitenbeek has developed indicators of ecologically sustainable development (ESD) for the Canadian Environmental Advisory Council. Ruitenbeek states that the five fundamentals given below are a manifestation of what can best be described as a more global outlook on achieving sustainable development:

1. A Broader Scope: ESD indicator design must acknowledge that the economy and human behavior are part of a broader ecosystem that supports them.

2. Distributive Elements: Social equity—in terms of the incidence of costs and benefits—must be an explicit component of ESD indicators.

3. Projective Applications: ESD indicators must be useful for forward-looking applications and not just descriptive of past or current conditions.

4. Explicit Linkages: Drawing connections between human economic behavior and broader ecosystem health is a vital function of ESD indicators.

5. Inherent Uncertainty: Unquantifiable uncertainty in ecosystem behavior and response requires that ESD indicators must explicitly communicate such uncertainty to decision-makers.

Note

1 For instance, per capita energy (safe, conventional, and nonconventional) availability may have been a more appropriate indicator of sustainable development than accessibility to water.

References

Adriaanse, A. 1993. Environmental Policy Performance Indicators, A Study on the Development of Indicators for Environmental Policy in the Netherlands.

Bechtel, T. J. and Copeland, B. J. 1970. Fish species diversity indices as indicators of pollution in Galveston Bay, Texas. *Contib. Mar. Sci.* 15, 103–32. Cited in Magurran, 1988.

Belgium Federal Planning Office. *Indicators of Sustainable Development for Decision-Making.* Report on the Workshop of Ghent, Belgium. January 9–11, 1995. submitted to the UN Commission on Sustainable Development.

Berger, A., and R. Hodge, *Natural Change in the Environment: A Challenge to the Pressure-State-Response Concept.* Presented at the SCOPE Scientific Workshop on Indicators of Sustainable Development, November 15–17, 1995. Wuppertal Institute, Germany.

Briguglio, L. 1995. Small Island Developing States and Their Economic Vulnerabilities. *World Development,* Vol. 23, No. 9, 1615–1632.

Bryant, D.; E. Rodenburg; T. Cox; and D. Nielsen. *Coastlines at Risk: An Index of Potential Development-Related Threats to Coastal Ecosystems.* World Resources Institute Indicator Brief.

Burlington, R. F. 1962. Quantitative biological assessment of pollution. *J. Water Pollut. Contr. Fed.* 36, 650–653. Cited in Washington, 1984.

Cairns Jr J. 1977. Quantification of biological integrity. *The Integrity of Water* R. F. Ballentine and L. J. Guarraia (eds.). EPA publications, New York. Cited in Washington, 1984.

Coates, E. L., and A. K. Mason, 1975. *Some practical problems in developing and presenting environmental quality indices to the public.* Proceedings of the International Conference on Environmental Sensing and Assessment. Las Vegas, NV: IEEE #75–CH 10007–1 ICESA, September.

Corvalan, C.; D. Briggs; and T. Kjellstrom. 1995. *Conceptual Issues in the Development of Environmental Health Indicators.* World Health Organization, presented at the SCOPE Scientific Workshop on Indicators of Sustainable Development, November 15–17, 1995, Wuppertal Institute, Germany.

Dahl, A. L. 1995. Towards Indicators of Sustainability, United Nations Environment Programme. Presented at the SCOPE Scientific Workshop on Indicators of Sustainable Development, November 15–17, 1995, Wuppertal-Institute, Germany.

Egloff, D. A. and W. H. Brakel. 1973. Stream pollution and a simplified diversity index. *J. Water Pollut. Contr. Fed.* 45, 2269–75. Cited in Magurran, 1988.

Environmental Agency of Japan. 1992. Activities on environmental indicators in Japan: Background Report for the World Resources Institute.

The Eurostat Pressure Index Project: Goals and Methodology. April, 1994. Commission of the European Union.

Fischer-Kowalski, M. and H. Habert, Tons, Joules and money: Modes of production and their sustainability problems. *Society and Natural Resources.* Vol. 6, 1996.

French, D. D. 1994. Hierarchical Richness Index (HRI): a simple procedure for scoring "richness" for use with grouped data. *Biological Conservation,* 69, 207–212.

Gutierrez-Espeleta, E. The Approximated Sustainability Index: A Tool for Evaluating Sustainability National Performance. Presented at Accounting for Change—A Network Seminar on Sustainable Development Indicators, 13–14 October 1994, London.

Harper, J. L. and D. L. Hawksworth. 1994. Biodiversity: Measurement and Estimation. Philosophical Transactions of the Royal Society of London B. 345, 5–12.

Homer, M. 1976. Seasonal abundance, biomass, diversity and trophic structure of fish in a salt-marsh tidal creek affected by a coastal power plant. In *Thermal Ecology II* G. W. Esch and R. W. McFarlene (eds.). US Energy Research and Development Administration, Washington, DC, 259–67. Cited in Magurran, 1988.

King, C. E. 1964. Relative abundance of species and MacArthur's model. Ecology, 45, 716–27. Cited in Magurran, 1988.

Lohani B. N. and G. Todino 1984. "Water quality index for Chao Phraya River" in Journal of Environmental Engineering, 110(6), 1163–1176.

Lohani, B. N. and N. Mustapha. 1982. "Indices for water quality assessment in rivers: A case study of the Linggi River in Malaysia" in Water Supply and Management, 6(6), 545–555.

MacArthur, R. H. 1960. On the relative abundance of species. *American Naturalist,* 94, 25–36. Cited in Magurran, 1988.

Magurran, A. E. 1988. *Ecological Diversity and its Measurement,* Princeton University Press, Princeton.

Mega, V. 1994. *Toward the Development of an Indicators Framework for the Sustainability Performance of European Cities.* HIID, Harvard University.

McKinley, T. 1995. Human Development Indicators: Sustainability, Equity and Poverty, Human Development Report Offices, UNDP, presented at the SCOPE Scientific Workshop on Indicators of Sustainable Development, November 15–17, 1995, Wuppertal Institute, Germany.

Muller, S. 1995. *Evaluating the Sustainability of Agriculture at Different Hierarchy Levels: A Framework for the definition of indicators.* Presented at the SCOPE Scientific Workshop on Indicators of Sustainable Development, November 15–17, 1995, Wuppertal Institute, Germany.

O'Connor, J. 1994. Topical approaches to environmental accounting. Draft.

Ott, W. *Environmental Indices.* Ann Arbor Science Publish Inc. Michigan, 1978.

Parker J. D. E. 1991. Environmental Reporting and Environmental Indices (doctoral dissertation).

Patrick, R. 1973. Use of algae, especially diatoms, in the assessment of water quality. American Society for Testing and Materials, *Special Technical Publication* 528, 76–95. Cited in Magurran, 1988.

Pfliegner, K. 1995. *Sustainable Human Development: Greening of the Human Development Index.* United Nations Development Programme, New York. Presented at the SCOPE Scientific Workshop on Indicators of Sustainable Development, November 15–17, 1995, Wuppertal Institute, Germany.

Planning Committee on Environmental Indices. 1975. Planning for Environmental Indices, NAS, Washington, DC.

Ruitenbeek, H. K. 1991. "Indicators of Ecologically Sustainable Development: Towards New Fundamentals." Canadian Environmental Advisory Council, Ottawa, Canada.

Serageldin, I. 1995. Sustainability and the Wealth of Nations: First Steps in an Ongoing Journey, Third Annual World Bank Conference on Environmentally Sustainable Development, September 30, 1995.

Taylor, L. R. 1978. *Bates, Williams, Hutchinson—a variety of diversities.* In Diversity of Insect Faunas: 9th Symposium of the Royal Entomological Society L.A. Mound and N. Warloff (eds.), Blackwell, Oxford: 1–18. Cited in Magurran, 1988.

Teixeira, I. M. 1995. *Brazilian Initiatives on Indicators of Sustainable Development—A Summary.* Presented at the SCOPE Scientific Workshop on Indicators of Sustainable Development, November 15–17, 1995, Wuppertal Institute, Germany.

Thomas, W. A. 1972. *Indicators of Environmental Quality.* New York: Plenum Press.

Tolbat, F. H., B. C. Rusell, and G. R. V. Anderson. 1978. Coral reef fish communities, unstable, high diversity systems? *Ecol. Monog.* 48, 425–440. Cited in Washington, 1988.

Tomascik, T. and Sander, F. 1987. Effects of eutrophication on reef building corals. II. Structure of scleractinian coral communities on fringing reefs, Barbados, West Indies. *Marine Biology.* 94, 53–75. Cited in Magurran, 1988.

Train, R. E., 1973. *Management for the future.* Presented at the National Conference on Managing the Environment, Washington, DC. 1973.

United Nations Environment Programme (UNEP). 1992. Convention on Biological Diversity, June 1992. Nairobi.

US Interagency Working Group on Sustainable Development Indicators. 1995. *An Endowment Framework for Sustainability Indicators.* Presented at the SCOPE Scientific Workshop on Indicators of Sustainable Development, November 15–17, 1995, Wuppertal Institute, Germany.

Washington, H. G. 1984. Diversity, Biotic and Similarity Indices: A Review With Special Relevance to Aquatic Ecosystems. *Water Research.* Vol. 18, No. 6, 653–694.

Whittaker, R. H. and C. W. Fairbanks. 1958. A study of copepod communities in the Colombia Basins, Southeastern Washington. *Ecology.* 39, 46. Cited in Washington, 1984.

Wilhm, J. L. 1967. Comparison of some diversity indices applied to populations of benthic macroinvertebrates in a stream receiving organic wastes. *J. Water Pollu. Contr. Fed.* 39, 1673–1683. Cited in Washington, 1984.

Wilhm, J. L. and T. C. Dorris. 1966. Species diversity of benthic macroinvertebrates in a stream receiving domestic and oil refinery effluents. *Am. Midl. Nat.* 76, 427–449. Cited in Washington, 1984.

World Resources Institute, 1992. Workshop on Global Environmental Indicators, Washington, DC.

Appendix IV

Some Theoretical and Technical Issues Regarding Environmental Elasticity and Environmental Diamonds

Measuring Environmental Quality in Asia

Xiang Yu [1]
Chang-Ching Yu

In addition to cost-of-remediation, we have also developed two supplementary indices useful for measuring environmental trend and state of the environment, namely, environmental elasticity and environmental diamond (see Chapter 3). In this appendix, we explore several technical and theoretical issues involved in the development of these two indices, and wherever possible, present alternative arguments and approaches. The purpose is to stimulate further discussion on the issues.

1. Issues Regarding Environmental Elasticity and an Alternative Index for Measuring Environmental Trend Relative to Economic Trend

The notion of sustainable development brings environment as a new dimension into economic development theories. The concept of environmental elasticity evolves from the aspiration for indices capable of describing both economic development and environmental changes (improvement or deterioration), as well as their interrelations.

In order to measure sustainable development, much has been done to devise indices reflecting both economic achievements and environmental performance. One such an example is given by Dufournaud and Rogers (1995) who employed the economic concept of elasticity to name their index of sustainability, i.e., environmental elasticity. In their work, they defined the environmental elasticity as the ratio of the percentage change in the environmental quality to the percentage change in the economy (see Chapters 3 and 5 of this volume).

1.1 Index Development and Economic Preference Theory

When trying to assess the performance of a nation or a region on more than one issue in a comprehensive way, an evaluator is in a situation similar to that a consumer facing the choice between bundles of goods and trying to determine the utilities, or levels of satisfaction, associated with the bundles. An index of development should also be able to measure the level of satisfaction of the evaluator toward a specific combination of economic and environmental changes. A higher value of the index should represent a more desirable situation. Although the numerical value of the index may have no obvious meaning, it should give the correct ranking for different combinations of the economic and environmental development. The evaluator's judgment is determined by its internal preference. If a set of assumptions is made about the evaluator's attitude toward bundles of economic and environmental development, and the assumptions are agreed to by the evaluator, we would then be able to model its preferences among different situations of development. For our purposes, we postulate that positive changes in both economy and environment are most preferred, and thus, be assigned the highest utility. The second highest preference would be given to those situations where one positive change and one negative change are observed. Negative changes in both economy and environment would be least preferred. To conduct quantitative analysis, we still need to make some more assumptions about the evaluator's internal preference. The assumptions are given below which may be modified in one way or another if the evaluator finds certain modifications are necessary to reflect its utility or satisfaction more precisely.

- The achievements in the economy and the environment are equally important and can substitute for each other. That is, a 5 percent increase in the economy accompanied by a 5 percent deterioration in the environment is regarded indifferently as a 5 percent decrease in the economy with a 5 percent improvement in the environment.

- A balanced development in both environment and economy is most preferred and a simultaneous degradation in the two is least preferred. The numerical values of the index should reflect such preferences.

- The preferences are continuous. It means that a sufficiently small change in one parameter should not change the utility dramatically.

- A higher value of the utility indicates a more desirable situation.

Once we agree upon these assumptions for index development, we should then try to develop indices that meet the assumptions as much as possible and whose numerical values can correctly reflect the utility or the levels of satisfaction toward a set of situations. In the next two sections, we will first demonstrate that environmental elasticity violates the assumptions above. We will then provide an alternative index which not only measures environmental trend relative to economic trend, as does the environmental elasticity, but also meets all the above assumptions.

1.2 Some Undesirable Properties of Environmental Elasticity

In Chapters 3 and 5, we have applied environmental elasticity to both developed OECD countries and developing Asian countries. With the aid of graphs, the environmental elasticity index appears to be quite indicative of their environmental changes relative to economic growth. We find, however, that the numerical value of environmental elasticity has some undesirable features. When used to reflect the extent of our satisfaction toward a specific situation, the index violates all of the above assumptions.

For example, in Appendix Figure 4.1, the five points indicate the following five situations:

A: 5 percent improvement in both the economy and the environment;

B: 0.1 percent increase in the economy and 5 percent improvement in the environment

---

APPENDIX FIGURE 4.1

Negative Properties of Environmental Elasticity

% Change in Environment

C (0.1, 5)   B (0.1, 5)   A (5, 5)

E (5, 0.1)

% Change in Economy

D (1.7, 1.7)

C: 0.1 percent decrease in the economy and 5 percent improvement in the environment;

D: 1.7 percent deterioration in both the economy and the environment;

E: 5 percent increase in the economy and 0.1 percent improvement in the environment.

Calculation on the environment elasticity index gives:

$$A = 1, B = 50, C = -50, D = 1, E = 0.02,$$

thus it would appear that

$$A(5, 5), A(5, 5) = D(-1.7, -1.7),$$
$$D(-1.7, -1.7) > E(5, 0.1) > C(-0.1, 5),$$

but,

- Assumption 1 indicates B(0.1, 5) = E(5, 0.1) due to substitution;

- Assumption 2 indicates A(5, 5) > D(-1.7, -1.7) and A should be the maximum and D the minimum, since a balanced development is most preferred and an even deterioration is the worst situation;

- Assumption 3 indicates B(0.1, 5) and C(-0.1, 5) should not be much different as they are very close;

- Assumption 4 indicates the complete order should be A > B, B = E, E > C > D.

Each situation corresponds to a point on the change in economy vs. change in environment coordinate system. We further find the environmental elasticity index is the tangent function of the angle established by that point and the origin, formed by the abscissa representing the economic changes and the line connecting the point and the origin. Since a tangent function varies between negative infinity and positive infinity, it has no definition on the vertical axis. Another problem with a tangent function is its 180^0 period, which makes the environmental elasticity index indiscriminate between the most and the least preferred situations.

In economics usage, the elasticity is dimensionless expressions typically used to portray the relationship between demand and price, or between demand and income. If such a relationship fits single term power function, the elasticity is a useful concept. For example, if demand Q and price P has the following functional relationship:

$$Q = aP^b, a \text{ and } b \text{ are constants}$$

we get:

$$b = \frac{dlogQ}{dlogP} = \frac{dQ/Q}{dP/P} = \frac{\% \text{ change of demand}}{\% \text{ change of price}}$$

in which parameter b is the own-price demand elasticity. Obviously, given a constant elasticity, we can forecast the demand for a good when its price changes. When the elasticity changes over time or among consumer groups, it is an indicator of changed consumer behavior.

When introducing the elasticity concept to make rankings in our case, we are faced with two problems. The first is that the relationship between the economy and the environment is relatively uncertain, so that use of the single term power function would be inappropriate. We have observed in Chapters 3 and 5 that the environment can either improve or deteriorate as the economy grows in different countries and in the same countries but over different periods. The second problem is that elasticity yields some undesirable results when used to rank countries, as shown by Appendix Figure 4.1.

If functional relationships do not exist, the elasticity concept becomes vulnerable in economics. Samuelson (1947) went as far as suggesting, "Not only are elasticity expressions more or less useless, but in more complicated system they become an actual nuisance, converting symmetrical expressions into asymmetrical ones, and hiding the definiteness of quadratic forms."

1.3 From Environmental Elasticity (EE) to the Economic-Environmental Change (EEC) Index

In this section, we propose an alternative index to assess the development of a nation or a region from the perspective of economic and environmental changes. One of the difficulties in introducing economic concepts such as utility or production functions into evaluating economic and environmental changes is that, in economics the amount of goods and products are usually assumed to be positive, and thus a Cobb-Douglas function confined to the positive quadrant is appropriate. However, changes in economy and environment can both be negative. Therefore, a utility function that goes through all four quadrants is needed. Also, due to difficulties in measuring the "utilities," the emphasis of our index development is placed on the "direction" of the development of a nation over a period of time. The criterion is based upon the notion that a balanced development in both economy and environment is most desirable. We call a condition in which both the economy and the environment are developing positively "dual improvement." "Economic-environmental surplus" indicates that either economy or environment is improving while the other is deteriorating, but the improving one has a higher change rate than the deteriorating one. "Economic-environmental deficit" also applies to where one is improving and the other is degrading, but the degrading rate here is higher

Classification of Economic and Environmental Changes

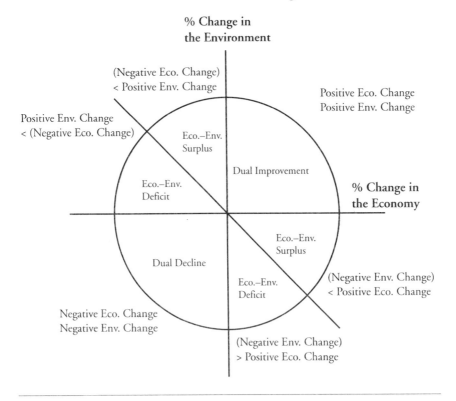

than the improving rate. "Dual decline" is defined as both the economy and the environment deteriorating. The four scenarios are shown in Appendix Figure 4.2.

1.3.1 The Origin of the Economic-Environmental Change Index

The index discussed in this paper is deeply rooted in consumer preference theory and production theory of microeconomics. In both consumer preference theory and production theory, the indifference curves and the production isoquants are assumed to be a set of curves convex to the origin. The typical curves are given by the Cobb-Douglas function with the shape shown in Appendix Figure 4.3

In order to construct an index to assess development from both environmental and economic perspectives, we assume economic development to be good X and environmental development to be good Y, and the decision-maker is the consumer who ranks the combinations of X and Y to reflect his or her levels of satisfaction. A higher rank should represent a higher level of satisfaction toward a specific condition of development, and thus a larger value of

The Shape of Typical Indifference Curves

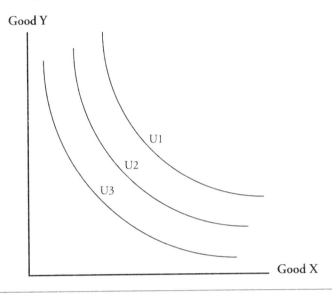

utility. However, the numerical value of the utility plays less of a role than the correct ranking, since what the consumer is concerned about is the ordinal utility, not the cardinal level of consumption.

A problem in introducing consumer preference theory to the ranking of development is that the typical utility functions are designed exclusively for positive consumption and inputs. In both consumer preference theory and production theory, all variables are positive. In our case, however, the changes in the environment and in the economy can either improve or deteriorate, showing positive and negative values. An expansion of the utility function is needed here. We must abandon the Cobb-Douglas function, which assumes that both X and Y are always positive and produces indifference curves confined to the positive quadrant for a proposed set of parabolas covering all four quadrants as indifference curves (Appendix Figure 4.4).

The mathematical expression of these curves gives the utility function described by them:

$$U = \frac{\sqrt{2}}{2}(x + y) - \frac{1}{2}a(x - y)^2 \qquad (4.1)$$

Equation (4.1) can be obtained from a normal parabolic function $y = ax^2 + U$ by rotating the coordinate system by 45^0. The parameter a is a positive constant determining the sharpness of the bend. Constant a is greater where the curve bends more sharply at its vertex (in this case, the vertex is the

The Shape of Proposed Indifference Curves

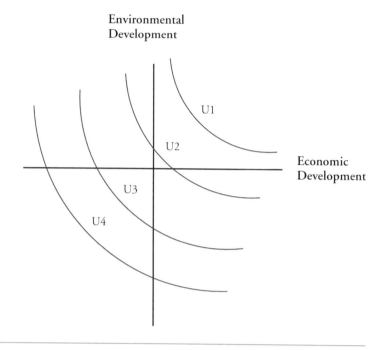

Environmental
Development

Economic
Development

U1

U2

U3

U4

intersection of a parabola and the straight line $x - y = 0$). When the curve becomes flatter, the constant a approaches zero. This constant is an important parameter as it determines the marginal rate of substitution of Y for X and can be modified according to the judge's internal rate of trade-off between the environment and the economy to represent varied tastes. When parameter a is set to zero, perfect substitution is obtained.

This scheme can be developed to rank combinations of situation where negative values exist. If the changes in the environment and the economy could be objectively measured and the substitution between the two be unanimously defined, such a utility function would be our final goal. Currently, we are using this simplified version of the utility function, leaving possible theoretical controversy aside.

In our case, since we are concerned about only the orientation of development, the relative relationship between the percentage changes in the environment and the economy is our focus. The algebraic values of the changes are not important here. Such an attitude makes it possible to simplify the algorithm of utility through projecting points to a unit circle.

Any point in the coordinate system represents a situation with specific percentage changes in the environment and the economy. As the sustainability index is designed to assess only the direction of development, the rates of

The Projection of Points on a Circle

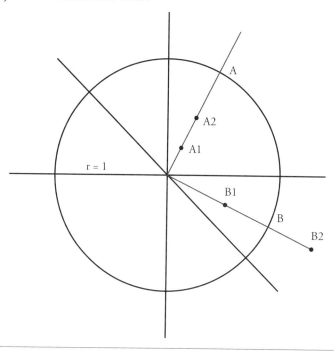

development are beyond our consideration. Only the relative relationship between the two concerned features is of concern. If the percentage changes are positively equal, the orientation of development is assigned the highest utility, no matter the changes are both 5 percent or both 10 percent. Therefore, all points on a radius vector have the same vectorial angle and are designated the same value of utility. Since we are not concerned about the distance between a point and the origin, we may suppose all points have a radius vector of 1 and are located on a unit circle. That is, all points are projected along their radius vectors to the circumference of a unit circle. In Appendix Figure 4.5, A1 and A2 are projected to A, and B1 and B2 are projected to B. After doing so, the utility values of points are only determined by their vectorial angles and the points on the unit circle give a complete set of possible utilities. So, to find the utility for A1, A2 and A, we may measure the utility only at A. All of A1, A2 and A have the same utility.

To find the values of utility for all points on the unit circle, we solve the following two equations simultaneously (see Appendix Figure 4.6 which shows the intersection points of the utility functions and the unit circle).

The utility function in Equation (4.1) and the equation of the unit circle:

$$x^2 + y^2 = 1 \qquad (4.2)$$

Utilities on a Unit Circle

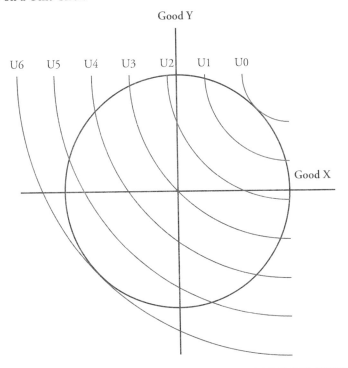

From these two equations we get:

$$U = \frac{\sqrt{2}}{2}(x + y) - \frac{1}{2}a(1 - 2xy)$$

For points on the unit circle, if (is the vectorial angle, are

$$x = cos\theta \; and \; y = sin\theta$$

Thus,

$$U = \frac{\sqrt{2}}{2}(cos\theta + sin\theta) - \frac{1}{2}a(1 - 2sin\theta cos\theta) \qquad (4.3)$$

As the exact value of the parameter *a* is not known, the assumption of perfect substitution between the percentage changes in the environment and the economy is assumed to avoid designating an arbitrary number. This implies that the marginal rate of substitution of Y for X is 1 and the parameter *a* is zero. The utility function is finally reduced to:

$$U = \frac{\sqrt{2}}{2}(cos\theta + sin\theta) \qquad (4.4)$$

We suggest using $cos\theta + sin\theta$, which can be interpreted as the same ordinal utility function since both represent an identical rank ordering. The index can also be expressed as:

$$\frac{X + Y}{\sqrt{X^2 + Y^2}}$$

(4.5)

in which X is the percentage change in the economy and Y is the percentage change in the environment.

The new index or Expression 4.5 can also be related to the environmental elasticity using the following formulas:

$$\frac{1 + EE}{\sqrt{1 + EE^2}} \text{ for } 0° < \theta < 90°, 270° < \theta < 360°$$

(4.6)

$$-\frac{1 + EE}{\sqrt{1 + EE^2}} \text{ for } 90° < \theta < 270°$$

(4.7)

Since we are concerned only about the shape or direction of development, we define the situations of development as points in a coordinate system whose coordinates are corresponding to the two percentage changes: the percentage change of the economy and the percentage change of the environment. For any situation, the polar coordinates of its corresponding point give the vectorial angle q of the point. While the environmental elasticity uses the tangent value of θ, the new index employs $cos\theta + sin\theta$. The environmental change axis is $90°$ lagged behind the economic change axis. This explains why both sine and cosine are used; sine and cosine functions also have a $90°$ difference of phase. The $cos\theta + sin\theta$ formula can be rewritten by supposing that the economy and environment have the same weight of 1:

$$economy' \; cos\theta + environment' \; cos(\theta - 90°)$$

(4.8)

where only the cosine is used.

We call this new index or Expression 4.8 the Economic-Environmental Change (EEC) index. In a "dual improvement" situation (see Appendix Figure 4.2), this index has a value between 1 and $2^{0.5}$ (1.414); when both the economy and environment are improving at the same rate, the index reaches its maximum $2^{0.5}$ (1.414). If one of either the economy or the environment is degrading while the other is improving, but the improving rate is higher than the degrading rate, the index gives a numerical value between 0 and 1. If the degrading rate is higher than the improving rate, a value between -1 and 0 is obtained. In the case both the economy and the environment are deteriorating, the index shows a number less than -1 but no less than $-2^{0.5}$ (-1.414). When the both are deteriorating at a same pace, the index arrives at its minimum $-2^{0.5}$ (-1.414). A sketch is given in Appendix Figure 4.7.

Classification of the Economic-Environmental Change Index

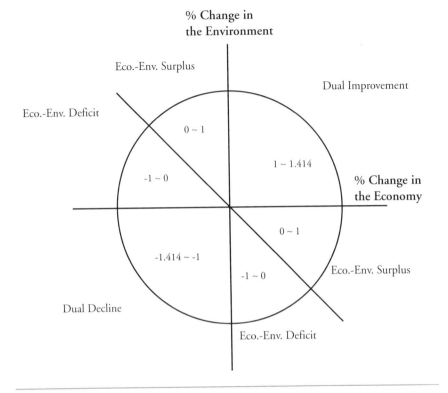

"Dual Improvement," the index Î (1, 1.414): both economy and environment are improving;

"Economic-Environmental Surplus," the index Î (0, 1): one's deteriorating pace is slower

than the other's improving pace;

"Economic-Environmental Deficit" the index Î (-1, 0): one's improving rate is lower than the other's degrading rate;

"Dual Decline" the index Î (-1.414, -1): both are deteriorating.

1.4 Discussions

We have introduced an index to assess the development of a nation from both environmental and economic perspectives, and have shown this index is a simplified version of expanded consumer preference theory, which allows negative quantities. The original and simplified versions of this ranking scheme would be useful in other cases with negative variables, including cardinal utilities and production functions, where the parameters making up the index can be objectively measured.

Several problems are associated with the EEC index. The first assumption of the index dictates a perfect substitution (or a constant marginal rate of substitution which is equal to 1) between changes in the environment and economy. This violates one of the axioms for indifference curves which assumes diminishing marginal rate of substitution. This axiom guarantees that the indifference curves are convex to the origin. In the case of constant marginal rate of substitution, the indifference curves are parallel straight lines. This implies that a fixed percent change of the environment can always be substituted for the same percent change of the economy. This departs from reality since the same percent change of environmental degradation or improvement may be worth different amounts of economic decline or growth at different stages of the development. Typically, people attach more importance to environmental improvement as the economy is more developed. Some may also find it hard to accept the second assumption of the index, which implies that very marginal improvements in both economy and environment, e.g., 0.1%, are deemed to be preferable to a situation in which one improves significantly but the other deteriorates marginally, e.g., 10% economic growth but 0.05% environmental deterioration.

2. Issues Related to Alternative Ways of Sub-Index Aggregation
2.1 Aggregating and Averaging Percentages
If water quality is improved by 10 percent and air quality is improved by 5 percent, what is the average percentage of the two improvements? In computing environmental elasticity in Chapters 3 and 5, and in developing the EEC index we have either used or implicitly assumed arithmetic averages for the sake of simplicity. Nevertheless, according to the index number theory, arithmetic averages would yield inconsistent results. A better choice for this situation is the geometric average. To prove this, we will introduce some basic concepts of the index number theory of classical economics.

An index number is defined as the average percentage change of prices from one point of time to another. All calculation is based upon "price relatives" (defined by Fisher 1922), which is the ratio between two prices of one particular commodity at two points in time. For the sake of simplicity, the base price (p_0) for any commodity at the starting year is usually set to 1.00. For example, if bread price increases by 100% and butter decreased by 50% from 1913 to 1918, their price relatives (P_0, P_1) were as shown in the following Appendix Table 4.1:

APPENDIX TABLE 4.1

The Concept of Price Relatives

	1913 (P_0)	1918 (P_1)
Bread	1.00	2.00
Butter	1.00	0.50

It is a classic topic in economics to measure the average price relatives over time and for a large number of commodities. Fisher (1922) identified many (at least 134) indices in an attempt to find an ideal way of averaging, and designed tests and criteria to examine the performance of those indices. Fisher's methodology was to design the indices by first identifying the simplest methods of averaging and then using different weighting schemes to develop the simple indices into more complicated ones. The difficulty facing Fisher was that both price relatives and quantity relatives should be averaged at the same time, and the result must be consistent with mathematical reasoning. In our case, environmental quality can be regarded as comparable to price in economics. If we assume that all major environmental components—air, water, ecosystems, and land—are equally important to the overall environmental quality, we may use the average quality changes as the overall change of the environment. Our major concern is thus to find a consistent way of averaging percentage changes of major environmental components.

In Fisher's work six types of averages were categorized as "simple averages." They were called simple because no weighting scheme (or equal weighting) was used in their construction:

1. The simple arithmetic: $0.5 (P1 + P2)$

2. The simple harmonic: $2/(1/P1 + 1/P2)$

3. The simple geometric: $(P1 \times P2)^{0.5}$

4. The simple median: Selecting the middlemost term

5. The simple mode: Selecting the commonest term

6. The simple aggregative: $\Sigma p_1 / \Sigma p_0$ where P's are price relatives and p's are prices.

It is noted that the geometric average of the simple arithmetic and the simple harmonic is the simple geometric index.

Two tests were designed to examine the validity of the simple averages above:

Preliminary test: The order of the commodities should make no difference, that is, any two commodities could be interchanged, i.e., their order reversed, without affecting the resulting index number. The rationale of this test is that it would be perverse to arbitrarily average the first half of the commodities by the arithmetic method and the other half by the geometric, or fancifully weight the sixth commodity by 6 and the ninth commodity by 9.

Time reversal test: Any point of time can be taken as the base, and the results based upon different points of time should be consistent, that is, the formula for calculating an index number should be such that it will give the same ratio between one point of time and another, no matter which of the two is taken as the base. For example, if taking 1913 as a base and going forward to 1918, we find, on the average, prices have doubled. Then, by proceeding in the reverse direction, we should find the 1913 price level to be half that of 1918. Thus, the index number reckoned forward should be the reciprocal of that reckoned backward, or, more useful for practical purposes, the forward and backward index number multiplied together should give unity.

Let us try the arithmetic average with this test, with 1913 as the base:

APPENDIX TABLE 4.2A
Time Reversal Test of Arithmetic Average

	Base year (1913)	Given year (1918)
Bread	1.00	2.00
Butter	1.00	0.50
Arithmetic average	1.00	1.25

But if 1918 is used as the base year and 1913 as the given year, we get:

APPENDIX TABLE 4.2B
Time Reversal Test of Arithmetic Average

	Base year (1918)	Given year (1913)
Bread	1.00	0.50
Butter	1.00	2.00
Arithmetic average	1.00	1.25

The first calculation indicates that the average price in 1918 is 25 percent higher than in 1913, while the second calculation indicates that the 1913 price is higher than in 1918 by the same margin. Clearly, this is an impossible situation and the arithmetic method fails to meet this test.

A similar thing can occur over locations. If Beijing's price is that of 1913 and Manila's price equals that of 1918, by arithmetic average, people in Beijing would say Manila's average price is 25 percent higher than theirs, while the people in Manila would insist on a reversed opinion.

Only the simple geometric method among the 6 simple methods is self-consistent when applied in reverse over time.

2.2 "The Larger the Diamond, the Better the Environment?"

As seen in Chapters 3 and 5, Environmental diamonds are a graphic tool for presenting four environmental sub-indices for air, water, land and ecosystem. They are easy to understand and visually appealing. By keeping the four individual components separate, environmental diamonds present the multi-dimensionality of the environment in a single graph.

A cautionary note is in order, however, in interpreting the sizes of the diamonds. In particular, the area within a diamond cannot be interpreted as a measurement of the overall environmental quality of the region or country that the diamond describes. We can approach this issue from the following two perspectives.

If we compute the area of a diamond and attempt to say "the larger the diamond, the better (or worse) the overall environmental quality," we could get conflicting results. The problem arises because, unlike a cube, the area of a diamond is dependent upon the ordering of axes. In Appendix Figure 4.8 we display the same environmental information in "Diamonds 1 and 2," or "Diamonds 3 and 4," but with the axes switched. If we exchange the location of land quality and ecosystem quality axes, or air and water quality axes, Diamonds 1 and 3 become environmental Diamonds 2 and 4, respectively. The areas within the diamonds change significantly while the values for the four subindices remain unchanged. This suggests that the area within a diamond is not a consistent measure.

One might argue that fixing the order of the axes would solve this problem. We could stop switching the axes and get single consistent value of diamond size for any given four subindices. The question remains, however, which order we should choose? If Country A has better water and land than air and ecosystem, it would prefer putting water and land at $90°$ directions, like the system in the chart "Diamond 1." In contrast, Country B, which has better water and ecosystem quality, may insist on the ordering in "Diamond 4."

If water = a, ecosystem = b, air = c, and land = d, the size of the diamond in "Diamond 1" is:

$$S1 = (1/2) (a + b) (c + d).$$

The size of the diamond in "Diamond 2" is:

$$S2 = (1/2) (a + d) (b + c).$$

The ratio of the two diamonds is:

$$\frac{S1}{S2} = \frac{(a + b)(c + d)}{(a + d)(b + c)}$$

Theoretically, this ratio can be infinite. For example, if a and c are significantly larger than 0 and b and d approach to 0, this ratio approaches infinity.

3. Summary

This appendix is a collection of several topics we have encountered and investigated in our index development efforts. Although no perfect index exists, the challenge is to develop indices to best meet the needs which must be

Limitations of Environmental Diamonds

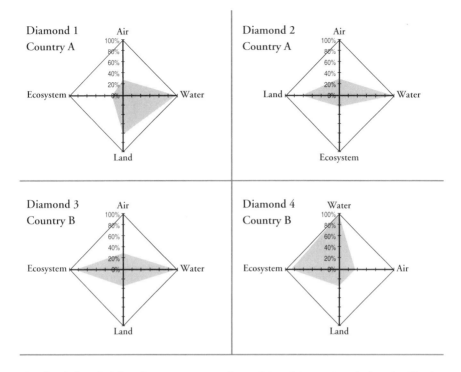

clearly defined. The discussions conducted in this section help clarify the theoretical and technical issues involved.

Note

1   This appendix draws heavily from two working papers produced by Xiang Yu, Ph.D. candidate, Harvard University. Some of the opinions expressed in the appendix are not shared by all authors, but are presented here in order to stimulate debate on the issues.

References

Binger, R. B. and E. Hoffman. *Microeconomics with Calculus*. Harper Collins Publishers, 1988.

Dufournaud, C. M. and P. P. Rogers. "A Computable Index of Sustainability." *The Working Papers of the Study of Environmental Indicators and Indices*. Division of Applied Sciences, Harvard University, 1994.

Dull, R. W. *Mathematics for Engineers*. 2d ed. New York and London: McGraw-Hill, 1941.

Fisher, I. *The making of index numbers; a study of their varieties, tests, and reliability*. Publications of the Pollak Foundation for Economic Research, no. 1. Boston, and New York: Houghton Mifflin Company, 1922.

Nicholson, W. *Intermediate Microeconomics and Its Application.* The Dryden Press, 1979.

Nordhaus, W. D. *Managing the Global Commons.* MIT Press, 1994.

OECD. Indicateurs d'environnement: une etude pilote, = *Environmental indicators: a preliminary set.* Paris: OECD; Washington, DC: OECD Publications and Information Center [distributor], 1991.

Ott, W. R. *Environmental Indices: Theory and Practice.* Ann Arbor Science, 1978.

Pindyck, R. S. *Microeconomics.* 3rd ed. Englewood Cliffs, NJ: Prentice Hall, c1995.

Rogers, P. P. and K. Jalal. "Used Cars, Used Environments: How to Choose One." *The Working Papers of the Study of Environmental Indicators and Indices.* Division of Applied Sciences, Harvard University, 1994.

Salvatore, D. *Microeconomics: theory and applications.* New York: Macmillan; London: Collier Macmillan, c1986.

Samuelson, P. A. *The collected scientific papers of P. A. Samuelson.* Cambridge, Mass.: M.I.T. Press 1966, vols 1 & 4. *Invariant Economic Index Numbers and Canonical Duality: Survey and Synthesis* (with S. Swamy) is in vol. 4, *A Note on the Pure Theory of Consumer's Behaviour* is in vol. 1.

Samuelson, P. A. *Foundations of economic analysis.* Harvard economic studies, v. 80. Cambridge, Harvard University Press, 1947.

Samuelson, P. A. *Microeconomics.* 15th ed. New York: McGraw-Hill, c1995.

Samuelson, P. A. "Consumption Theory in Terms of Revealed Preference." *Economica* n.s. 15 (November, 1948), pp. 243–253.

Stuvel, G. *The index–number problem and its solution.* Basingstoke: Macmillan, 1989.

Theory and applications of economic indices. Proceedings of an International Symposium held at the University of Karlsruhe April–June 1976. Wurzburg: Physica-Verlag, 1978.

UNDP, *Human Development Report.* Oxford University Press, 1992.

UNDP, *Environmental data report 1989–1990.* Oxford, UK; Cambridge, Mass.: B. Blackwell.

World Bank, *World Development Report.* 1978 [New York] Oxford University Press.

World Bank, *Social indicators of development.* Washington, DC: World Bank.

World Bank, *World tables* (and computer files). Washington, DC

World Resources Institute and the International Institute for Environment and Development. *World resources: a report by the World Resources Institute and the International Institute for Environment and Development.* 1986. New York: Basic Books, c1986. Institute for Environment and Development.

Yu, C. C., C. M. Dufournaud, and P. P. Rogers, "How Many Indices Do We Need?" *The Working Papers of the Study of Environmental Indicators and Indices,* Division of Applied Sciences, Harvard University, 1995.

7712　49